Taking Your iPhone to the Max, iOS 5 Edition

Michael Grothaus

Steve Sande

Erica Sadun

Apress®

President and Publisher: Paul Manning
Lead Editor: Michelle Lowman
Technical Reviewer: Dave Caolo
Editorial Board: Steve Anglin, Mark Beckner, Ewan Buckingham, Gary Cornell, Morgan Ertel, Jonathan Gennick, Jonathan Hassell, Robert Hutchinson, Michelle Lowman, James Markham, Matthew Moodie, Jeff Olson, Jeffrey Pepper, Douglas Pundick, Ben Renow-Clarke, Dominic Shakeshaft, Gwenan Spearing, Matt Wade, Tom Welsh
Coordinating Editor: Kelly Moritz
Copy Editor: Kim Wimpsett
Compositor: MacPS, LLC
Indexer: BIM Indexing & Proofreading Services
Artist: SPi Global
Cover Designer: Anna Ishchenko

Distributed to the book trade worldwide by Springer Science+Business Media New York, 233 Spring Street, 6th Floor, New York, NY 10013. Phone 1-800-SPRINGER, fax (201) 348-4505, e-mail orders-ny@springer-sbm.com, or visit www.springeronline.com.

For information on translations, please e-mail rights@apress.com, or visit www.apress.com.

Apress and friends of ED books may be purchased in bulk for academic, corporate, or promotional use. eBook versions and licenses are also available for most titles. For more information, reference our Special Bulk Sales–eBook Licensing web page at www.apress.com/bulk-sales.

Any source code or other supplementary materials referenced by the author in this text is available to readers at www.apress.com. For detailed information about how to locate your book's source code, go to www.apress.com/source-code/.

Dedicated to the memory of Steven P. Jobs, without whom the iPhone and this ebook would never have existed.

— Steve, Erica, and Mike

Contents at a Glance

Contents v

About the Authors xiv

About the Technical Reviewer xv

Part I: Setup 1

▓ Chapter 1: Selecting, Buying, and Activating Your iPhone 3

▓ Chapter 2: Putting Your Data and Media on the iPhone 27

Part II: Meet the Phone 63

▓ Chapter 3: Interacting with Your New iPhone 65

▓ Chapter 4: Placing Calls with iPhone 101

Part III: Getting Online 125

▓ Chapter 5: Browsing with Mobile Safari 127

▓ Chapter 6: Staying in Touch with FaceTime and Messages 157

▓ Chapter 7: iPhone Mail 183

Part IV: Media and Shopping 213

▓ Chapter 8: Touching Your Music 215

▓ Chapter 9: Shopping at the iTunes Store 239

▓ Chapter 10: Shopping at the App Store 257

▓ Chapter 11: Reading Books and Newspapers with iBooks and Newsstand.... 275

Part V: Photos, Video and the Camera 319

▓ Chapter 12: Touching Your Photos and Videos 321

▓ Chapter 13: Photographing and Recording the World Around You 365

Part VI: Accessories 383

▓ Chapter 14: Staying on Time and Getting There with Clock,
Calendar, and Maps 385

▓ Chapter 15: Using Your Desk Set: Contacts, Calculator, Notes,
Weather, Stocks, Voice Memos, and Reminders 425

Part VII: Preferences 455

▓ Chapter 16: Customizing Your iPhone 457

Index 487

Contents

Contents at a Glance.. iv

About the Authors..xiv

About the Technical Reviewer xv

Part I: Setup... 1

▓Chapter 1: Selecting, Buying, and Activating Your iPhone............................ 3

Selecting Your iPhone...3

Considering System Requirements..5

Buying Your iPhone...5

Returns and Exchange Policies..7

Bringing Home Your iPhone 7

iPhone 4S Feature Overview...9

Activation at the Store 10

Preparing for Activation Through iTunes 11

Connecting Your iPhone to Your Computer...14

Activating Your iPhone (Nonstore Version) 15

The Activation Process 17

"PC-Free" Activation...18

Insuring and Repairing Your iPhone..20

Accessorizing Your iPhone...20

iPhone Bumpers and Cases 21

iPhone Skins 22

Power Adapters 23

Docks 23

Cables 24

Summary 25

▓Chapter 2: Putting Your Data and Media on the iPhone 27

Syncing 27

The iPhone iTunes Device Window 28

A Word on Syncing Your Data 30

Where Do I Get My Media From? 30

Remember to Apply Your Changes 32

The Tabs 32

The Summary Tab 33

The Apps Tab 40

The Ringtones Tab 44

Synchronization Options 45

The Music Tab..45

The Movies Tab 46

The TV Shows Tab 48

The Podcasts Tab...49

The Books Tab 51

The Photos Tab 53

The Info Tab 54

iTunes Device Settings 58

Restoring...61

Syncing via iCloud...61

Summary 62

Part II: Meet the Phone **63**

Chapter 3: Interacting with Your New iPhone **65**

Interaction Basics 65

The iPhone Language 66

The iPhone Sensors 69

iPhone Power Tricks 74

Changing iPhone Wallpapers 81

Organizing Apps with Folders 82

Using the iPhone Keyboard 84

Dictating Text...92

Using a Bluetooth Keyboard with Your iPhone..93

Using the iPhone Stereo Headset 95

Talking to Siri...97

Summary 98

Chapter 4: Placing Calls with iPhone **101**

Checking the Cell Network Indicator 101

iPhone Basics 102

Launching the Phone app 102

Placing Calls 103

GSM versus CDMA 106

Placing Calls with Siri 107

Placing Calls with Voice Control 108

Answering Calls 109

Managing Calls 111

Managing Favorites 114

Using Visual Voicemail..115

Setting Up Your Voicemail Passcode 115

Choosing Your Greeting 116

Managing Voicemail Messages 116

Accessing Voicemail Files...118

Sending Voicemail Indirectly 118

Managing Ringtones and Other iPhone Alerts 119

Adding Custom Ringtones..119
Advanced Phone Preferences 121
iPhone Codes 121
Basic iPhone Information 122
Service Shortcuts..122
Summary 122

Part III: Getting Online 125

■ Chapter 5: Browsing with Mobile Safari 127
Getting Started with Wi-Fi 127
Checking Your Wi-Fi Connection...128
Choosing a Wi-Fi Network 128
Connecting to a Protected Network 129
Asking to Join a Network 130
Getting Started with 3G Data Connections...131
Getting Started with the Safari Web Browser 133
Entering URLs 135
Searching the Web..136
Searching for Text on a Web Page..137
Entering Text...138
Following Links 139
Changing Orientation 141
Scrolling, Zooming, and Other Viewing Skills 141
Working with Pages 142
Working with Bookmarks...143
Selecting Bookmarks...144
Editing Bookmarks..145
Saving Bookmarks and Sharing Web Pages 147
Eliminating Clutter with Reader 149
Building Up Your Reading List..150
Customizing Safari Settings...152
The iPhone and Flash Videos 154
Summary 155

■ Chapter 6: Staying in Touch with FaceTime and Messages 157
The Camera Hardware 157
Front Camera 157
Rear Camera 158
Getting Started with FaceTime 158
Signing In..158
Navigating Your FaceTime Contacts 164
Favorites 164
Recents 166
Contacts 167
Placing and Receiving a FaceTime Call 167
Other FaceTime Calling Options...170
FaceTime Settings 172
Getting Started with Messages...173
Reading Conversations 174

Deleting and Forwarding Individual iMessages 175
Deleting Entire Conversations 177
Sending a New iMessage 177
Attaching a Photo, Video, or Contact to an Messages 178
Messages Settings..180
Using Messages with Siri 181
Summary 182

Chapter 7: iPhone Mail 183
Compatibility..183
POP 183
SMTP 184
IMAP 184
Microsoft Exchange 185
Adding Mail Accounts to iPhone 185
Adding Accounts with iTunes 186
Adding Accounts from Your Phone 187
E-mail Provider Setup 188
Removing Accounts from iPhone 190
Mail Basic Settings 191
Audible Mail Alerts 194
Getting Started with iPhone Mail 194
Inboxes 195
Accounts 196
Using Mailboxes...196
Reading and Navigating Through Mail 198
Bottom Icons 199
Top Icons 199
Embedded Links 200
Viewing Attachments 203
Sending Mail 205
Addressing E-mail...206
Entering a Subject...207
Editing the Message 207
Saving a Draft 208
Sending E-mail 208
Writing and Sending Mail with Siri 208
Creating Mail 208
Checking Mail 210
Responding to Mail 210
Summary 211

Part IV: Media and Shopping 213
Chapter 8: Touching Your Music 215
The Music Application..215
Browsing Media 216
Editing Your Browse Buttons 218
Navigating the Category Screens...219
Playing Audio 220

Album View 223

Cover Flow 225

Creating Playlists 226

Searching 231

Going Beyond the Music App 232

Saving Energy 232

Display Music Playback Controls When in Another App 233

Adding a Sleep Timer 233

Adjusting Music Settings 234

Choosing Headphones 236

Summary 236

Chapter 9: Shopping at the iTunes Store **239**

Connecting to the iTunes Store...239

Signing in to Your iTunes Account 240

Browsing Through the iTunes Store 241

The Music Store 242

Exploring the Top Tens 243

The Video Store 246

The Podcasts, Audiobooks, and iTunes U Stores..248

Searching the iTunes Store...248

Purchased 249

Downloads 250

Redeeming Codes 251

Transferring Purchased Items to Your Computer...251

Getting Free Music and Videos 252

Getting Social with Ping...252

Summary 255

Chapter 10: Shopping at the App Store **257**

Connecting to the App Store 257

Signing in to Your App Store Account 258

Browsing Through the App Store..259

Featured..259

Categories...261

Top 25 262

Exploring an App's Information Page 263

Buying and Downloading Apps 265

Searching the App Store 266

Downloading Updates and Previously Purchased Apps...267

Redeeming Gift Certificates and Codes 270

Transferring Purchased Items to Your Computer..270

Buying Apps Through iTunes on Your PC..270

Getting Your Game on in Game Center 271

Summary 272

Chapter 11: Reading Books and Newspapers with iBooks and Newsstand.... 275

iBooks App 275

View a Book's Info Page 276

Syncing Books 276

iBookstore 277

   View a Book's Info Page 282

   ePub Books 283

Navigating Your Bookshelf 285

   Rearranging the Order of Your Books 288

   Deleting Your Books 288

Sorting Your Books into Collections 289

   Creating New Collections 290

   Navigating Between Your Collections 293

Reading Books 295

   Turning Pages 297

   Adjusting Brightness 298

   Adjusting Font, Font Size, and Page Color 299

   Searching Text 300

   Bookmarking a Page 301

   Interacting with Text 302

   Accessing the Table of Contents, Bookmarks, and Notes 305

Having a Book Read to You 307

Syncing PDFs 307

Navigating the PDF Bookshelf 309

Navigating and Reading PDFs 310

   Using the Contact Sheet 311

Settings 314

Newsstand 316

Summary 317

Part V: Photos, Video and the Camera **319**

▓ **Chapter 12: Touching Your Photos and Videos** **321**

Working with Photos 321

   Syncing Photos from Your Computer 321

   Saving Photos from Mail and Safari 322

Navigating Your Photos in the Photos App 323

Touching and Viewing Your Albums and Photos 328

   Touching and Viewing Albums 328

   Touching and Viewing Photos 329

   Viewing Your Photos as a Slideshow 331

   Other Slideshow Settings 332

Sharing Your Photos 333

   Managing Photos 337

Editing Your Photos 339

iPhone Video Applications 343

Video Playback 346

YouTube 348

   Playing YouTube Videos 349

   Finding YouTube Videos 350

   Customizing the YouTube Buttons Bar 351

   Viewing Video Info Screens 353

The Videos App 354

Deleting Videos on the Go 356
Getting Videos 356
Video Settings 357
Watching Videos on the Web with Safari 358
Streaming Video to Your Apple TV with AirPlay 359
Video Accessories 361
Summary 362

Chapter 13: Photographing and Recording the World Around You 365
The Camera Hardware 365
Front Camera 366
Rear Camera 366
Real-World Use 367
Navigating the Camera App 367
Taking Still Pictures 369
Recording Video 372
Accessing Your Camera from the Lock Screen 373
Viewing Your Camera Roll 374
Viewing Individual Photos 375
Viewing Videos...377
Editing Your Video 378
Sharing Your Video 379
Uploading Images to Your Computer 381
Summary 382

Part VI: Accessories.. 383

**Chapter 14: Staying on Time and Getting There with Clock,
Calendar, and Maps 385**
Using the Clock Tools..385
World Clock 386
Alarm 388
Stopwatch 390
Timer...391
Working with the Calendar 392
Switching Calendar Views 393
Adding Events 397
Editing and Removing Events 401
Synchronizing Calendars with Your Computer 401
Exploring with Maps 402
Getting Around the Maps Screen 402
Navigating Maps 404
Gestures...404
Changing Map Views 405
Finding Locations 406
Current Location 410
Bookmarking and Viewing Saved Locations 412
Dropping a Pin 412
Bookmarking 413
Directions and Traffic..414

Directions...414
Traffic...418
Maps Tips 420
Find a Lost iPhone 420
Find a Friend 422
Summary 423

**Chapter 15: Using Your Desk Set: Contacts, Calculator, Notes,
Weather, Stocks, Voice Memos, and Reminders 425**
Synchronizing Your Address Book with Your Computer 425
Choosing Sync Options 426
Replacing Contacts 426
Working with the Contacts Application 527
Finding Contacts 427
Adding Contacts 429
Managing Custom Labels 432
Editing and Removing Contacts 433
Using the Calculator 433
Taking Notes 435
Syncing Notes 436
Checking the Weather..437
Viewing Weather Info 438
Weather Tips 439
Monitoring Stocks 439
Dictating Voice Memos 443
Setting Reminders 448
Summary 452

Part VII: Preferences... 455

Chapter 16: Customizing Your iPhone 457
Six Important Settings 458
Airplane Mode..458
Twitter..459
Sounds...460
Brightness..462
Wallpaper...463
Location Services...464
Other Good-to-Know Settings 466
"About" Your iPhone 467
Software Update 467
Usage...468
iTunes Wi-Fi Sync 469
Network 469
Bluetooth..470
Auto-Lock...470
Restrictions..471
Date and Time..473
Keyboard..474
International..475

Accessibility 476

    VoiceOver 477

    Zoom 478

    Large Text 478

    White on Black 478

    Speak Selection 479

    Speak Auto-text 479

    Mono Audio 479

    Assistive Touch 479

    Triple-Click Home 480

Reset 481

iCloud 483

Third-Party App Settings 484

Summary 484

Index **487**

About the Authors

 **Michael Grothaus** is an American novelist and journalist living in London. He was first introduced to Apple computers in film school and went on to use them for years to create award-winning films. However, after discovering many of Hollywood's dirty little secrets while working for 20th Century Fox, he left and spent five years with Apple as a consultant. He's since moved to London and earned his MA in Creative Writing. His first novel, *Epiphany Jones*, is a story about trafficking and America's addiction to celebrity. Currently, Michael is a staff writer at AOL's popular tech news site The Unofficial Apple Weblog (TUAW.com), where he writes about all things Mac. Additionally, Michael has written several other books for Apress, including *Taking Your iPod touch to the Max, Taking Your OS X Lion to the Max,* and *Taking Your iPhoto '11 to the Max.* When not writing, Michael spends his time traveling Europe, Northern Africa, and Asia. You can reach him at www.michaelgrothaus.com and www.twitter.com/michaelgrothaus.

 **Steve Sande** has been a loyal fan of Apple technology since buying his first Mac in 1984. Originally trained as a civil engineer, Steve's career as an IT professional blossomed in the 1990s. A longtime blogger, Steve is the features editor at Aol's The Unofficial Apple Weblog (TUAW.com), the author of three books about Apple's iWeb application, a collaborator on **Taking Your iPad to the Max** and **Taking Your iPhone 4 to the Max**, and **Taking Your OS X Lion to the Max.** You can join Steve every Wednesday for the popular TUAW TV Live show, and follow his exploits at www.twitter.com/stevensande. He lives with his wife of 32 years in Highlands Ranch, Colorado.

Erica Sadun is the bestselling author, coauthor, and contributor to several dozen books on programming, digital video and photography, and web design, including the widely popular The iPhone Developer's Cookbook: Building Applications with the iPhone 3.0 SDK, Second Edition. She currently blogs at TUAW.com, and has blogged in the past at O'Reilly's Mac DevCenter, Lifehacker, and Ars Technica. In addition to being the author of dozens of iOS-native applications, Erica holds a Ph.D. in Computer Science from Georgia Tech's Graphics,Visualization and Usability Center. A geek, a programmer, and an author, she's never met a gadget she didn't love.When not writing, she and her geek husband parent three geeks-in-training, who regard their parents with restrained bemusement, when they're not busy rewiring the house or plotting global dominance.

About the Technical Reviewer

 **Dave Caolo** is an author and the Managing Editor at The Unofficial Apple Weblog, TUAW.com. Previous to his career as a writer, Dave spent 8 years as the IT Director at a Mac-friendly residential school in Massachusetts. Today, Dave can be found geeking out with his Macs and spending time with his kids, wife, and Boston Terrier, Batgirl. Learn more at http://davecaolo.com.

Setup

Chapter 1

Selecting, Buying, and Activating Your iPhone

Now that Apple's iPhone has been out for a number of years, you may have seen horror stories in the press about how an iPhone is going to cost you thousands of dollars over its lifetime. You have to buy the iPhone, pay for activation, and fork out money for expensive monthly service voice, data, and text plans (not to mention taxes and other fees). If you decide to back out any time during the standard two-year mobile phone contract, you're going to hand over even more money in early termination fees.

Well, there's more than a grain of truth to what you read. Since you're going to be spending a couple thousand dollars over the next few years, you need to know what you're doing when you buy that iPhone. If you're weighing the choice of whether to purchase an iPhone and trying to figure out exactly how much you're going to be paying, this chapter is for you. You'll also discover the down-and-dirty secrets of iPhone activation, plan selection, and even return policies. This chapter contains all the basic facts you need to select, buy, and activate your iPhone.

Selecting Your iPhone

At any given time, there are relatively few models of iPhones available. As of the publication of this book, all of them come with iOS 5, representing a new generation of the operating system software that powers the features of the iPhone. Usually you'll see an entry-level iPhone or two with fewer features and less storage, as well as a new top-of-the-line model.

How do you choose the model that's right for you? It all comes down to two factors: cameras and storage. The iPhone 4S has a high-resolution 8-megapixel camera with a flash that can shoot 1080p high-definition (HD) video, while the original iPhone 4 has a 5-megapixel camera (also with a flash) that will shoot 720p HD video. If you don't need a front-facing camera that allows you to take self-portraits or make FaceTime video calls, you can even get an iPhone 3GS with a 3-megapixel camera. As for storage, you need to decide whether you want to double the purchase price of your phone for a few more gigabytes of storage. I recommend getting as much storage as you can. If you load a lot of movies and videos onto your device, you can run out of space on a top-of-the-line iPhone very quickly.

The iPhone 4S tops out storage at a whopping 64 GB, while the iPhone 4 and iPhone 3GS are now available with only 8 GB of storage. iPhone 4S devices are also available in 16 GB and 32 GB models.

Here are some questions to ask yourself while selecting the model of iPhone to purchase:

> *How big is your music library?* If your library is small, a unit with less storage might be fine. If it's large, the extra space on some iPhone models helps to store additional music and podcasts.

> *How many videos do you want to carry around?* A single two-hour movie may occupy more than a gigabyte of storage. If you travel a lot, especially on airplanes, you may want to pay more to store additional movies and TV shows with those extra gigabytes.

> *Do you plan on using your iPhone as your primary camera and camcorder?* If you do, then look at the more sophisticated models with higher resolution, flash, and HD video capabilities. If you already carry a digital camera or camcorder with you on a regular basis or don't frequently shoot photos or video with your existing phone, a free (in many countries) iPhone 3GS or low-cost iPhone 4 may be fine. For budding videographers who plan to take a lot of HD video or photographers who want the best possible optics and resolution, the iPhone 4S is the right choice.

> *Is the thought of making video calls exciting to you?* For some people, just answering a regular cell phone call is a challenge. But if you love to have regular face-to-face conversations with friends and relatives, then you may want to consider the iPhone 4 or 4S with the built-in FaceTime video-calling feature and front-facing camera.

> *Do you need to carry lots of data?* Many iPhone apps use iTunes data storage and can synchronize files with your computer. Whether that data consists of presentation slideshows, project management files, or some other information that you need at your fingertips, the size of the data being stored can add up quickly. If you think you might need to do this, maybe the extra gigabytes on a more expensive iPhone model could be put to good use.

How long do you intend to keep this iPhone? If you're an early adopter who likes to trade up at the earliest possible opportunity whenever Apple offers a new model of iPhone, you may want to "buy in cheap" each time the new models are released and sell your old iPhone on the aftermarket. If you'd rather get the most use out of the iPhone over the longest period of time, then paying more up front means you won't outgrow the iPhone quite as fast.

Considering System Requirements

With the release of the fifth-generation iPhone operating system, iOS 5, you no longer need to think about your computer system requirements. In fact, iOS 5 makes it possible to live in a post-PC world—use an iPhone for your mobile device and an iPad for work requiring a larger screen, synchronize the two through Apple's iCloud, and everything works out beautifully.

However, you'll most likely want to synchronize your iOS 5 phone with either a Mac or a PC, since most people still own personal computers and want to keep all of their devices synced with the latest information. To do so, you'll want to have iTunes installed on your Mac or Windows PC in order to have control over the various synchronization options.

For the versions of iTunes available at the time of publication, the computer system requirements are as follows:

- A Mac computer running OS X 10.5, or a Windows computer with Windows 7, Vista, or XP Home or Professional with Service Pack 2 or newer.
- iTunes Store account.
- Broadband Internet access to use the iTunes Store.
- If you own an older computer, you may want to check the latest hardware requirements for iTunes at www.apple.com/itunes/download.

Buying Your iPhone

Once you've decided what iPhone model to buy (Figure 1–1), you're probably ready to pull out your credit card and buy that phone as quickly as possible. So, where you should buy it? At an AT&T store or at an Apple Store? A "big box" store like Best Buy? How about a discount store like Target or Walmart? Or should you purchase it online? You might be surprised to learn that your choice does matter.

Figure 1–1. *The Apple iPhone 4S (bottom) and iPhone 4 (top) are typical of the models of iPhones available at any particular point in time.*

Although it's possible to purchase an iPhone from any number of online stores, I recommend buying your iPhone in person at a store. You can ask questions. You can make human connections. You can have your iPhone activated and ready for calling when you leave the store. If something goes wrong with your purchase, you have a person who's there to help you work through it.

The sad fact of the matter is that a significant, although small, percentage of iPhone purchases go awry. Some people end up with a screen flaw, such as dead screen pixels. It's not an uncommon problem, and if found soon after purchase, it may involve a trade-in for a new unit. Others may have problems with their antennas or with activating their service. The chances of resolving these issues may be better if you have a real person to help.

As for the question of Apple or a carrier, I lean slightly toward buying at an Apple Store. It's an Apple product you're buying, and the Apple staff members are more knowledgeable about their products. Apple employees are happy to activate and set up your iPhone for you.

Apple Stores usually replace defective iPhones regardless of their point of purchase, and if you have problems with your phone service, you can go to any of the carrier's store locations whether you purchased your phone there or not; it's the service you're dealing with, not the physical iPhone unit.

Returns and Exchange Policies

The return policy for iPhones has improved since the release of the phone. If you're not happy with your iPhone purchase, you can return the undamaged phone to an Apple Store or the Apple online store within 30 days of purchase for a full refund. You must return the phone in the original packaging, including all the accessories, manuals, and documentation, and you won't be charged a restocking fee.

If you purchased your iPhone at a cellular carrier store, things aren't as rosy. A restocking fee will generally be applied to the return, unless you purchased it without service and the phone box was never opened.

As for discount and "big box" stores, the return and exchange policy varies. Before you make your purchase, be sure that you know exactly how returns and exchanges are handled. My personal preference is to get that policy in writing; it's usually printed out on the receipts that accompany your purchase.

Any return might involve an early termination fee (ETF) being levied against you by your cellular carrier. iPhones are available on many different carriers around the world. I recommend talking with your carrier or at least visiting their web site to determine the exact return policy and applicable ETF for your situation. An ETF can be quite expensive—for AT&T Wireless, canceling your contract after 30 days can cost you $315.

Bringing Home Your iPhone

Once you buy your iPhone, it's time to take it home, unpack it, and set it up. iPhone packaging (see Figure 1–2) is a small work of art. The iPhone ships in a box containing the phone, a USB connector cable, a USB power adapter, those famous white earbuds, and a packet of documentation. Each of these items is important and will help you in your day-to-day use.

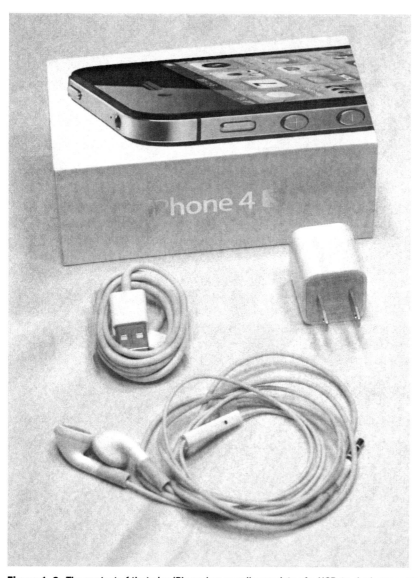

Figure 1–2. *The content of that nice iPhone box usually consists of a USB-to-dock connector cable (left), a USB power adapter (right), and a stereo headset (bottom). You can find your complimentary Apple sticker in a packet inside the box.*

Cable: The USB cable attaches your iPhone to either your computer or the USB power adapter. With past versions of the iPhone, the cable was useful for charging the battery and for activating and syncing the phone. Now it's possible to activate your phone without syncing to a computer, but you'll still need to use the cable for charging.

USB power adapter: The power adapter included with your iPhone plugs directly into the wall and allows you to charge your iPhone. It offers a single USB port. To use it, just connect your iPhone to the adapter using the USB cable. The adapter supplies the 5 volts required for powering USB devices. Third-party power adapters are also available for charging multiple devices or charging in an automobile.

Stereo headset (earbuds): The earbuds included with the iPhone differ slightly from those included with iPods. This stereo headset contains a built-in microphone and switch. The microphone allows you to take calls on your iPhone without holding the phone up to your ear, and the switch allows you to end calls as well as control music playback. The switch is also used to initiate the Siri Intelligent Assistant or Voice Control of your iPhone.

NOTE: The features of older or newer models of the iPhone may vary from what you see in the following feature overview.

iPhone 4S Feature Overview

The iPhone 4S is similar to earlier iPhones in terms of external features. The top of the iPhone houses a jack into which you can plug your earbuds and a Sleep/Wake button that is used to power on and off certain features. The bottom of your iPhone has a built-in speaker and microphone and an indented slot for connecting to a dock or USB cable. The iPhone's front has a receiver (earpiece) on top, which you use to listen to phone calls, a large touchscreen, and a single Home button. On the right side of the iPhone as you look at the screen is a Subscriber Identity Module (SIM) tray where your phone's SIM card is stored. You do not see the interactive screen shown in Figure 1–3 until you have activated your iPhone.

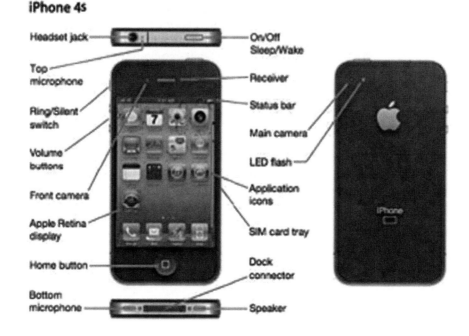

iPhone 4S

Headset jack
Top microphone
Ring/Silent switch
Volume buttons
Front camera
Apple Retina display
Home button
Bottom microphone

On/Off Sleep/Wake
Receiver
Status bar
Main camera
LED flash
Application icons
SIM card tray
Dock connector
Speaker

Figure 1–3. *iPhone 4S feature overview*

Activation at the Store

If you purchase an iPhone at an Apple or cellular service provider store in the Apple Stores in the United States and many other countries, you'll find that the activation process is taken care of in the store at the time you pay for the phone.

After you've made your choice as to the model of iPhone you want to purchase and have picked out accessories (cases, cables, and other goodies) to go with it, it's time to pay for the goods. When the Apple Store associate scans the iPhone box with an iOS-based point-of-sale device, the device immediately starts asking questions that you'll need to answer. Among those questions are the following:

- Are you a current customer of a particular mobile phone company that features the iPhone? If so, what is your telephone number?

- Are you coming over from another cell phone company? If so, what company, and what is your telephone number?

- What voice, data, and text plan would you like to sign up for?

- If you are not eligible for a phone upgrade on your existing plan, are you willing to pay the extra cost to buy the unsubsidized phone? (Many carriers subsidize the cost of the phone, knowing that you'll more than pay them back in your monthly subscription fees.)

In the case of an existing iPhone owner upgrading to a newer iPhone, the point-of-sale device checks your existing phone number and immediately lets the Apple Store associate know whether you're eligible for an upgrade. There's usually a nominal fee associated with the upgrade, and you are asked whether you want to accept that fee. The associate then displays your existing voice, data, and text plans, and you are asked whether you want to stay with those plans or change to a different plan. Of course, you'll also need to swipe the credit card that you'll use to pay for the phone and the plan, and your signature is required on the point-of-sale device.

After you agree to the terms and conditions of the carrier's plan and the use of Apple's hardware and software, your new iPhone is activated. Note that if you have an existing phone, the service to it is cut off immediately.

Activating your iPhone at an Apple or a carrier store has another benefit. Most of the stores have a set of cables and special software that are used to transfer all your settings, data, addresses, photos, and more from your existing phone to the iPhone. This is especially important if you are getting your first iPhone and coming over from another phone platform.

Until the iPhone has been fully activated, you are not able to make calls except for emergency (911) calls. With iOS 5, activation can now be done completely on your iPhone without requiring synchronization to a computer. In the next section, I describe how to activate your phone through iTunes on a computer, and the "PC-free" activation follows that.

Preparing for Activation Through iTunes

You have unpacked your iPhone but haven't yet connected it to iTunes. Now is a good time to review the data on your computer. When your iPhone is activated for the first time, it synchronizes with iTunes and, depending on your computer, to your e-mail accounts, your calendars, and so forth. Before you begin, here are some items you may want to review and clean up so your iPhone begins life with the freshest possible data:

> *Contacts*: The iPhone can sync with Microsoft Outlook 2007 or 2010 on Windows, Address Book, Outlook or Entourage on a Macintosh, and Yahoo! Address Book on the Internet. To prepare for your first sync, review your existing contacts, and make sure they're up-to-date with current phone numbers and e-mail addresses. If you use another program to manage contacts, consider migrating your contacts to one of these solutions. If you'd rather not, that's OK too. You can add contact information directly to your iPhone, although it's not as convenient as having the information automatically loaded for you.

Calendar: Your iPhone can synchronize with computer-based calendars just like it does with contacts. iPhone supports iCal, Outlook, Gmail, and Entourage calendars on the Mac and Outlook 2007 and 2010 calendars on Windows. Get your calendars into shape before your first synchronization, and you'll be ready to immediately manage your schedule both from your computer and from your iPhone.

E-mail: Your iPhone works with most e-mail providers including Yahoo! Mail, Gmail, AOL, and of course Apple's iCloud mail. If your e-mail provider uses the industry-standard POP3 and IMAP services, your service will work with iPhone. You may want to establish new accounts with these providers before you activate your iPhone. That way, they'll load onto your unit the first time you synchronize. You can always add new e-mail accounts later, but it's nice to have them all set up and available for use right away.

> **NOTE:** iPhone owners who use Microsoft Exchange as an e-mail, contacts, and calendar server will be happy to hear that their phone can tie into a Microsoft Exchange ActiveSync server with no problems.

Media: Current iPhone models offer relatively small storage space when compared to, for example, iPod Classic's generous 160GB hard drive. To make the most of this limited space, set up playlists for your favorite songs and podcasts, and consider removing TV shows and movies from your device once you've watched them. You can store all of your media in iCloud and download it when needed, so why load all items onto your iPhone at once? Since, in all likelihood, you won't be able to synchronize your entire media library to your new iPhone because of storage constraints, invest time now in organizing your media to find those items you most want to have on hand.

Software and OS: You should update to iTunes 10.5 or newer before you attempt to activate your iPhone. And, if you're using a Macintosh, updating your computer to Mac OS X 10.7 "Lion" ensures that you'll be able to take advantage of all the latest features. It is possible to run iTunes 10.5 on a Mac running OS X 10.5.8, so that is the oldest version of the Mac operating system that is usable with the iPhone. You can download the latest version of iTunes from Apple at `www.apple.com/itunes/download`. Remember that the system requirements may change at any time, so be sure to check the web page mentioned earlier: `www.apple.com/iphone/specs.html`.

iTunes account: Apple requires a current iTunes account to activate your iPhone. If you do not already have one, you must sign up for a U.S. account with the iTunes Store. This requires a U.S. address and credit card. Here are the steps you'll need to follow in order to create that new iTunes account:

1. Launch the iTunes application, and wait for it to load.

2. Locate iTunes Store in the sidebar on the left side of the iTunes window. Click iTunes Store, and wait for the store window to load. Your Windows computer or Mac must be connected to the Internet for this to happen, since all storefront information is stored on Apple's servers.

3. Find and click the Sign In button in the top-right corner of the screen. iTunes displays the sign-in screen shown in Figure 1–4. If you currently have an iTunes account, enter your Apple ID and password, and then click the Sign In button to sign into iTunes. No iTunes account? Click the Create New Account button, and follow the remaining steps to create your iTunes account.

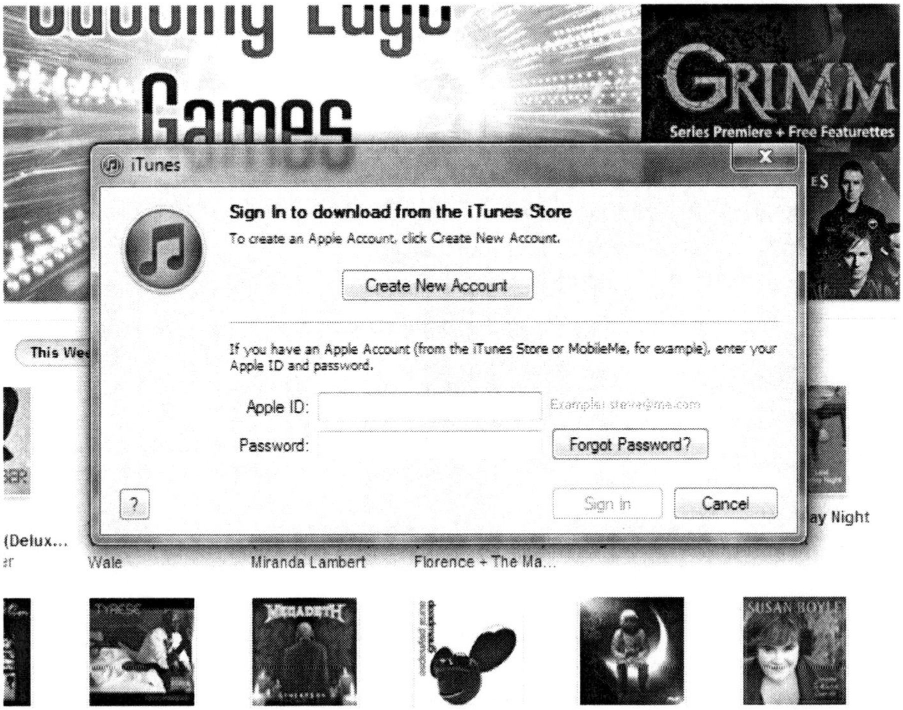

Figure 1–4. *Use the iTunes Sign In window to access iTunes with your existing account or begin the process of creating a new account.*

4. Click Create New Account. The screen clears and displays a message welcoming you to the iTunes Store. Click Continue to start the process of creating your account.

5. Review the terms of service, check the box that says "I have read and agree to the iTunes Terms and Conditions and Apple's Privacy Policy," and then click Continue. A new window appears prompting you to create your account.

6. Enter your e-mail address and a password. You must enter the password twice to verify that it was typed correctly. You also need to enter a security question—something only you would know the answer to, such as "What was the name of my third-grade teacher? or "What color was my first car?" Supply the answer to that question in the next space, and then enter your date of birth. Finally, review the questions about opting into e-mail notifications, and then click Continue.

7. A payment information screen now appears. You'll need to enter a valid form of payment, either a credit card or a PayPal account. For a credit card, you must enter the card number, CVV number, and billing information. Those must match in order to complete account creation. If you choose to use PayPal, your web browser launches, and you're asked to log into the PayPal account to verify that you're a valid member. Finally, you can also choose to use an iTunes gift card or certificate as a form of payment by entering the redemption code on the card. Once the payment information has been entered, click the Continue button.

After following these steps, iTunes displays a screen congratulating you on creating the new account, and you'll also receive a confirmation e-mail at the address you specified during sign-up. The e-mail welcomes you to the iTunes Store and thoughtfully provides the customer service web address. In case you ever need it, that address is `www.apple.com/support/itunes/`.

Connecting Your iPhone to Your Computer

Once you have an active iTunes account, it's time to unpack your iPhone and connect it to your computer. Follow along with these steps of connecting to your computer in preparation for service activation:

1. Remove the iPhone from its box, take off the plastic factory wrapping, and remove the USB-to-dock connector cable.

2. Locate the two ends of the USB-to-dock connector cable. One is thin and marked with a standard three-pronged USB symbol, while the other is wide and marked with a rectangle with a line inside of it.

3. Connect the thin end of the cable to a spare USB 2.0 port on your computer.

4. Orient your phone with the screen facing you and the Home button pointing toward you (see Figure 1–5).

Figure 1–5. *Plug the USB-to-dock connector cable into the iPhone with the rectangle mark facing you.*

5. Locate the universal dock connector on the bottom of your iPhone. It's that rectangular hole about an inch wide that is located under the Home button. Gently yet firmly push the cable into the dock connector without twisting or forcing the connection. iTunes launches, and your iPhone should automatically power on.

If your iPhone doesn't automatically power on and display either a white Apple logo or a Connect to iTunes message, press and hold the Sleep/Wake button on the top of the iPhone—it's the button on the top right of the iPhone. After a few seconds, the iPhone should wake up and display the white Apple logo as it powers on. If the iPhone doesn't respond with some sort of message on the display, contact the store where you purchased the phone.

Activating Your iPhone (Nonstore Version)

Until you activate your iPhone, you won't be able to use it for anything except calls to emergency services. All you'll see initially is a prompt directing you to connect to iTunes. Activating the iPhone involves nothing more than selecting a service plan and registering your phone with your cellular carrier. In theory, this process is simple, and it works properly for the vast majority of new iPhone owners. However, if you're porting a number from another carrier or selecting a less popular plan, it can take a while to get your iPhone "on the air."

> **TIP:** If you run into significant delays during iPhone activation, call your carrier's customer service team. They'll usually refund the activation charge as a courtesy.

Since the process of activation varies somewhat depending on what mobile carrier you're using, I recommend following the prompts that are displayed on your iPhone screen. The activation process also changes over time, so I am not describing the process in detail here.

Your most important decision prior to activation is to select a monthly rate plan that provides a certain number of minutes of voice calling as well as text or multimedia messages and data transfer. These plans vary by carrier.

Voice Plans

Voice plans are for those times when you're not playing with your iPhone but instead having a conversation with others using the Phone app on your device. As an example, AT&T customers in the United States have a choice of several plans ranging from a low-cost minimum number of minutes per month (450) up to an unlimited calling plan. The difference in price between 450 minutes of talk time and unlimited was, at the time of publication, only $30. If you do a lot of talking, an unlimited voice plan may be perfect for you.

Cellular carriers often provide other features with the voice plans. Visual Voicemail, which is Apple's proprietary way of implementing a voice mail inbox on the iPhone that you can see and interact with, is included. Carriers may also provide rollover minutes, which means that unused plan minutes can be used in future months, as well as provide "free" night and weekend minutes in excess of the plan minutes.

If you're having difficulty making your mind up about a voice plan, consider how much total time you currently spend per month talking on your existing mobile or landline phone. Most cellular providers will provide you with exact usage statistics. Also consider if you're going to be replacing a landline with your new iPhone. Many people are doing this, and it can increase your monthly usage.

Regardless of the plan you select, know that most cellular carriers allow you to adjust your plans for more or less minutes while you're in a contract. They understand that your needs can change and are usually more than willing to provide you with a more or less expensive plan in order to keep you as a customer.

Data Plans

Data plans charge you for every little bit of information that you send or receive from your iPhone. Data is what you're consuming when you access the Internet, surf the Web, or check e-mail. Many cellular service providers sell "packages" containing a specific amount of data—say 200MB or 2GB—to be used during a month. If you use more, you're charged an extra amount for the extra usage. If you don't use all your data, you won't be able to carry over those extra megabytes.

How much data will you use in a month? That's dependent totally on what you use your iPhone for. For many users, 2GB of data transfer per month will be more than enough, especially if you're using your iPhone in an environment where you can use a Wi-Fi connection for most of your data needs. As with voice plans, many carriers offer a way to change your requirements up or down depending on your actual usage. Once you've used your iPhone for a few months, you'll be able to see your usage patterns and adjust accordingly.

There's one other feature that is offered by most carriers—Personal Hotspot. Personal Hotspot allows you to share the 3G data connection on your iPhone with your Windows laptop, MacBook, iPad or other Wi-Fi device and connect to the Internet. While your iPhone is set up as a Personal Hotspot, you may still be able to send and receive data and make phone calls, although this does not work for the CDMA-based iPhones used on the Verizon and Sprint networks. Depending on the carrier, Personal Hotspot may be included as part of your data plan, or it may be an additional cost per month.

Messaging Plans

If you're planning to use text or multimedia messages to contact your friends, you'll also need to add a messaging plan. These plans vary; in some cases, you will pay a set charge per text (SMS) or multimedia (MMS) message. Multimedia messages are used for sending pictures or video through the iPhone Messages app. Note that Apple's iMessage service uses a traditional data plan, and if you plan on using iMessage only, an SMS/MMS plan is not required. iMessage works for international messaging as well; with SMS or MMS, special international messaging rates will apply.

Some carriers sell "buckets" of messages. You pay a set fee for a certain number of messages per month, and if you send or receive more messages than that number, you a charged per additional message. Most carriers also offer unlimited messaging packages for those customers who are addicted to text or multimedia messages.

The Activation Process

Now, you've selected a plan, made sure you have the latest version of iTunes installed on your computer, have your iPhone connected to your computer, and you're anxious to get it all working. Let's activate the phone on your carrier's network. Since the process varies from carrier to carrier and is frequently changed, I'll give you a general idea of what to expect. The process is quite easy to follow and simply requires that you register your iPhone with Apple, agree to terms and conditions of usage for both Apple and your carrier, and notify the carrier if you're coming over from another phone on their network, activating a new account, or transferring a number from another carrier.

If at any time you feel uncertain or confused about a step in the activation process, grab another phone and call your carrier. They'll be more than happy to step you through the process.

When the activation of your iPhone is nearing completion, a Completing Activation screen appears exclaiming, "Congratulations, AT&T is activating your iPhone" (assuming you're an AT&T customer, of course). If you're an existing AT&T customer and upgrading your phone, this screen displays the number that is being transferred to your phone. If it's a new number or you're having a number transferred from another cell phone provider, you'll see that number on this screen.

"PC-Free" Activation

As noted earlier in this chapter, you don't need a PC anymore to activate and use an iPhone. It's now possible to pull an iPhone out of its box, press the power button, follow some simple instructions, and be on the Web and making phone calls within minutes.

In the first part of the activation process, the iPhone connects to the cellular carrier that you will be using and verifies the voice, data, and text plans you have chosen. You can make changes if necessary; for example, you may decide that you'd like to add the Personal Hotspot service to your data plan.

Once your phone is on the cellular network, you'll be asked whether you want to join a Wi-Fi network. If you're in your home or workplace and know the network name and password, choose the proper network and sign in.

Apple then asks you to agree to the iOS Terms and Conditions. You can read them, if you're either a lawyer or just bored and have nothing better to do. Most people agree to them without ever reading the pages of legalese.

Next, you'll be asked whether you want to have your iPhone automatically send diagnostics and usage information to Apple. This information, which is completely anonymous, is used to determine problems with the iPhone firmware that need to be resolved and to help design future iPhones. For privacy, you may want to decline sending that information, and that's your right.

Once this is complete, your iPhone displays notification that everything is ready to go (Figure 1–6).

Figure 1–6. *After answering a lot of questions, your iPhone is set up and ready to use. Tap the Start Using iPhone button to begin making calls, playing with apps, listening to music, watching videos, and doing the almost infinite number of things you can do with an iPhone.*

Those aren't all the questions your iPhone will ask, however. For example, there's a screen that asks whether you want to enable Location Services. This allows applications to know your approximate location, which can be helpful if you're using a navigation app or annoying if you're using a third-party app that displays ads based on your location. I suggest turning on Location Services but then configuring your apps (Chapter 16) separately.

During the process, you'll also be asked whether you want to set up your iPhone as a new device, restore it from an iCloud backup, or restore it from an iTunes backup. If this is your first iPhone, the answer is simple—just set it up as a new iPhone. If you have previously owned an iPhone and made your backups to iTunes on a computer, tap the "restore from iTunes backup" button to get step-by-step instructions on how to reload all of your personal information, apps, and media from iTunes to the iPhone.

The newest feature allows you to restore your iPhone from an iCloud backup. If you had an iPhone 4 that you upgraded to iOS 5 and iCloud prior to purchasing a newer iPhone, chances are good that you allowed your phone to make automatic backups to iCloud. If this is the case, then tap the "restore from iCloud backup" button to restore your information, apps, and media to the iPhone.

Note that restoring your iPhone from the iCloud backup happens over a wireless connection. Even over a fast Wi-Fi network, the restoration of your data takes much longer than if you're restoring from an iTunes backup using a USB cable. This is a time-consuming process in either situation, so be patient, and you'll be rewarded with a fully loaded iPhone that's ready to roll.

Insuring and Repairing Your iPhone

Insurance plans for your iPhone can be offered by your mobile carrier, your insurance company, or Apple.

Your iPhone is covered under Apple's Limited Warranty for one year. That warranty covers problems with the device. If you drop your iPhone or lose it, you're out of luck unless you have additional insurance. You can add one extra year of iPhone AppleCare for $69. This extends your hardware repair coverage to two years in total. If interested, you can purchase this option online at the Apple Store (http://store.apple.com). Once the warranty has expired, your best bet is to have any repairs done at an authorized Apple repair center.

Beginning with the iPhone 4S, Apple now provides AppleCare+ ($99), which extends protection to accidental damage caused by dropping your device. AppleCare+ must be purchased at the time you buy your iPhone, and it extends repair coverage and technical support to two years from the original purchase date of your iPhone and adds coverage for up to two incidents of accidental damage because of handling, each subject to a $49 service fee.

With AppleCare+ for iPhone, Apple can troubleshoot issues over the phone or at an Apple Retail Store. If your iPhone needs service under the plan, Apple technical support representatives can set up a repair during the call.

If you can, be sure to back up your iPhone by syncing it to iTunes *before* bringing it in for service. Apple usually restores your iPhone to factory condition, which means you'll lose any data stored on the iPhone during the repair and service process. I recommend doing a backup and full erase of your iPhone before bringing it in for service so that the private information stored on the phone remains private. You can perform a full erase by selecting **Settings ➤ General ➤ Reset ➤ Erase All Content and Settings**.

Whether you buy an AppleCare protection plan or not, be aware that many mobile phone customers are provided with up to two years of complimentary telephone support (1–800-MY-IPHONE) during the term of their contract. You can find a complete list of ways to contact Apple Support at http://apple.com/support/contact.

Accessorizing Your iPhone

The iPhone accessory business is a huge and thriving economy. A visit to the iPhone accessories pages on the Apple online store shows just a small fraction of the iPhone cases, cables, docks, and other accessories that have been developed.

If you purchase your iPhone in an Apple Store, your Apple sales associate will show you many accessories that are available for it. These accessories are from Apple and third-party sources, and they provide your iPhone with protection and added functionality. Let's talk about some of the accessories that can make your iPhone experience more pleasant and fun.

iPhone Bumpers and Cases

One of the most popular categories of products for the iPhone consists of cases or, in the case of the iPhone 4 and 4S, bumpers. A case is exactly what it sounds like—something that encases the iPhone in fabric, plastic, carbon fiber, or metal to protect the phone from scratches or accidental damage because of a drop.

The phone-surrounding metal antenna of the iPhone 4 caused a stir when initial buyers of the phone complained of issues with signal strength. Apple responded shortly with an acknowledgment that most cell phones exhibit the same loss of signal when held a certain way by offering initial buyers a free iPhone 4 Bumper (Figure 1–7). The Bumper ($29) is an attractive two-tone band that wraps the external stainless steel antenna in hard plastic.

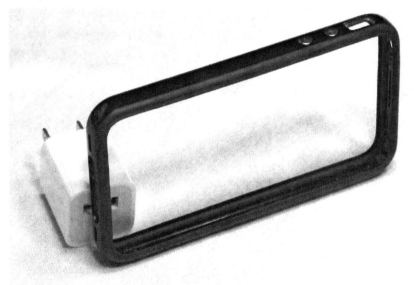

Figure 1–7. *The Apple Bumper fits around the perimeter of the iPhone 4 or 4S, providing protection to the stainless steel antenna on the edges of the phone. That's the Apple USB Power Adapter at left, providing support to the iPhone 4 Bumper.*

The iPhone 4 Bumper does not protect the screen or back of the iPhone. Those are made of hard aluminum-doped glass that is almost metallic in strength. The material can withstand impacts, can withstand drops, and is virtually scratch-proof, but that doesn't keep iPhone owners from wanting to protect their devices.

The iPhone 4S doesn't suffer from the same antenna issues, but a Bumper protects your investment just the same.

There are hundreds, if not thousands, of cases made for the entire family of iPhones. Some popular models are made by OtterBox (www.otterbox.com), LifeProof (www.lifeproof.com), Incipio (www.myincipio.com), Griffin (www.griffintechnology.com), and Marware (www.marware.com).

iPhone Skins

Skins are another popular form of protective gear for the iPhone. Instead of a thick shell of some other material encasing the device, skins stick to the iPhone like a second skin. Some are brightly decorated, while others are completely transparent.

GelaSkins (www.gelaskins.com) makes colorful designs from a number of artists, and you can also create your own designs from photos or original artwork. The skins are inexpensive, provide protection against scratches, and turn your iPhone into a movable feast of art (Figure 1–8).

Figure 1–8. *GelaSkins are one of several skins made for iPhone. These skins feature dynamic custom artwork designed for the company and classic art like "Artist's Garden at Giverny" by Claude Monet, but you can supply your own photos or art. Image courtesy GelaSkins.*

Many other manufacturers are also making skins for the iPhone at this time, some of which dispense with artistic good looks in favor of invisible protection. Zagg (www.zagg.com) makes Invisible Shields that you can either install yourself or have installed for you at thousands of retail locations.

Power Adapters

Even though newer iPhones tend to get better battery life than the older models did, you still need to keep your battery charged. Apple sells the $29 USB Power Adapter (see Figure 1–6), which is exactly what comes with your new iPhone. Why would you want another one? It's always nice to have an extra to keep in your office for away-from-home charging or to take with you when you travel.

Speaking of travel, you'll want to keep your iPhone charged when you're in the car, so why not consider a car charger? Several models are popular, including the Griffin PowerJolt Plus ($24.99, Figure 1–9) and the Belkin Car Micro Charger ($19.99).

Figure 1–9. *The Griffin PowerJolt Plus is one of a number of car chargers available for iPhone. Image courtesy of Griffin Technology.*

Your computer can also charge your iPhone through the regular Dock Connector to USB cable that comes with the device. However, some people prefer the vertical orientation and ease of plug-in that comes with a dock.

Docks

Docks come in a variety of sizes, shapes, and capabilities. The most bare-bones dock that you'll find is the $29 Apple iPhone Dock, which allows you to place an iPhone onto the dock connector for charging and syncing while putting the device into a portrait orientation for easy viewing.

From there, your imagination and wallet are the limit. Higher-end models are equipped with speakers to turn your sleek little iPhone into a loud "clock radio" or boom box. The latter category is well represented by the $300 Harmon Kardon Go + Play Micro Portable

Loudspeaker Dock for iPod and iPhone, while the former category is described by the Stem Innovation TimeCommand (http://steminnovation.com; Figure 1–10; $99.95).

Figure 1–10. *Looking for something that can wake you up and charge your iPhone at the same time? This Stem Innovation Time Command dock is functional and looks good enough to sit on your nightstand.*

Cables

Although the only cable you may ever need for your iPhone is the included USB-to-dock connector cable, there are other cables that can provide video-out functionality—perfect for watching photo slideshows or video stored on your iPhone on a big-screen TV.

Apple makes the Component AV Cable ($39) and Composite AV Cable ($39) for connecting an iPhone to either Component (Y, Pb, and Pr video and red/white analog audio ports) or Composite (composite video, red/white analog audio cables) television inputs.

The $29 Apple VGA Adapter also works with the iPhone 5, iPhone 4, and newer models to provide a VGA attachment to a television, projector, or VGA display.

> **CAUTION:** Not all applications support these connection cables, so be sure to contact app developers for assurance that their app will drive your TV, projector, or display prior to purchase.

Summary

In this chapter, you've learned how to select and purchase your iPhone. You've discovered what's involved in activating your iPhone and become aware of the various service plans that you'll need to choose from. To wind things up, here is a quick overview of some key points from this chapter:

- Only a handful of iPhone models are available at any time. Whatever model you select, buying it at the Apple Store (retail or online) provides you with the best opportunities for returns and repairs if necessary.

- Make sure your computer is compatible with iTunes before you buy your iPhone by comparing it to the system requirements listed in this chapter. Remember, you don't need a computer to activate your iPhone, but if you want to keep it synced with your Mac or Windows PC, you'll need to sync via Wi-Fi or USB cable with iTunes.

- When activating, know in advance what kind of plans are available and which ones you want to use. Deciding in advance can save you many activation headaches.

- iPhones are not cheap. Protect your investment by insuring your phone. Also consider adding AppleCare for an additional year's coverage against hardware repairs or AppleCare+, which covers accidental damage to your iPhone for two years (subject to a $49 repair fee).

- iPhone technical support is free for two years. Take advantage of it at 1–800-MY-IPHONE (1–800-694-7466).

Chapter 2

Putting Your Data and Media on the iPhone

So, you've unboxed your iPhone and connected it to iTunes. Now what? Chapter 1 briefly introduced the basics of syncing your iPhone with your music, movies, photos, and other data via iTunes. Now this chapter explores the options you have for syncing your data with your iPhone. Whether you've bought your songs and videos from the iTunes Store or have imported them into the program from CDs and DVDs, iTunes can synchronize your iPhone to nearly any content in its library. If you want a rich media and applications library on your iPhone, you need to sync those contents from the library on your computer.

iTunes determines which app, music, and video files transfer to and load onto your iPhone. You're about to discover how to bring all this content together in iTunes and send it to your iPhone via the USB-to-dock connector data cable. You'll see how to choose which items you want to synchronize and how to keep your iPhone content fresh and up-to-date.

With iOS 5, you don't need to own a computer to use an iPhone. The Apple Store will help you set up your device wirelessly out of the box. You can back up and restore your device automatically using iCloud. For the most part, this chapter isn't about that kind of device management. You'll read about using iTunes to synchronize and control your iPhone content using the traditional synchronization cable, with a few words toward the end regarding iCloud-based computer-free operation.

Syncing

Before you begin to choose which songs, videos, podcasts, and audiobooks will be synchronized using iTunes, you physically connect your iPhone to your computer and launch the iTunes application. Use the USB cable that shipped with your iPhone (or an equivalent dock) to connect your device to a spare USB port on your system. Launch iTunes by clicking the iTunes application icon on your computer. If your iPhone uses a lock code, you must unlock your device before iTunes can connect to it

The first time you sync your iPhone with your iTunes library, you need to do it via the USB docking cable. After that, you can sync it with your iTunes library via the USB cable that came with it or do so wirelessly as long as the iPhone is on the same wireless network as your computer is. Once connected via either of these methods, your iPhone appears in the list on the left side of the iTunes window (you can see it later in Figure 2–3). This light blue column, called the *source list*, is divided into several sections for your media library, the iTunes Store, your devices, and your playlists.

If you do not see your iPhone in this list, make sure you've physically connected it with the USB cable. Verify that the cable is firmly inserted into both the computer and the iPhone if you are doing a hard-line connection, or make sure that your iPhone and computer are both connected to the same wireless network. Be sure your iPhone is powered on. It is listed in iTunes when it's active or asleep, but it won't show up if powered down.

The iPhone iTunes Device Window

When the iPhone is plugged into your computer, it automatically appears in your iTunes source list under Devices. Click the name of your iPhone in the source list to open its preferences in the main iTunes window (see Figure 2–1). You'll see a series of tabs along the top of the window that allow you to set options associated with your iPhone. The tabs you'll see (from left to right) include Summary, Apps, Ringtones, Music, Movies, TV Shows, Podcasts, Books, Photos, and Info.

Along the bottom of the iPhone preferences window you'll find a long, colorful Capacity bar (see Figure 2–2). This bar appears regardless of what tab you have selected, displays the total storage capacity of the iPhone, and breaks down the amount of data you have on the device in color-coded segments along the bar. Blue is for audio, purple is for video, orange is for photos, green is for apps, lighter purple-pink is for books, yellow is for other stuff (mostly data and the operating system), and gray is for the remaining free space you have on your iPad. The key just below the Capacity bar shows what each color segment represents and the amount of space occupied per category.

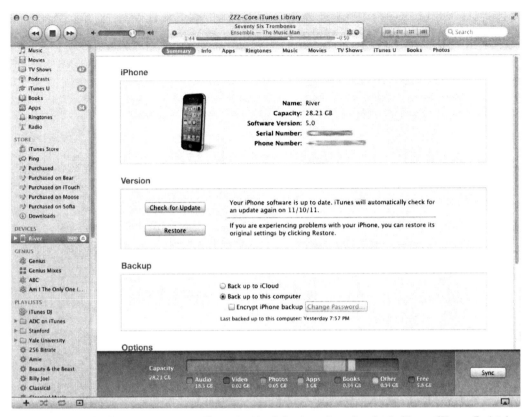

Figure 2–1. *iTunes allows you to manage the content loaded onto and synchronized with your iPhone. Each tab at the top of the window offers a variety of controls, allowing you to choose what information is loaded onto your iPhone at each sync.*

Figure 2–2. *The Capacity bar is a visual representation of the different types of files occupying space on your iPhone.*

NOTE: The Capacity bar breakdown is pretty self-explanatory. Still, some people are thrown by yellow—the color that represents Other. What is "Other," exactly? This includes database files (which keep track of your music, video, and podcast libraries), which can be 100MB to 200MB in size; album artwork (which can be 500KB per track); and preference files for the applications you have on your iPhone. Preference files let the apps remember in-app settings you've configured every time you launch them. If you store a lot of data inside your applications, the green Apps segment increases accordingly.

A Word on Syncing Your Data

The current iPhones hold a lot of data. But many of us have music or movie libraries that are far larger than even the storage in the most capacious iPhone. Apple devised sync preferences to help organize and select your most important data and move it to the iPhone.

If you have a 32GB iPhone and a 40GB music library, not only will you *not* be able to fit all your music onto the device, but if you filled that 32GB with your music library, you'd have no room for photos, movies, books, or apps. The following tabs that I discuss can help in selecting what to sync to your iPhone.

> **NOTE:** Applications like Air Video, Dropbox, LogMeIn, and Air Sharing Pro provide ways to offload local storage to remote servers, letting you free up space on your iPhone. Instead of synchronizing entire movies, Air Video streams media from your home computer to your device wherever you have an available Internet connection. Dropbox, LogMeIn, and Air Sharing Pro each let you transfer data to and from remote servers (Dropbox and Air Sharing Pro) or your home or office desktop (LogMeIn and Air Sharing Pro).

Although you most likely won't be able to fit all of your music, photos, and movies onto the iPhone, you don't have to do so. You can keep changing what you put on the iPhone. For example, once you've watched a movie on your iPhone, you can remove it and replace it with another one. Also, some files are larger than others. For example, don't worry about syncing all of your contacts, calendars, and book collections onto your iPhone. These are all text-based files, and text takes up very little storage.

Where Do I Get My Media From?

The iPhone is a great device for consuming media. But where do you get that media? The easiest and most direct way to get movies, music, TV shows, and books onto your iPhone is through the iTunes Store (see Figure 2–3). In the iTunes Store, you can buy music (a song or an entire album), rent or purchase movies, download your favorite TV shows by the episode or subscribe to a Season Pass, and download free podcasts and iTunes U content.

Figure 2–3. *The iTunes Store is the world's largest music store. You can also download movies, TV shows, apps, podcasts, and books from it.*

You can also import music and movies from your own collections. Importing music from CDs is straightforward using iTunes, as is importing video. One way to get movies onto your iPhone is to rip them from your DVD collection.

> **NOTE:** *Ripping* a DVD means copying content from the disc into a format that's playable on other devices, including iPhone devices. To load video from your DVDs onto your iPhone, download a copy of HandBrake from `http://handbrake.m0k.org` (for both Windows and Mac), and convert your DVD content to an iPhone-friendly format. HandBrake is free and easy to use. Insert your DVD into your computer, run the application, and follow the directions in the program. After your movie has finished ripping, you must then add it to iTunes by dragging and dropping the movie file onto your Movies library in the source list.

The only Apple-approved consumer-specific way to get applications onto your iPhone is by using the iTunes App Store. You can easily browse for apps from the desktop version of iTunes or in the dedicated App Store app on the iPhone.

You can build your iPhone e-book library in a variety of ways. Perhaps the easiest is to buy titles through Apple's iBookstore, which is part of Apple's free-to-download iBooks app. You can also take advantage of the more than 33,000 free e-books at Project Gutenberg (www.gutenberg.org) by downloading books to your downloads folder and then dragging them into iTunes. There are also many e-book stores and publishers that sell e-books directly online. For a good list of web sites that sell e-books, go to www.epubbooks.com/buy-epub-books.

iBooks also supports PDF files. You can purchase inexpensive PDF versions of popular titles from many vendors. Some publishers, like Baen Books, sell DRM-free PDF editions directly on their web site. They also offer an extensive free eBook collection (www.baen.com/library/) that's well worth checking out.

> **NOTE:** E-books come in many formats. The format compatible with the iPhone's iBooks app is ePub. Make sure when buying an e-book outside the iBookstore that it is in ePub or PDF format, or else you'll need to find another app that reads the format your e-book is in. Books from Amazon's Kindle Store are an example of this. Kindle books can be read on the iPhone, but not in the iBooks app. You need to download Amazon's Kindle app for the iPhone to read e-books purchased from Amazon or use Amazon's Cloud Reader web app. The latter is available at http://read.amazon.com and allows quick downloading of your books to the iPhone for offline reading.

Remember to Apply Your Changes

After making any of the choices I discuss in the following sections, note that they do not become finalized until you click the gray Apply button to the right of the Capacity bar (see Figure 2–4). Don't worry if you forget to click it, because iTunes automatically reminds you before you navigate away from the iPhone preferences window. Don't panic if you make a change in the preferences by mistake because you can always click the Revert button that sits above the Apply button.

Figure 2–4. *The Revert and Apply buttons (boxed) allow you to accept or negate any of the changes you have made in iTunes' iPhone preferences window.*

The Tabs

The tabs (see Figure 2–5) running along the top of the iPhone preferences window are how you navigate all your iPhone settings. There are ten tabs in total: Summary, Apps, Ringtones, Music, Movies, TV Shows, Podcasts, Books, Photos, and Info. To begin configuring the settings under any tab, just click the tab to select it.

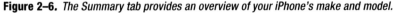

Figure 2–5. *Each setting tab offers a different way to control the way that iTunes synchronizes your iPhone to your home media library.*

The Summary Tab

The Summary tab (see Figure 2–6) is the first tab visible in the iPhone preferences window. It displays an overview of your iPhone including its name, capacity, currently installed firmware version, and serial number. From this page, it's also possible to check for firmware updates, restore your iPhone to a pristine factory-installed condition, and set options to help you manage the way your data is synced. The page is broken up into several boxes: iPhone, Version, Backup, and Options.

iPhone

Name:	River
Capacity:	28.21 GB
Software Version:	5.0
Serial Number:	
Phone Number:	

Version

Check for Update — Your iPhone software is up to date. iTunes will automatically check for an update again on 11/10/11.

Restore — If you are experiencing problems with your iPhone, you can restore its original settings by clicking Restore.

Backup

○ Back up to iCloud
◉ Back up to this computer
   ☐ Encrypt iPhone backup [Change Password...]
Last backed up to this computer: Yesterday 7:57 PM

Options

☐ Open iTunes when this iPhone is connected
☐ Sync with this iPhone over Wi-Fi
☐ Sync only checked songs and videos
☐ Prefer standard definition videos
☐ Convert higher bit rate songs to 128 kbps AAC
☐ Manually manage music and videos

Figure 2–6. *The Summary tab provides an overview of your iPhone's make and model.*

iPhone Box

In this box, an image of your model of iPhone is displayed along with its name, capacity, software version, and serial number. The iPhone image should match the model and color of your device.

> *Name*: This is whatever name you have given your iPhone. To rename it, click the iPad in the source list. This opens a text edit field around the name. Edit the name as desired (see Figure 2–7), and then press Return or Enter to confirm your change.

> *Capacity*: This number indicates the actual data capacity of your iPhone. As with all data storage, the advertised capacity (32GB, for example) never quite matches the actual capacity (28.21GB).

> *Software Version*: The iPhone regularly updates its software with bug fixes and improvements. iTunes indicates which firmware release is currently installed on your iPad. Click the phrase Software Version to switch to the Build Version display, showing which firmware build you are using.

> *Serial Number*: This unique serial number identifies your iPhone to Apple. Click the phrase Serial Number to reveal your unit's UDID, or unique device identifier.

> *Phone Number*: This is the phone number associated with your iPhone. For GSM units, you can click the phrase to reveal the unit ICCID (where appropriate), the number used to identify your Subscriber Identity Module (SIM). This is a unique number assigned to a SIM card in a GSM phone.

The only things that could ever change in this box are your iPhone's software version number and your iPhone's name. When you perform a software update on the iPhone, the new version number appears in this box. It's an easy way to tell which version of iOS (the operating system used on Apple's iPod touch devices, iPhones, and iPads) you are using. If you change the name of your iPhone by double-clicking its name in the iTunes source list (see Figure 2–7), the name change is updated here. Your iPhone's capacity and serial number never change.

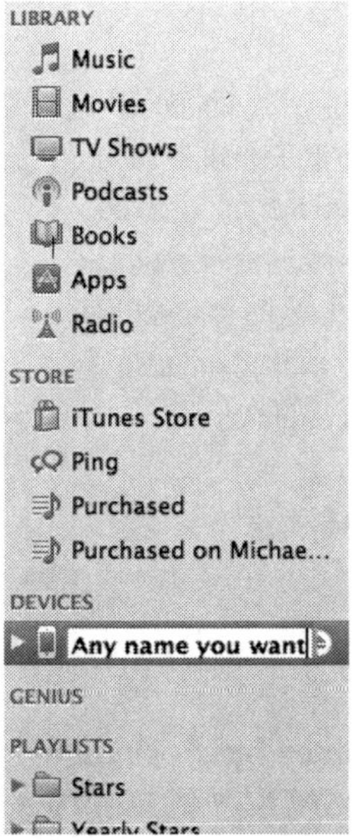

LIBRARY
- ♫ Music
- 🖿 Movies
- 🖵 TV Shows
- 🎙 Podcasts
- 📖 Books
- 🖼 Apps
- 📡 Radio

STORE
- 🛍 iTunes Store
- ⊂Ọ Ping
- 🎵 Purchased
- 🎵 Purchased on Michae...

DEVICES
- ▶ 🖳 Any name you want ⊳

GENIUS

PLAYLISTS
- ▶ 🗀 Stars
- ▶ 🗀 Yearly Stars

Figure 2–7. *Double-click your iPhone's name in the iTunes source list. You can rename it to anything you want. The name change will be reflected on the Summary tab.*

NOTE: You bought a 32GB iPhone, but you notice that the capacity states your device has only 29.21GB of storage. What gives? Whenever you buy an electronics device that offers storage capacity, the advertised amount of storage is always more than the actual storage available to you. Why? Several reasons. One is because the device's operating system must be stored on the same disk as your files. Without the OS, your device could not function. In this case, the iPhone's OS takes up almost 2GB of space. Another, more technical reason is because storage size can be measured in binary or decimal measurements. Binary says 1KB is equal to 1,024 bytes, while decimal says 1KB is equal to 1,000 bytes. When advertising storage space, companies choose to use the decimal measurement, which ends up showing more space than is actually available to you.

TIP: Use the serial number to check your current warranty status at the Apple Self Solve web site (https://selfsolve.apple.com/GetWarranty.do). There, you can see whether you have properly registered your device, whether you have active telephone technical support service, whether you are covered for repairs and service, and the details about your AppleCare protection plan. If you have not yet signed up for AppleCare service for your new iPhone, you can do so directly at the Self Solve site. It prompts you for billing information and processes your credit card payment. AppleCare extends your iPhone coverage to two years from the purchase date of your hardware. AppleCare+, which adds accidental damage coverage, can be purchased only at the same time as your device.

> **NOTE:** You can use the UDID to register your iPhone for certain developer beta tests (called *ad hoc builds*). Copy this value to memory via **Edit ➤ Copy** and then paste it into an e-mail to send your UDID to a developer. Although your UDID is not a particularly sensitive piece of information, you probably should not share it freely with others, just in case some as-yet-unknown exploit finds a use for UDIDs. Send it only to trusted developers, who will register it at Apple to enroll you in their ad hoc distribution program. Another, simpler way to share your UDID with others is to download the free Ad Hoc Helper application from the App Store. You can get to the proper iTunes page by loading this URL into your web browser:
> `http://itunes.apple.com/app/ad-hoc-helper/id285691333?mt=8.`

Version

The Version box allows you to manually check for iOS software updates by clicking the Check for Update button. Next to the button is text notifying you if your iPhone software is up-to-date or if there is an update available. Sometimes iTunes notifies you that there is a software update available before you've even clicked the Check for Update button. It knows this because iTunes automatically checks for iOS updates once a week. You'll also see text to your right that tells you when iTunes is going to automatically check for an update. If there is an iOS software update available, always install it. Sometimes updates provide new features; other times they provide simple bug fixes. Apple rigorously tests these updates before releasing them to the public, so it's usually safe to assume the updates will improve your device (whether you notice it or not).

> **NOTE:** Just what is iOS? iOS is the name Apple gave to the operating system that runs on all of its touchscreen mobile devices (iPhones, iPhone devices, and iPads). The latest version of iOS is iOS 5. Previous versions were referred to as "iPhone OS" 1, 2, or 3 since the iPhone's operating system was based on it. But now Apple has thankfully decided to take "iPhone" out of the OS name, and it's been called "iOS" for the last two versions. This book explores everything you can do with your iPhone running iOS 5.

> **NOTE:** If there is an iOS software update available, you should install it. Sometimes updates provide new features; other times they provide simple bug fixes. Apple rigorously tests these updates before releasing them to the public, so it's safe to assume the updates will make your device better (whether you notice it or not). Confused between the Restore and Update options? Updates offer newly released firmware from Apple. Installing an update leaves your data and applications unchanged. Restoring your iPad returns it to a factory-fresh state, removing all apps and data.

Below the Check for Update button is the Restore button. Clicking the Restore button allows you to restore your iPhone to a factory-new condition. You will rarely, if ever, use this feature. The only time to restore your iPhone is if you are having technical difficulties with it or if you decide to sell the iPhone or give it away and want to make sure all your personal data is removed from the device. Before the restore commences, you'll be shown a dialog box asking you to confirm the restore (see Figure 2–8).

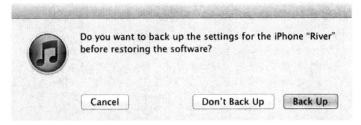

Figure 2–8. *After a restore, you have the option of putting all your data back onto the iPhone.*

Backup Box

This box allows you to choose how you want to back up your iPhone system and application data. You can back up to Apple's iCloud or to the local computer. Apple offers 5GB of cloud storage for free. You can easily consume that with backed-up data, let alone with application cloud-based documents. Additional iCloud storage costs $20/year for 15GB total (including your free 5GB), $40/year for 25GB total, and $100/year for 50GB total.

If you back up to your computer instead of the cloud, you'll save a bit of space—and potentially money. At the same time, you'll lose the "it just works" convenience of that backup. Also, if your computer dies for any reason, you will not have the off-site security of knowing your data is safe in the cloud. You'll need to tether your iPhone to your computer and allow the backup to occur during a tethered sync.

You may want to encrypt your iPhone backup by checking the "Encrypt iPhone backup" option. This allows you to set a password for your backed data. Be aware, if you lose that password, your data will be *gone*. You cannot recover your password through e-mail.

Options

You have several preferences in the Options box. To enable or disable any of the features, simply check or uncheck the box next to it.

> *Open iTunes when this iPhone is connected*: This option is selected by default. It tells your computer to open iTunes when it detects that your iPhone is connected via USB. If this option is not selected, iTunes doesn't open when you connect your iPhone, and no data is synced to your device until you manually open iTunes and click the Sync button next to the Capacity bar.

> **NOTE:** Even though iTunes does not launch or sync your data when this box is not selected, the iPhone is still charged.

Sync only checked songs and videos: When this option is selected, iTunes syncs only the songs in your library and playlists that have a check mark next to them in the iTunes library (see Figure 2–9).

Let's say you have a Greatest Hits playlist set to sync with the iPhone. In the playlist you have two copies of Michael Jackson's "Man in the Mirror" from two separate albums. You want to have only one copy of the song on the iPhone, but you don't want to remove the extra copy from the playlist. If you deselect one version of "Man in the Mirror" in the playlist and have "Sync only selected songs and videos" selected, the playlist syncs to your iPhone minus the extra "Man in the Mirror," but the song remains in your playlist in your iTunes library.

✔ In the Closet	Michael Jackson
✔ Jam	Michael Jackson
✔ Man in the Mirror	Michael Jackson
Man in the Mirror	Michael Jackson
✔ P Y T (pretty young thing)	Michael Jackson
✔ Remember the Time	Michael Jackson

Figure 2–9. *Selected songs and an unselected song in iTunes*

Sync with this Phone over Wi-Fi connection: This box must be checked if you want to sync the iPhone with your iTunes library over a Wi-Fi connection. This is why you need to sync your iPhone via a wired connection (the USB dock connector cable) the first time, so you can select this Sync over Wi-Fi connection box. Without this box being checked, your iTunes library has no way of knowing that it should be syncing with your iPhone over Wi-Fi.

Prefer standard definition video: When this box is checked, only the standard-definition version of any video in your iTunes library that has both standard and high-definition copies is synced. It's a good idea to keep this checked if you don't have a lot of space on your iPhone. A standard-definition version of a movie can save you up to four times the space of a high-definition movie.

Convert higher bit rate songs to 128 kbps AAC: Digital music comes in many formats and sizes, with the most popular being MP3 and AAC. Depending on how you obtained your music, whether buying it from the iTunes Store or ripping your collection from old CDs, your songs most likely have different encoding settings. A song encoded at 256Kbps takes up twice the space as a song encoded at 128Kbps. With the "Convert higher bit rate songs to 128 kbps AAC" option selected, any music synced to your iPhone is converted on the fly to the 128Kbps AAC format. The advantage of doing this is to save space on your iPhone by reducing higher bit rate songs to a perfectly acceptable 128Kbps.

NOTE: Unless you are an extreme audiophile with a gifted ear, you probably won't notice a difference between 128Kbps AAC file and 256Kbps versions of a digital music file.

Manually manage music and videos: With this option selected, music and videos are never automatically synced with your iPhone. The only way to add music and videos on the iPhone under this option is by dragging the songs or videos from the iTunes library onto the iPhone in the iTunes source list. Likewise, with this option selected, the only way to remove music or videos from your iPhone is by clicking the drop-down triangle next to the iPhone in iTunes' source list, navigating to your playlists selecting the song or video, and then pressing the Delete key on your computer's keyboard.

NOTE: Manually adding or removing music or video from your iPhone does not affect the files on your computer. Whenever a file is added to or deleted from the iPhone, it is just a copy of the file in your iTunes library. The original file always resides in your iTunes library until you delete it from there.

Configure Universal Access: The last thing on the Summary page is a Configure Universal Access button. Clicking this button opens a Universal Access box (see Figure 2–10) for setting visual and audible device assistance options for people who are hard of sight or hearing.

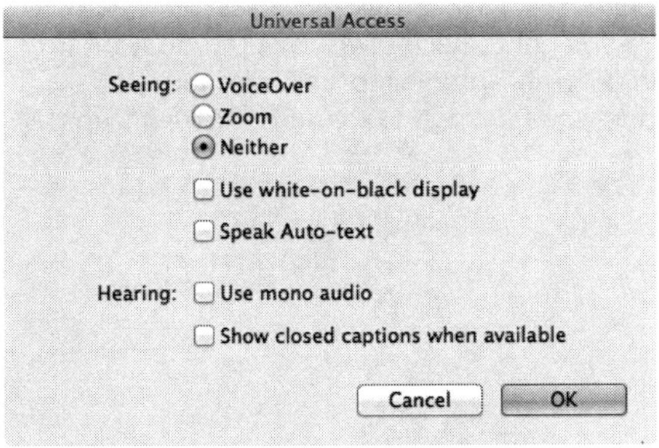

Figure 2–10. *The Universal Access settings*

Seeing: You have the option of selecting one of three radio buttons: Voice Over, Zoom, or Neither.

- *VoiceOver* makes your iPhone speak the name of a button or its function when the user touches it. It also speaks text. I explore the VoiceOver features in Chapter 16 of this book.

- *Zoom* allows the user to zoom into parts of the screen that normally don't support a magnifying or zoom function. When this option is selected, the user can double-tap any part of the iPhone's screen with three fingers to automatically zoom in at 200 percent. When zoomed in, you must drag or flick the screen with three fingers. Also, when you navigate to a new screen, Zoom always returns to the top middle of the screen.

Use white-on-black display: Selecting this option inverts the colors of the iPhone's screen so text appears white on a black background. The iPhone's entire screen looks like a photograph negative.

Speak Auto-text: With this option selected, autocorrected text is spoken aloud. An example of this is when spell check popups appear during typing.

Hearing: There are two accessibility features for the hearing impaired.

- *Use mono audio*: When this is selected, the stereo sounds of the left and right speakers are combined into a mono (single) signal. This option lets users who have a hearing impairment in one ear hear the entire sound signal with the other ear.

- *Show closed captions when available*: When this is selected, any video you have on your iPhone automatically displays closed captions if that video has captions embedded in it.

The Apps Tab

This is my favorite tab. It's the place where you get to decide which apps you want to put on your iPhone and arrange them with drag-and-drop simplicity. This tab is composed of two main sections: Sync Apps (see Figure 2–11) and File Sharing (see Figure 2–13). Let's get started.

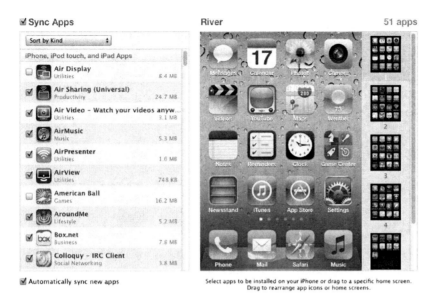

Figure 2–11. *The Apps tab is where you choose the apps to put on your iPhone and how they are arranged.*

Sync Apps

Under the Sync Apps heading is a scrollable list of all the applications you have in your apps library in iTunes. You can sort the list by name, kind, category, or date downloaded. There's also a search field in the upper-right corner of iTunes if you're one of those people who has downloaded thousands of apps and can't scroll through all of them quickly.

In the apps list there is a check box to the left of the app's icon. To the right of the icon is the app's name, and below that are the app's category listing and the file size of the individual application. Any app that has a selected check box means the application is set to sync with the iPhone. Below the apps list is a check box labeled "Automatically sync new apps." When this is selected, any new apps you've downloaded through iTunes are automatically synced with your iPhone on the next connection.

Next to the apps list is a visual representation of the screen of your iPhone. To the right of that are one or more smaller black screens with icons representing apps that are already on, or set to be synced with, your iPhone. You'll also see a completely gray screen below the last black one.

The easiest way to get apps on your iPhone is to find them in the apps list and simply drag them onto the virtual screen. As soon as you do, the app's check box is automatically selected in the app list.

You can drag around the apps on the virtual iPhone screen until you've arranged them in the order you like. It's also possible to grab the smaller black screens and move them up or down in the list, rearranging entire pages of apps on your iPhone. The black screen at the top of the list is the home page on your iPhone, and each one below that is a subsequent swipe away. The gray screen at the bottom is an extra screen should you want to create a new screen with apps.

To remove an app, hover your computer cursor over the app, and a little *X* appears in the upper-left corner. Click the *X*, and the app disappears from the screen. On the next sync, the app is removed from your iPhone. Don't worry; you can always get an app back by dragging it to the virtual iPhone's screen or by clicking the app in the list to the left.

> **NOTE:** Apps that Apple ships on the iPhone cannot be removed from the device—they can only be repositioned.

Creating Folders

There's a way to create folders of apps on your iPhone home screen as well. Folders help you avoid constantly swiping screens to the left or right and make it easy to group similar apps together. To create a folder in the Apps tab, drag one app onto another on the virtual iPhone screen and release it. A folder is created with the two apps in it, and you can name the folder whatever you want. Drag more apps to the folder and release them to add them. In the folder in Figure 2–12, I've created a folder called Travel & WX that contains some of my favorite travel and weather apps.

To remove apps from the folder, drag them out or click the *X* that appears when you move your pointer over the app's icon. Folders contain up to 12 applications, and there can be up to 20 folders on a page. Similarly, each screen holds 20 apps (or folders of apps) including the ones docked at the bottom of the screen. The dock holds anywhere between zero and four apps. Any apps placed in the dock appear at the bottom of the iPhone no matter what app screen you've swiped to. Since the docked apps always appear at the bottom of any app screen, it's best to put the ones you use most frequently down there for quick access.

River   51 apps

Select apps to be installed on your iPhone or drag to a specific home screen.
Drag to rearrange app icons or home screens.

Figure 2-12. *Creating a folder full of apps*

File Sharing

iTunes enables you to easily share files between the iPhone and your computer. Beneath the File Sharing heading is an Apps box and a Documents box (see Figure 2–13). Any apps that are currently on your iPhone that support drag-and-drop file sharing appear in the Apps list here. To share a file with an application, select the application in the Apps list, find the file on your computer you want to share, and drag it into the Documents list. You can also click the Add button at the bottom of the Documents list to browse for the file on your computer.

To transfer a file from your iPhone back to your computer, select the file in the Documents list, click the "Save to" button at the bottom, and choose where you want to save the file on your computer. Alternatively, drag the file from the Documents list to your desktop.

To delete a file from an app that contains it, select the file in the document list, and press the Delete key on your computer. iTunes prompts for confirmation when deleting or replacing files. Click the Delete button in the confirmation dialog to complete the deletion. At this time, you cannot delete folders or read the contents of files stored in folders in the documents list.

As long as a file is shared inside an app, it is always backed up when you sync your iPhone to your computer.

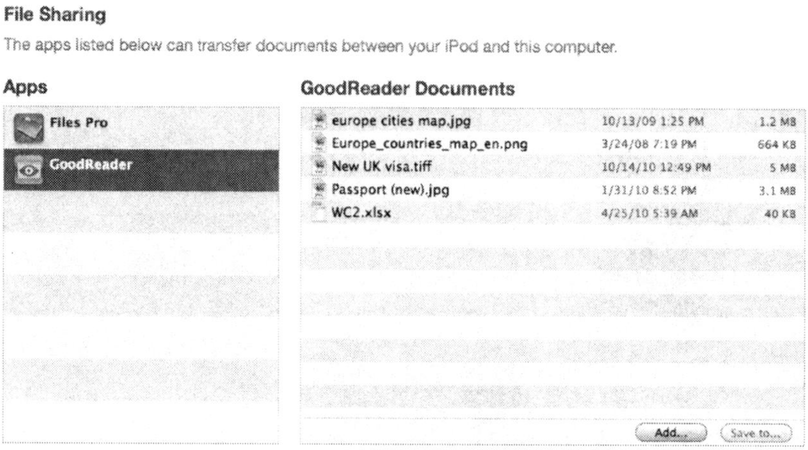

File Sharing

The apps listed below can transfer documents between your iPod and this computer.

Apps	GoodReader Documents		
Files Pro	europe cities map.jpg	10/13/09 1:25 PM	1.2 MB
GoodReader	Europe_countries_map_en.png	3/24/08 7:19 PM	664 KB
	New UK visa.tiff	10/14/10 12:49 PM	5 MB
	Passport (new).jpg	1/31/10 8:52 PM	3.1 MB
	WC2.xlsx	4/25/10 5:39 AM	40 KB

Add...   Save to...

Figure 2–13. *Apps that support drag-and-drop file sharing and their enclosed documents*

NOTE: Just because you can drag a file to an app's Documents box doesn't mean that the app can open it. Apps are limited to working with files that the iPhone supports. For example, the iPhone does not support Microsoft's WMV video files. If you drag a WMV movie to an app, the app contains it but is still not able to play it. To work around this issue, you need to download the Yxplayer app—it recognizes the WMV files and plays them.

The Ringtones Tab

The Ringtones tab (Figure 2–14) allows you to import custom ringtones you've purchased from the iTunes Store and use them to notify you not only of incoming phone calls but also of FaceTime video calls.

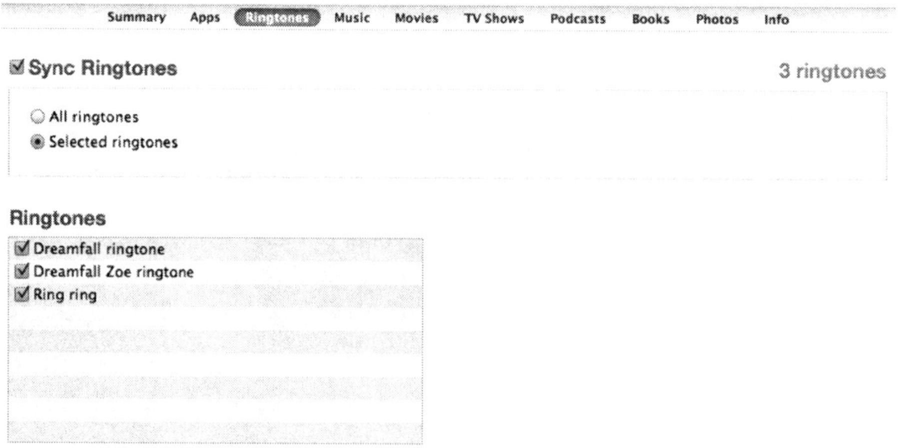

Summary   Apps   **Ringtones**   Music   Movies   TV Shows   Podcasts   Books   Photos   Info

☑ **Sync Ringtones**   3 ringtones

○ All ringtones
◉ Selected ringtones

Ringtones

☑ Dreamfall ringtone
☑ Dreamfall Zoe ringtone
☑ Ring ring

Figure 2–14. *The Ringtones tab*

To sync ringtones, select the Sync Ringtones box. Next, choose whether you want to sync all of your ringtones or just selected ones. If you choose "Selected ringtones," the Ringtones box appears, listing all of the ringtones you have stored in iTunes. Check the ringtones you want to sync.

Synchronization Options

In many of the remaining tabs, iTunes offers a primary checkbox allowing you to sync items or not. You can sync music, movies, TV shows, podcasts, iTunes U classes, books, and photos. For the first four of these, you'll be given the option to synchronize items automatically.

To choose that automatic option, check the appropriate box in each tab ("Sync Music," "Sync Movies," and so on), check the automatic box ("Automatically include"), and then choose how you want iTunes to select those items.

- *Recent items*: Select some number of recently added items (typically one, three, five, ten, or all) to synchronize to your device.

- *Unplayed or unwatched items*: When selected, you can choose from all unplayed/unwatched items or some. Pick some number of the most recent selections, or if you want to catch up with media that's been sitting around for a while, choose the least recent unplayed selections.

- *New items*: These work in much the same way as unplayed items in that you can pick a certain number of items. The difference between new and unplayed/unwatched is that an item is considered "unplayed" (or "unwatched") until it's been fully listened to or watched. After that, it is played/watched. New means the item has never been accessed at all. This ensures the material synced to your device is completely fresh.

Further automatic options allow you to decide whether these choices are selected from the entire collection or from selected items. This varies by tab.

To choose items manually, uncheck the "Automatically include" option and use the on-screen selection elements for each tab to pick which items you want to synchronize to your iPhone.

The Music Tab

The Music tab is used to—what else? Set up syncing of music (see Figure 2–15). Make sure the Sync Music check box is selected at the top. In the box below it are two radio buttons.

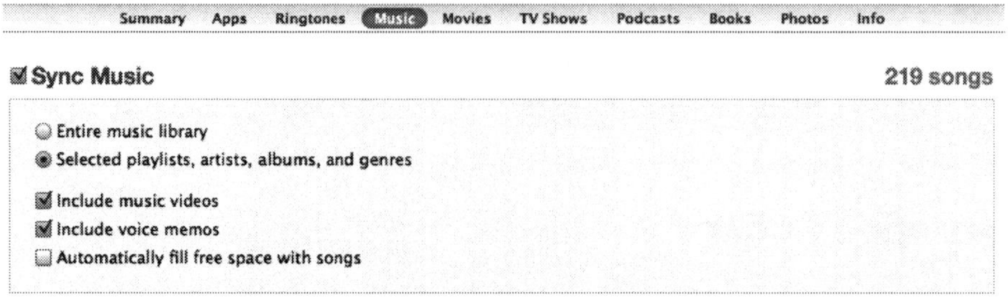

| Summary | Apps | Ringtones | Music | Movies | TV Shows | Podcasts | Books | Photos | Info |

☑ Sync Music   219 songs

○ Entire music library
◉ Selected playlists, artists, albums, and genres

☑ Include music videos
☑ Include voice memos
☐ Automatically fill free space with songs

Figure 2–15. *The Music tab allows you to select which songs, playlists, and artists you want to sync to your iPhone.*

Entire music library: When this is selected, the entire music library is synced to your iPhone. Note that your entire library is synced only if you have the storage space available on your iPhone. If you have more music than the iPhone can hold, the remainder of the music stops syncing once the iPhone is full.

Selected playlists, artists, albums and genres: Selecting this option displays four boxes listing all of the playlists, artists, and genres in your iTunes library. Go through and select the check boxes of the playlists, artists, and genres you want on your iPhone.

Include music videos: Selecting this check box transfers any music videos associated with playlists, artists, or genres to the iPhone.

Include voice memos: If you select this check box, any voice memos stored in your iTunes library are synced with your iPhone.

Automatically fill free space with songs: This check box appears only if you've chosen the "Selected playlists, artists, and genres" radio button. If it's selected, once all your other files (movies, books, photos, and so on) have been synced to your iPhone, any leftover free space is filled with music. I don't recommend selecting this option. It severely limits your ability to create any new documents or store any photos you take on your iPhone since there won't be any space left in which to store them.

The Movies Tab

The iTunes Store offers a large collection of movies for rent or purchase that you can download and sync to your iPhone. The Movies tab, shown in Figure 2–16, provides several ways of transferring your movies onto the iPhone.

Summary   Apps   Ringtones   Music   **Movies**   TV Shows   Podcasts   Books   Photos   Info

☑ **Sync Movies**   6 movies

☐ Automatically include | all   ⬦ | movies

Figure 2–16. *The Movies tab allows you to select which movies you want to sync to your iPhone.*

To sync your movies, first make sure the Sync Movies check box is selected (see Figure 2–16). Three check boxes are displayed on the Movies tab:

> *Automatically include*: If this check box is selected, you'll be able to access a pop-up list of preset options to make your movie syncing experience easier. From the pop-up list, you can choose to sync all your movies (not a good idea because one hour of video can take up to half a gigabyte of space) or decide to save some space.
>
> If you'd like to go the space-saving route, select the one, three, five, or ten "most recent movies" preset. You also have the option of selecting the "all unwatched" movies preset, which adds all the movies in your library that have not been watched yet. Other preset options include syncing one, three, five, or ten of your "most recent unwatched movies" or one, three, five, or ten of your "least recent unwatched movies."
>
> *Movies*: If the "automatically include" check box is selected and the drop-down list is set to anything but "all," you also have the option of selecting additional movies from your iTunes library. With the "automatically include" box unchecked, you can manually select as many of your movies as you want (see Figure 2–17).

Movies

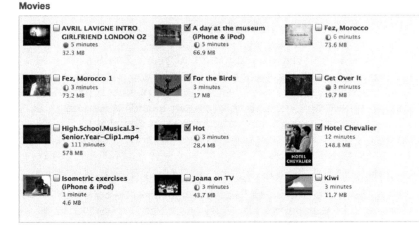

Figure 2–17. *The Movies check box allows you to select individual movies to sync to your iPhone.*

> *Include Movies from Playlists*: This box, shown in Figure 2–18, provides the option of including movies found in your iTunes playlists.

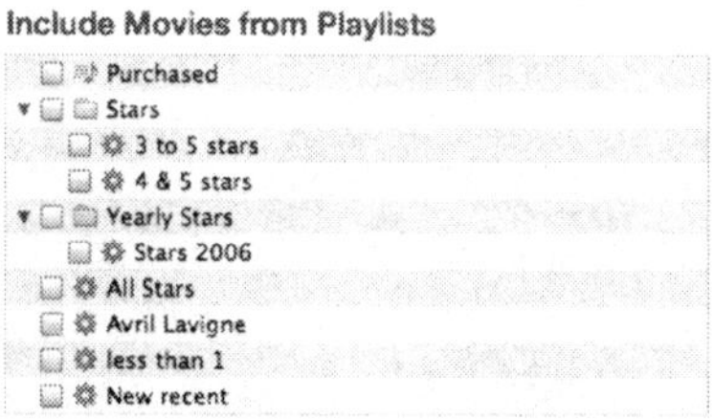

Include Movies from Playlists

Figure 2–18. *This box allows you to sync movies from your iTunes playlists.*

The TV Shows Tab

The iTunes Store offers large collections of TV shows available for purchase and download. All of these shows can be synchronized to your iPhone for viewing. You can purchase individual episodes *à la carte* or buy a Season Pass. With the latter choice, you pay for the entire season at once, often at a slight discount, and new episodes are automatically downloaded when they are available.

To sync TV shows, first make sure that the Sync TV Shows check box is selected (see Figure 2–19). On the TV Shows tab below are three check boxes similar to those on the Movies tab.

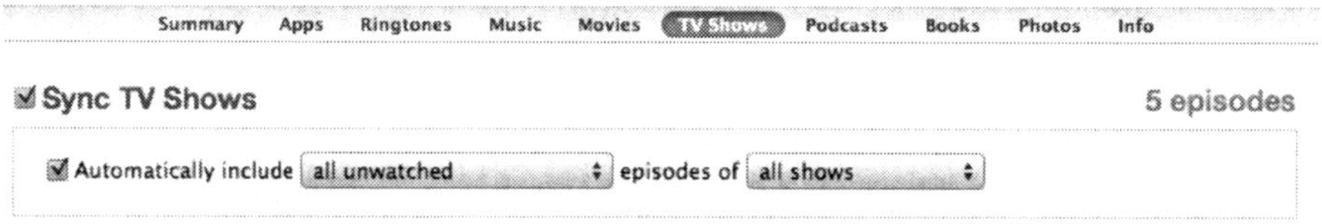

Figure 2–19. *The TV Shows tab is used to select the shows you want to sync to your iPhone.*

> *Automatically include*: Select this check box to access a pop-up displaying preset options to simplify your TV show syncing experience. From the drop-down list, you can choose to sync all your TV shows; again, this is not a good idea if you watch a lot of TV on your iPhone since an hour of video can occupy up to half a gigabyte of space). There is also an "all unwatched" option and several presets including syncing only the newest shows, the newest unwatched shows, or the oldest unwatched shows. With all these options, the presets can be applied to all shows or just selected TV shows.
>
> *The Shows and Episodes boxes*: If the "automatically include" check box is selected and set to anything but "all," you also have the option of selecting additional TV shows from your iTunes library (see Figure 2–20). With the "automatically include" check box deselected, you are able to manually select as many of your TV shows as you want.

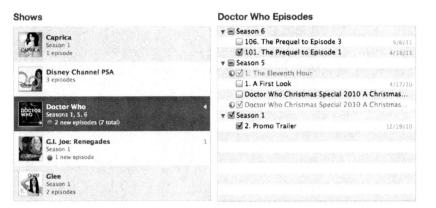

Figure 2–20. *The Shows check box allows you to select TV series to sync to your iPhone. In the box to the left you can select the episodes to sync.*

> *Include Episodes from Playlists*: This box gives you the option of including any TV show episodes found in your iTunes playlists (see Figure 2–21).

Include Episodes from Playlists

- Purchased
- Stars
  - 3 to 5 stars
  - 4 & 5 stars
- Yearly Stars
  - Stars 2006
  - Stars 2007
- 2003
- All Stars
- Christmas
- less than 1
- New recent
- Recently Played
- Smallville

Figure 2–21. *This box allows you to sync any TV shows found in your iTunes playlists.*

The Podcasts Tab

Many people use iTunes to subscribe to their favorite podcasts. *Podcasts* are audio and video programs delivered over the Internet on a subscription basis; that is, you subscribe to a podcast for free and receive a series of episodes on a particular topic. Numerous podcasts are available, with topics including entertainment and advice, tech shows, politics, news, and much more. iTunes monitors your podcast subscriptions and automatically downloads new episodes when they become available. The Podcasts tab gives you control over which shows are synchronized to your iPhone.

The Podcasts tab (see Figure 2–22) has a similar look and feel to the Movies and TV Shows tabs. To sync podcasts, first make sure the Sync Podcasts check box is selected. Below the check box are three boxes on the Podcasts tab.

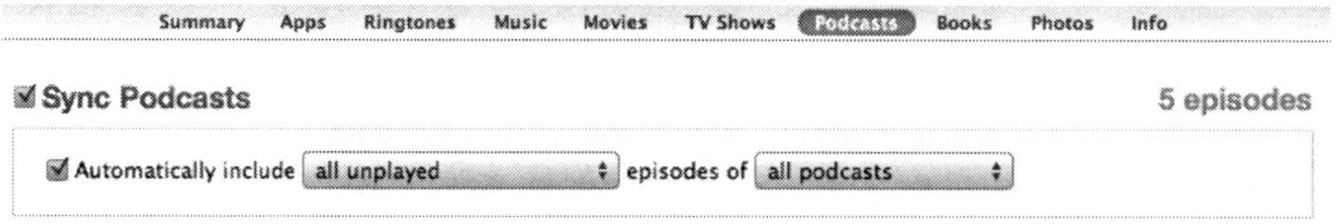

| Summary | Apps | Ringtones | Music | Movies | TV Shows | Podcasts | Books | Photos | Info |

☑ **Sync Podcasts**   5 episodes

☑ Automatically include [all unplayed ‡] episodes of [all podcasts ‡]

Figure 2–22. *The Podcasts tab allows you to select the podcasts to sync to your iPhone.*

> *Automatically include*: Selecting this check box displays a pop-up list with several options, the first of which is to sync all of your podcasts. If you're subscribing only to audio podcasts, this might not be a bad idea, but be sure to keep in mind the space limitations that come with syncing video.
>
> Other options include syncing all unplayed or all new podcasts. Apple thoughtfully provided presets for syncing only the newest, the most or least recent unplayed podcasts, or the most or least recent new podcasts. Those presets can be applied to all podcasts or just to those that you've selected.
>
> *The Podcasts and Episodes boxes*: If the "automatically include" check box is selected and set to anything but "all," you also have the option of selecting additional podcasts from your iTunes library (see Figure 2–23). With the check box deselected, manually select as many or as few podcasts as you want.

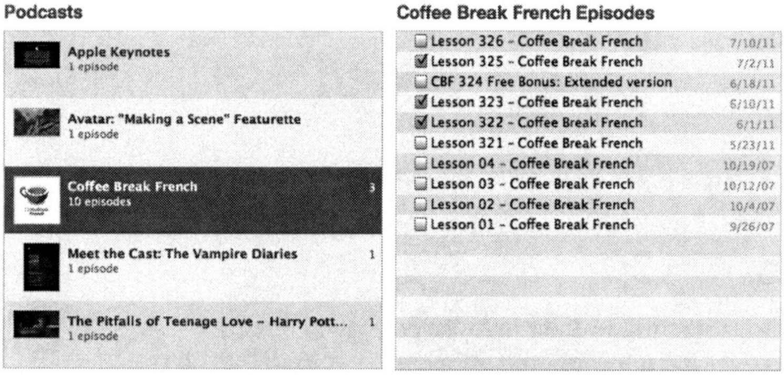

Podcasts   **Coffee Break French Episodes**

Apple Keynotes 1 episode	
Avatar: "Making a Scene" Featurette 1 episode	
Coffee Break French 10 episodes	3
Meet the Cast: The Vampire Diaries 1 episode	1
The Pitfalls of Teenage Love – Harry Pott... 1 episode	1

☐ Lesson 326 – Coffee Break French	7/10/11
☑ Lesson 325 – Coffee Break French	7/2/11
☐ CBF 324 Free Bonus: Extended version	6/18/11
☑ Lesson 323 – Coffee Break French	6/10/11
☑ Lesson 322 – Coffee Break French	6/1/11
☐ Lesson 321 – Coffee Break French	5/23/11
☐ Lesson 04 – Coffee Break French	10/19/07
☐ Lesson 03 – Coffee Break French	10/12/07
☐ Lesson 02 – Coffee Break French	10/4/07
☐ Lesson 01 – Coffee Break French	9/26/07

Figure 2–23. *The Podcasts check box allows you to select podcasts to sync to your iPhone. In the dialog to the left you select episodes of a podcast series to sync.*

> *Include Episodes from Playlists*: This dialog (see Figure 2–24) provides the option of including any podcast episodes found in your iTunes playlists.

Include Episodes from Playlists

| ☐ ⚙ Last 30 days |
| ☐ ⚙ Music Videos |
| ☐ ⚙ New recent |
| ☐ ⚙ Recently Added |

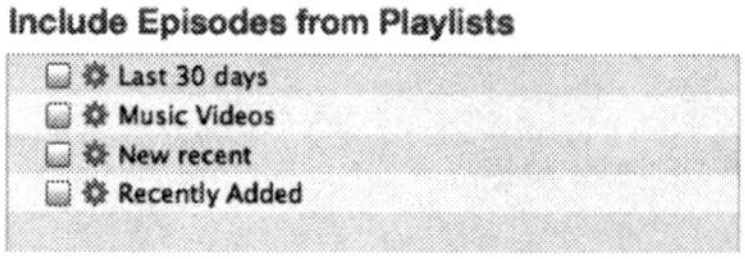

Figure 2–24. *Have podcasts in your iTunes playlists? Here's where you can choose to sync those episodes to your iPhone.*

The Books Tab

With the iBooks app installed on your iPhone, you have the ability to buy and read e-books or view PDF files on your device. I'll explore the iBookstore and iBooks app in Chapter 11, but for now you just need to know that the Books tab in the iPhone preferences window is where you control the books and PDF files that are synced to your iPhone (Figure 2–25).

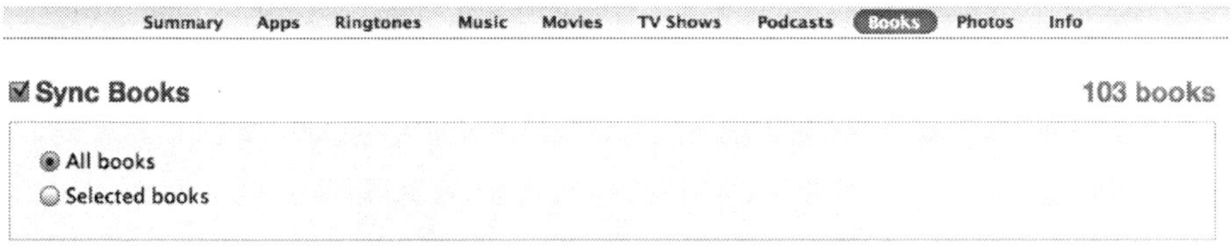

Figure 2–25. *The Books tab allows you to select which books and PDF files you want to sync to your iPhone.*

Make sure the Sync Books check box is selected. In the area below it are two radio buttons; "All books" syncs every book in your iTunes library, and "Selected books" allows you to sync only the books and/or PDFs selected in the Books box further down the page (see Figure 2–26).

> **NOTE:** Even if you have 300 books in your iTunes library, you might as well sync them all. An e-book takes up very little storage. As a matter of fact, *War and Peace*, one of the largest books ever written, takes up only a tiny 1.2 MB of storage. That's less than 50 percent of the size of a single three-minute 128Kbps AAC music file. Illustrated books take up more space, but even then they won't take up much more storage than a few song files. Don't worry about a cluttered library, either. You'll learn how to organize your books in Chapter 11.

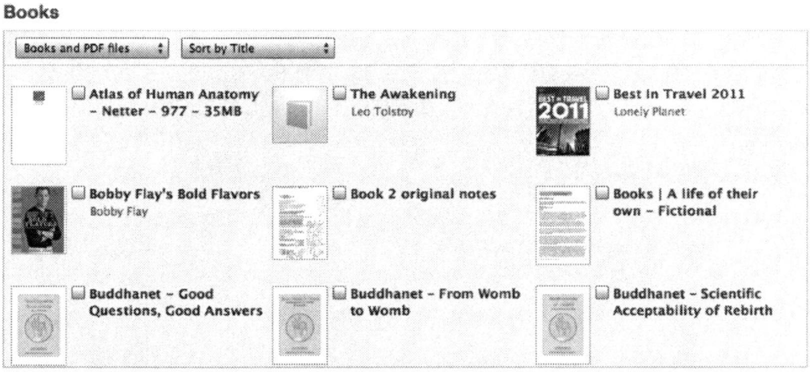

Figure 2–26. *The Books check box allows you to select individual books to sync to your iPhone.*

Below the Books box is a Sync Audiobooks check box (see Figure 2–27) and two options: "All audiobooks" or "Selected audiobooks."

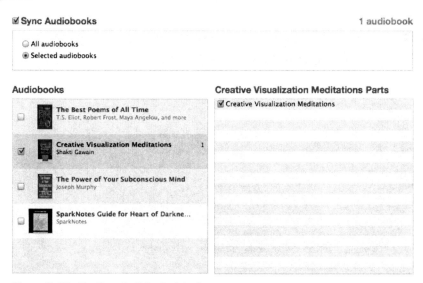

Figure 2–27. *The Sync Audiobooks interface*

As you'd expect, selecting "All audiobooks" syncs all audiobooks in your iTunes library with your iPhone, while choosing "Selected audiobooks" displays the familiar layout you've seen on the other media tabs.

> *Audiobooks and Parts*: In the Audiobooks box, you manually select the audiobooks you want to sync. Some audiobooks have separate files, or *parts*, that usually designate chapters (see Figure 2–27). You can select only the parts you want to sync for any audiobook in the Parts box. If the "automatically include" check box is selected and set to anything but "all," you also have the option of selecting additional audiobooks from your iTunes library. With the "automatically include" check box deselected, feel free to manually select as many or as few of your audiobooks or parts as you want.

> *Include Audiobooks from Playlists*: This box gives you the option of syncing any audiobooks included in your iTunes playlists (see Figure 2–28).

Figure 2–28. *This box allows you to sync any audiobooks found in your iTunes playlists.*

NOTE: Audiobooks are different from their e-book brethren, since the former are long audio files that can be quite large. If you have dozens of audiobooks, consider transferring only a select few from iTunes to your iPhone to save space.

The Photos Tab

The ability to view photos on my iPhone was pretty low on my list of reasons to buy one. Ironically, viewing photos is now one of my favorite things to do with my iPhone. I'll discuss viewing photos on your iPhone in Chapter 12, but for now I'll say that the experience is delightfully different than viewing photos on your desktop. There's nothing like physically holding digital photos in your hand and swiping through them on the gorgeous display of the iPhone.

To get photos onto your iPhone, make sure the "Sync Photos from" check box on the Photos tab is selected (see Figure 2–29), and then choose where you want to sync your photos from. On the Mac, your options will be iPhoto 4.0.3 or newer, Aperture 3.0.2 or newer, or any folder on your computer. On a Windows computer, your options will be Adobe Photoshop Elements 3.0 or newer or any folder on your computer.

Figure 2–29. *The Photos tab allows you to select which photos you want to sync to your iPhone.*

In the box below the check box, there are three options:

> *All photos, albums, events, and faces*: Selecting this option syncs every photo from your selected photo application or folder onto the iPhone. Again, I recommend against this if your photo collections are as large as mine (I have somewhere around 80GB of travel photos on my Mac). If you have only a few thousand photos, load 'em up!

NOTE: You can add photos from another iPhone or digital camera to your iPhone via the Camera Connection Kit. The $29 kit (available at http://store.apple.com) includes two adapters—one for connecting a camera through a USB 2.0 cable and the other for reading SD memory cards.

Selected albums, events, and faces, and automatically include: Selecting this option displays boxes for albums, events, and faces further down the page (see Figure 2–30). From these boxes you can choose which iPhoto albums and events to sync. You can also choose whether you want to sync faces. Faces is a feature in iPhoto that uses facial recognition capabilities to create collections of photos in which a certain person appears.

When you select any of the check boxes next to a certain album, event, or face, the photo count of that selection is displayed to the right. Choosing the "Selected albums, events, and faces, and automatically include" option, you are presented with a list of options allowing you to select all, none, or a preset date-specific range of iPhoto event collections.

Include video: When this check box is selected, any videos made with your digital camera that appear in any of your selected albums are transferred to the iPhone. Keep in mind that video can quickly use up storage space.

Figure 2–30. *Choose which iPhoto photo albums, events, and faces to sync.*

The Info Tab

The final tab to discuss (although it's actually listed second in iTunes) is the Info tab (see Figure 2–31), and it's all about you. This is the tab that allows you to sync your most personal information with the iPhone, including contacts, calendars, and e-mail. This tab has five sections: Sync Address Book Contacts, Sync iCal Calendars, Sync Mail Accounts, Other, and Advanced.

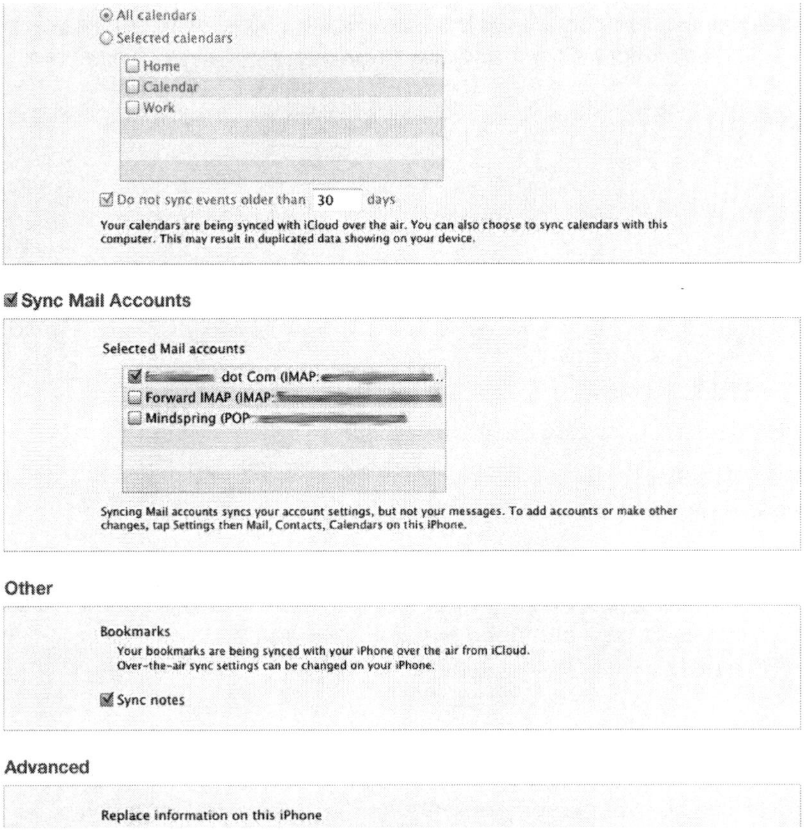

Figure 2–31. *The Info tab allows you to sync mail accounts, contacts, calendars, bookmarks, and notes. The tab is way too long to show entirely in a single image.*

If you have been using Outlook on Windows or Mail, iCal, and Address Book on a Mac, then you'll already have everything you need to sync your information to your iPhone. You just need to tell the iPhone how you want to sync that information.

> **NOTE:** If you are using Apple's iCloud service (www.icloud.com), the Sync Address Book Contacts and Sync iCal Calendars options are deselected after your first iPhone sync, and a message states that your contacts and calendars are being synced over the air via iCloud.

Sync Address Book Contacts

To sync address book contacts, you need to be using one of the following applications: Address Book or a recent version of Microsoft Entourage on a Mac or Windows Address Book or a recent version of Microsoft Outlook on Windows.

Select the Sync Address Book Contacts check box (see Figure 2–32), which gives you the option of syncing all the contacts in your address book or just those from selected groups.

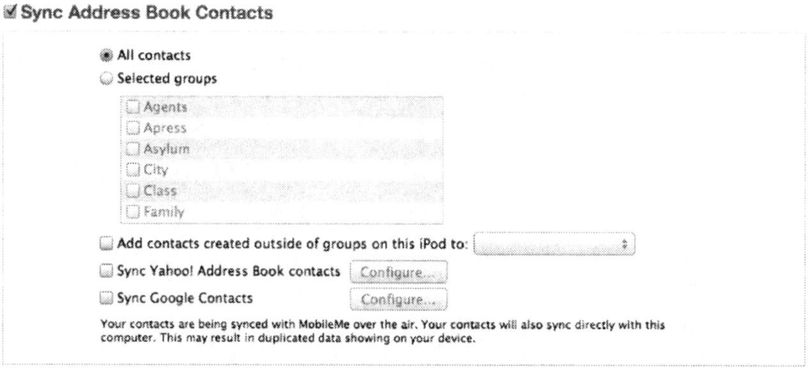

☑ Sync Address Book Contacts

    ◉ All contacts
    ◯ Selected groups

      ☐ Agents
      ☐ Apress
      ☐ Asylum
      ☐ City
      ☐ Class
      ☐ Family

    ☐ Add contacts created outside of groups on this iPod to: [⬍]
    ☐ Sync Yahoo! Address Book contacts   [Configure...]
    ☐ Sync Google Contacts   [Configure...]

    Your contacts are being synced with MobileMe over the air. Your contacts will also sync directly with this computer. This may result in duplicated data showing on your device.

Figure 2–32. *Your address book syncing options*

Add contacts created outside of groups on this iPhone to: When this check box is selected, a drop-down list of all your address book groups appears. If you create a new contact on your iPhone and don't assign the contact to a group, that contact is automatically put into the group you select here.

Sync Yahoo! Address Book contacts: When this check box is selected, Yahoo! Address Book contacts are automatically synced with your iPhone address book. You must agree with the dialog box that asks you to acknowledge that you are allowing the iPhone to sync to your Yahoo! account. Next, you are asked to enter your Yahoo! ID and password. Once you've done this, your contacts are set to sync. Clicking the Configure button allows you to enter a different Yahoo! ID.

Sync Google Contacts: When this check box is selected, Google contacts are automatically synced with your iPhone address book. You must agree with the dialog box that asks you to acknowledge that you are allowing your iPhone to sync to your Google account. Next, you are prompted to enter your Google ID and password. Once you've done this, your contacts are ready to sync. Clicking the Configure button allows you to enter a different Google ID.

Sync iCal Calendars

To sync your calendars, you need to be using one of the following: iCal or a recent version of Microsoft Entourage on a Mac or a recent version of Microsoft Outlook on Windows.

To set up calendar syncing, select the Sync iCal Calendars check box (see Figure 2–33). Just like with contacts, you then have the option of syncing all your calendars or just selected ones.

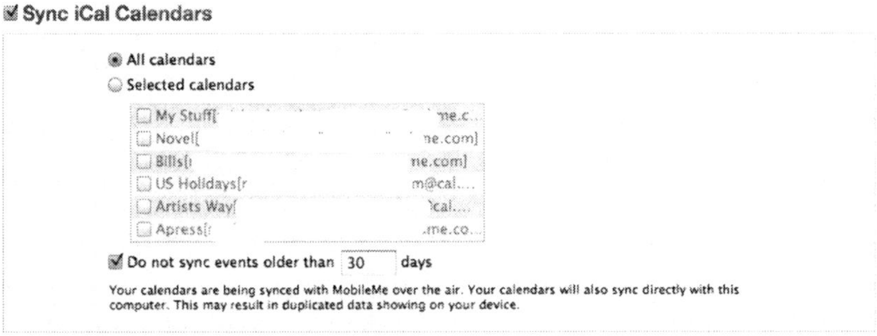

☑ Sync iCal Calendars

- ⦿ All calendars
- ◯ Selected calendars

  - ☐ My Stuff[ne.c...
  - ☐ Novel[ne.com]
  - ☐ Bills[ne.com]
  - ☐ US Holidays[r m@cal....
  - ☐ Artists Way[ical....
  - ☐ Apress[: .me.co...

☑ Do not sync events older than 30 days

Your calendars are being synced with MobileMe over the air. Your calendars will also sync directly with this computer. This may result in duplicated data showing on your device.

Figure 2–33. *Your calendar syncing options*

> *Do not sync events older than*: With this check box selected, events that are more than a specified number of days old are not synced. The default number of days is 30, but you can enter anything up to 99,999 days.

NOTE: A great place to find premade calendars for holidays, school events, or your favorite sporting teams is at www.icalshare.com.

Sync Mail Accounts

All of the mail accounts you have set up in Mac OS X Mail or Microsoft Outlook appear here (Figure 2–34). You have the option of selecting or deselecting any of the accounts. Accounts that are not selected do not appear in the iPhone's Mail app.

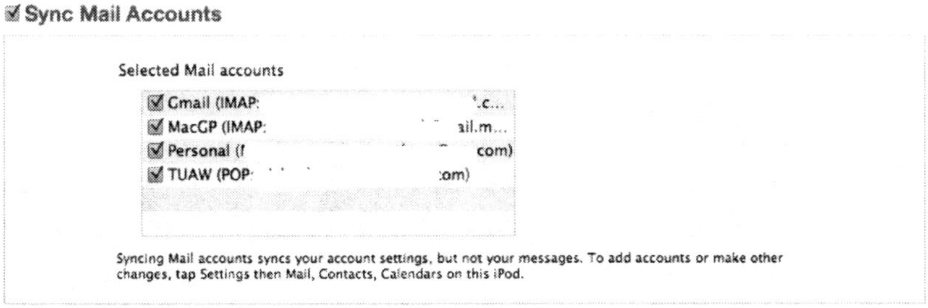

☑ Sync Mail Accounts

Selected Mail accounts

- ☑ Gmail (IMAP: '.c...
- ☑ MacGP (IMAP: ail.m...
- ☑ Personal (f ~ com)
- ☑ TUAW (POP· :om)

Syncing Mail accounts syncs your account settings, but not your messages. To add accounts or make other changes, tap Settings then Mail, Contacts, Calendars on this iPod.

Figure 2–34. *Your e-mail account syncing options*

Other

Apple should really have named this section "Bookmark and Notes Syncing," but Apple opted for "Other." Here you can sync bookmarks from the web browser on your computer to the Safari web browser on the iPhone (see Figure 2–35). Again, if you have an iCloud or MobileMe account, your bookmarks are synced over the air. If not, select the Sync Bookmarks check box, and choose your browser from the drop-down menu. On the Mac, bookmark syncing is supported for Safari. On a Windows computer, bookmark syncing supports Safari and Microsoft Internet Explorer 8 or newer.

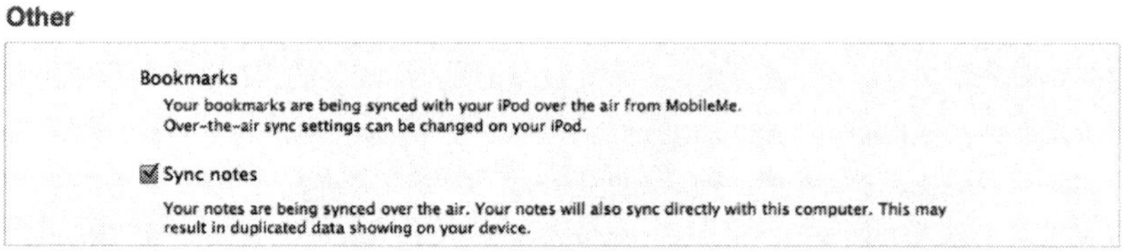

Other

Bookmarks
Your bookmarks are being synced with your iPod over the air from MobileMe.
Over-the-air sync settings can be changed on your iPod.

☑ Sync notes
Your notes are being synced over the air. Your notes will also sync directly with this computer. This may result in duplicated data showing on your device.

Figure 2–35. *Your bookmark and note syncing options*

This section also allows you to sync notes to your iPhone. Note syncing works only with Mac OS X Mail on a Mac, Outlook on Mac, or Microsoft Outlook 2003 or 2007 on Windows. To enable note syncing, select the check box.

Advanced

When selected, this section allows you to replace contacts, calendars, mail accounts, and notes on the iPhone with information from your computer (see Figure 2–36). This is a handy feature if your information gets out of sync and you want to make sure that everything you see on your computer matches what is on the iPhone.

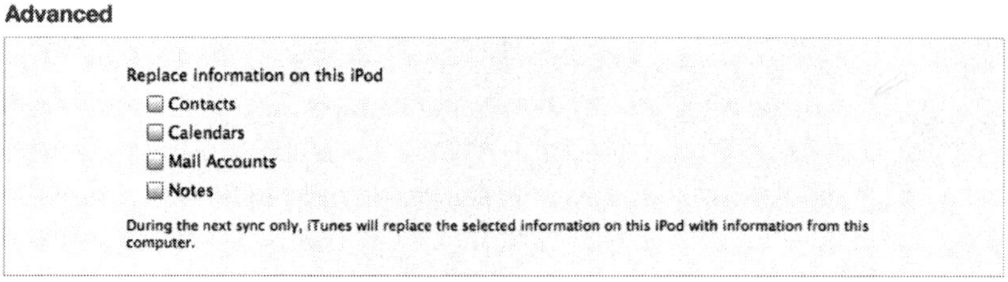

Advanced

Replace information on this iPod
☐ Contacts
☐ Calendars
☐ Mail Accounts
☐ Notes

During the next sync only, iTunes will replace the selected information on this iPod with information from this computer.

Figure 2–36. *Your advanced syncing options*

When you select the respective check boxes, iTunes overwrites the information on your iPhone during the next sync only. After that sync, normal syncing resumes between your iPhone and computer.

> **NOTE:** If your calendars and contacts are being synced via iCloud, you will not be able to select their check boxes in the Advanced section.

iTunes Device Settings

iTunes has several preferences for the iPhone. To access these on a Mac, launch iTunes and select **iTunes ➤ Preferences** from the menu bar, or select **Edit ➤ Preferences** from the menu bar if you are using Windows. The Preferences window pops up with a series of icons running along the top. The only one we are interested in for the iPhone is the Devices icon. Click the Devices icon (it looks like an iPhone), and you'll be presented with the Devices preferences window (see Figure 2–37).

Here you'll find settings for devices that interact with iTunes. These devices can include the iPhone, iPad, iPhone, Apple TV, and AirPort Express.

> *Device backups*: Any time your iPhone is synced, iTunes creates a backup of its contents. Any backups of iPad, iPhone, or iPhone devices are listed under "Device backups." The name of the device is listed along with the date it was last backed up. Hover your cursor over the name of the iPhone to view its serial number.

> Although iTunes keeps multiple dated, partial backups of your device, it's still a good idea to make copies of your backups on an external hard drive. iTunes places the original backup files in the following locations:

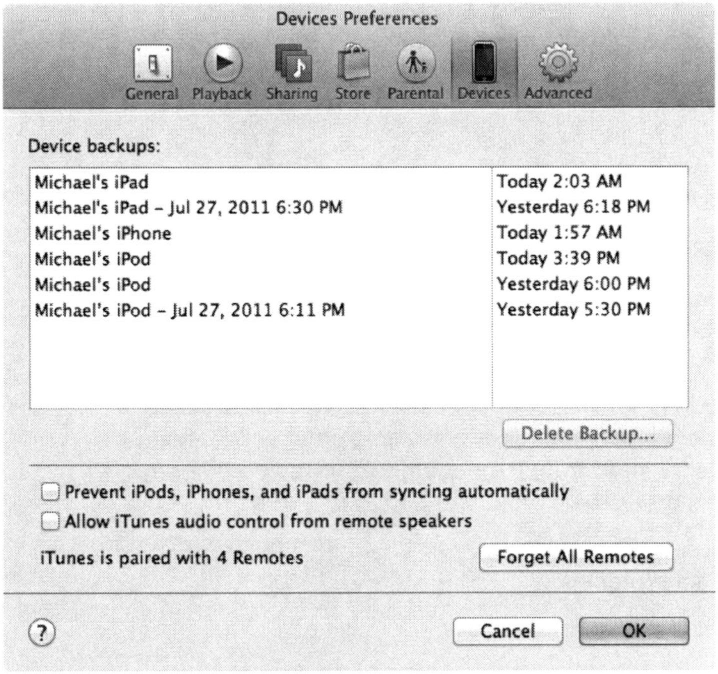

Figure 2–37. *The iTunes Devices preferences window*

- *Mac*: ~/Library/Application Support/MobileSync/Backup/

- *Windows XP*: \Documents and Settings\(username)\Application Data\Apple Computer\MobileSync\Backup\

- *Windows Vista*: \Users\(username)\AppData\Roaming\Apple Computer\MobileSync\Backup\

The list of information backed up by iTunes is a long one:

- Safari bookmarks, cookies, history, and currently open pages
- Map bookmarks, recent searches, and the current location displayed in Maps
- Application settings, preferences, and data
- Contacts
- Calendars
- CalDAV and subscribed calendar accounts
- YouTube favorites
- Wallpapers
- Notes
- Mail accounts
- Autocorrect dictionaries
- Camera Roll
- Home screen layout and web clips
- Network settings (saved Wi-Fi hotspots, VPN settings, network preferences)
- Paired Bluetooth devices (which can be used only if restored to the same iPhone that did the backup)
- Keychain (This includes e-mail account passwords, Wi-Fi passwords, and passwords you enter into web sites and some other applications. The keychain can be restored from backup only to the same iPhone. If you are restoring to a new device, you will need to fill in these passwords again.)
- Managed configurations/profiles
- Email account configurations
- App Store application data (except the application itself and its tmp and Caches folders).
- Per-app preferences allowing use of location services
- Offline web application cache/database
- Autofill for web pages
- Trusted hosts that have certificates that cannot be verified
- Web sites approved to get the location of the device
- In-app purchases

To delete an iPhone backup, select it from the "Device backups" list, and click the Delete Backup button. Confirm the deletion by clicking the Delete Backup button in the dialog that appears.

Prevent iPhones, iPhones, and iPads from syncing automatically: Select this box if you want to disable automatic syncing when the iPhone is connected to your computer. To sync, you'll need to manually click the Sync button at the bottom of the iTunes preferences window for iPhone.

Restoring

If you ever experience problems with your iPhone, you can choose to restore it. There are two restore options: restore to factory default and restore from backup. Restoring to factory default restores your iPhone to its original factory settings, as if you've just turned it on for the first time. Restoring from backup restores the iPhone from its last saved backup file.

To restore to factory settings, select the iPhone from the devices list in iTunes, select the Summary tab, and then click Restore (this deletes all data on iPhone and restores to factory settings). When prompted by iTunes, select the option to restore your settings.

To restore from backup, right-click (or Ctrl+click) the iPhone in the devices list in iTunes and select Restore from Backup. The iPhone is restored from the backup selected from the "Device backups" list.

> **NOTE:** If you've set up password encryption on your iPhone backups (covered earlier in this chapter), you cannot restore from the encrypted backup if you forget the password. Be sure to choose passwords that are easy to remember!

Syncing via iCloud

If you want, you need never connect to your iPhone to a home computer. You can activate it at an Apple store and then use iCloud synchronization, updates, and backups. To enable your iPhone to synchronize directly through iCloud, set **Settings ➤ iCloud Storage & Backup ➤ iCloud Backup** to ON. Keep in mind that backups will occupy a large part of your initial 5GB free storage. You may want to move up to a paid tier if you take this route with your iPhone.

You can update your iPhone to new firmware without ever using iTunes. Choose **Settings ➤ General ➤ Software Update**. New updates appear here and can be installed "over the air" using a Wi-Fi connection.

To reset your iPhone, select **Settings ➤ General ➤ Reset ➤ Erase All Content and Settings**. This returns your iPhone to a factory-fresh state.

Summary

In this chapter, you explored options for syncing media and data with your iPhone. You discovered where to get your media and how to make sure your iPhone/iTunes sync preferences stick. To wind things up, here is a quick overview of some key points from this chapter:

- The Capacity bar is always visible in the iPhone preferences and is an easy indicator of how much storage is available on your iPhone.

- No change made to the iPhone preferences is complete until you click the Apply button. Likewise, if you accidentally make a change you don't want, you can always click the Cancel button.

- It is important to manage what data you sync with your iPhone. Syncing all of your music may not leave enough storage for photos and videos.

- Syncing and organizing apps is easy to do when you use the visual representation of your iPhone under the Apps tab. If you have a lot of apps, syncing can be a slow process. Waiting can be a pain, but it's best never to interrupt a sync.

- Syncing of movies, music, TV shows, podcasts, books, and photos is pretty straightforward, and once you've mastered how to sync one form of media, the rest are a cinch.

Meet the Phone

Chapter 3

Interacting with Your New iPhone

If your previous mobile phones have not been iPhones, you're in for a treat. Your iPhone's touchscreen uses a revolutionary new way to interact. It responds to the language of your touch. Its vocabulary includes taps, drags, pinches, and flicks. With these motions, you control your iPhone as easily as using a trackpad or mouse with your personal computer.

There's more to those touch gestures than just single-finger interactions; the iPhone offers multitouch technology. That means the iPhone can recognize and respond to more than one touch at a time. In this chapter, you're about to discover different ways you can interact with your iPhone—zooming in and out of maps and photos, using the iPhone's built-in touch keyboards, and playing with its sensors. You'll learn how all these features work and how to take advantage of some secret ways of interacting with your iPhone.

Interaction Basics

Whether you're a Windows user, a friend of the Linux penguin, or a Mac fan, you know that a mouse or trackpad is the way to interact with a computer. On the iPhone and iPad, your fingers provide the tools for interacting with the device. The iPhone requires real finger contact. It doesn't sense pressure; it detects the small electrical charge transferred from your skin. You can use your iPhone with your fingers, your knuckles, your toes, or, if you're feeling up to it, your nose, but you can't use a pencil eraser, Q-tip, or one of those old nonconductive plastic PDA styluses. The electrical charges in your touch make it possible for the iPhone to detect and respond to one or more contacts at a time, otherwise known as Multi-Touch technology.

The iPhone Language

The ways in which you touch your iPhone screen are the words in your communication vocabulary. Here's a quick rundown of the many ways you can speak to your iPhone:

Pressing the Home button: The iPhone's Home button lives below the touchscreen and is marked with a white or gray square. Press the Home button at any time to return to your Home screen with its list of applications. Double-pressing the Home button displays icons in a row at the bottom of the screen for all apps that are currently running and, with a flick to the right, displays a set of controls for operating the iPod app. Press and hold the Home button to launch Siri, the iPhone's voice navigator. (On older devices, pressing and holding Home launches VoiceControl instead. Siri was launched exclusively on the iPhone 4S and newer.) If you've enabled VoiceOver, the iPhone's screen narration accessibility feature for the visually impaired, a triple-click of the Home button can jump into or out from VoiceOver mode.

Tapping: Tap your iPhone by touching your finger to the screen and removing it quickly. Tapping selects web links, activates buttons on the screen, and launches iPhone apps. When typing text on the iPhone's virtual keyboard, you may want to tap with your forefinger or, if it's more comfortable, your thumb.

Double-tapping: Double-tapping means tapping your iPhone's screen twice in quick succession. Double-clicking may be important on your personal computer, but double-tapping isn't used all that much on the iPhone. In Safari, you can zoom into columns of text or pictures on a web page by double-tapping them, and then you can zoom back out by double-tapping again. In the Photos app, double-tapping is used to zoom into and out from pictures.

Two-fingered tap: The iPhone's Multi-Touch technology means you can tap the screen with more than one finger at a time. To do this, tap the iPhone display with your forefinger and middle finger at the same time. In Maps, double-tapping zooms into the map, while a two-fingered tap zooms out.

Rotoring is a variation of the two-fingered tap. To rotor, you place two fingers on the screen and rotate them as if you were turning a wheel with both fingers. You can rotor in the Photos app while cropping images to align the picture just so.

Holding: This gesture consists of putting your finger on the screen and leaving it there until something happens. Holding brings up the magnifying glass while you're typing. You can also move app icons around on your iPhone by holding an icon until the app icons begin to "wiggle." They can then be moved around the display and between Home screens to organize your apps, and they can be fixed in place by pressing the Home button. For apps that you've installed on your iPhone, holding an app icon also displays a small circle with an *X* in it in the upper-left corner of the icon. Tap that icon to delete the app from your iPhone.

Dragging: Drag your finger by pressing it to the screen and moving it in any direction before lifting it. Use dragging to position the view in Maps or to scroll up or down a list of messages in Mail. Some apps offer an alphabetical index on the right side, such as the one shown in Figure 3–1. To use this index, drag your finger along it until the item you want becomes visible.

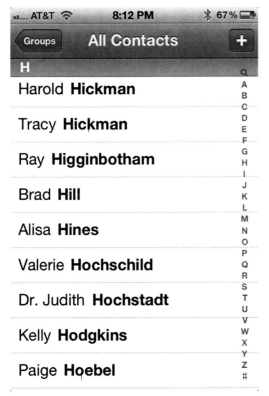

Figure 3–1. *Use dragging to move quickly through an index. In the Contacts screen shown here, dragging on the index allows you to jump through the alphabet to find the name you're searching for. You can also tap a letter to jump to it.*

Flicking: When you're dealing with long lists, you can give the list a quick flick. Place your finger onto the screen, and then move it rapidly in one direction—up, down, left, or right. The display responds by scrolling quickly in the direction you've indicated. Use flicking to move the names in your Contacts app quickly.

Stopping: During a scroll, press and hold your finger to the screen to stop the scroll. Apple's legal text provides a great place to practice flicking, dragging, and stopping. To get there, select **Settings** ➤ **General** ➤ **About** ➤ **Legal**. Have fun with its endless content of legalese that you can flick, drag, and stop to your heart's content. If you don't want to stop a scroll, just wait. The scroll will slow and stop by itself.

Swiping: To swipe your iPhone, drag a finger from the left side of the screen toward the right or from the right side to the left. Swiping is used to unlock your phone and to indicate you want to delete list items, such as an e-mail item or contact (see Figure 3–2). You can also swipe notifications on your iPhone's lock screen. Each notification, when swiped, opens up the application that created the notification in the first place. If you missed a call, swiping returns you to the Phone app. If you received a text, swipes lead to the Messages app.

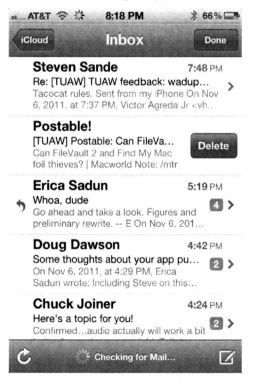

Figure 3–2. *To swipe, drag your finger from left to right or right to left across an item you want to delete. After, the Delete button (shown here) appears for the item you swiped. To delete, tap Delete. Otherwise, tap anywhere else to hide the Delete button again.*

> **TIP:** Flicking and dragging will not select or activate items on the iPhone's display. You can try this yourself by dragging and flicking on the Home screen.

Pinching: On the iPhone, you pinch by placing your thumb and forefinger onto the screen with a space between them. Then, with the fingers touching the screen, move the two fingers together as if you're pinching the screen. Pinching allows you to zoom out in many iPhone programs, including the photo viewer, Safari, and Maps.

Unpinching: To unpinch, you perform the pinch in reverse. Start with your thumb and forefinger placed together on your screen and, with the fingers touching the screen, spread them apart. Unpinching allows you to zoom into those same iPhone applications that pinching zooms out of.

> **NOTE:** Several multitouch gestures that appeared in iOS 5 beta versions failed to make it to release on the iPhone 4S, specifically four-fingered swipes to move between applications and to reveal recent applications. One further gesture, a four-fingered pinch would have taken you back to your home page. Ideally these gestures will reappear in future iOS releases because they were extremely handy to use.

About the iPhone Home Screen

The iPhone's Home screen allows you to launch any application with a single tap. The Home screen, named SpringBoard internally in iOS, provides app-launching abilities. Tap the Home button to return to the Home screen at any time.

A Back button appears on many iPhone screens in the upper-left corner. Tap this button to return to the previous screen in the application. This is different from pressing Home. A Back button moves you between screens within an application. The Home button leaves an application and returns you to the Home screen.

Returning to the Home screen from an app does not necessarily quit the app. Later in this chapter, you'll read how to properly quit apps that are running.

The iPhone Sensors

In addition to the touchscreen, your iPhone contains a variety of important sensors. These sensors vary depending on the model. The iPhone 3GS and newer contain a proximity sensor, an ambient light sensor, a tilt sensor (also known as an *accelerometer*), a digital compass, and a Global Positioning System (GPS) receiver. The iPhone 4 and newer also add a built-in three-axis gyroscope and a noise-cancellation microphone to the mix. These sensors give your iPhone some science-fiction-grade features that set it apart from the crowd.

Proximity Sensor

The proximity sensor is located on your iPhone right near the earpiece. Its job is to blank the screen when the iPhone is held up to your ear. This means your ear and chin won't accidentally hang up your calls with their stray touches, and it means you'll save some power during those phone calls.

You can see the proximity sensor in action by going to **Phone ➤ Voicemail**. Set Speaker to off (on is a brighter blue; off a dimmer blue), and then play a voicemail message by tapping the name or phone number of the person who left it. With the speaker off, place a finger just above the earpiece. The iPhone display goes dark. Remove the finger, and the screen returns.

Test the sensor range by placing your iPhone on a flat surface and holding your finger in the air about an inch above the earpiece. Move the finger up and down slightly, and you'll discover exactly where the sensor gets triggered.

The proximity sensor works by shooting out an infrared (IR) beam, which is reflected back and picked up by the iPhone's light sensor. If the range is short enough, the iPhone switches off the screen.

You can also *see* the IR source for the proximity sensor by using a digital camera. The IR beam is visible to the camera's CCD detector. To take the picture shown in Figure 3–3, we switched off a camera's flash, enabled its Macro settings (because we needed the camera to be pretty close to the iPhone), and waited for the source to flash red. You can't see it with your eyes, but you can with your camera's IR-sensitive detectors.

Figure 3–3. *You can "see" the iPhone's IR light from its proximity sensor if you own a digital camera. Its IR beam is visible to the camera's detector. Make sure to cover the iPhone's screen when you take the photograph, because it's bright and the IR light is dim.*

Tilt Sensor

The iPhone uses an accelerometer (what we're going to call the *tilt sensor*) to detect when your iPhone tilts. Many apps, including Safari, update their displays when you turn the iPhone on its side. This allows you to use your iPhone in both portrait and landscape modes.

If you feel like playing with the tilt sensor, try this: go into Photos, and select a favorite picture. Hold the iPhone up normally in portrait orientation, press one finger onto the screen, and then tilt the phone into landscape orientation. The picture will not change. Now, lift the finger off the screen. Presto—the iPhone finally rotates the display.

Many iPhone games use the accelerometer for user interaction. For example, with the very popular Flick Fishing game, you "cast" a line out to catch fish by moving your hand and arm in the motion of casting. Many driving games let you use your iPhone as a steering wheel as you drive along a virtual course.

Ambient Light Sensor

The ambient light sensor detects whether you're in bright or dark lighting conditions and then adjusts the overall brightness of your iPhone display to match. For example, if it's extremely bright outside and you pull out your iPhone to make a call, the light sensor will judge the surrounding brightness when you unlock the phone and let the iPhone know that it needs to compensate by making the display brighter so you can read it. Going the other way, the screen will dim when you're in a dark room to protect your eyes from the glare of a bright screen as well as save some battery power.

Want to have fun with this sensor? When you cover the sensor (found just above the ear speaker on the top front of the phone) with a finger and then unlock the phone, you'll find that the screen brightness is quite dim. On the other hand, if you shine a bright light at the sensor when you unlock the iPhone, you'll see the screen at a very bright setting.

You can toggle the autobrightness feature off and on in **Settings ➤ Brightness**. This setting also offers direct control over the brightness of the iPhone's screen, which is handy when you need immediate results instead of playing with bright lights, fingers, and unlocking your iPhone.

Digital Compass

The digital compass (also known as a *magnetometer*; see Figure 3–4) built into the iPhone 3GS and newer models is similar to a magnetic compass. In other words, if you happen to be near a strong magnetic field such as the magnets contained in the iPhone earbuds, the compass needle may not be pointing toward true or magnetic north. On occasion, the digital compass may need recalibrating.

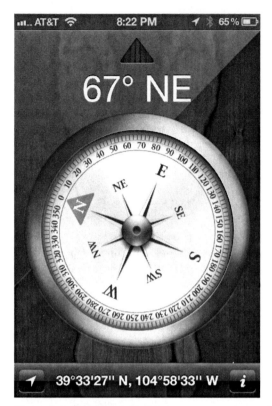

Figure 3–4. *The iPhone's digital compass can get you pointed in the right direction, but be sure to recalibrate it when it asks you to do so.*

The iPhone Compass app informs you of those rare occasions by displaying a message that says "Re-calibrate compass. Wave in a figure 8 motion." That's your cue to hold the iPhone out in front of you and draw a big figure eight, with the eight lying on its side. Keep moving the iPhone until the calibration message disappears. Yes, you look like a total geek while doing this, but it's better than getting lost, right?

If you're in a car and driving around, you don't need to wave the iPhone at the windshield. Just make a few turns, and the compass recalibrates itself. That's much safer for everyone in and outside of your car.

GPS Receiver

Not only is your iPhone an amazing, powerful pocket computer and a very capable phone, but it's also a state-of-the-art navigation tool. Built inside the latest iPhones is a GPS receiver that is capable of pinpointing your exact location on the globe within about 30 feet (10 meters).

> **NOTE:** The Global Positioning System consists of a constellation of 24 to 32 satellites in precisely known orbits about 12,550 miles above the earth's surface, all equipped with extremely accurate clocks and powerful radio transmitters. GPS receivers determine their location by timing the reception of signals from four or more satellites and then performing a series of complex calculations.

In fact, your iPhone has an advantage that many dedicated GPS receivers do not. Since it is constantly in touch with cell phone towers with precisely known locations, it can determine your approximate location within several seconds of being turned on. Once the iPhone has locked onto several GPS satellites, it pinpoints the location with even more accuracy. This capability of blending the GPS satellite signals and known cell tower locations is known as Assisted GPS (A-GPS).

The GPS receiver is used in most iPhone apps that contain some sort of geolocation feature. Some examples of these apps include Maps, the Navigon, Tom Tom, and AT&T navigation apps, and the official Geocaching (`www.geocaching.com`) app.

Three-Axis Gyroscope

The iPhone 4 was the first mobile phone to contain a miniaturized three-axis gyroscope. The iPhone 4S continues that tradition, offering a sensor that can determine the precise orientation of the phone at every moment. This is handy in gaming apps that may need to track the motion of the phone more accurately than the tilt sensors can. That's because the gyroscope can sense motion to the left and right, not just tilting. It's highlighted in apps such as You Gotta See This! (`www.boinx.com/seethis`). The latter is an iPhone 4 (and newer) app that creates photo collages simply by waving the phone around in front of you. The iPhone shoots photos as it is moving, and since the app knows the orientation of the iPhone's camera as each photo is being taken, it can easily stitch them into an attractive collage in seconds.

The gyroscope can be used by iPhone developers to capture movement that isn't sensed by the accelerometer, specifically nontilted motion along the major axes. Although the accelerometer does a good job of detecting whether the iPhone has been tilted one way or another, the gyroscope allows the device to be moved left or right, up and down, or forward and back, and that motion can be understood by apps. These additional movements provide another layer of precise control to the gestures that the iPhone understands.

Noise Cancellation Microphone

A glance at the top of a recent iPhone reveals a tiny hole next to the headset jack. This hole is actually a microphone, given the name *top microphone* by Apple. What's it used for? It's for improving the quality of your voice phone calls.

The Noise Cancellation microphone samples the ambient noise level around you. It then subtracts much of that ambient noise from the signal being sent to the person on the receiving end of your phone call. The result is much more clarity when you're making phone calls in noisy conditions.

iPhone Power Tricks

There are many ways to switch your iPhone on and off. The following are the most important methods that every iPhone owner should know.

Unlocking Your iPhone

When your iPhone has been idle for a while, it automatically locks, and the screen goes dark. When this happens, press Home. The locked iPhone screen shown in Figure 3–5 appears. To unlock your phone, swipe the slider from the left to the right. The lock screen clears, and the Home screen springs into place.

Screen locking is a form of power saving. If your iPhone never turned off its bright display, it would go through a battery charge much faster. Shutting down the screen and going into lock mode extends your battery life and optionally allows you to protect your iPhone by requiring a passcode to use the device after it has been locked.

If it seems like your iPhone is locking too frequently, you can adjust how long it should wait before locking. Tap your way to **Settings ➤ General ➤ Auto-Lock**, and select how many minutes you want your iPhone to wait before going dark. Sometimes you may want to just power the iPhone off by yourself and disable autolocking. There's a choice for that in the autolock settings, when you set the duration to Never. Make sure you have a good power source available at all times if you disable autolocking, since autolocking is a power-saving feature. Disabling it means your iPhone will use up battery power more rapidly.

Figure 3–5. *This is the lock screen from an iPhone with a custom wallpaper. To unlock your phone, swipe the slider from left to right. If the default wallpaper that is installed on new iPhones is too boring for your tastes, you can change it in Settings ➤ Wallpaper*

Putting Your iPhone to Sleep

For iPhones, sleep mode offers a power-saving way to use your device. Press the Sleep/Wake button once. The screen turns off, and your iPhone locks and enters its low-power mode. You can still listen to music and receive phone calls and incoming text messages. Your device alerts you for timers, calendar appointments, and reminders. You can even take photos from the lock screen. The volume control buttons on the left side of your iPhone work, and the switch on your iPhone headset continues to control music playback and allows you to answer calls.

Some apps can continue to run in the background even when the device is asleep, including most run tracking applications like RunMeter and RunKeeper. As an example, some location-aware apps continuously update the location of the iPhone although it is asleep.

To wake up your iPhone again, press Home, and swipe to unlock.

NOTE: You can use Siri from your iPhone's lock screen by pressing and holding the Home button even though the unit has been locked. You may be required to authenticate if your unit is set to use a passcode. Passcodes are discussed in the following section. As shown in Figure 3–6, you can also disable this capability in Settings to prevent access to Siri from the lock screen.

Securing Your iPhone with a Passcode Lock

For security, you can assign a passcode lock for your iPhone. There are two types of passcodes: a simple passcode, which consists of four easily remembered and typed numbers, and a regular passcode, which can include text. When locked, your iPhone cannot be used except for emergency calls. Go to **Settings ➤ General**, and tap Passcode Lock to establish a new passcode. As you can see in Figure 3–6, there's a button that turns the passcode lock feature on and off. If a four-digit simple passcode is all you'd like to enter, make sure that the Simple Passcode switch is set to the default value of on. If you'd rather enter a text passcode, flip that switch to the off position.

Figure 3–6. *Securing your iPhone with a passcode lock is a good idea so that personal information isn't compromised in case of loss or theft of your phone.*

Once you've decided what kind of passcode you want, tap Turn Passcode On to enter it. If you have chosen a simple passcode, you're prompted to enter four digits twice— once to enter the numbers and again to verify that you entered it correctly the first time (see Figure 3–7, left). For regular passcodes, you're prompted to enter your passcode with text, symbols, and numbers (Figure 3–7, right). Once again, you'll have to enter the passcode twice to make sure it has been entered properly.

As soon as you've set a passcode, you can change some other settings that are related to the passcode lock. Tap the Require Passcode button to set the time interval before your iPhone requests the passcode. Shorter times are more secure, although you'll need to enter your passcode more frequently as a result.

If you like to use Voice Control and your iPhone or Bluetooth headset to do voice dialing or control the iPod app, slide the Voice Dial switch to on to make sure that Voice Control is always enabled, even when the phone is locked. This makes it handy for you to use a Bluetooth headset to dial and control your phone, even when it's sitting in your pocket or in a briefcase or purse.

Figure 3–7. *On the left is the standard keypad for entering a simple passcode, while the full iPhone keyboard appears for typing a regular passcode.*

The final button on the Passcode Lock screen ensures absolute security in case your iPhone is lost or stolen. Sliding the Erase Data button to on will erase the contents of the iPhone if someone incorrectly enters the passcode ten times. Before you engage this setting, be sure that you know your password.

How can you test your passcode? Press the Sleep/Wake button once to put your iPhone to sleep, wait for the time interval to pass, and then wake the iPhone by either pressing the Sleep/Wake button again or pressing the Home button. A passcode challenge screen appears (Figure 3–8 shows the challenge screen for a simple passcode). Enter your passcode correctly, and your iPhone unlocks.

To remove the passcode from your iPhone, go back to the Passcode Lock screen. Tap the Turn Passcode Off button, and then reenter the passcode one more time to confirm that the rightful owner of the iPhone is making the request.

What can you do if you forget your passcode or a mean-spirited colleague adds one to your iPhone without telling you? Unfortunately, you will have to connect the iPhone to your computer and use iTunes to restore the iPhone to factory defaults. Why? Well, for security reasons, there's absolutely no way to reset the passcode since that would defeat the purpose of the passcode.

Figure 3–8. *With passcode lock enabled, you'll be prompted to enter the passcode before you can use your iPhone to do anything other than make an emergency phone call. This figure shows the passcode keypad for a simple passcode.*

Multitasking and Quitting Applications

Prior to iOS 4, iPhones could not perform more than one task at a time. Well, they *could* play music from the Music app while performing some other tasks, but that was about it.

iOS now acts more like a modern multitasking operating system by allowing multiple apps to run simultaneously. One example that many people pointed at as proof of the need for iOS multitasking was being able to play tunes using the popular Pandora music-streaming app while performing other tasks, such as reading e-mail, at the same time.

When you're using an app, pressing the Home button returns you to the Home screen, but the app is either suspended or may actually be running. In fact, if the app has been written to take advantage of backgrounding, it will continue to run when you're viewing the Home screen or running other apps. In other words, don't assume that when an app is out of sight, it's shut down.

To see what's currently running on your iPhone, double-click the Home button. The current Home screen becomes transparent, and a side-scrolling list of active and recent apps appears at the bottom of the screen.

Flicking the active apps to the right, you'll eventually get to a control panel for whatever music app happens to be active at the time. This control panel is equipped with play, pause, fast-forward, and fast-reverse buttons, as well as a screen orientation lock button. The far-right icon on the control panel shows which music app you're currently controlling.

Flick once more to reveal the AirPlay mirroring controls, which are to the left of the music playback controls. AirPlay allows you to play music and video wirelessly to AirPlay-enabled devices including the Apple TV (audio and video) and numerous audio-only AirPlay-enabled speakers. AirPlay also allows you to wirelessly mirror your iPhone 4S's display to Apple TV. It's a great way to demonstrate applications or use your HDTV as a wireless external monitor. Many games now take advantage of AirPlay video connections to transform your iPhone into a game controller, as you watch the actual game play on a large-screen TV.

Having multiple apps running in background can increase usage of the processor to the point that your iPhone heats up, the device uses much more power, and the response of the phone becomes sluggish. Even with the fast and powerful processors on newer iPhones , too many apps running simultaneously can slow things down dramatically. Idle applications occupy your iPhone's memory, which may eventually cause it to balk when you try to open another app.

So, how do you quit apps? Double-click the Home button, and at the bottom of the iPhone display you'll see a side-scrolling list of all the apps that are currently running (Figure 3–9). To turn off an app, tap and hold an app icon in the list until it begins to jiggle. A small minus sign in a red circle appears at the top-left corner of the icon. Tap the minus sign to quit the application.

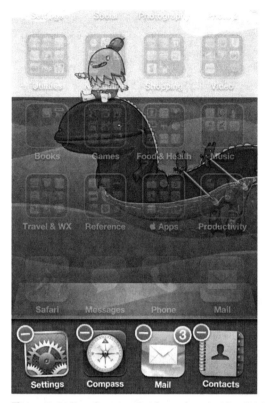

Figure 3–9. *To quit an app that is running, double-click the Home button to display all the currently active apps, and then tap and hold one of the apps. When the small minus sign in the red circle appears, tap it to quit the app. Some apps appear in this list that are neither running nor suspended. This list includes all recent apps that have been used in order they were last accessed. If so, the red circle minus sign simply removes that app from the recent apps list.*

Powering Your iPhone Off and On

To power off your iPhone, press and hold the Sleep/Wake button for about five seconds. A slider appears prompting you to slide the red button that appears to the right in order to power off. To cancel, either tap Cancel or just wait about ten seconds. The iPhone automatically returns you to the Home screen if you don't power down within that time.

When your iPhone is powered off, it ceases to function. You cannot listen to music. You cannot receive phone calls. You must power your iPhone back on for it to do these things.

To power on your iPhone, press and hold Sleep/Wake for two to three seconds. Release the button when you see the white Apple icon. The iPhone starts up and returns you automatically to the unlock screen.

Rebooting Your iPhone

At times, you may need to reboot your iPhone. Although you can reboot just by powering down and then powering back up, Apple provides a much easier way do this. Press and hold the Sleep/Wake button for eight to ten seconds. Ignore the "slide to power off" message, and keep holding the button until the white Apple logo appears. Once it shows up, release the button, and let the iPhone finish its reboot. You will return automatically to the unlock screen.

Changing iPhone Wallpapers

An iPhone comes out of its box with a default picture installed as "wallpaper." Wallpapers are the pictures that are used as a background on your iPhone's Home and lock screens. On the iPhone 4, the standard wallpaper looks like glass with raindrops on it. Although it does a great job of showing just how good the iPhone 4's Retina Display is, since it looks like real water on your screen, it's not unique to you.

Changing the wallpapers is an easy way to customize your iPhone:

1. If you have a favorite artwork or photo that you want as wallpaper on your iPhone, make sure it's in the Photo Library first. You can move photos and artwork to your iPhone by e-mailing them to your phone's e-mail address and then tapping and holding the photo. A Save Image button appears; tap that, and the photo is saved into your iPhone's Photo Library.

2. Select Settings ➤ Wallpaper. A screen appears showing the current lock screen and Home screen wallpapers.

3. Tap the image of the current wallpapers. Two buttons appear; one is marked Wallpaper and contains a number of built-in textures and photos that can be used as wallpapers, while the other is marked Camera Roll and includes the photos that are in your Photo Library.

4. Tap either one of the buttons to preview the pictures that can be used as wallpaper. If you select a photo from your Photo Library, you'll be asked to move and scale the photo before you tap Set to assign it to a wallpaper (Figure 3–10).

Figure 3–10. *When you assign one of the images in your Photo Library to be a wallpaper, you'll be asked to move and scale the image so that it looks its best. Once that's done, tap the Set button.*

5. If you choose one of the built-in wallpapers or have moved and scaled your photo, you're now asked whether you want to make the picture your wallpaper for your Home or lock screen or for both. Tap the appropriate button, and the image appears as wallpaper.

Organizing Apps with Folders

iOS 4 brought a smile to the face of many longtime iPhone users with the addition of folders. Previously, app icons could not be organized except by locating them all on the same page. Each page could contain up to 16 apps, so if you had a lot of apps, you were often flipping through ten or more screens of apps to find the one you needed.

iOS 5 also provides folders. Each folder can hold up to 12 apps, and each Home screen can have up to 12 folders—that's 144 apps per screen, not including those in the Home row at the bottom of the iPhone display.

Here are some tips on creating and using folders:

- To organize similar apps into folders, tap and hold one app until it begins to wiggle, and then drag and drop it on another app of the same type. For example, to create a game folder, you can tap and hold the Angry Birds app icon until it wiggles and then drag it over to the Chopper 2 icon and drop it. Since both apps are in the Games category of the iTunes App Store, the iPhone automatically selects Games as the name of the folder.

- Once a folder is created, you can add any other app (up to a total of 12) to it by repeating the process of dragging and dropping icons. You cannot add the Newsstand to folders; we encourage you not to try. The Newsstand is a special kind of folder.

- To rename a folder, tap and hold the folder icon until it wiggles. Tap the folder icon, and the folder opens with an editable title at the top. When you're done renaming the folder, press the Home button to save the new name.

- You can also organize your apps and folders in iTunes. With your iPhone connected to your computer, click its name under Devices in the iTunes sidebar, and then click the Apps tab. In the image on the right side of the iTunes screen (Figure 3–11), drag and drop app icons to organize them the way that you want them.

Figure 3–11. *That simulation of your iPhone display on the right side of the iTunes screen is a fast way to organize your apps into folders or pages.*

Using the iPhone Keyboard

Let's start talking about the iPhone keyboard by quoting verbatim from an early iPhone e-mail written by one of the authors:

I would like to sat that the iPhone has turned me into a tupong expert, but that would ne far far far from the truth. The fact is that I type on the iPhone like a cow, working with the iPhone keyboard is norm hard and frustrating. Foe all this Rhine is supposed to be smart and press five, I find that in actual use it is slow and mistake-prone. Will my accuracy improve as I get more experience? Probably. Will my fingers become smaller and less oqlike?almost certainly nor.

That e-mail was written within the first 24 hours of ownership, causing a lot of consternation about the whole iPhone keyboard thing. Within a week, however, iPhone typing progressed from horrible to readable, and within another week, from readable to pretty darn good. The entire paragraph in Figure 3–12 was written on an iPhone and transferred to this manuscript (see Figure 3–12).

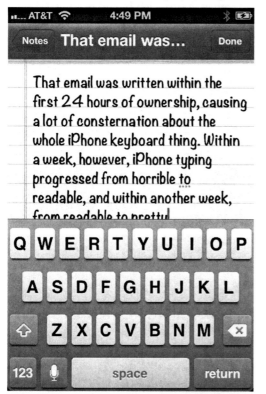

Figure 3–12. *The iPhone keyboard grows easier to use with more experience. Within a couple of weeks, you'll master its quirks. Notice the Shift key (arrow pointing up) to the left of the Z key and the Backspace/Delete key (pentagon pointing left with an X in it) to the right of the letter M. The .?123 button switches the keyboard to a number and symbols layout, and the Return button lets you add carriage returns to your text. The microphone to the left of the spacebar is new to the iPhone 4S and represents a voice dictation option provided by the Siri service.*

The secret to success is that the iPhone keyboard is smart—so smart, in fact, that it corrects a lot of typos and compensates for misaligned fingers. It automatically capitalizes the beginning of sentences. It suggests corrections for misspelled words and uses something called *predictive zones* to make it easier to hit the right keys. Here are some of the key technologies that make the iPhone keyboard work:

Dictionary: The iPhone has an onboard dictionary that learns frequently used words as you type. It also picks up names and spellings from your address book. This means it gets better at guessing your intention as it builds its data.

Automatic correction: As you type, the iPhone looks for words similar to what you're typing and guesses them, placing the guess just below the word you're typing. To accept the word, tap the spacebar. (You don't have to finish typing the word. The iPhone puts it in there for you.) To decline the correction, tap the word itself. The iPhone will not make a substitution, even when you press the spacebar.

Predictive mapping: The iPhone uses its dictionary to predict which word you're about to type. It then readjusts the keyboard response zones to make it easier for you to hit the right letters. Likely letters get bigger tap zones; unlikely letters smaller ones.

Offset correction: The iPhone understands that people sometimes misalign fingers. So, if you mean to type *pizza* but you press O instead of P and U instead of I (that is, ouzza), the iPhone is smart enough to know that the typing pattern you used matches a known word in its dictionary.

Getting Started

When you're new to the iPhone, start by typing slowly. Pay attention to those confirmation pop-ups that appear every time you tap a key. We find it easiest to use our fingertips to type. Others prefer to use their thumbs. Whatever method you use, make sure to go at a pace that allows you to keep track of what you're typing and make corrections on the go.

Automatic corrections: The iPhone displays suggested corrections just below the word you're typing (see Figure 3–13). To accept the suggestion, tap the spacebar. To disable correction for the current word, tap the word itself in the text area, and iPhone will leave the word exactly as you have entered it. You can also turn off autocorrection by opening **Settings** ➤ **General** ➤ **Keyboard** and sliding the autocorrection switch to off.

Figure 3–13. *iPhone suggestions appear just below the word you type. Tap the spacebar to accept the suggestion, or tap the word you're typing to disable autocorrection for that word.*

Using the magnifying glass (loupe): While you're typing, you can adjust the cursor by using the iPhone's built-in magnifying glass feature, also known as the *loupe* (see Figure 3–14). Hold your finger somewhere in the text area until the loupe appears, and then use the magnified view to drag the cursor exactly where you need it.

Summoning the keyboard: To make the keyboard appear, tap in any editable text area on the iPhone screen.

Dismissing the keyboard: There's no standard way to dismiss the keyboard, but many programs offer a Done button indicating that you're done typing. In Safari, tap Go instead of Done.

Select/Select All: You can select either a single word or all text in an editable area on the iPhone by using Select or Select All. In a text area, tap and hold your finger until the loupe appears. When you remove your finger, a small pop-up menu appears (Figure 3–15), allowing you to select either a single word or all the text on the page. If any text has been copied or cut, you may also see the Paste command in the menu (see next item).

Figure 3–14. *iPhone's loupe offers a magnified view that makes it easy to position the cursor exactly where you need it to be.*

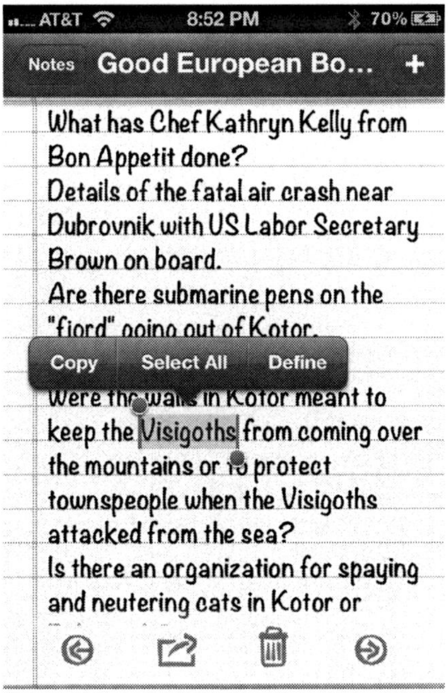

Figure 3–15. *If you need to select a word or phrase to copy, double-tap a word to bring up this pop-up menu. You can copy the word, select all text on the page, or tap Define to get a dictionary definition of the selected word.*

Cut/Copy/Paste/Suggest: Like a computer, there are functions within the iPhone that allow you to cut, copy, and paste text. To enable these, double-tap a word in a text area. The word is selected, with small "handles" on either side that can be moved left or right to expand the area that is selected. In addition, a pop-up menu appears with the commands Cut, Copy, Paste, and Suggest to select from (Figure 3–16).

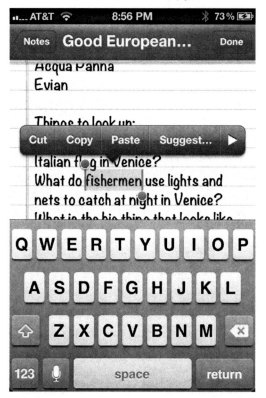

Figure 3–16. *Just like in a word processing application on a computer, the iPhone can cut, copy, and paste text. It can suggest similarly spelled words.*

Cut removes the selected text and keeps it stored in the iPhone's clipboard until you paste it somewhere else. Copy saves a copy of the selected text in the clipboard but does not remove it from the existing text file. Paste takes whatever text is currently in the clipboard and pastes it at the cursor point in any text field. Suggest (Figure 3–17) displays a list of words that are spelled similarly to the selected word so that accidentally misspelled words can be replaced with the correct word with a tap of a finger.

Figure 3–17. *If the app you're typing in has replaced your word with something that is spelled similarly, use the Suggest command to display a list of words that you can insert with a tap of a finger.*

iPhone Typing Tricks

Once you're comfortable with the keyboard, there are further ways to make typing easier. Here are a few more iPhone typing tricks you can use to make your keyboard entry faster and easier.

Contractions

When you want to type a contraction like *can't* or *shouldn't,* don't bother putting in the apostrophe. The iPhone is smart enough to guess that *cant* is *can't*. Of course, if you're referring to a slope or tilt, be sure to tap the word itself to decline the change from the noun to the contraction.

If you're typing a word like *we'll*, where the uncontracted word *well* is a common word, just add an extra *l*. The iPhone corrects *welll* to *we'll* and *shelll* to *she'll*.

> **TIP:** Other contraction tricks include *itsa*, which gets corrected to *its*, and *weree*, which gets corrected to *we're*.

Punctuation Dragging

If you plan to use only one item of punctuation at a time, such as a comma or period, save time by dragging. Drag from the 123 button to the item you want to include. By starting the drag at 123, the iPhone switches momentarily to the numbers and punctuation view. After selecting your item, the keyboard automatically bounces back to the alphabet.

> **TIP:** Another punctuation trick for the end of sentences is to tap 123, the punctuation item you want to use, and then the spacebar. The iPhone is smart enough to recognize the end of a sentence and put you back in alphabet mode. You can also double-tap the spacebar to add a period followed by a space.

Accents

Tap and hold any keyboard letter to view accented versions of that letter. For example, tapping and holding N presents you with the option of adding n, ´n, or ñ. This shortcut makes it much easier to type foreign words.

If you need to do a lot of typing in a foreign language, you can add new keyboards to your iPhone by going to **Settings ➤ General ➤ Keyboard**, tapping International Keyboards, and then adding the keyboards you need from a palette of 51 that are available. To use the keyboards to enter text, open a keyboard, and then tap the small globe to the left of the spacebar, which will display a list of the international keyboards you have installed. Yes, you too can write in Russian on any iPhone (Figure 3–18).

Figure 3–18. *The Russian keyboard has been enabled in Notes, and the keyboard is full of Cyrillic characters. Tap the globe to the left of the spacebar to choose another keyboard or return to your default keyboard.*

Caps Lock

To enable Caps Lock, go to **Settings ➤ General ➤ Keyboard** Preferences. When that's enabled, you can double-tap the Caps button to toggle the lock on and off.

Deleting Multiple Words at a Time

When you press and hold the Delete key, it starts off by deleting one letter and then the next. But if you hold it for longer than about a line of text, it switches to word deletion and starts removing entire words at a time, making it easier to clear text quickly.

Autocapitalization

Autocapitalization means the iPhone automatically capitalizes the start of sentences. So, you can type *the day has begun*, and the iPhone is smart enough to capitalize *the*: "The day has begun." This means you don't have to worry about pressing the Shift key at the beginning of every sentence or even when you type *i* because *i went to the park* becomes *I went to the park*.

TIP: Enable or disable autocapitalization in **Settings ➤ General ➤ Keyboard Preferences**.

iPhone Typing Test

You may be curious just how fast you can type on your iPhone keyboard. There are several apps in the App Store that can test your typing speed. Search the App Store for *typing test* to find those apps.

Dictating Text

The microphone button, found just to the left of the space bar on the iPhone 4S, allows you to dictate text instead of typing it. To use this option, tap the microphone button, speak, and then tap the Done button. As you speak, a purple microphone shows you the levels as you speak. Once you tap Done, your audio is sent over the Internet to Apple's data processing center and is returned to you as text.

When dictating to your iPhone, speak slowly and clearly. Over enunciate words and pause more than might feel natural. If you want to include punctuation, you must speak it as part of your dictation. For example, you'd say "Hello there comma Steven full stop" to produce the sentence "Hello there, Steven."

You can dictate up to about 30 seconds at a time; a beep interrupts you when you have filled the talk buffer. We recommend taking things slowly and speaking one phrase at a time. Although you can go on longer, it's easier to catch and respond to errors when working in stages than trying to proofread and correct longer dictations.

iPhone dictation follows many of the same rules used by the popular Dragon Dictation software. If you want to learn more about the finer points of dictation, consult the Dragon Dictation Users Manual on the Nuance web site (http://support.nuance.com).

At times, the iPhone may encounter trouble choosing between multiple interpretations. In this case, you'll see a blue underline under words. Tap that phrase to open a bubble showing the alternate interpretation. Tap that bubble to accept the alternate or tap the background to continue using the original text.

Speech-to-text on the iPhone 4S is phenomenal, to the point where you'll find yourself typing less and less and using dictation more and more in your e-mails, notes, and other typed material. You can dictate into any text element on your iPhone. The microphone on the keyboard does not care which application is running. If you can type with the keyboard, you can speak with the microphone button.

Using a Bluetooth Keyboard with Your iPhone

That little iPhone virtual keyboard can be annoying for typing large amounts of text. Can you imagine writing a book on an iPhone, tapping away with one finger or two thumbs?

Thankfully, iPhones running iOS 4 or higher can use with Bluetooth keyboards. Apple's Wireless Keyboard is a perfect example of a compact, battery-powered keyboard that links to the iPhone and works well for typing e-mails or writing books. Here are some instructions on setting up your Bluetooth keyboard with your iPhone:

> *Make sure that your Bluetooth keyboard is not paired with another device*: Pairing is the act of making the two devices (a computer and a keyboard) aware of each other. If you've been using your Apple Wireless Keyboard with a Mac, for example, you'll want to unpair the two before pairing the iPhone and the keyboard. To do that, open **System Preferences ▶ Bluetooth** on your Mac, find the listing for your Bluetooth keyboard, and then click the gear icon at the bottom of the Settings pane (Figure 3–19). Click Disconnect to break the connection between the keyboard and Mac, and then click the minus sign to delete the keyboard from the Bluetooth settings.

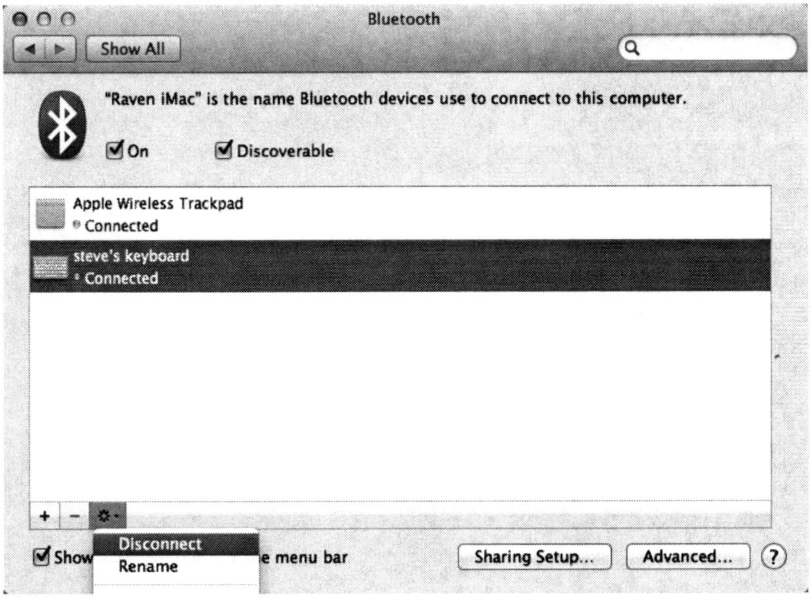

Figure 3–19. *To unpair your Bluetooth keyboard from a Mac, disconnect it first, and then click the minus sign to delete the keyboard from the list of Bluetooth devices.*

Make your Bluetooth keyboard discoverable: When a Bluetooth device is discoverable, it can be discovered by other devices like your iPhone and paired to them. Continuing the previous example with the Apple Wireless Keyboard, you make the keyboard discoverable simply by pressing the power button on the right side of the keyboard. The tiny green LED on the keyboard begins to blink, signaling that the keyboard is now discoverable.

Pair your iPhone and the Bluetooth keyboard: Once more using the Apple Wireless Keyboard example, go to **Settings ➤ General ➤ Bluetooth**, slide Bluetooth to on if it's currently turned off, and then tap the name of the keyboard in the list of discoverable devices. When the two devices begin to talk, the iPhone displays a four-digit number that you need to type on the keyboard (Figure 3–20). Once the number has been entered, the two devices are paired, and you can use the Bluetooth keyboard anywhere on the iPhone that you'd normally use the on-screen virtual keyboard.

Figure 3–20. *To pair your iPhone to a Bluetooth keyboard, make the keyboard discoverable, find it in the iPhone's Bluetooth settings, and then tap the keyboard name. To consummate the pairing, you'll need to type in a random passkey created by the iPhone.*

The standard Apple Wireless Keyboard works much like it does on a Mac when it's being used on an iPhone. The brightness keys (F1 and F2) brighten and dim the iPhone screen, the play/pause/fast-forward/rewind keys F7 through F9 work with the iPod app, and the volume keys (F10 through F12) adjust the volume of sounds playing on the iPhone. If at any point you need to use the iPhone's virtual keyboard, just tap the Eject button (top-right corner of the keyboard), and it appears. Tap it again to make the virtual keyboard disappear.

Used with an app like Pages (`www.apple.com/iphone/from-the-app-store/apps-by-apple/pages.html`) or Quickoffice Pro (`www.quickoffice.com/quickoffice_pro_iphone/`), a Bluetooth keyboard makes writing large documents on an iPhone a reality.

Using the iPhone Stereo Headset

If you look carefully at the headset packaged with your iPhone, you'll discover a small, thin cylinder about 6 inches below one of the two earpieces. This cylinder contains both a microphone and a switch. Go ahead and squeeze it, and you can feel the switch react. This switch has several functions:

Music: When listening to music, squeeze once to pause the music; squeeze again to resume playback. Double-squeeze (two quick squeezes in a row) to skip to the next song.

TIP: You can also pause your music by pulling out the headset plug from the iPhone jack.

Phone calls: When an incoming call rings on your iPhone, squeeze once to answer the call. Squeeze again to hang up. In theory, you can double-squeeze to send the call to voicemail, but I find that *really* difficult to do. It's much easier in my opinion to use the Sleep/Wake button. Press the Sleep/Wake button once to silence an incoming call and twice to send the incoming call to voicemail.

Siri and Voice Control: Did you know that it's possible to control your iPhone by talking to it? If you squeeze the headset switch until you hear a double-tone in the earbuds, you can talk to Siri on the iPhone 4S or command the iPhone to either make a phone call or play music using older iPhone units. Siri is introduced in the next section, but here are a few words first about Voice Control, which appears on a wider range of iPhone device installations. If you are looking at the iPhone screen when it goes into Voice Control mode, the various voice commands are visible floating across a blue background (Figure 3–21).

For example, squeezing the switch until you hear the prompt and then saying "Call Joe Smith at Home" causes the phone to call Joe at his home phone number, provided that his name and home number are in your Contacts list.

If you simply say "Call Joe Smith" and Joe has more than one phone number, you'll be asked which number to call—"Home, Work, or iPhone?" The iPhone prefers for you to tell it which number to call, and voice recognition is improved drastically. Use the short form of this voice command only in those situations where you aren't sure that there are multiple numbers for a contact.

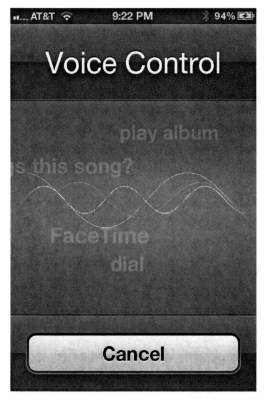

Figure 3–21. *The iPhone's Voice Control capability is a futuristic and useful way to call people or listen to music on older iPhones that do not have access to the new 4S Siri feature.*

Voice Control can be very useful when you are walking or running. Rather than stopping to pick a song in the iPod app, just squeeze the headset switch, and tell your iPhone what you want to hear. The following is a list of the voice commands that your iPhone understands:

- "Call [contact name]"
- "Dial [name or phone number]"
- "Shuffle"
- "Pause music"
- "Play more music like this"

- "Play playlist"

- "Next song"

- "Play songs by"

- "Next track"/"previous track"

- "What group is this song by?"

- "What is this song?"

Talking to Siri

Debuting on the iPhone 4S, the voice-operated Siri assistant uses natural-language processing to answer questions, respond to commands, and provide other kinds of assistance. With Siri, you can set up meetings, call friends, ask about appointments, check e-mail, find friends, and do a lot more.

Siri is incredibly convenient, going way beyond what you can do with Voice Control. You'll find yourself using your iPhone in ways you never did before because Siri makes things so much simpler. "Wake me up at 8:30 a.m.," "Tell my wife I'm on my way home," "Remind me to stop by the dry cleaners when I leave here": Siri offers virtual concierge services that simplify your life.

You launch Siri by pressing and holding the Home button or by squeezing the control button on your iPhone headset. (You can also use Bluetooth headsets to launch the Siri assistant.) A chime tells you that Siri is listening and ready to follow your commands. Make sure that Siri is enabled and that you have a good Internet connection. You'll be ready to take off and start exploring this amazing voice-driven service.

To enable Siri, navigate to **Settings ➤ General ➤ Siri**. Switch Siri to ON. When disabled, you can still use the older Voice Control technology but you miss out on all of Siri's amazing features.

The more you use Siri, the better it becomes at recognizing your speech and responding to your particular tones, inflections, and accents. That's because Siri sets up a personal account for you at Apple's servers and learns your vocabulary as well as the names of the songs in your music library and those of your contacts and acquaintances. Siri builds up a profiles of you and your data, so its recognition improves over time.

To find out what Siri can do for you, say "Help." Siri will respond with a screen like the one shown in Figure 3–22. Here, you'll see examples of things you can see to place phone calls (tap the phone option) or to adjust your calendar (tap the Calendar one). Each sample phrase leads to another screen full of examples.

Take messages, for example. If you have a meeting, you can say "Tell Susan, I'll be right there." Or you might "Send a message to Jason saying how about tomorrow." Got a conference call early tomorrow morning? Tell Siri to "Wake me up tomorrow at 7:30 a.m." and "Remind me to check my schedule at 8 a.m. tomorrow."

If Siri ever misunderstands what you've said, you can tap the talk bubble that represents your side of the conversation. There, you can re-dictate your request or use the keyboard to edit it directly. You can always tell Siri to "Cancel" what you've said or to "Change it" to some other choice.

It is our personal opinion that Siri is truly the stand-out feature on the iPhone 4S and the one most likely to make people consider early upgrades from older equipment.

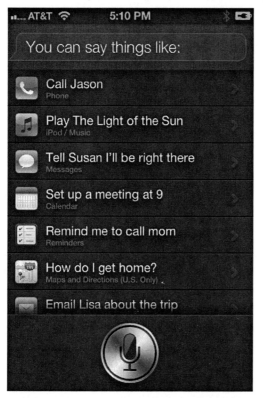

Figure 3–22. *If you're new to Siri, you can ask for suggestions of what to say. Say "Help," and Siri presents this screen, which leads to category-by-category examples.*

Summary

This chapter has explored many of the ways you can interact with your iPhone from taps to buttons to switches to dictation. You've read about the touchscreen and how you can communicate with it as well as about other sensors built into the phone. You've discovered how to put your phone to sleep, how to lock it, and how to power it off completely. After finishing this chapter, you will have been introduced to all the basic ways you and your iPhone can communicate with each other. Here are a few key lessons to carry away with you:

- Build up your working iPhone interaction vocabulary. You'd be surprised how often one of the lesser-known gestures, such as the two-fingered tap, will prove useful.

- Understand how the iPhone sensors are supposed to work so you won't be surprised when they're doing their job. Are you wondering why the iPhone is so dim when you wake it up in a dark room? Knowing about the light sensor will put you on the path to adjusting the phone to the brightness you need.

- Know the difference between powering your iPhone down and putting it to sleep. When it's powered off, you can't receive any calls, but you'll conserve battery power. When it's asleep, you can still listen to music and take calls.

- If you forget your iPhone's passcode, you'll need to restore the iPhone at your computer.

- Do you need to do a lot of text entry on an iPhone? Consider using a Bluetooth keyboard with the iPhone to make fast and more accurate typing a breeze. Dictation is a big timesaver as well, as long as you use your iPhone in a relatively quiet place. Trying to dictate on mass transit during rush hour is going to be difficult.

- On older devices, Voice Control can do the job of dialing a number or playing music when your hands are too busy to keep them on the iPhone. Just remember that Voice Control's ability to recognize your voice isn't perfect and that your iPhone may not necessarily do what you intend it to do.

- On newer systems, Siri is the answer. It does everything that Voice Control does and adds a huge range of concierge features that make your iPhone understand your appointments, text messages, calendars, contacts, and more. Siri is the assistant you never knew you needed, making life simpler for you on your iPhone.

Chapter 4

Placing Calls with iPhone

iPhones are versatile devices. They can surf the Web, check the latest stock prices, request a weather report, play thousands of games, and map out directions. But at its core, the iPhone remains a cell phone and that means that making phone calls is its primary function. In this chapter, you'll learn the essential things you need to know in order to maximize your iPhone use for placing and receiving calls. You'll discover ways you can get up to speed and make the most of your iPhone as a cell phone.

Checking the Cell Network Indicator

The bars at the top-left corner of your iPhone screen indicate how strong a signal you're receiving from the local cellular network. Five bars indicate the strongest signal. No bars or the words "No Service" indicate a complete lack of signal strength: no bars means no calls.

Reception problems can stem from many causes: distance to the nearest cell tower, hills and trees blocking reception, or even wiring or ducts inside your building. When you're not receiving a good signal, you'll need to move. Go to a place where the signal is stronger. This can mean anything from moving around a room, getting closer to a window, stepping outside your building, or driving toward a tower. Can they hear you now?

> **NOTE:** The iPhone 4 had a well-publicized design issue in which holding a bare phone a certain way causes a dramatic drop in signal quality. As a result, Apple recommended the use of an iPhone case or the Apple Bumper to reduce the issue's effect on your calls. These issues don't seem to affect the iPhone 4S, but a case will help protect your unit against physical impacts and may help your signal quality as well.

Finding good reception can be an art, but most mobile phone carriers try to help by making coverage maps on their websites that show where you should be able to receive service. Just google up your carrier and the phrase *coverage map*. In the United States, each carrier (AT&T, Sprint, and Verizon) offers interactive tools to help you determine whether coverage extends to particular locations. A network provider that offers excellent coverage in one region might provide only spotty reception in another.

> **TIP:** When attempting to place calls, make sure you haven't enabled Airplane Mode, which turns off all of the radios on your iPhone – the cell phone radio, Wi-Fi, and Bluetooth. If you can't make a call, check for an orange airplane at the top-left of your screen. If you see it, go to Settings and make sure that Airplane Mode is set to Off.

iPhone Basics

As with all Apple products, there's never just one way to do anything. In this section, you'll find many ways to perform the most basic iPhone tasks including answering calls, sending calls to voicemail, and even hanging up. You may be surprised to discover just how many options Apple has built into your iPhone to get the job done.

Launching the Phone app

By default, the green phone icon appears in the lower-left corner of your iPhone's Home screen. It looks like a white old-style handset slightly tilted to the left. Labelled Phone, this is the app that you use to place and receive phone calls, check your voicemail, review recent calls, and more. You may see a red bubble with a number on the Phone app icon. This number indicates the total number of missed calls and unheard voice mails. If you missed three calls and have one unlistened-to message, the bubble will show the number 4.

Once tapped, the green icon launches the Phone application and opens to the main screen. Once launched, take a look at the bottom of the screen. There's a shortcut bar at the bottom that offers the following key features:

- *Favorites* allows you to create a list of the most frequently called contacts for instant dialing.

- *Recents* lists all of your recent incoming, outgoing, and missed calls. To call back, tap any phone number in the list. You may see a red bubble with a number over the Recents icon. That number indicates any missed calls. Missed calls appear in your Recents list displayed in red.

- *Contacts* provide access to your complete address book. You can sync it to your PC or Mac, and also to Apple's iCloud and other online services. To call a contact, tap the Contacts icon, choose a contact from the address book and tap any phone number listed for that contact. You can store numbers for home, for work, for mobile (cell) phones, and more.

- *Keypad* is used to manually call phone numbers, and also to press keys during a phone call. If you ever call up the local pharmacy to refill a prescription, for example, you'll want to use the keypad to respond to the auto-fill robots that many drugstores now offer to their clients.

- *Voicemail* is the gateway to Visual Voicemail, and where you can listen to voice messages left when you missed phone calls. Like Recents, you may see a number in a red bubble. This indicates the number of unheard voicemail messages that await you.

To leave the Phone app, press the Home button. This suspends the application but does not cause it to quit. You'll still be able to receive phone calls.

Placing Calls

The simplest way to place calls is by dialing in numbers directly. Tap Keypad to enter the iPhone dialing screen shown in Figure 4–1. From here, you can place a call by tapping in a number to dial. Tap the green Call button to place the call with the number you have entered.

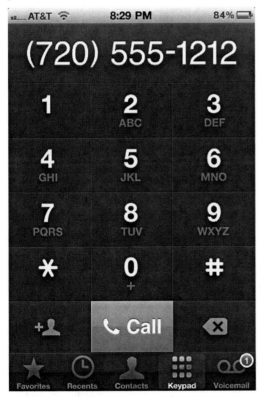

Figure 4–1. *The iPhone keypad, from which you can dial numbers and make phone calls.*

Here is an overview of the many ways the Phone app can be used to place calls:

Dial directly: To place a call manually, tap the Keypad icon at the bottom of the Phone app. Use the keypad to enter the phone number, then tap Call to place the call. If you make a mistake while typing, tap the backspace key. It's just to the right of the Call button, and looks like a sideways-pointing pentagon with an "X" in it.

Add contacts: The Add Contact button sits just to the left of the Call button. It looks like a face with a + sign next to it. This button provides a fast way to create a new contact using the number you just entered. Enter a phone number, press the Add Contact button, and a details screen opens (Figure 4–2). On the details screen, enter the details for the new contact, such as name, address, and company. If you need to add the number to an existing contact rather than create a new contact, choose Add to Existing Contact instead.

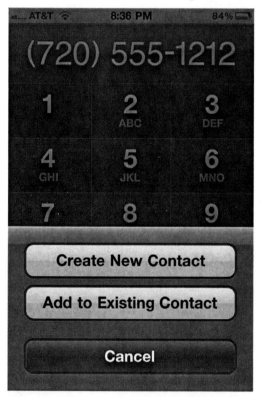

Figure 4–2. *When you tap the Add Contact button, you're given the choice of creating a new contact with the phone number you just entered, or adding that phone number to an existing contact. "Add to Existing Contact" is a great feature to use when someone you know gets a new phone number.*

Select a contact: To call someone in your address book, tap Contacts. The scrolling Contacts screen opens. Search down the list of names until you find the person you want to call. To speed this along, you can drag through the alphabet at the right side of the screen. Tap a name to display its address book entry, and then tap a phone number to place your call.

Call favorites: The Favorites screen lets you add your most frequently called contacts to a quick-call list. To call, just tap any name in the list. Since the Favorites screen stores a preferred number for your contacts, you don't have to select a specific phone number (for example, home or work) each time the way you do with the Contacts screen.

Reply to recent calls: Tap the Recents icon to open a list of your most recent incoming, outgoing, and missed calls. Missed calls appear in red, while incoming and outgoing calls are listed in black. Tap any number to instantly place a call back to that number.

> **NOTE:** Buttons at the top of the Recents screen let you view All calls, only the Missed calls, and to Clear the list entirely.

Call via email, calendar, note, and web links: The iPhone knows what a phone number looks like, and it will automatically add links to your emails, calendar events, notes, and web links using a technology called "data detectors". Telephone links show up as blue underlined text in emails, calendar events, and on web pages. In notes, they show up in brown underlined text. To call an embedded phone number, just tap it.

Place international calls: Mobile phone carrier policies range widely in terms of placing international calls and using the iPhone while roaming. Be sure to call your carrier before leaving on a foreign trip or placing international calls. Avoid the horror stories of thousand-dollar phone bills or the disappointment in finding that your phone doesn't work at all overseas by checking your facts before you use your iPhone in unconventional ways and locations. As a rule, you can usually add international calling to an iPhone plan, and will need to shop the current deals to find the best rates for your package. These details vary by country and carrier.

Using your iPhone for international calls adds a few more features and rules that you should be aware of. Here are a few tips to keep in mind regarding international calling:

- Use the plus (+) symbol to prefix international calls, for example +44 800 555 1212. To add + to a phone number, press and hold the 0 button on the iPhone keypad for about 2 seconds (note the + symbol under 0 in Figure 4–1). A tone sounds as you hold the button. Just ignore it. After a second or two, the 0 turns to a +, and you're ready to continue entering the number.

▨ When traveling outside the United States, add +1 to your numbers to call back to America, for example, +1 (212) 555 1212. If you do foreign travel regularly, use this style for all your contacts. Calls placed with +1 work both inside and outside the United States. Calls without +1 work only inside the United States. Your iPhone is smart enough to know when you're dialing from the United States, and you won't be charged extra for using +1.

▨ Check with your carrier for international calling rates. These vary wildly and can range from reasonable to outrageous. You may want to consider using alternative ways of connecting overseas, such as by using FaceTime or Skype or other Voice-over-IP (VoIP) solutions to save money.

▨ If you're a fan of SMS text or MMS multimedia (picture and video) messaging, you may want to text friends abroad. Once again, rates are dependent on the carrier. You may want to use use IM clients instead of texting to save money.

▨ When you're using your using your iPhone in a foreign country, be aware of data roaming costs. These can easily add up without you really knowing what's happening, as the iPhone often sends and receives data behind the scenes. If you don't want to get accidentally charged for data roaming, it can be disabled by selecting **Settings ➤ General ➤ Network** and sliding Data Roaming to Off.

▨ If, on the other hand, you do wish to use data services while abroad, consider using Wi-Fi only. Many hotels, restaurants, and bars offer free Wi-Fi to visitors, or you can pay a nominal fee for access. If you must use a 3G or EDGE network in a foreign country, check with your carrier for a discounted rate plan or use an unlocked iPhone with a locally-purchased subscriber card. You can purchase unlocked world GSM-only iPhone 4S units from Apple's online store. The next section discusses unlocked contract-units from Sprint and Verizon.

▨ Find out if cell phone carriers abroad provide short-term pay-as-you-go plans or iPhone rentals. This can reduce your cost significantly as the iPhone you're using is tied to the local carrier in the country you're visiting.

GSM versus CDMA

In the United States, you can purchase the iPhone 4S from AT&T, from Sprint, from Verizon, or Apple. The iPhone 4S use two kinds of technology: GSM (Global System for Mobile Communications, the most common international standard) and CDMA (Code Division Multiple Access). These are different technologies using distinct cellular network standards. (The unlocked international "world phone" 4S ships with GSM technology only onboard.)

Each US carrier-based iPhone is *carrier locked*. This means that you cannot use the phones with third party carriers, even when they use the same network technology. You cannot take a US AT&T iPhone to Germany and expect to use it with T-Mobile's GSM service, even though they are both built on GSM technology. Apple and its official carriers cannot unlock these carrier-locked units. From the time they are purchased, they are set to only work with the approved carrier.

That's where unlocked phones come in. Apple now sells unlocked GSM World-service iPhones (but not CDMA), which allow you to use those units overseas or with different carriers in-country. Because they sell them unlocked and without contract subsidies, they cost far more than the ones you purchase from AT&T, Sprint, and Verizon. Normally, a large part of the purchase price is paid off over the lifetime of the contract and is not reflected in the initial upfront costs for the phone.

Sprint's policy allows customers in good standing to use the GSM technology on their iPhone 4S outside the United States. Sprint writes that they will allow those customers to unlock unit for international travel. Verizon added a sixty-day waiting period, specifying that customers must be in good standing for two months before they would issue an unlock. AT&T had not issued statements by the time this book went to press on the matter.

You can use unlocked phones, including the unlocked Apple world phone 4S or unlocked units from Sprint or Verizon with other GSM carriers like T-Mobile, both domestically and overseas, O2, Orange, and so forth. However, you may not be able to access full data speeds on these units. That's because each carrier licenses different frequencies for their data connections. The iPhone's internal antennas may or may not be able to tune into these. In the United States, you can use an unlocked GSM iPhone with T-Mobile data service, but only for the slower EDGE service, not with the faster 3G.

Placing Calls with Siri

The Siri voice assistant can help you place phone calls to contacts. To invoke Siri, raise the iPhone to your face or press and hold the Home button for a few seconds. You can also squeeze the stereo headset button for two seconds.

Siri uses your address book contact information to simplify the way you place phone calls. For example, you might say one of the following phrases to initiate calls with one of your personal contacts. If a person is not listed in your address book, you can explicitly speak out the number.

- Call Jason
- Call TJ (Yes, Siri works with nicknames too)
- Call Jennifer Wright mobile
- Call Susan on her work phone
- Call 408 555 1212
- Call home

Be aware that Siri does *not* confirm phone calls before placing them. It initiates the call directly and immediately switches to the phone application. You can cancel the call in that application as needed, but you may use an airtime minute in the process.

When calling a person with multiple numbers, Siri may ask you to specify whether you wish to to call the home number or work number, etc. Telling Siri in advance which number you wish to use, e.g. "Call John Appleseed at home".

If Siri cannot find a home number for this example, it will offer an alternative number, such as the mobile number or work number if one is available.

Relationships form an important part of the Siri/Address Book story. Siri allows you to personalize your relationships with others and use those relationships as shortcuts when making requests.

Here are some relationship examples you could use with Siri.

- My mom is Susan Park
- Michael Manning is my brother
- Call my brother at work
- Text my assistant

These phrases help establish those connections between your contact information and other entries in your address book. You can then use them when placing calls to instantly know exactly whom you're talking about. You may know 20 Mary's, but you probably only have one Mom.

Placing Calls with Voice Control

Older iPhones include a very helpful and mostly hands-free method of interaction called Voice Control. Not only is Voice Control fun to use, but it can also be very useful for making phone calls with or without the iPhone stereo headset. To enable voice control, press and hold the Home button for two seconds or squeeze the stereo headset button for two seconds. The Voice Control screen appears, and you can begin speaking to your iPhone to dial a number.

To place a call to someone who is in your Contacts list, simply say:

Call Bob Smith at Work / Home / iPhone / Mobile: For the best possible recognition, always tell the iPhone which destination to call.

Call Bob Smith: You can get away without specifying a destination when there's more than one number for Bob, and the iPhone will prompt you for the proper phone, but the recognition rate does go down quite a bit with this approach.

Dial Bob Smith at Home: This works identically to "Call Bob Smith at Home".

Dial 1-720-555-1212: If dialing internationally, you can preface the first number with the word "plus". This dials the number you read to the phone. Although you *can* use this approach, the error rate is high enough to make it inconvenient while driving. You'd be better off waiting for a red light and typing in the numbers directly.

Answering Calls

When your iPhone receive calls, it rings, playing back whatever ringtone you have selected and, if you've set it up that way, vibrates. The screen updates and tells you (to the best of its ability) who is calling by showing you a contact name and picture. If you're using the iPhone when a call comes in, the screen offers you the option of answering or declining the call (see Figure 4–3, left).

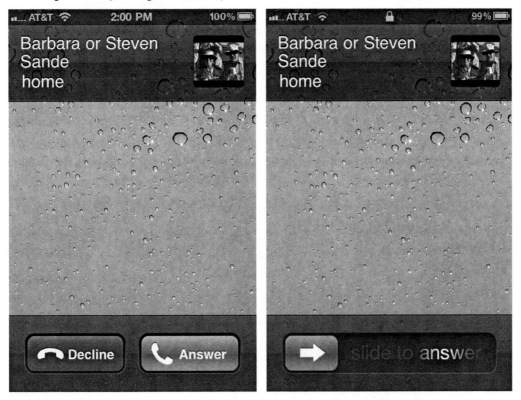

Figure 4–3. *When you receive a call, your iPhone identifies the caller with a name (if possible), contact photo, and the phone (work, home, iPhone, etc.) from which the call was placed. Tap Answer (or slide the green arrow button to the righ), to accept the call and talk, or Decline to send the call directly to voicemail. When two or more contacts share the same number (as seen here), your iPhone lists each possible caller.*

When your iPhone is in sleep mode, you'll see a different screen when there's an incoming call (Figure 4–3, right). To answer the phone when it wakes from sleep and is ringing, slide the green arrow button to the right.

Here are the ways you can answer and manage your calls:

> *Answering calls*: Tap the green Answer button to accept the call. The iPhone connects you to the caller, and you proceed with your call. You can also answer calls by squeezing the iPhone headset control once. If you are using a Bluetooth headset, you can usually click an onboard button to answer the call. Both the phone and the earpiece will ring. During the call, you may tap the Audio Sources button to re-route audio from the earpiece to the phone, to the speaker, or back. Tap Hide Sources to leave the audio selection as-is.

> *Sending calls to voicemail*: To decline a call, sending that call to voicemail, tap Decline. Your Voicemail account must be set up in advance for this to work, otherwise your caller may hear a message about a voice mailbox that has not yet been set up. Alternatively, press and hold the headset control for about two seconds, or press the Sleep/Wake button. AT&T's automated answering service prompts your caller to leave a message, which you can check later at your convenience.

> *Silencing the ringer*: Sometimes you forget to power off your phone before meetings. When this happens to you, silence the ringer by pressing one of the volume buttons. The iPhone stops ringing immediately. You can still answer the call for the normal period of time until it gets sent to voicemail. And don't forget to switch the Ring/Silent switch off before that next call comes through!

The iPhone's Ring/Silent switch is located just above the volume controls on the top-left side of the phone. Toggle your iPhone between ring mode (all black) and silent mode (red dot) by flipping the switch. You can set whether the iPhone vibrates upon receiving a call in **Settings ➤ Sounds**, where you'll find two vibrate settings: one for silent mode and another to make the phone vibrate when it's in ring mode.

Managing Calls

During conversations, your iPhone provides several ways to handle calls from muting your caller to handling call waiting (see Figure 4–4).

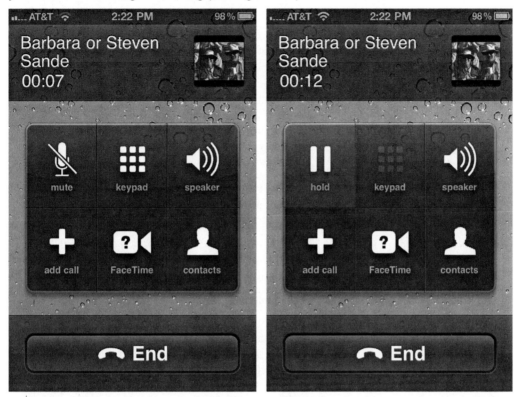

Figure 4–4. *The iPhone options available while you're on a call allow you to mute the microphone, place a call on speaker, establish a conference call, and more.*

When you need control your conversation, here are the options available to you:

> *Mute the microphone*: Tap Mute to temporarily disable your microphone. You can still hear your caller, but your caller will not be able to hear you until you tap Mute a second time. When enabled, the Mute button turns blue. This is a particularly great feature when you're using your phone with a multiparty conference, and a spouse or child walks into the room. You can keep listening to the ongoing call but no one will hear what's going on from your end.

Use the keypad: Tap the Keypad icon to bring up the iPhone keypad during a call. The keypad lets you navigate through automated voice systems (e.g., "Press 1 for English") or enter a PIN number. Tap Hide Keypad to return to the options shown in Figure 4–4. Use this for any keypad-driven menu system, such as contacting your insurance company, your pharmacy, or your bank.

Use the speakerphone: Tap the Speaker icon once to switch sound output from the earpiece to the built-in iPhone speaker. Like Mute, the Speaker icon turns blue when enabled. Tap a second time to return sound to the earpiece. Like the iPhone 4, the iPhone 5 has a terrific speaker, which is far improved from the iPhone 3GS and earlier models. Unfortunately, pickup is never as good as the speaker. If people complain that you're sounding too soft, you may want to switch off speaker and hold the handset to your face.

> **NOTE:** Your iPhone uses its proximity sensor to determine when the phone is held up to your ear. This blanks the screen but has no effect on the speaker. If you've enabled the speakerphone and hold the iPhone up to your ear, it remains on speakerphone but with a black screen. Unfortunately, both the iPhone 4 and iPhone 5 have some issues with proximity detection. If you find that your cheek keeps muting your call, or creating a secondary call, bring your device into the Genius Bar to be checked by a technician. This is called "cheek dialing", even though it's rare to actually place a second outgoing call by accident.

Placing a call on hold: To place a call on hold, tap and hold the mute button for two seconds. It will turn blue and display the hold icon seen in Figure 4–4, right. To take a caller off of hold, tap the hold button again. Use the hold feature rather than muting as a courtesy to provide privacy to the person who is calling you. It's rude listen to personal conversations while the other party thinks they're on hold.

Conference calling: To add another party to your call, tap the Add Call button. This places your current call on hold and allows you to place a new call. Use the keypad or the contacts list to place the call. After establishing the new call, tap Merge Calls to add the new call to the on-hold call. If needed, repeat these hold, call, and merge actions to bring additional parties into the conference call. On AT&T, the iPhone offers spectacular conference calling; this is one of the most powerfully useful features the phone offers. And it does so as a part of the built-in calling package for most carriers. On Verizon, you may be limited to adding a single third party into your call. Please check with your carrier for details about this feature.

Begin a FaceTime video chat (iPhone 4 or later, and iPod 4th generation or later, and iPad 2 and later only): FaceTime is Apple's unique videophone application that works only with very recent devices. It was first introduced as a feature on the iPhone 4. Chapter 4 introduces FaceTime in more detail. You can start a FaceTime chat with another iPhone 4 caller by tapping the FaceTime button. FaceTime uses the Internet to connect, and does not charge against your account minutes on your cell plan. You may, however, use cellular data so it's best to always connect to WiFi when you plan to FaceTime.

Accessing Contacts: Tap the Contacts icon to look up another contact during a call. Tapping a contact's phone number is equivalent to tapping Add Call and then selecting that contact.

TIP: You can run normal iPhone applications during your calls. Click the Home button, and select an application to open. To return to the call screen, tap the green bar that appears at the top each screen during an active call.

Responding to Call Waiting: When receiving a new call during a conversation, the iPhone asks whether to switch to that new call. You can choose to answer or decline that call in several ways.

- To end your current call and answer the new one, tap the red End Call and Answer buttons.

- Tap Ignore to continue with your current call. Alternatively, squeeze and hold the headset control for about 2 seconds and then release. Your iPhone beeps twice to confirm.

- Tap Hold Call and Answer to place your conversation on hold and answer the incoming call. Once answered, you can merge calls into the call on hold.

- Squeeze the headset control once to place the current call on hold and answer the incoming call. Squeeze again to toggle back and forth between the first call and the new one.

TIP: When using headphones or Bluetooth earpieces, your iPhone rings through both the handset and the attached headset—very convenient when you've put the iPhone down with the headphones still plugged in.

Ending a call: Tap End Call to hang up. You can also end calls by squeezing the iPhone headset control once.

TIP: Living in an age of quick-dial and disposable phone numbers, you might not always remember your iPhone's number. Fortunately, Apple makes it easy to look up. Scroll all the way to the top of the Contacts list or select **Settings ➤ Phone**. Your number appears at the top of each of these: "My Number: 1 (555) 555-1212". You can also check your iPhone's telephone number by docking it to your computer. Select your iPhone from the Sources list (the blue column on the left side of the iTunes screen), and check the number on the Summary page. It appears toward the top of the page, just under the serial number.

Managing Favorites

The Favorites screen offers one-touch access to your most often-used phone numbers. It can be a little counterintuitive to manage your favorites, because this one-tap behavior means you can't select a contact and then edit it. When you tap a name, the iPhone immediately calls it. Instead, here are the ways you should use to keep your Favorites list in line:

> *Adding a favorite*: In the Favorites screen, tap the plus (+) button in the top-right corner. Select a contact and then a phone number from that contact. The iPhone adds the number to Favorites and returns you to the Favorites screen.

> *Removing a favorite*: Tap Edit to place Favorites into edit mode (see Figure 4–5). Red circles with minus signs appear next to each contact. To delete a contact, tap the red circle and then confirm by tapping Remove. To cancel without removing the selected favorite, tap anyplace else on the screen. Tap *Done* to leave edit mode.

> *Reordering favorites*: Tap Edit at the top-left corner of the Favorites screen. In addition to the red circles to the left of each name, notice the gray bars to the right of each name. Drag these handles to move names into new positions. Tap *Done* when finished.

TIP: Although you can edit contact information on your iPhone—as when you add a new phone number on the go—the easiest place to manage contacts is on your computer. Your iPhone updates its contact information every time you synchronize. In iTunes, make sure you've chosen to sync your contacts by checking the appropriate option in the iPhone Info tab. You can also sync contact information over the air using Apple's iCloud service.

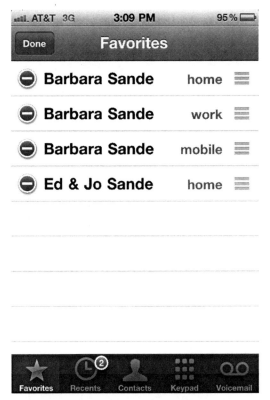

Figure 4–5. *In Edit mode, tap the red buttons to delete contacts and use the gray drag handles on the right to reorder contacts. Your favorites list can quickly grow long. Using these management features helps you keep your quick-access contacts list lean and ordered.*

Using Visual Voicemail

When someone calls and you can't or don't answer, they're transferred to your carrier's voicemail system and prompted to leave a message. Your iPhone's Visual Voicemail allows you to see a list of messages that have been left for you, where you can select which ones you want to hear. A small red bubble with a number in it may appear on the Voicemail icon at the bottom of the Phone app. This number indicates the number of voicemail messages that you have not yet heard.

If you purchase an unlocked iPhone from Apple and use it with a phone plan that is not an official iPhone account, tapping on the voicemail button takes you directly to the voicemail service for your carrier. You will not have access to visual voicemail except for official iPhone plans.

Setting Up Your Voicemail Passcode

The first time you enter the Voicemail screen, your iPhone prompts you to enter a new voicemail passcode (PIN). Select a number you will remember and make a note of it some place secure and private, i.e., not in your wallet or on a stick-it note attached to your computer.

To change your passcode at a later date, go to **Settings ➤ Phone**, and tap Change Voicemail Password. The iPhone prompts you for the current passcode. Enter it, and tap Done. Then enter the new passcode, and tap Done. To confirm the new passcode, enter it one more time, and tap Done.

> **TIP:** Advanced iPhone users should note that the **Settings ➤ Phone** screen also allows you to specify a SIM PIN. This number locks your SIM card, so it can't be used in other phones. When enabled, you must enter the SIM passcode every time you power on your iPhone.

Choosing Your Greeting

To set the message that plays when your mobile carrier transfers a call to voicemail, tap Greeting at the top-left of the Voicemail screen. Select Default to use the standard message or tap Custom to record a greeting as follows: tap Record; speak your message; tap Stop. You can review your recording by tapping Play and save it by tapping Save.

Managing Voicemail Messages

As mentioned earlier in this chapter, the small number in a red circle that appears on the green Phone icon on your Home screen indicates the combined number of accumulated missed calls and voicemails. When you tap the icon and enter the Phone application, these numbers break down individually, as shown in Figure 4–1. Tap the Voicemail icon to open the Voicemail screen and see your message list (Figure 4–6).

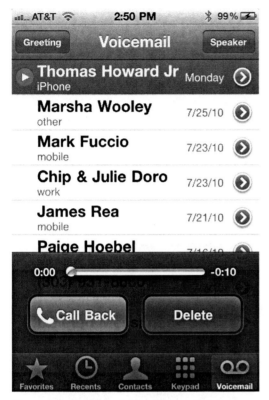

Figure 4–6. *The iPhone's Visual Voicemail lists your messages. To play back a message, select it and tap the play button to the left of the name or number.*

From the Voicemail screen, you can perform the following functions:

Toggling the speaker: By default, voicemail audio plays back through the iPhone's earpiece. Tap the Speaker button to play back voicemail through the iPhone's built-in speaker system instead. It turns a brighter, lighter blue when enabled. Tap again to redirect audio back to the internal earpiece.

Playing messages: To listen to voicemail, select a message, and tap the Play button that appears to the left of the contact name or phone number, as shown in Figure 4–6. The button switches to a two-lined Pause indicator, which you can tap again to pause playback. You also can rewind and fast-forward by adjusting the playhead on the scrubber bar that appears just above the Call Back and Delete buttons.

Removing voicemail: Tap Delete to remove the currently selected message. The iPhone moves that item into its Deleted Messages list. To undelete, select Deleted Messages, tap the item you want to restore, and tap Undelete. Permanently remove deleted voicemail by tapping

Clear All in the Deleted Messages list. When the iPhone prompts you, confirm by tapping Clear All again.

Reviewing contact information: The Disclose button at the right of each message links to the informational page for that contact. If you haven't assigned a phone number to a contact, use this page to add the selected number to an existing contact or to create a new contact for the number. Tap the Voicemail button in the upper left corner to return to the Voicemail screen.

Returning a call: Select any message from the list, and tap Call Back to return the call.

Accessing Voicemail Files

If you have a need to save important voicemail that you've received, you may want to look into a third-party Mac application from Mark/Space called The Missing Sync for iPhone (www.markspace.com/products/iphone), or PhoneView from ecamm (www.ecamm.com/mac/phoneview). With these applications, you can move voicemail messages to your Mac for future reference. There are similar application for Windows including WideAngle's TouchCopy (www.wideanglesoftware.com/touchcopy/index.php).

Another way you can save those messages on just about any computer is to play the voicemails on the iPhone through the speaker, and use a sound recording application to record the voicemail to the PC or Mac. On most Windows machines, you can use the Sound Recorder accessory, found in the list of All Programs under Accessories, to record the voicemail. On the Mac, the GarageBand application (part of iLife) is useful for recording and editing voicemail messages.

Sending Voicemail Indirectly

AT&T customers can uncover their AT&T message center phone number by opening the Phone application. Tap Keypad, enter *#61# (i.e., star, pound, 6, 1, pound), and tap Call. The iPhone responds with "Please wait". After a few seconds, the screen updates with overlaid text. One message will read, "Setting interrogation Succeeded. Voice Call Forwarding When Unanswered Forwards to" followed by a number. This number is the AT&T voice-messaging center. When you call this number, AT&T welcomes you and asks you to enter a ten-digit phone number. By entering the phone number for your iPhone, it's as if you'd dialed the iPhone directly. You hear the greeting you've set and can leave a message for your iPhone.

Managing Ringtones and Other iPhone Alerts

The Sounds pane (**Settings ➤ Sounds**) allows you to choose how your iPhone responds to incoming calls and other events. Here, you can both set the volume of the ringtone and choose which ringtone to play when calls arrive.

To switch to a new sound, tap Ringtone, and choose any of the sounds listed. The iPhone plays it back for you to hear. When you're satisfied with your selection, tap Sounds to set the ringtone and return to the previous screen.

> **Note** In addition to setting ringtones, the Sounds pane allows you to choose whether to play sounds for new voicemail, new text messages, new mail, sent mail, calendar alerts, locking your iPhone, and keyboard clicks.

The iPhone allows you to assign custom ringtones to individual contacts. This allows you to instantly know which contact is calling: a happy song for your spouse or an alarm for your boss (or vice versa, depending on how much you like your job). Choose **Phone ➤ Contacts**, and select a contact. Scroll down the contact information page, and tap Assign Ringtone. Select a ringtone, and tap Save to select that sound, or select Cancel to use the default ringtone for this contact.

Adding Custom Ringtones

The iPhone uses m4a audio files (AAC format) as ringtones but renames them as m4r, which allows iTunes to know that they are to be used as ringtones. While almost any sound file can be converted to this format in iTunes, third-party applications such as Ambrosia Software's iToner2 (www.ambrosiasw.com/utilities/itoner/) make this simple. Make sure you limit your ringtones to 30 seconds in length. Any unprotected m4a AAC file (i.e. doesn't use digital rights management) that's shorter than 30 seconds long can be renamed with an m4r extension, imported into iTunes, and used on your iPhone.

You can also turn a short segment of some songs that you've purchased from the iTunes store into a ringtone. Here's how:

1. Launch iTunes on your Mac or PC.

2. To find songs that you've purchased in iTunes, click the Purchased icon under the Store listing. You will also see a Purchased icon for each device that you've used to buy iTunes content.

3. Click a purchased song in the list, and then select Store ➤ Create Ringtone. If it's possible to convert a portion of the song into a ringtone, a small ringtone editor appears at the bottom of the iTunes screen (Figure 4–7). You can drag the highlighted area to any point of the song, make the ringtone longer (up to 30 seconds) or shorter, and choose to loop the ringtone over and over. There's an adjustable time gap between rings as well.

Figure 4–7. *The ringtone editor in iTunes provides a way to turn some purchased songs into iPhone ringtones.*

4. When you've edited the ringtone to your satisfaction, click the Buy button to purchase the ringtone for $0.99. It is saved to your Library under a section titled Ringtones.

5. Connect your iPhone to your computer. Under the Ringtones tab for your iPhone, make sure that Sync Ringtones is selected and that you have chosen either "All ringtones" or "Selected ringtones" to sync.

6. Click Apply, and the ringtones are transferred to your iPhone.

NOTE: Not all songs in iTunes can be purchased as ringtones. Apple previously put a small icon next to songs in iTunes that could be made into ringtones, but has stopped doing that recently. The only way to determine if a song can be turned into a ringtone is to try it. You can also create your own ringtones in Garage band from your own audio and export them in a format that you can bring into iTunes for use on your phone.

Advanced Phone Preferences

The Phone Settings pane (**Settings ➤ Phone**) allows you to enable and disable several key features including call forwarding, call waiting, and caller ID (that is, showing your caller ID information to other cell phones). Each of these preferences leads to a toggle switch, which selects whether the feature is enabled or not. In addition, the Call Forwarding setting lets you specify which number to forward calls to when the feature is in use. Choosing to hide your Caller ID means that others will not be able to see either your name or phone number when you call them or answer their calls.

TIP: The **Settings ➤ Phone** pane allows you enable iPhone use with a teletype machine. To use a TTY system with your iPhone, you must purchase a separate iPhone TTY adapter cable at the online Apple Store.

iPhone Codes

Every GSM phone (in the US, this means an AT&T or unlocked iPhone, and not a Verizon- or Sprint-provisioned one) has a "secret" vocabulary, codes that you can type into the number pad that provide backdoor access to phone information. To use these codes, open the Phone application, and tap Keypad. Next, enter the codes exactly as stated, including any stars and pound signs. Tap Call after entering the code. The iPhone implements a large subset of the standard GSM service codes as well as a number of carrier-specific ones. Here is a sampling of the codes you can use on your iPhone in the US on the AT&T network. To learn more, Google for *GSM codes*. If you are a Verizon customer, you will want to download the free My Verizon Mobile application, which allows you to access your account, check your usage, and pay your bills on the go. Sprint should have an iPhone app out shortly, now that it has joined the iPhone club with its new 4S.

Basic iPhone Information

Use these shortcuts to view information about your iPhone's core functionality:

> *#06#: Displays your iPhone IMEI, the unique identifier for your cell phone hardware. (No need to tap Call.) Together with your SIM information, it identifies you to the provider network.

Service Shortcuts

These shortcuts provide quick access to information about your US account:

> *225#: Current bill balance. (Postpaid service only; the acronym is BAL for balance. For prepaid units, use *777# instead.)

> *646#: Check remaining minutes. (Postpaid service only; the acronym is MIN for minutes.)

> *3282#: Check your data usage. (Postpaid service only; the acronym is DATA.)

> *729: Make a payment. (The acronym is PAY.)

> 611: Connect to customer service.

Summary

They don't call it an iPhone for nothing. This chapter introduced the "phone" part of the iPhone. In it, you have read about placing calls, receiving calls, and managing your iPhone contacts. You've learned about some of the ways to access and control calling features, and you've seen a few added features like adding ringtones and using GSM codes. Before you go away, here are a few key points that you may want to remember about making calls with the iPhone:

- AT&T, Sprint, and Verizon are the current US iPhone providers, although you can now purchase an unlocked world iPhone 4S and use it with any compatible GSM carrier. If you do not spend the extra money on an unlocked unit, your iPhone will be locked to its carrier. Both Sprint and Verizon offer courtesy unlocking to customers in good standing. In the U.S. and other countries, be sure to check with local carriers to determine if service at your most frequently-visited locations is good before purchasing an iPhone.

- It takes only a few seconds to get acquainted with many of the advanced iPhone calling features like multiway conference calling. If you're unsure how to proceed, just look at the menus on the iPhone screen. They are clear, explicit, and indicate what you need to do next.

These features are truly amazing, simplifying single and multi-party calling in ways that just work, and work well.

▓ It's easy to purchase an inexpensive application to add ringtones to your iPhone or even, if you feel comfortable doing so, rolling your own using Garage Band. Just remember to keep those ringtones under 30 seconds in length.

▓ If you have a lot of music in your iTunes library that has been purchased from iTunes, you may be able to create, edit, and transfer your own ringtone to your iPhone for a small fee.

▓ The GSM iPhone code shortcuts are both safe and convenient to use. Check your balance or your minutes directly from your iPhone without fear or download an application from the App Store for your current carrier.

Part III

Getting Online

Chapter 5

Browsing with Mobile Safari

Every iPhone has 3G and Wi-Fi networking capabilities. With these networks, you can connect to the Internet and view web pages directly on your iPhone.

The iPhone's mobile version of Safari is a near twin to the computer-based version that runs on both Mac and Windows. The iPhone's Retina display touchscreen shows web pages just as their designers intended. When it comes to browsing, there's nothing else like Safari on any other smartphone.

In this chapter, you'll discover how to get the most from Safari with all its awesome full-browser powers. You'll learn how to navigate to pages, manage bookmarks, and use both portrait and landscape orientations. You'll also discover some great finger-tap shortcuts, useful Safari web sites, and Safari's handy Reader and Reading List functions.

Whether you use the slower, but ubiquitous 3G cellular data network or choose to stay near a Wi-Fi hotspot for your Internet connection, the iPhone and Safari make handheld web browsing a pleasurable experience. In the next section, I'll describe how to get connected to a Wi-Fi network. After that, I'll focus on making a 3G data connection.

Getting Started with Wi-Fi

With your iPhone's Wi-Fi connectivity, you can connect to web sites such as YouTube and the iTunes Music Store, and you can pretty much do everything over the Internet that you desire. Read on to learn more about setting up your iPhone to connect to a Wi-Fi network.

> **NOTE:** Wi-Fi is a wireless networking technology. Your iPhone is compatible with three kinds of Wi-Fi standards known as IEEE 802.11b, 802.11g, and 802.11n. What's the difference? 802.11n is the newest standard and provides both the best speed and highest levels of security, while b and g are slower, less secure networking standards.

Checking Your Wi-Fi Connection

Before you use Safari, you need to have a Wi-Fi or 3G connection. You cannot connect to the Internet without it. In this section, I'll talk about the faster Wi-Fi connection.

You can tell in an instant whether your Wi-Fi connection is up and running. Look at the very top-left corner of your screen. When you see the three semicircle-like arcs next to the name of your cellular carrier, as shown in Figure 5–1, you have a live connection. When the arcs are more blue (and less black or gray), you have the strongest connection possible. Having three blue arcs is ideal. Seeing one or more black—or worse, gray—arcs means that your connection is weak. Moving closer to the Wi-Fi source is the best way to ensure a strong connection.

.ıl. AT&T 🤶   1:04 PM   ⚡ 93% 🔋

Figure 5–1. *The three arcs shown here indicate a strong Wi-Fi connection. Blue arcs indicate the strongest connection. Black arcs mean a weak connection. Very light gray arcs show the worst connection.*

Choosing a Wi-Fi Network

If your iPhone shows no Wi-Fi service, you'll need to connect to a local network. Navigate to the **Settings ➤ Wi-Fi** screen, shown in Figure 5–2. From here, you can enable your Wi-Fi service and specify whether you want your iPhone to search for local networks.

To connect to any network, set Wi-Fi to On. When Wi-Fi is switched to On, your iPhone scans the immediate area and lists all active networks. When it is Off, your iPhone shuts down Wi-Fi service and does not actively seek connections.

You can connect to any Wi-Fi network listed by tapping its name. As with the network strength indicator in the iPhone title bar, the arcs next to each network indicate the strength of its signal.

Figure 5–2. *Set Wi-Fi to On to connect to local networks. A lock icon next to a network name indicates that you must use authentication to connect.*

Tap the blue > buttons to see information about each network, including IP addresses, Domain Name System (DNS) server information, and so forth. You'll find all the standard kinds of information you would expect to see on any computer client for any Wi-Fi network. The iPhone offers the same information and capabilities in a handheld package.

Connecting to a Protected Network

When you see a lock next to the network name on the Wi-Fi Networks settings screen (Figure 5–2), this indicates that the network is protected and requires authentication. When you select a protected network, you must log in to the network with a password to use it.

Figure 5–3 shows a typical authentication screen. Enter the network password, and click Join. If you succeed, just go ahead and start using your connection. If you fail, make sure your password is up-to-date and that you typed it correctly. Be aware that you can only briefly see the last letter that you just typed before it changes into a black dot. This is a security feature so people can't steal your password by looking over your shoulder as you type it. Use extra care, and check the keyboard feedback carefully as you type.

Figure 5–3. *The password-entry screen allows you to join networks using WEP, WPA, or WPA2 authentication.*

You can also add an unlisted network to your iPhone network list. Tap Other on your main Wi-Fi settings screen. Enter the network name, choose the kind of encryption in use (None, WEP, WPA, WPA2, WPA Enterprise, WPA2 Enterprise), and then tap Join.

> **NOTE:** The WEP, WPA, and WPA2 acronyms refer to three common data encryption standards, listed in order of their security and strength from weakest to strongest: Wired Equivalent Privacy, Wi-Fi Protected Access, and Wi-Fi Protected Access version 2. Each standard was created to enhance wireless network security. Enterprise WPA encryption is used in business settings.

Asking to Join a Network

Your Wi-Fi Networks settings screen offers an option at the very bottom that prompts you to "Ask to Join Networks," as shown in Figure 5–4. This option allows your iPhone to automatically scan the local area and search for available networks. When it finds one, it offers to join it—with your permission. If you've already joined that network before, it automatically goes ahead and does so again.

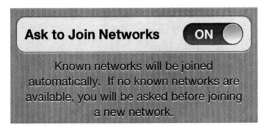

Figure 5–4. *The Ask to Join Networks feature facilitates rejoining known networks and searching for networks in areas where you haven't previously made a connection.*

This option is both a bonus and a possible security problem. On one hand, it's extremely convenient to join networks you already know about and trust. On the other hand, airports and other high-traffic transit areas are known for offering free Wi-Fi services that are easily pirated. Another possible threat comes from Wi-Fi traffic sniffers (also called *packet sniffers*), which are devices that track your online activity while you're connected via Wi-Fi. Both services that masquerade as official service providers and Wi-Fi traffic sniffers are designed to compromise your security and might endanger personal information and passwords. Fortunately, such exploits are rare.

In the end, the decision of when and whether to enable the Ask to Join Networks feature is up to you. For the most part, places like Starbucks, Panera Bread cafes, and many airports offer safe connections, but be aware that your iPhone network activity *can* be tracked.

Getting Started with 3G Data Connections

While you're out and about, you can still be connected to the world via the 3G (GPRS) data network. An easy rule of thumb to remember when you're going to use the 3G data connection—is that any time you are able to make a phone call via 3G, you also have access to the 3G data network.

How can you tell that you're connected to the network? In the top-left corner of your iPhone screen are several indicators (Figure 5–5). The first shows one to five bars of increasing height. This is your 3G network signal strength, with one bar being a barely acceptable connection and five bars indicating a strong, fast network connection. The next indicator shows the carrier you're connected to (in the figure, it's AT&T), and the final indicator shows the type of network connection.

Figure 5–5. *On the status bar at the top of this image, you see the bars indicating the cellular network signal strength (four bars), the carrier name (AT&T), and the type of network the iPhone is connected to (3G).*

Most of the time, you'll see the letters *3G* in this spot, but occasionally—most likely when you're out of a major urban area—an *E* appears. That stands for EDGE, an older and slower cellular wireless networking standard. On increasingly rare occasions, you may see an "o" in the network type—that indicates that you're currently connected to a 2G GPRS (General Packet Radio System) network.

Any time you're on a 3G data connection, you're going to be paying for the privilege. If you use a lot of Internet service, you may want to get an "unlimited" data plan with your wireless provider. These plans are generally more expensive but usually do allow you to use as much data as you want. The reason I say "usually" is that some providers throttle (slow down) your data speeds after you've reached a specified level of usage. Be sure to read the fine print on your data plan.

If you're ever in the mood to spend a ridiculous amount of money, use your 3G data connection overseas to do "data roaming" on a network other than the one you usually use. I recommend that you disable data roaming unless you absolutely must have a data connection and spending money is not an issue. To do this, launch the Settings app and select General ➤ Network ➤ Data Roaming ➤ Off.

Getting Started with the Safari Web Browser

Once you're assured of a strong Wi-Fi or 3G data connection, tap the Safari application icon to open the program. It's the icon on your Home screen marked with a white compass on a blue background (see Figure 5–6). The Safari application launches and opens a new Internet browser window.

Figure 5–6. *The Safari icon*

Many elements of the Safari window may look familiar, especially to anyone experienced using web browsers. Familiar items include the address bar, the reload icon, the search field, and the history navigation arrows. Figure 5–7 shows a typical Safari browser window in portrait and landscape modes.

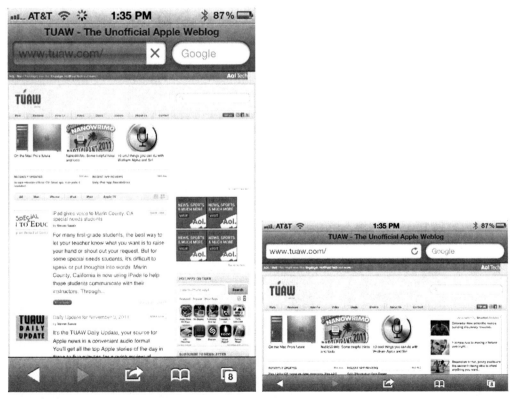

Figure 5–7. *The Safari browser window displays many familiar features, including the address bar, the Reload button, and the History button. Portrait orientation (left) allows you to see further down the page, while landscape (right) provides a wider page view.*

Here are interactive elements you'll find arranged around the screen and what they do:

Address bar: Use the address bar at the top center of the Safari window to enter a new web address (URL).

Reload button: The arrow bent in a semicircle to the right in the address bar is the Reload button. Tap it to refresh the current screen.

Stop button: As a page loads, Safari replaces the Reload button with a small *X* (you cannot see this in Figure 5–7). If you change your mind after navigating to a page, tap this button. It stops the current page from loading any further.

Search field: This is the white field with the word *Google* in it next to the address bar. Tap this field to enter your search query. You can also change your default search provider to Yahoo! Search or Microsoft's Bing using a process I'll describe shortly.

History buttons: Located at the bottom of the screen, the two triangles, facing left and right, navigate through your page history. When grayed out, you haven't yet created a history. The arrows turn from gray to white once you start browsing, and you can move back and forth through your history to the previous and next pages. Each page maintains its own history.

Share button: Found just to the right of the history buttons, this arrow breaking out of a box-shaped button adds the current page to your bookmark collection as well as gives you other sharing options. You can read more about bookmark creation and management in the "Working with Bookmarks" section later in this chapter.

> **NOTE:** You cannot use the History button to go back to a page you were viewing in another window. Use the Pages button to select another window, and then use the arrows there to navigate through that page history.

Bookmarks button: Tap the book-shaped icon to open your Bookmarks screen.

Pages button: The button at the bottom right that looks like two squares superimposed on one another allows you to open the page-selection browser and select one of your Safari sessions. You can open up to eight browser windows at a time. With more than one session active, a number appears on this icon. It indicates how many sessions are in use. You can read more about viewing and adding pages in the "Working with Pages" section later in this chapter.

Safari lets you do all the normal things you expect to do in a browser. You can tap links and buttons, enter text into forms, and so forth. In addition, Safari offers iPhone-specific features you won't find on your home computer; for example, tilting the iPhone on its side toggles the browser window from portrait to landscape orientation. The following how-to sections guide you through Safari's basic features.

> **NOTE:** Although Safari allows you to browse the Web in full resolution, some web sites detect that you're surfing with an iPhone and (wrongly) present a lighter, mobile version of their web pages. This should change as the iPhone's capabilities become better known and web sites become accustomed to receiving visits from iPhone users.

Entering URLs

Tap the address bar to open the URL entry screen, as shown in Figure 5–8. The navigation section appears at the top of your screen, and a keyboard opens from below. Between these, the screen dims, and you can still see part of the current page.

Figure 5–8. *The URL-entry screen allows you to enter the address that you want Safari to visit.*

Tap the white URL field, and use the keyboard to enter a new URL. Apple provides both the forward slash (/) and a .com key to help you type, but not a colon (:) key. Safari is smart enough to know about http://, so you don't need to type it each time.

> **TIP:** To access secure web pages, be sure to type the full address, including the `https://` prefix. Mobile Safari assumes that any address without a prefix uses `http://`. Secure web sites using the `https` prefix encrypt data being sent to and received from your computer using a Secure Socket Layer (SSL) certificate.

When you're finished typing, tap Go, and Safari navigates to the address you've entered. To return to the browser screen without entering a new URL, tap Cancel instead.

As you type, Safari matches your keystrokes to its existing collection of bookmarks. The space between the top of the keyboard and the bottom of the URL field turns white and displays a list of possible matches. To select one, just tap it. Safari automatically navigates to the selected URL. This matching ability is much more useful in portrait orientation than in landscape orientation, because there's more vertical space in which to view matches.

When entering URLs, you can use the tap-and-hold trick discussed in Chapter 2 to invoke the magnifying glass. Use the magnifying glass to move the insertion point and edit URLs to fix any mistakes made while typing.

> **TIP:** When you see a white *X* in a gray circle in a text-entry field, you can tap it to clear the field.

Searching the Web

A search bar appears just to the right of the address bar, as shown in Figure 5–9. Tap it to begin entering text into the URL field. As you do, search suggestions start to appear between the search field and the keyboard. To use a search suggestion, tap it—you don't need to finish typing the entire query. To start a search query of your own, tap the Search button next to the spacebar. Safari navigates to the search page of your selected search engine (for example, `www.google.com`) and searches for that term.

Figure 5–9. *Type in the search field for easy access to the Google, Yahoo!, or Bing search engines.*

If you would rather search with Yahoo! or Bing than Google, use Settings ➤ Safari to change your default search engine.

Searching for Text on a Web Page

Safari also allows you to search for specific text on a web page. To search for text, tap inside the Google search field and enter the word or words you are looking for on the Web. At the bottom of the list of possible search terms is the phrase "On This Page (X Matches)" (Figure 5–9). Tap that and scroll up just a bit, and you'll see *Find [search term]*. Tap the search term, and Safari displays the web page with the first occurrence of the text you're searching for highlighted in yellow (Figure 5–10).

Figure 5–10. *Searching for text on a web page*

If there is more than one match for the search term on the current web page, a set of arrows for the next (right arrow) or previous (left arrow) match appears at the bottom of the display. When you're finished searching for text on a web page, tap the blue Done button.

Entering Text

To edit a text entry (other than in the address bar), tap any text field on the currently displayed web page. Safari opens a new text-entry screen (Figure 5–11). Although this screen is superficially similar to the URL-entry screen (Figure 5–8), it presents a few differences, notably the text-entry buttons in a black bar above the keyboard:

- A *Done* button hides the keyboard and returns you to the web page after you have entered your text.

- *Previous* and *Next* buttons search for other text fields on your web page so you can jump to them without having to tap into each new field. Enter text in one field, tap Next, enter more text, and so on.

■ An *AutoFill* button uses information from your address book card to fill in relevant information such as your name, phone number, and e-mail address. The AutoFill button saves you time.

To submit a form after you've entered all the text, tap the Go or Search button next to the spacebar instead of the Done button in the text-entry bar. This is like pressing the Enter or Return key on a computer.

Figure 5–11. *Entering text in text-entry fields on a web page. Note the text-entry bar above the keyboard.*

Following Links

Hypertext links are used throughout the World Wide Web. Text links are marked with underlines and are usually a different color from the main text. Image links are subtler, but they can also move you to a new location.

Tap a link to navigate to a new web page or, for certain special links, to open a new e-mail message or view a map. When a link leads to an audio or video file with a format that the iPhone understands, it plays that file. Supported audio formats include AAC, M4A, M4B, M4P, MP3, WAV, and AIFF. Video formats include H.264 and MPEG-4.

To preview a link's address, touch and hold the link for a second or two. A link screen slides up, showing you the full URL. Below the URL you'll see four buttons, as shown in Figure 5–12:

Open: Opens the link in the current Safari window

Open in New Page: Opens the link in a new Safari page

Add to Reading List: Adds the selected page to your Reading List (discussed later in this chapter)

Copy: Copies the URL so you can paste it in another document later

Cancel: Returns you to the page you were just on

Figure 5–12. *Touch and hold either an image or a text link for a second or two to view the URL link screen. This bubble reveals the link's full URL and allows you to choose whether to continue following the link or to stop.*

TIP: To detect image links on the screen, tap and hold an image. If the image is also a link, a dialog similar to the one in Figure 5–12 appears and allows you to decide what you want to do with the link, including saving the image to your Photo Library. If the image is just an image, your only choices are to save the image or copy it to your iPhone clipboard.

Changing Orientation

One of the iPhone's standout features is its flexible orientation support. When you turn your iPhone on its side, it flips its display to match, as you can see in Figure 5–7. A built-in acceleration sensor detects the iPhone's tilt and adjusts the display. Tilt back to vertical, and the iPhone returns to portrait orientation. It takes just a second for the iPhone to detect the orientation change and to update the display.

The iPhone's landscape view offers a relatively wider display. This is particularly good for side-to-side tasks such as reading text. The wider screen allows you to use bigger fonts and view wider columns without scrolling sideways. The portrait view provides a longer presentation. This is great for reading web content with more narrow columns. You don't need to keep scrolling quite as much as you do in landscape view.

Whether in landscape or portrait view, Safari features work the same, including the same buttons in the same positions. In landscape view, you enter text using a wider, sideways keyboard. In portrait view, the smaller keyboard provides more space for you to view possible address completions while entering URLs.

Scrolling, Zooming, and Other Viewing Skills

Safari responds to the complete vocabulary of taps, flicks, and drags discussed in Chapter 2. You can zoom into pictures, squeeze on columns, and more. Here's a quick review of the essential ways to interact with your screen:

> *Drag*: Touch the screen, and drag your finger to reposition web pages. If you think of your iPhone as a window onto a web page, dragging allows you to move the window around the web page.

> *Flick*: When dealing with long pages, you can flick the display up and down to scroll rapidly. This is especially helpful when navigating through search engine results and news sites.

> *Double-tap*: Double-tap any column or image to zoom in, automatically sizing it to the width of your display. Double-tap again to zoom back out. Use this option to instantly zoom into a web page's text. The iPhone recognizes how wide the text is and perfectly matches that width.

> *Double-drag*: When you need to scroll a text entry field in a form or a scrollable frame in a multiframe web site, use two fingers to drag at once. This tells your iPhone to scroll just that page element and not the entire web page at once.

> *Pinch*: Use pinching to manually zoom in or out. This allows you to make fine zoom adjustments as needed.

> *Tap*: Tap buttons and links to select them. Use tapping to move from site to site and to submit forms.

Page down: When zoomed in on a column, double-tap toward the bottom of the screen while staying within the column. The page recenters around your tap. Make sure not to tap a link!

Jump to the top: Tap the very top of the screen (for instance, between the Wi-Fi signal strength indicator and the time display) to pop instantly back to the top of the page.

Stop a scroll: After flicking a page to get it to scroll, you can tap the page at any time to stop that movement. Don't forget that you can also manually drag the screen display to reset the part you're viewing.

Working with Pages

Safari allows you to open up to eight concurrent browser sessions at once. To review your open windows, tap the Pages button (the two squares) at the bottom-right corner of your browser. Safari's pages viewer opens, as shown in Figure 5–13.

Figure 5–13. *The pages viewer allows you to select which browser session to display.*

This viewer allows you to interactively select a browser session:

- To select a window, scroll horizontally from one window to the next. The brightest dot along the line of dots shows which item you're currently viewing. In Figure 5–13, the viewer is showing the sixth of eight open pages. Tap either the window or the Done button to select that window and display it full-screen.

- To close a window, tap the Close button—the red circle with an *X* in it at the top left of each page. The pages viewer slides the remaining pages into the gap left by the closed window.

- To add a new page, tap New Page. Safari creates a new session and opens a new, blank page. You can add up to eight pages, after which Safari grays out the New Page button.

Working with Bookmarks

One of the great things about the iPhone is that it lets you take your world with you: contacts, calendars, and bookmarks. You don't need to reenter all your favorite web pages into Safari on the iPhone. It loads them through iCloud.

Once you've set up your iPhone to sync to your other devices through iCloud, look at **Settings ➤ iCloud** and make sure that the toggle next to Bookmarks is set to On. On your Mac, open **System Preferences ➤ iCloud** and make sure that there's a check mark next to Bookmarks. Now any time you edit, add, or delete a bookmark on either your Mac or your iPhone, the changes are synchronized through iCloud. You'll always have the same bookmarks on all of your Apple devices.

For Windows PCs, install and configure the iCloud Control Panel (it's a free download from http://support.apple.com/kb/DL1455). You have the choice of syncing your bookmarks with either Safari for Windows or Internet Explorer 8. On the iPhone, you just need to check that **Settings ➤ iCloud** shows Bookmarks as On. On the Windows PC, check the box next to Bookmarks in the iCloud Control Panel (Figure 5–14) and use the Options button to select the browser you want to sync to.

Figure 5–14. *Syncing bookmarks between your iPhone and Windows PC. Install the iCloud Control Panel for Windows, and then make sure that the check box next to Bookmarks is selected.*

Selecting Bookmarks

Most standard bookmark collections contain dozens of individual URLs. That's one reason I really appreciate Safari's simple bookmarks browser, shown in Figure 5–15. It uses the same folder structure that you've set up on your personal computer. You can tap folders to open them and tap the Back button (top-left corner) to return to the parent folder. To access your bookmarks, tap the bookmarks icon in the lower part of any Safari window.

Identifying bookmarks is easy. Folders look like folders, and each bookmark is marked with a small, open book symbol. Tap one of these, and Safari takes you directly to the associated page.

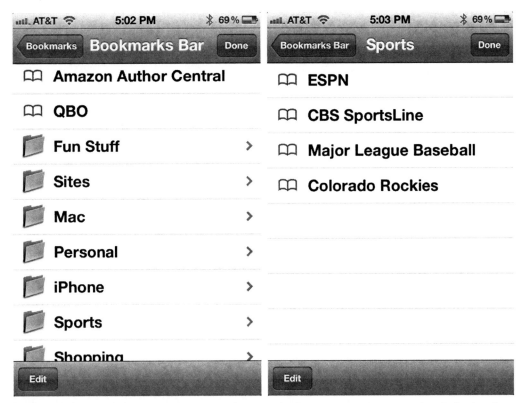

Figure 5–15. *Use Mobile Safari's interactive bookmarks navigation to locate and open your favorite bookmarks. This figure shows folders full of bookmarks (left) and individual bookmarks in those folders (right).*

Editing Bookmarks

As Figure 5–13 shows, an Edit button appears at the bottom left of the Bookmarks screen. Tap this to enter edit mode, as shown in Figure 5–16.

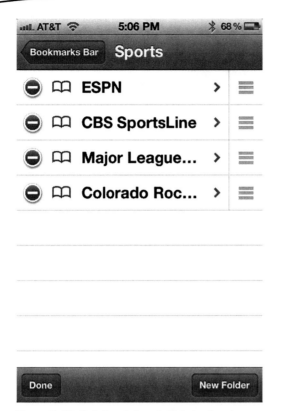

Figure 5–16. *Safari contains a built-in bookmark-management system that allows you to edit and reorder your bookmarks.*

Edit mode allows you to manage your bookmarks on your iPhone just as you would on your personal computer:

> *Deleting bookmarks*: Tap the red delete circle to the left of a bookmark to delete it. Tap Delete to confirm, or tap elsewhere on the screen to cancel.

> *Reordering bookmarks*: Use the gray grab handles (the three lines on the far right) to move folders and bookmarks into new positions. Grab, drag, and then release.

> *Editing names*: Tap the gray reveal arrow (the > symbol to the right of each name) to open the Edit Bookmark or Edit Folder screen. Use the keyboard to make your changes. Tap the Back button to return to the bookmarks editor.

> *Reparenting items*: You can move items from one folder to another by tapping the gray reveal arrow and selecting a new parent from the bookmark folder list (just below the name-editing field). Select a folder, and then tap the Back button to return to the bookmarks editor.

Adding folders: Tap New Folder to create a folder in the currently displayed bookmark folder list. The iPhone automatically opens the Edit Folder screen. Here, you can edit the name and, if needed, reparent your new folder. Tap the Back button to return to the editor.

Finishing: Return to the top-level bookmarks list (tap the Back key until you reach it), and then tap Done. This closes the editor and returns to Safari.

Saving Bookmarks and Sharing Web Pages

To save a new bookmark, tap the Share button at the bottom of any Safari web page. The Sharing menu appears, giving you six choices (see Figure 5–17).

Figure 5–17. *The bookmark creation menu*

Add Bookmark: Tapping this lets you enter a title for the bookmark and then optionally select a folder to save to (Figure 5–18). Tap the currently displayed folder to view a list of all available folders. The root of the bookmark tree is called Bookmarks. After making your selection, tap Save. Safari adds the new bookmark to your collection. If you want to return to Safari without saving, tap Cancel.

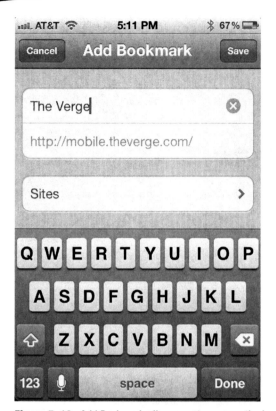

Figure 5–18. *Add Bookmark allows you to rename the bookmark before you save it.*

Add to Reading List: Tapping this adds the current page to your Reading List. I'll talk about Reading List in a moment.

Add to Home Screen: This is a cool feature. Tapping this adds an icon of the web page to your iPhone Home screen. Apple calls these web page icons *Web Clips*. Before you save a Web Clip, you have the option of renaming it. Keep the names short so you can see the entire name under the Web Clip icon on the Home screen.

> **NOTE:** Some web sites create an iPhone-optimized site icon when you add a Web Clip to your Home screen. Others just show you a thumbnail of the page in the shape of an iPhone app icon.

The Web Clips look just like app icons, and when tapped, they launch Safari and automatically take you to the web page. One handy hint is to keep a Home screen on your iPhone full of your favorite Web Clips so you can quickly navigate directly to your most frequently visited web sites. In many cases, this is much faster than using the bookmarks feature of Safari.

In iTunes, the Web Clips appear in the virtual iPhone screen on the Apps tab (see Chapter 2), but you cannot delete them from within iTunes; you can only rearrange them. To delete a Web Clip icon on the iPhone, press and hold it until it jiggles, and tap the X in the upper-left corner.

Mail Link to this Page: Tapping this button opens a new mail message window in Safari and automatically inserts the link into the body of the message.

Tweet: Tapping this button composes a Twitter message to send to all your followers (Figure 5–19). You must have a Twitter account to use this feature.

Figure 5–19. *Tweeting a web page*

Print: This allows you to print the web page to an AirPlay-compatible wireless printer.

Eliminating Clutter with Reader

Safari has an awesome built-in feature that all other mobile web browsers lack. It's called Reader (not to be confused with Reading List—another awesome feature that I'll explain shortly). Reader allows you to eliminate all the clutter on web pages—the ads, the comments, the links—and read the content of that page as if you were reading it from a piece of paper. You can see Reader in action in Figure 5–20.

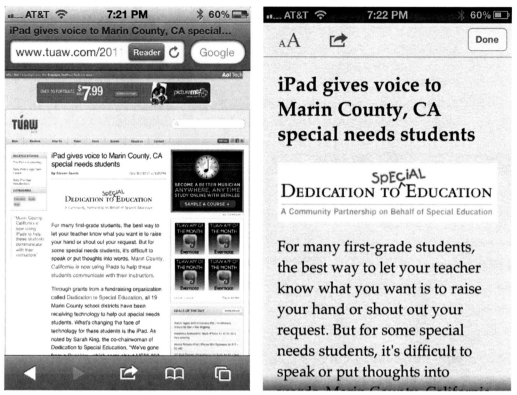

Figure 5–20. *Safari's Reader feature. Left: a web page as it normally appears. Right: the same web page when viewed through Reader.*

As shown in Figure 5–20, viewing the text on a web page through Reader is much easier because all the distractions are eliminated. To activate reader, click the gray Reader button that appears in the address bar. The Reader document slides up onto the screen. To exit Reader mode, click the Done button. Notice that the Reader button appears only when you are on a web page that has a single article. You won't see a Reader button on the front page of The Unofficial Apple Weblog web site, for example; you'll see it only when viewing single articles on the site.

Building Up Your Reading List

Reading List is another new feature of Safari in iOS 5 on the iPhone. It allows you to save web pages to read when you have the time, even when you're not connected to the Internet. I know, that sounds a lot like adding a bookmark, right? It's similar, but Reading List is more of a temporary bookmark. It's for that cool article you find about a small town in Andorra, which you want to read but don't have time to right now. It's not a bookmark you want to keep forever; it's just something you want to make sure you read.

To activate Reading List, tap the Share button at the bottom of Safari's window. The Sharing menu appears. Tap Add to Reading List. The web page has now been added to your Reading List.

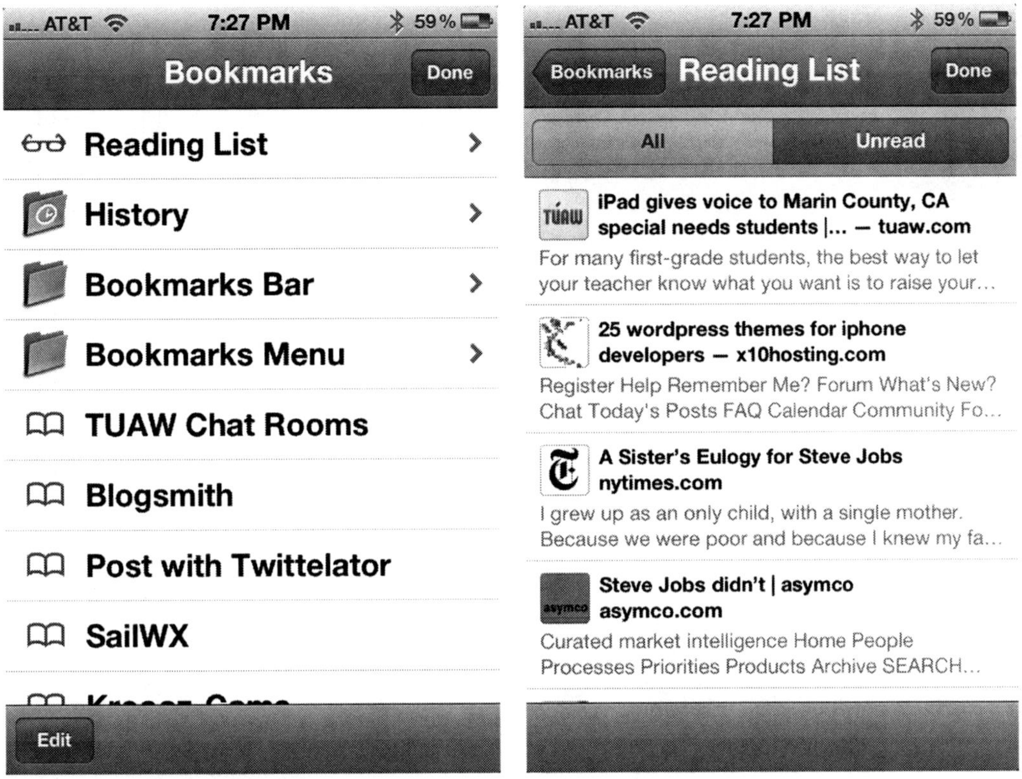

Figure 5–21. *Safari's Reading List*

To access your Reading List, tap the Bookmarks button in Safari. In the bookmarks screen you'll see an icon that looks like a pair of reading glasses labeled Reading List at the top (Figure 5–21, left). Tap it to view your Reading List. The Reading List panel contains all the web articles you've added to it. You can tap a tab to see all the articles you've added or just the ones you haven't read yet. Tap an article in the Reading List to read the saved web page.

Once you've read a page on the Reading List in its entirety, it disappears from the list of Unread items on your list. To permanently remove pages from the Reading, swipe left or right over an article description, and then tap the red Delete button that appears.

One of the best features about Reading List is that is synced across all your computers and iOS devices that use Safari. This allows you to find an interesting article on Safari on your iPhone, save it to Reading List, and then read it on your iPad or Mac when you get home. Just open up Safari, and the article appears in Reading List no matter what device you are on. It does this by syncing Reading List via your iCloud account.

Customizing Safari Settings

Like many of the apps on the iPhone, Safari can be customized. Customize your Safari settings by launching the Settings app on your iPhone Home screen, and then tap Safari. This screen, shown in Figure 5–22, allows you to control a number of features, mostly security-related. Here's a quick rundown of those features and what they mean:

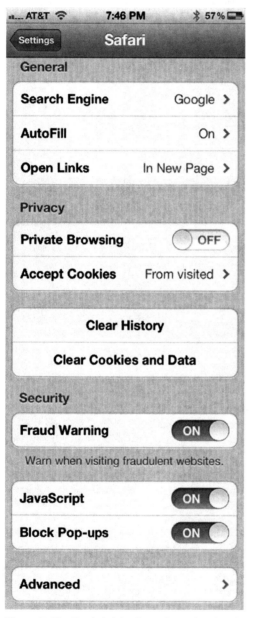

Figure 5–22. The Safari Settings window is primarily concerned with security features.

Search Engine: This setting determines which search engine is used for the search field you saw back in Figure 5–9. Choose from Google, Yahoo!, or Bing.

AutoFill: This allows you to turn on AutoFill for use in filling out forms on web pages. In the My Info box, select your address book card to take the AutoFill information from. Here you can also select to turn on Names & Passwords. With this on, Safari remembers login names and passwords to web sites you visit. You might not want to enable name and password saving if you share your iPhone with people because they could then easily access your personal web accounts such as e-mail and bank accounts. Tap Clear All to wipe all saved names and passwords from your iPhone.

Open Links: Here you can choose to open links in a new browser page or in the background. When New Page is selected, tapping a link in an e-mail, for instance, causes you to jump immediately to the Safari app. When In Background is selected, tapping a link in an e-mail opens the page in Safari in the background while you remain in the Mail app.

Private Browsing: When private browsing is enabled, your web history is not saved, nor are any of the user names, passwords, web searches, or text you enter on a web page.

Accept Cookies: Cookies refer to data stored on your iPhone by the web sites you visit. Cookies allow web sites to remember you and to store information about your visit. You can choose to always accept cookies, never accept cookies, or accept cookies only "from visited" web sites.

Clear History: Tap and confirm to empty the page navigation history from your iPhone. This keeps your personal browsing habits private to some extent, although other people are still able scan through your bookmarks if they so desire.

CAUTION: Clearing your history does not affect Safari's page history. You can still tap its Back button and see the sites you've visited.

Clear Cookies and Data: Tap and confirm to clear all existing cookies and cache from your iPhone. Your iPhone's browser cache stores text and graphics from many of the web sites you visit. It uses the cached information to speed up page loading the next time you visit. As with cookies and history, your cache may reveal personal information that you'd rather not share. Tap Clear Cache and Confirm to clear your cache.

> **TIP:** Clearing your cache may also help correct problem pages that are having trouble loading. By clearing the cache, you remove page items that may be corrupted or only partially downloaded.

Fraud Warning: Turn this preference on, and you'll be presented with a warning before navigating to potentially fraudulent web sites. Unfortunately, fraudulent sites are rampant on the Internet (like bogus PayPal sites). This feature helps you recognize and avoid those sites.

JavaScript: JavaScript allows web pages to run programs when you visit. Disabling JavaScript means you increase overall surfing safety, but you also lose many cool and worthy web features. Most pages are safe to visit, but some, sadly, are not. To disable JavaScript, switch from On to Off.

Block Pop-ups: Many web sites use pop-up windows for advertising. It's an annoying reality of surfing the Web. By default, Safari pop-up blocking is On. Switch this setting to Off to allow pop-up window creation.

Advanced: This preference gives you control over databases and debugging. Most people never use this preference. Some sites like Gmail use databases to store local information on your iPhone for offline browsing. Emptying databases can clear up problems you may be having on certain web sites. The debug console helps developers who are working to optimize their web sites for the iPhone.

The iPhone and Flash Videos

If you've ever watched a video or animation on the Web, chances are the video was encoded using Adobe Flash. Ever since Apple unveiled the iPhone to the world, there has been growing tension between Apple and Adobe. The reason is because Apple does not allow Adobe's proprietary and resource-intensive Flash plug-in to run on the iPhone.

Flash, in Apple's estimation, is a slow, buggy, and archaic technology. The late Apple CEO Steve Jobs even posted a letter on Apple's web site effectively telling the world the same thing (www.apple.com/hotnews/thoughts-on-flash/). His letter was the final word for anyone hoping to see Flash on the iPhone.

What many people misunderstand when they hear "no Flash on the iPhone" is that they think the iPhone can't play web videos. There's nothing further from the truth. Sure, if a video is encoded in Flash, you can't view it on the iPhone, but most videos on the Web (about 75 percent of them, according to former Apple CEO Steve Jobs) are encoded in Flash but also in a new, universal web standard called HTML5. HTML5 videos don't require a plug-in to play. HTML5 is also much less power hungry than Flash—an important feature when dealing with mobile devices that consume battery power.

The world is moving to HTML5, and Apple chose to support it—and open standards—instead of Adobe's aging and proprietary Flash. Most of YouTube's videos have already been reencoded to support HTML5, and many other major web sites have chosen to drop Flash in favor of the new HTML5 web standard. Apple even has a dedicated page to spotlight the advantages of the new HTML5 web standard: `www.apple.com/hmtl5/`.

Should you need to view Flash-enabled web sites, there are third-party browser apps that you may want to install on your iPhone. These apps usually work through a server that is able to play Flash on the fly and then translate it to a format that is visible on your iPhone. Examples of Flash-friendly browsers are Skyfire (`www.skyfire.com/en/for-consumers/iphone/iphone`) and Puffin (`www.cloudmosa.com/puffin-ios.php`).

Summary

Safari on the iPhone puts the power of a real Internet browser into your pocket. There's nothing half-cocked or watered down about it. You can browse the real Web and read real sites without major compromise. It's such an amazing step forward in technology that you'll find yourself shaking your head with disdain when you remember the old days when your cell phone could only make phone calls.

Here are a few tips to keep in mind as you move on from this chapter:

- iPhones work in more orientations than just vertical. Go ahead and flip your iPhone on its side. Your Safari pages automatically adjust.

- Nope, there's no Flash support. There never will be. And you don't need it.

- Web Clips are a great way to access your favorite web sites right from your iPhone's Home screen.

- Lost your address bar? Use the "double-tap to the top" trick.

- Use the power of iCloud to sync your Bookmarks between your iPhone, iPad, Mac, or Windows PC.

- Safari's page management tool lets you navigate back and forth between several Safari windows at once. This functions like the way tabs function on desktop browsers.

- Don't confuse Reader and Reading List. Reader lets you strip away ads and read a web page's text as if you were reading a newspaper. Reading List allows you to save interesting articles to come back to at your leisure.

Chapter 6

Staying in Touch with FaceTime and Messages

Are you ready to learn what the future feels like? Want to reach out and connect with friends, family, and colleagues in new ways? Remember this: the iPhone's cameras aren't for just taking pictures and recording video. They can bring people together using a new technology called FaceTime. FaceTime introduces easy and intuitive video calling for your handset. And video chatting isn't the only way you can stay in touch. The newly introduced iMessage app allows you to text anyone who owns an iOS device. For free. It doesn't matter if they own an iPhone, iPod touch, or iPad. In this chapter you'll read about these apps and learn how to use them to stay in touch on your iPhone.

The Camera Hardware

The iPhone 4S features two cameras—one front and one rear. These cameras allow you to snap photos and record video. The cameras aren't created equal, however. As you'll see, each one has been designed for different uses.

Front Camera

The front iPhone camera is located at the top left of the device's upper bezel across from the unit's Home button. Behind a rather hard-to-see dot lies the front-facing camera.

This front camera is meant primarily for FaceTime video calls, but you can also take photos and record video with it. For example, you might use the front-facing camera to snap a profile picture for your Facebook account or to record yourself and a friend singing "Happy Birthday" to a special someone. With the front camera, there's no shooting pictures in a bathroom mirror or turning a camera around and hoping you frame yourself into the shot. The front camera allows you to see and compose the shot as you take it.

The front-facing camera isn't as powerful as the rear camera: it cannot record high-definition (HD) video. High-definition video refers to video that has at least 720 lines of resolution. With video, the more lines of resolution you have, the sharper the picture will be. Although the front camera can record video, its resolution is limited to standard-definition (SD). SD video, also called VGA, uses a resolution of 640x480. The VGA acronym refers to an old computer monitor standard and is actually a higher resolution than the 525 lines that was originally broadcast over commercial television stations in the original NTSC standard.

Why didn't Apple use an HD camera in the front? Well, it would be unnecessary. The front camera was designed for FaceTime video calling, not recording video. The image quality while video calling on a portable device like the iPhone is more than good enough using an SD camera.

Rear Camera

The iPhone's powerful rear camera allows you to take photos, to record video, and to work with third-party augmented reality applications. When you flip your iPhone over, you can easily spot the rear camera in the top-left corner of the device.

The rear camera records videos in 1080p HD resolution at 30 frames a second; that's enough resolution to show pictures in beautiful quality on a large HDTV screen.

Getting Started with FaceTime

With the FaceTime app on the iPhone, you can video call anyone with an iPhone 4 (or newer), an iPad 2 (or newer), a fourth-generation iPod touch (or newer), or a Mac running OS X 10.6 or newer.

Apple wants to make FaceTime the de facto standard for video calling, and in order to do so, Apple has made the FaceTime technology an open standard. That means other phone manufacturers can build the technology in their phones, so one day, ideally, you'll be able to place a FaceTime video call on your iPhone to someone on an Android phone.

To use FaceTime, you'll want access to a Wi-Fi Internet connection and have your Apple ID on hand, even if you are calling on an iPhone with cellular data service. FaceTime is data intensive. Even if you *can* use cellular data for your conversations, you probably do not want to, particularly if you use a metered data plan.

Signing In

To begin using FaceTime, tap the FaceTime icon on your home screen. The icon looks like a white video camera with a blue lens on a metallic background (Figure 6–1). If this is the first time you've launched the app, you'll be presented with the FaceTime Get Started screen (Figure 6–2).

If you click the "Learn more about FaceTime" link, Safari will open, and you'll be taken to Apple's iPhone FaceTime page on Apple's web site.

Figure 6–1. *The FaceTime icon*

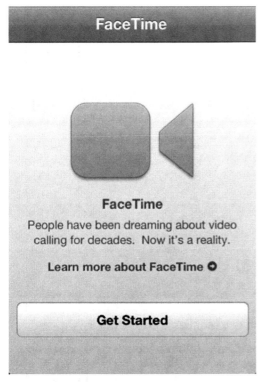

Figure 6–2. *The FaceTime Get Started screen*

Once you are ready to sign in, tap Get Started. You'll be taken to the sign-in screen (Figure 6–3) where you can sign in with your existing Apple ID or create a new account.

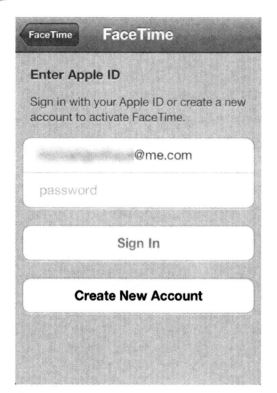

Figure 6–3. *The FaceTime sign-in screen*

Signing In with Your Existing Apple ID

To sign in with your existing Apple ID, fill in the e-mail and password fields, and tap Sign In. You already have an Apple ID if you use the iTunes Store, the App Store, or the iBookstore. You also have an Apple ID if you have a MobileMe account.

When you sign in for the first time, FaceTime notifies you that people will call you using your e-mail address (Figure 6–4). It asks you which e-mail address you would like to use. You can keep the same e-mail address that is your Apple ID, or you can enter another e-mail address.

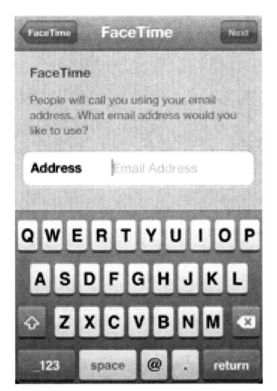

Figure 6–4. *Choose which e-mail address you want to act as your FaceTime "phone number" and enter it into the Address field. Tap Next to continue.*

Once you have specified the e-mail address you want associated with FaceTime calls, tap the Next button. A short verification screen appears as FaceTime verifies your e-mail address authenticity. Once this finishes, a Check Mail button appears; tapping it navigates you to your selected e-mail account in the iPhone's mail app. Look for an e-mail with the subject "Please verify the contact email address for your Apple ID," and then tap the Verify Now link in the e-mail. A Safari window opens, taking you to the My Apple ID page. Enter your Apple ID and password again to verify your FaceTime e-mail address. This may sound complicated, but it's actually quite easy to do.

Once you are presented with the "Email address verified" web page, you know that you have successfully associated your email address with your FaceTime application. Hop out of Safari and return to the FaceTime app. This time, you'll be presented with the standard FaceTime screen (Figure 6–5), which you'll see each time you launch the app from now on. On this screen, you'll see a list of your contacts, providing you a jumping-off point for new FaceTime conversations.

This first time you sign in, the process may seem arduous and time-consuming, but once you have signed in, you won't have to do it again, even if you leave the app or shut down and restart your iPhone.

Please be aware that the authorization procedure for FaceTime, which is subject to change, went like this at the time the book was being written. Apple could always change its account creation and authorization process in the future.

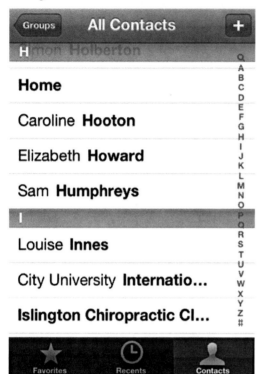

Figure 6–5. *The FaceTime app*

Creating an Account

If you don't already have an Apple ID, you can create one by tapping the Create New Account button, which you saw back in Figure 6–3. The New Account screen slides up (Figure 6–6). On this screen, you enter your first and last names, your e-mail address (which will become your new Apple ID), and a password of at least eight characters. This password does not have to be the same as the password for your e-mail account.

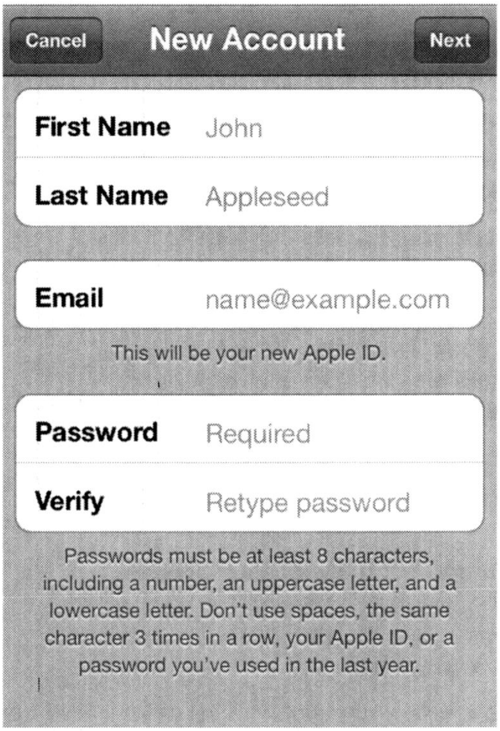

Figure 6–6. *The New Account screen*

Lower on the New Account screen, you'll also need to choose a security question and enter the answer for that question. This question and answer pair is used to verify your identity should you forget your Apple ID password. Finally, enter your month and day of birth, choose which country you reside in, and select whether you want to subscribe this e-mail to Apple marketing. (You can say no.)

Once you have entered this information, tap Next. You return to the Sign In screen with your Apple ID and password already entered. The FaceTime signing in will commence. A short verification screen appears as Apple verifies that your e-mail address is authentic. Then a Check Mail button will appear; tapping it navigates you to your selected e-mail account in the iPhone's mail app.

Look for an e-mail with the subject "Please verify the contact email address for your Apple ID," and then tap the Verify Now link in the e-mail. A Safari window opens and takes you to the My Apple ID page. There you'll need to enter your Apple ID and password to verify your FaceTime e-mail address.

Once you are presented with the "Email address verified" web page, return to the FaceTime app. You'll be presented with the standard FaceTime screen (Figure 6–5), which you'll see every time you launch the app from now on.

Navigating Your FaceTime Contacts

Each time you launch the FaceTime app after the initial setup, you are presented with your contacts screen (Figure 6–5). The contacts screen is divided into three sections, accessible by tapping the buttons in the contact bar at the bottom of the screen.

> *Favorites*: This screen allows you to add your favorite contacts to it. It's a handy shortcut to the people you FaceTime call the most often, letting you start a new chat with a single tap.

> *Recents*: This screen lists the recent FaceTime calls you've made or received. If you get interrupted, you can pick up your chat later by tapping any of the names you find here.

> *Contacts*: This screen lists all the contacts in your address book. Use this screen for connecting with anyone you've added to your iPhone's contact list.

The sections that follow provide a closer look at each of these contact options.

Favorites

The Favorites screen (Figure 6–7) allows you to create and maintain a list of your favorite contacts. Favorite contacts generally encompass anyone you call the most, such as family and friends and important work contacts. This screen acts as a shortcut to their FaceTime e-mail addresses or phone numbers. One tap, and you're ready to start chatting.

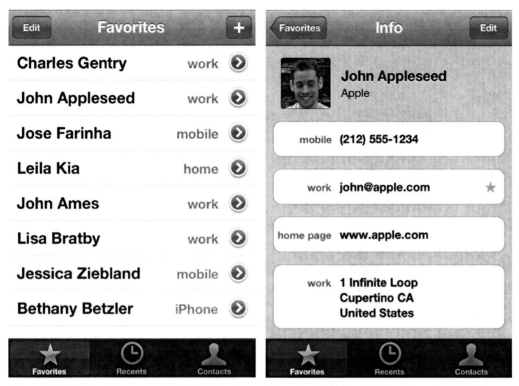

Figure 6–7. *The Favorites screen (left). Selecting the e-mail or phone number of a Favorites contact (right).*

Adding a contact to Favorites: To add a new favorite, tap the + button in the upper-right corner. Select any contact from the address book list that slides up on screen.

Choosing the contact's FaceTime info: From your selected contact's information screen, tap the FaceTime e-mail address or phone number for the contact. If your contact is using an iPad or iPod touch, you must choose their associated FaceTime e-mail. If you contact is using an iPhone, you can choose their iPhone phone number as well. Once you have selected the contact's FaceTime info, a blue star (Figure 6–7) appears by their FaceTime e-mail or number.

Calling a Favorite: Once you have set up your favorites, simply tap their name in the Favorites list, and a FaceTime call will be initiated.

You can tap the blue-and-white chevron next to a favorite's name to view or edit their contact information.

Recents

The Recents screen (Figure 6–8) gives you a list of recently made or received FaceTime calls. This list can be sorted into two categories via the tabs at the top of the screen:

All: Shows you all the FaceTime calls you have made, received, or missed. Missed calls show up in red. The time of the call is shown to the right of the name of the person called. You can tap the blue-and-white chevron next to a favorite's name to view or edit their contact information.

Missed: Shows only the FaceTime calls you have missed.

To clear your Recents list, tap the Clear button in the upper-right corner of the screen.

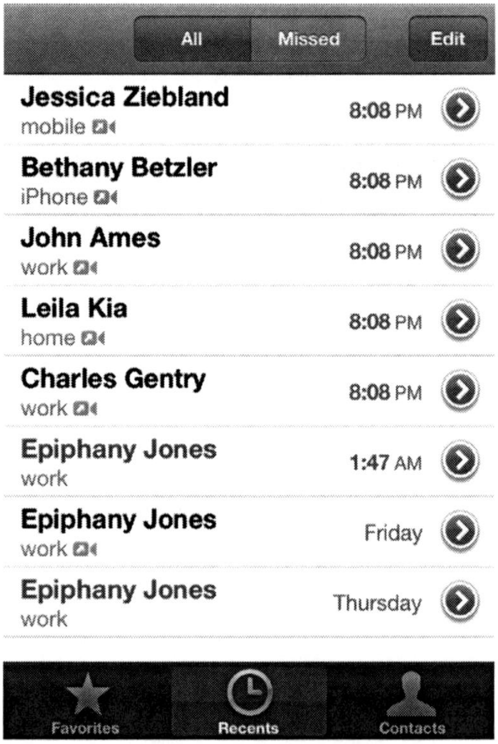

Figure 6–8. *The Recents list*

Contacts

The contacts screen features your entire address book (Figure 6–9). It works just like your stand-alone Contacts application. You can navigate it by all the contacts or by just a group of contacts. When you find the contact you want to call, tap their name, and their contact information card will be displayed. Tap their FaceTime e-mail or FaceTime phone number, and your call will begin.

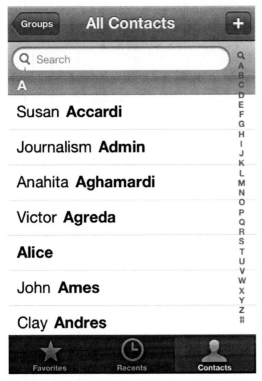

Figure 6–9. *The contacts screen*

When you find the contact you want to call, tap their name, and their contact information card will be displayed. Flick down the screen until you see their FaceTime e-mail or FaceTime phone number. Tap the correct one, and your FaceTime call will begin.

Placing and Receiving a FaceTime Call

To place a FaceTime call, simply select a contact from your Favorites, Recents, or Contacts list, or tell Siri to "FaceTime *contact name*." Tapping a name in the Favorites or Recents list will initiate the FaceTime call (Figure 6–10, left). To start a call using your Contacts list, you'll need to tap the contact's name and then tap either a FaceTime phone number or e-mail. To cancel a call before the person has picked up, tap the END button.

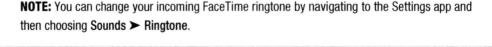

NOTE: You can change your incoming FaceTime ringtone by navigating to the Settings app and then choosing **Sounds ➤ Ringtone**.

Figure 6–10. *Initiating a FaceTime call (left) and receiving a FaceTime call (right)*

When you receive a FaceTime call, a message appears on-screen telling you that a friend would like FaceTime with you (Figure 6–10, right). The front camera automatically activates so you can see what you look like. To accept, tap the green Accept button. To reject the call, tap the red Decline button.

Figure 6–11 shows you what it looks during a FaceTime call. The speaker's image takes up a majority of the screen, while your image appears in a rectangle at the corner of the screen. Below your image is the FaceTime control bar. This gives you several options.

Figure 6–11. *A FaceTime video call. This image highlights the always-challenging issue of up-the-nose camera coverage produced by an iPod or iPhone held too low during a FaceTime chat.*

Mute: Tap the microphone icon to switch between muting and unmuting a call. While you call is muted, you can still hear the person you are calling, and they cannot hear you. The other person can still see you, though, so be careful what you do! This is definitely not a time to attend to nasal hygiene issues.

Switching cameras: Tap the Switch Camera icon in the bottom right of the screen to switch between the front and rear cameras. The icon looks like a traditional still camera with swirling arrows on either side. Switching cameras changes what the person you are talking to sees. When the camera is switched, your friend will see what the rear camera on the device is pointed at.

Switching cameras during a call is a handy feature. It allows your friend to see what you are looking at, like your newborn crawling on all fours, for example.

Ending the call: To end a FaceTime call, tap the End button.

> **NOTE:** You know that the iPhone has two cameras, but did you know the front one is perfectly designed for FaceTime? Apple made sure it has just the right focal length and field of view to focus on your face at arm's length.

Other FaceTime Calling Options

FaceTime gives you several advanced options while on a call that help with its usability features:

> *Change orientation*: You can rotate your device into landscape mode, and the image your caller sees will change to match. Landscape mode while FaceTime calling is useful if you want to show your caller a wide shot of something using the rear camera, like a beautiful sunset from your backyard.

> **TIP:** To avoid unwanted orientation changes as you move the camera around, lock your iPhone in portrait orientation by pressing the Home button twice and flicking right until you see the portrait lock button.

> *Moving picture-in-picture*: That little square in the corner that shows you what your caller is seeing can be moved around. Tap and hold the square and drag it to any of the four corners of the screen. This is useful if the square is blocking something on the screen that you want to see.

> *Multitasking during a FaceTime call*: You can use any app on your device while on a FaceTime call. To do so, while in a FaceTime call, press your Home button once to be taken to the home screen. You can then launch any app you want. To return to your FaceTime call, tap the glowing green "Touch to resume FaceTime" bar at the top of the screen (Figure 6–12).

Figure 6–12. *You can use other apps while on a FaceTime call. Touch the green bar at the top of the screen to return to the FaceTime call when you're done.*

The multitasking feature is particularly nice when you are on a FaceTime call. It allows you to check the Yelp app for restaurants while you're making dinner plans with your FaceTime caller, for example.

While you are multitasking, you can still talk to your FaceTime caller, but neither of you can see the other.

FaceTime Settings

FaceTime has several settings. You can find them in the Settings app under FaceTime (Figure 6–13).

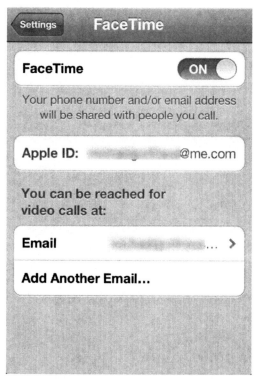

Figure 6–13. *FaceTime settings*

Switch FaceTime on or off: Tap the FaceTime switch to ON or OFF. While off, you cannot make or receive FaceTime calls, which means you may miss a special treat while you are busy getting work done. When enabled, however, other people can call you, interrupting whatever you are doing.

Change your FaceTime geographic location: Tap your blue Account e-mail. From the pop-up menu, tap Change Location. Choose your location's new region from the list of regions.

View your FaceTime account settings: Tap your blue Account e-mail. From the pop-up menu, tap View Account. The account settings screen you saw earlier in this chapter in Figure 6–6 will show up on-screen. Tap any field to change your account settings, such as your name or security question.

Sign out of FaceTime: Tap your blue Account e-mail. From the pop-up menu, tap Sign Out. This will immediately sign you out of FaceTime without any more warnings. To sign back in, reenter your Apple ID password on the Sign In screen.

Remove a FaceTime e-mail address: You can deassociate your FaceTime e-mail address by tapping it and then tapping the Remove This Email button.

Adding more e-mail addresses: FaceTime allows you to associate more than one e-mail address with your FaceTime account. This is handy if you use several e-mails for different purposes in your life. For example, you might have one for friends and one for work colleagues, and so forth. When multiple e-mails are associated with your FaceTime account, people can initiate a FaceTime video call with you using any one of them.

To add additional e-mails, tap the Add Another Email button, and then enter your other e-mail address. Repeat this step for each e-mail address you have. With each e-mail added, you'll need to check that e-mail account for the FaceTime verification e-mail from Apple and click the link in that e-mail before the e-mail address can be added to your FaceTime account.

Getting Started with Messages

The Messages app enables you to send text messages, called iMessages in iOS, to anyone with an iPhone, iPod touch, or iPad running iOS 5 or newer for free. If you've ever sent a text message from an iPhone before, you know exactly how to use Messages because both traditional texting and sending iMessages are done through the exact same app: Messages (Figure 6–14). The Messages icon is the same white text speech bubble on a striped green background that iOS has been using for years, but it has a new name and exciting new features.

Figure 6–14. *Use the Messages app to send iMessages.*

Upon launching the Messages app, you'll be presented with a list of any previous iMessage conversations you've engaged in (Figure 6–15). The most recent conversation appears at the top of the screen, so when you receive new messages, that conversation is promoted accordingly.

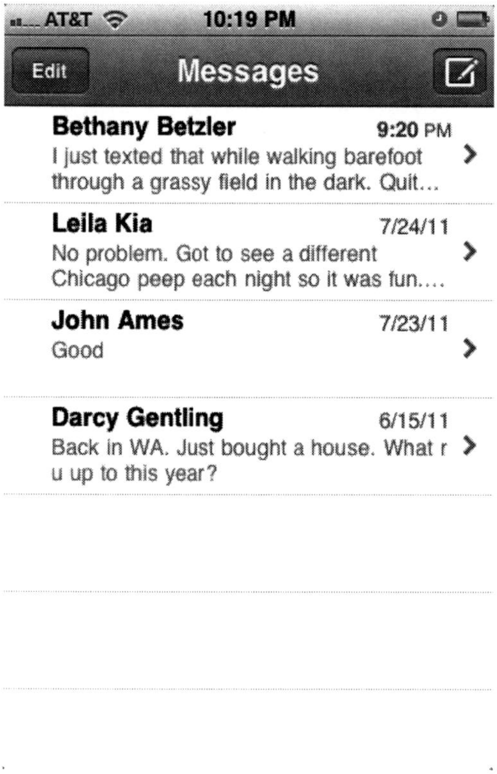

Figure 6–15. *All your iMessages in one place*

Reading Conversations

iMessages transforms conversations into a beautiful visual presentation, as you can see in Figure 6–16. Tap any conversation item in Figure 6–15 to open this view. As you can see, conversations are made up of individual iMessages between you and one other party. Your messages appear on the right of the screen, and your friend's messages appear on the left.

Figure 6–16. *Reading conversations*

Have something new to say? Tap the reply field at the bottom of the screen and enter your message. Tap Send to send it, and iMessage transmits that information to your buddy, while adding it to the visual conversation above the reply field.

Deleting and Forwarding Individual iMessages

Each iMessage conversation window lets you delete or forward individual iMessages. The Edit button at the top right of the conversation window enables you to enter a special editing mode. During this mode you'll find a red Delete button and a blue Forward button at the bottom of the screen. These buttons let you choose what actions you want to apply.

In Figure 6–17, notice the dots next to each message. The first two dots are clear, and the third and fifth are colored red, with a check mark shown inside. Checked items can be deleted or forwarded using the buttons at the bottom of the screen.

Figure 6–17. *Deleting and forwarding conversations*

To delete one or more iMessages, tap each message you want to get rid of. A red checked dot appears next to each one. Tapping the dot again removes the checked selection, returning the dot to clear. To delete these items, tap Delete. WARNING: the messages will be deleted right away, and you cannot undo this action. You do not get to confirm your deletion; there's no "Are you sure dialog." The messages are deleted immediately, and you're done.

To forward one or more iMessages, tap each message you want to forward. The same red dots are used for forwarding messages as well as deleting them. The color red does not mean "delete" here. It just means "selected message." When you're finished selecting your messages, tap Forward. A new iMessage screen appears allows you to forward the selected iMessage(s) to one or more people.

> **NOTE:** When you are in an active conversation and someone is typing a reply, you'll see a grayed-out chat bubble with three dots in it. That way, you know the person on the other end is in the middle of replying to you. This is something that may be familiar to you in instant messaging applications but one that might surprise you if you expected only SMS-style texting in this application.

Deleting Entire Conversations

There are times you want to clean up an entire conversation. Perhaps you were chatting about your boss. Or maybe you were comparing notes regarding Justin Bieber or *Twilight*. There are many reasons you might want to remove a text history from your device. Besides showing you all your previous conversations, on the main screen (Figure 6–15), Messages allows you to delete entire conversations. Tap the Edit button at the top right of the screen and then tap the red and white minus sign that appears next to the conversation you want to delete. Unlike individual message deletions, you will be prompted to confirm deletion for an entire conversation. Tap the red Delete button to confirm your deletion.

Sending a New iMessage

To initiate a new conversation, tap the compose button in the top-right corner of the main Messages screen. This button looks like a pencil over a piece of paper. Messages' new message screen appears (6–18), ready for you to start up a new conversation.

Your first task is to address your message. You can send your iMessages to one or more people at once. At the top of the screen, start typing the name of the person you want to send the message to. Messages automatically fills in their information from your contacts. You can also tap the blue + button to bring up a list of all your contacts. As you can see in Figure 6–18, you can send group messages to multiple people.

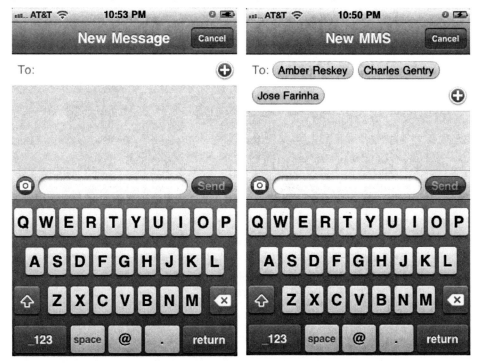

Figure 6–18. *Creating a new iMessage. A blank message, left, and sending a group message, right.*

Tap the text field above the keyboard and start entering your text (Figure 6–19). When you are done, tap the Send button, and your message is on its way!

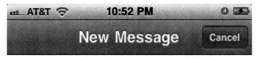

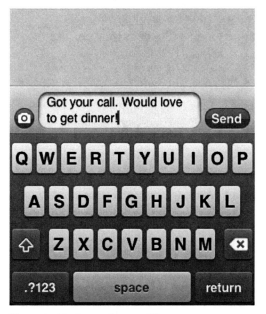

Figure 6–19. *Composing your iMessage*

Attaching a Photo, Video, or Contact to an Messages

With Messages, you can send not only text, but photos, videos, and contacts. Adding a any of them are as easy as a few taps. You can send a photo, video, or contact information card with text or just by itself. To add an attachment to an iMessage, tap the camera icon next to the text entry field (Figure 6–19). The attachment dialog box appears, letting you choose whether to use an existing photo or video or shoot a new one (Figure 6–20).

Choose Take Photo or Video to record an new video or take a new picture with your camera, or choose Choose Existing and select a photo or video from your photo albums or Camera Roll on your device. After you have selected your attachment, it appears as a thumbnail in the text entry field (Figure 6–21). Tap send to send the message on its way, along with the media you just attached.

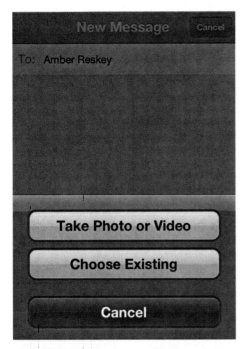

Figure 6–20. *Composing your iMessage*

Figure 6–21. *An attached photo in an iMessage*

Messages Settings

You can customize Messages in the Settings app (Figure 6–22), allowing you to tweak a few essential features. Here is a quick rundown of those features and what they mean to you.

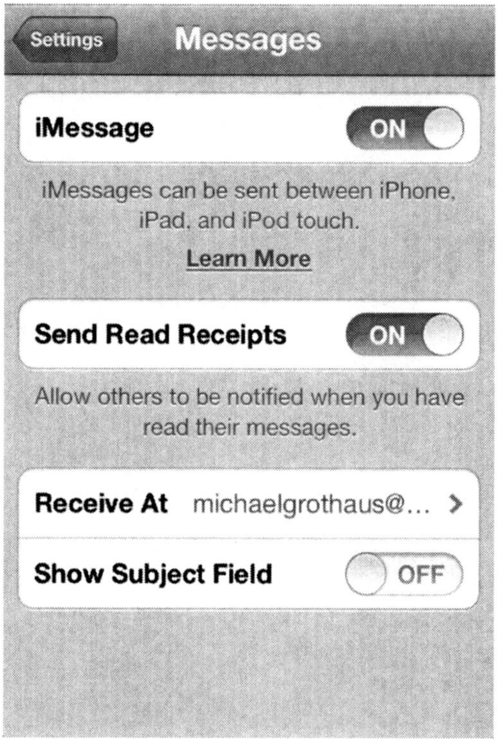

Figure 6–22. *The Messages settings are where you adjust iMessage settings.*

iMessage: When you need to get work done or are on the road, you can enable or disable messaging, switching them on or off. Toggle the switch to Off to disable iMessages. Doing so will prevent any messages from being sent to or from your device. Toggle the switch to On to restore messaging capabilities.

Send Read Receipts: When this is set to On, others will be notified when you have read a message they've sent. This feature is most of use with work colleagues who might want to know that you've received directions but do not need a personalized message in return.

Receive at: You can associate more than one e-mail address with your iMessage account. Use the "Receive At" option to choose identities. This is handy if you use more than one e-mail, one for friends and one for work colleagues, for example. When multiple e-mails are associated with your iMessage account, people can initiate a iMessage chat with you using any of your e-mails.

To add additional e-mails, tap *Receive At* and then tap the Add Another Email button, and then enter your other e-mail address. Repeat this step for each e-mail address you have. With each e-mail added, you'll need to check that e-mail account for a iMessage verification e-mail from Apple and click the link in that e-mail before the e-mail address can be added to your iMessage account.

Show subject field: When this is set to On, you'll have the option of adding a subject field to your iMessages. This is handy if you are sending iMessages in a more formal manner, say to professional contacts.

Using Messages with Siri

The Siri voice assistant on your iPhone 4S helps you use your voice to check your messages, reply to them, and start new conversations. With Siri, you can perform many of your iMessage tasks from anywhere on your iPhone. Just press and hold the Home button and tell Siri what you need to do.

When new messages arrive, tell Siri "Read my new messages." Want to hear it another time, tell it "read it again." Siri will fill you in on all the new messages while keeping your hands free for other tasks.

You can reply to your messages in a variety of way. When you listen to a message, Siri knows what conversation you are in the middle of. This context allows you to say "Reply, that is great news" or "Tell him I will be there in a few minutes." If the matter is urgent, you can say "Call her," and Siri will use the contact information associated with the message you just received to look up the user's phone number.

To create a message, instruct Siri to tell someone something. "Tell Steve, I'll be right there. " You can also "text" or "send a message". For example, you could say "Send a message to Mike saying how about tomorrow" or "Text Anthony where are you I have been waiting for twenty minutes."

If you don't have an entry in your Contacts for someone, you can specify their phone number. For example, say "Send a message to 408-555-1212." Siri will prompt you for the text contents. Speak your message.

Siri will ask you to confirm what you said. You can reply by asking it to read the message back to you with "read it to me" or "read it back to me." You can also speak to correct text messages or mail contents that you have composed. The following examples let Siri know that you're not satisfied with what you've said. Notice how you can change the contents completely, add new material, and so forth.

- "Change it to: Let's meet at 3 p.m."

- "Add: Can't wait exclamation point." (You can do this, by the way, even if Siri does not mention it explicitly as an option.)

- "No, send it to Megs."

- "No." (This keeps the message without sending it)

- "Cancel."

When you are satisfied with your text or email message, you can say something like "Yes, send it" to start it on its way.

Summary

FaceTime is a terrific feature to use for communicating visually with others. Its popularity is sure to grow as more devices become FaceTime-compatible and iMessages bring free texting and chatting to any device running iOS 5 or newer. In this chapter, you learned how to set up your FaceTime account and send and receive calls and send and receive messages using iMessages. Here are a few more tips for using FaceTime:

- If you are planning to make a lot of FaceTime calls at home or in the office, you may want to invest in a dock so you don't have to keep holding your device at arm's length. A dock helps you eliminate those horrible up-the-nose and double-chin points of view that happen when holding the camera at arm's length.

- Use FaceTime from the sky! If you're on a plane that offers Wi-Fi service, you can use FaceTime to talk to your friends and family back on the ground!

- Don't forget to use the rear camera to show your caller what you are looking at. You don't have to turn your unit around to show them!

- FaceTime can be a life-changing feature for those who can't speak. The screen resolution is crisp enough where sign language can easily be read and for grandparents to make that all-important eye-contact with preverbal grandchildren, especially at a distance.

- Watch out for bright backgrounds. If light is glaring in through the window behind you, it's likely to cause your viewer to see you in silhouette. To fix this, move your camera just a tiny way away from the light source, and your face should show up just fine.

iMessages provide a great way to keep in touch with your friends who live long distances away. It's like always-on instant messaging. Individual messages are delivered as texts to your friends no matter if they are on an iPod touch, iPad, or iPhone. The only requirement is a Wi-Fi or 3G connection.

Chapter 7

iPhone Mail

Unlike many other smartphones, your iPhone can send, receive, and browse e-mail without getting weighed down with compromise. The iPhone doesn't settle for cramped, odd presentations. Your e-mail looks the way it should—the way it would if you were reading it on your home computer. That's because the iPhone provides an HTML-compatible rich-text client. Mail looks better because the client is better. It's made to work right.

iPhone Mail works with most industry-standard e-mail systems. With it, you can send and receive photos; view Excel spreadsheets, PDF files, and Word documents; manage your accounts; and more. This chapter introduces you to many features of the iPhone Mail application. You'll discover how to set up and use your iPhone with new and existing e-mail accounts. You'll learn how to manage your mail, how to compose new mail, and how to get the most out of the iPhone's e-mail settings. If you have questions about using mail with your iPhone, this chapter is for you.

Compatibility

iPhone Mail is surprisingly compatible. It works with virtually all major e-mail providers, including Apple's own iCloud mail, Gmail, AOL, Yahoo!, and cable and DSL Internet providers. For businesses, iPhone plays well with Microsoft Exchange. This high level of provider support is because of the iPhone's support of industry-standard protocols. The iPhone understands the most popular e-mail standards, namely, POP, IMAP, SMTP, and Exchange. If you're not already familiar with these standards, here's a brief overview.

POP

POP (aka POP3) stands for Post Office Protocol. It's probably the most common e-mail retrieval protocol in use today. It allows mail clients to connect to a server such as Gmail or AOL, retrieve messages, and disconnect afterward. This usually happens on a set schedule, such as every ten minutes or every hour; you do not receive mail until your client connects to the server and requests that new mail.

POP works by checking in with a server, downloading your e-mail, and optionally leaving the original copies of your e-mail on the server. This leave-on-server option works well with the iPhone, because when you're on the go, you probably want to check your mail on the iPhone and retrieve it again later when you get back to the office or return home. POP also has its downsides. Unlike the newer and more sophisticated IMAP protocol, POP downloads entire messages all at once, so it's a bit of a space hog on portable devices.

> **NOTE:** The 3 in POP3 indicates the third version of the protocol standard; POP1 and POP2 are obsolete.

SMTP

Mail clients use one protocol for receiving mail and another for sending mail. Your iPhone uses Simple Mail Transfer Protocol (SMTP) to send outgoing messages. SMTP contacts a mail server and transmits messages you've written along with any attachments including text, photos, and so forth. A common kind of SMTP, called SMTP-AUTH (AUTH stands for authorization), allows you to send secure, authorized mail. You provide your account name and a password. Your mail client authenticates itself to the server, and your e-mail is sent on its way.

The iPhone makes sending authenticated e-mail easy. Enter your account name and password into the Mail settings pane. Once you've done this, just use outgoing mail to send a note, share a web page's URL, or pass along a photo that you've just snapped with the iPhone's built-in camera. The iPhone takes care of all the protocol issues. You decide what to send and to whom to send it.

IMAP

IMAP stands for Internet Message Access Protocol. Like POP3, it allows you to receive e-mail on the iPhone. It's a newer and more flexible protocol. As the name suggests, IMAP was built around the Internet. It introduces advanced ways to connect to the mail server and use the limited bandwidth of mobile connections in the most efficient way. The key to understanding IMAP is to recognize that messages are meant to live on the server rather than go through a retrieve-and-delete cycle. You manage your mail on the IMAP server. You read your mail on a client, like the iPhone.

When you download mail with POP, you download entire messages. When you download mail with IMAP, you download headers instead, at least initially. Headers are the bit that tells you who the mail is from and what it's about. You don't download the main body of the message until you explicitly request it from the server. Since the header occupies only a fraction of the space of the message, you can download IMAP data a lot faster than you download POP. The rest of the message stays on the server until you're ready to read it.

The same thing goes for attachments. Say that someone sends you a 10MB video. It doesn't get downloaded to your iPhone. It stays on the server until you're ready to watch it on your home computer. If you'd downloaded the message with POP, the entire video would have transferred with the message. With IMAP, you can read the message that came along with the video without having to download the video file itself until you're ready to watch it. The video attachment waits for you on the mail server.

IMAP also offers a feature that's called *push e-mail*. Geeks will tell you that *technically speaking* IMAP is not exactly the same thing as push e-mail. True push e-mail reaches out and tells your e-mail client whenever new mail arrives in the system. Instead, your iPhone IMAP client connects to and checks the server until new mail arrives. This kind of always-on connection allows the iPhone to receive mail almost as soon as it arrives on the server. In practice, there's better intention there with push-style mail than actual results. Yahoo! and Gmail offer free IMAP accounts for iPhone users. To sign up for an account, point your browser to `http://mail.yahoo.com` or `http://gmail.com`.

Microsoft Exchange

Microsoft Exchange provides e-mail along with other enterprise-level services intended to support Outlook on the Web, personal computers, and mobile devices. Past versions of the iPhone did not support Exchange without, well, jumping through hoops. Exchange Server administrators had to open all sorts of security holes to get it to work, and they usually weren't too happy about doing that. Fortunately, iOS 5 provides much better compatibility with Microsoft Exchange, to the point that you can now configure multiple Microsoft Exchange ActiveSync accounts on your iPhone for business use.

Exchange is more than just e-mail, though—it's also about sharing calendars and contacts. Since iOS 4, iPhones can receive push e-mail from an Exchange Server, access a company-wide global address list, accept or create calendar invitations, and even search e-mails that are stored on the server.

If you're using your iPhone in a corporate setting that uses Microsoft Exchange Server, it's best to work with your IT department to ensure that your device is connected to the server in the most secure way possible. If they're not familiar with how the iPhone works with Exchange, Apple has provided a white paper on Exchange deployment that is free to download: `http://images.apple.com/iphone/business/docs/iPhone_EAS.pdf`.

Adding Mail Accounts to iPhone

You can add accounts to your iPhone in two ways. First, you can synchronize with iTunes. The first time you connect your iPhone to your computer and sync (whether through a USB cable connection or Wi-Fi), iTunes searches your computer for mail accounts and adds them to your phone. Second, you can add accounts directly on your iPhone using the Mail, Contacts, Calendars settings. It takes a few more steps than using iTunes, but it's not at all complicated. Here are both ways to do this.

Adding Accounts with iTunes

iTunes takes most of the work out of setting up your iPhone with your existing mail accounts. It looks at programs on your computer like Outlook and Apple Mail, finds account information, and offers to synchronize those account settings with your iPhone (see Figure 7–1). This makes it really easy to get your iPhone up to speed. A single sync puts these account details on your iPhone, and you're pretty much ready to roll.

NOTE: If you use a third-party e-mail app or web mail on your computer, this isn't going to work for you. Only those e-mail apps that are supported, like Apple Mail and Outlook, pass account information to iTunes.

To select which accounts to add, launch iTunes, and connect your iPhone. Select your iPhone from the source list—that's the column at the left of the iTunes window; your iPhone appears under the Devices heading. The iTunes screen updates and displays a summary of your iPhone, including its name, its phone number, the software version, and so forth. Locate the tabs at the top of this window, and select the Info tab. Scroll down the Info pane to Sync Mail Accounts.

The Sync Mail Accounts settings area allows you to choose whether to synchronize your Mail accounts to your iPhone. Ensure the Sync Mail Accounts check box is checked, and also check the accounts you want to use.

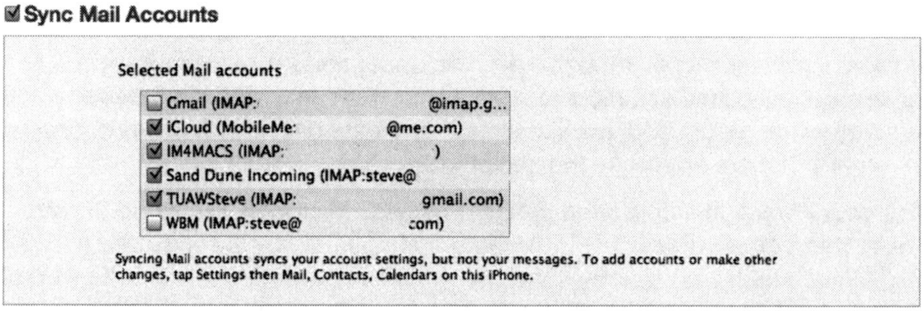

Figure 7–1. *The Sync Mail Accounts settings appear on the Info tab in iTunes. Select your iPhone device, click Info, and scroll down to find the Sync Mail Accounts settings.*

Next, scroll down further on the Info tab, below Sync Mail Accounts and Other, to the Advanced settings area (see Figure 7–2). As a rule, your iPhone won't add new accounts until you force things. Unlike normal syncs that just update data, when you select to replace your mail accounts on your iPhone, iTunes updates your iPhone with all the accounts you just selected in the Mail Accounts settings.

Replacing mail accounts isn't something you do all the time. You'll want to do this account replacement with new iPhones that you want to initialize, when you've moved your iPhone's home to a new computer, and after you've restored your iPhone's firmware to factory settings. If you just want to add a new e-mail account, add it directly on your iPhone rather than using iTunes. It's easier.

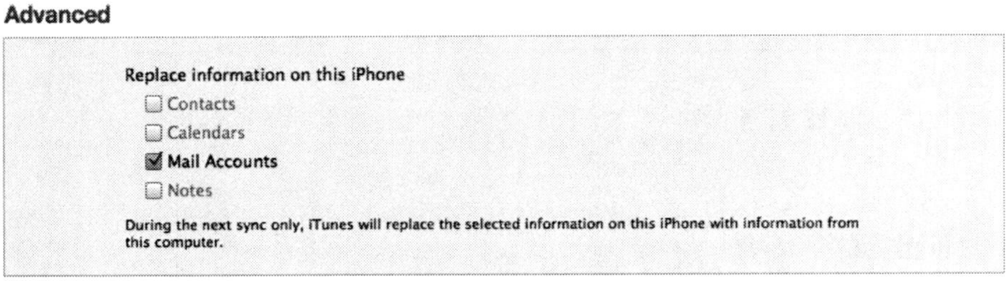

Advanced

Replace information on this iPhone
☐ Contacts
☐ Calendars
☑ **Mail Accounts**
☐ Notes

During the next sync only, iTunes will replace the selected information on this iPhone with information from this computer.

Figure 7–2. *Use Advanced settings to replace mail accounts during the next sync. You can also choose to update Contacts, Calendars, and Notes from this settings pane.*

Adding Accounts from Your Phone

It takes just a few steps to add a new account to your iPhone. It's especially easy when you use one of the preferred providers: iCloud, a Microsoft Exchange Server, Gmail, Yahoo!, Windows Live Hotmail, or AOL. Here are the steps to take, whether you're using a preferred provider or another provider that does not appear on the list:

1. From the Home screen, tap Settings, and navigate to **Settings ➤ Mail, Contacts, Calendars**.

2. Tap Add Account.

3. Select the kind of account you will use *or* tap Other if your provider is not listed (see Figure 7–3). Note that Apple's MobileMe is not visible in this figure but will remain available until July 2012 at which time all MobileMe e-mail accounts must be transferred to iCloud.

Figure 7–3. *When you use a preferred provider, the e-mail setup process is vastly simplified to entering a few items of information. Tap Other to set up e-mail with another provider.*

E-mail Provider Setup

Setting up account information for preferred providers is very easy. Your iPhone already knows how to contact the mail servers and which protocols they use.

1.   Preferred providers require just four items of information, as shown in Figure 7–4.

   a.   For Name, enter the name you want to appear in your From line, usually your full personal name.

   b.   For Address, enter your full e-mail address (for example, yourname@yahoo.com).

   c.   In the Password field, enter your password. Make sure to type carefully and slowly, and look at the key confirmations as you type. You will *not* be able to see the password itself as you type it. Try not to make mistakes.

   d. Finish by entering an account description. Your iPhone uses the text you type into the Description line as a label in the Accounts list, so enter something meaningful, such as Work Yahoo! Account or Home AOL.

2. Tap Save, and wait as the iPhone verifies your account information. You automatically return to the Mail settings, and you are done setting up your account.

3. For iCloud mail, only your Apple ID and password are required to set up a new account. If you don't already have an Apple ID (it's what you use to purchase items in the iTunes Store), Apple conveniently provides a button to acquire a free Apple ID.

4. What if your e-mail provider isn't on the list? For example, I use Comcast Internet service, which provides e-mail accounts to customers. To add an e-mail provider that isn't listed on the main e-mail screen in Figure 7–3, tap the Other button. You'll be asked to enter the same information as in step 4, and when you're done, tap Save, and the iPhone verifies your account information.

5. If the iPhone's automated setup doesn't work for you, you have several options:

   a. If the account is set up correctly on your Mac or Windows computer, use the method described earlier in "Adding Accounts with iTunes" to sync the settings to your iPhone.

   b. Still no luck? Tap the recalcitrant e-mail account in the list of accounts in **Settings ➤ Mail, Contacts, Calendars**. On the screen that appears, tap Account. A display similar to Figure 7–4 appears.

Figure 7–4. *The Account Info screen is available for tweaking incoming or outgoing mail server settings and changing server port numbers.*

    c. On this screen, you can change the name of the incoming and outgoing mail servers. You may need to contact your e-mail provider for the details of your account. Some important settings to know are the host (server) name, your full username (sometimes it's the full e-mail address instead of just the first part of the e-mail address), whether or not SSL is enabled, the type of authentication used by the server, and the server port number.

> **TIP:** Setting up an Exchange account can be difficult, because no two Exchange Server configurations seem to be the same. We recommend contacting your IT department or mail service provider for specific instructions on the exact settings you should use to set up your Exchange account.

Removing Accounts from iPhone

To remove an e-mail account from your iPhone, go to **Settings ➤ Mail, Contacts, Calendars**, and tap one of the items in your Accounts list. Scroll all the way down to the bottom of the account screen, and tap the red Delete Account button. To be safe, the iPhone prompts you to confirm account deletion. Tap Delete Account one more time to remove the account, or tap Cancel to leave the account alone.

At times, you may want to disable an account without removing it from your iPhone. To do this, go to **Settings ➤ Mail, Contacts, Calendars ➤** *the name of the account*. Locate the Mail switch at the top of the screen. Set this from On to Off to disable the account or from off to on to reenable it.

Mail Basic Settings

You're ready to start using Mail, but there are just a few more steps you'll want to take first. Navigate to **Settings ➤ Mail, Contacts, Calendars,** and scroll down to the Mail section (see Figure 7–5). Here, you'll find preferences that control the way your iPhone checks for and displays mail. You'll find that Mail works far more smoothly and predictably when you customize these settings *before* using your new accounts.

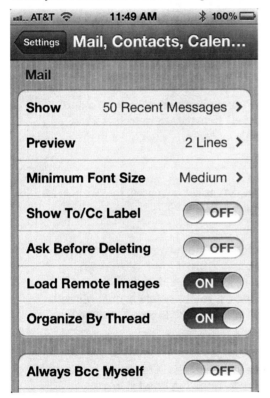

Figure 7–5. *The Mail pane contains many basic settings you'll want to configure before using your mail accounts.*

Here is a rundown of the settings you'll want to look over:

> *Show*: How many messages should the iPhone download and display at once? Choose from 50, 100, 200, 500 or 1,000 recent messages. Choosing fewer messages speeds downloads of messages from your server and saves space on your device, but if you get a lot of e-mail, you may want to see them all in one fell swoop.

> *Preview*: Your inbox, which you can see in Figure 7–9, displays information about each message. It shows who sent the message, the time it was sent, the message subject, and a brief preview of the message itself. In addition to all this information, you choose how many lines to show. Choices are None (no message preview), 1, 2, 3, 4, and 5 lines. The example in Figure 7–9 shows two lines per message. The more lines you choose to see of each message, the bigger the preview you get; however, fewer messages can fit on each screen.

> *Minimum Font Size*: If your eyes have issues with small print, the default font size on the iPhone might be difficult to read. The iPhone lets you choose a minimum font size, so you can make sure text displays no smaller than what you can read. Choose from Small, Medium, Large, Extra Large, and Giant. I use Large.

> *Show To/Cc Label*: By default, your iPhone does not show the To and Cc lines from e-mail. The iPhone normally hides them to save screen space. If you want to override this behavior for your mail, switch this option from Off to On.

> **TIP:** You can view the To and Cc lines even if you haven't enabled this option. Tap Details in the From line of the e-mail to reveal the extra information. Tap Hide to hide them again.

> *Ask Before Deleting*: You might think that asking for confirmation before allowing the iPhone to delete a message is a great idea. When working your way through 100 messages in your inbox, this idea quickly becomes less attractive. The iPhone allows you to delete e-mail without confirmation by default. If you want to add an extra layer of protection, switch this option on.

> *Load Remote Images*: Many e-mail messages contain images. These images are not actually sent with the e-mail; instead, the image is actually a link to an image file on a server. Enabling Load Remote Images ensures that the images are downloaded from the server and displayed within the body of the e-mail message when you open it. The trade-off is speed; loading images can slow down the receipt of e-mail.

Organize by Thread: Do you ever get into e-mail conversations, with many e-mails flying back and forth? If so, enabling Organize by Thread can make some sense of your inbox. When it is enabled, e-mail conversations are signified by a number on the right side of the message indicating how many e-mails are in the thread (Figure 7–6, left). Tapping the number and arrow displays the messages in the thread (Figure 7–6, right).

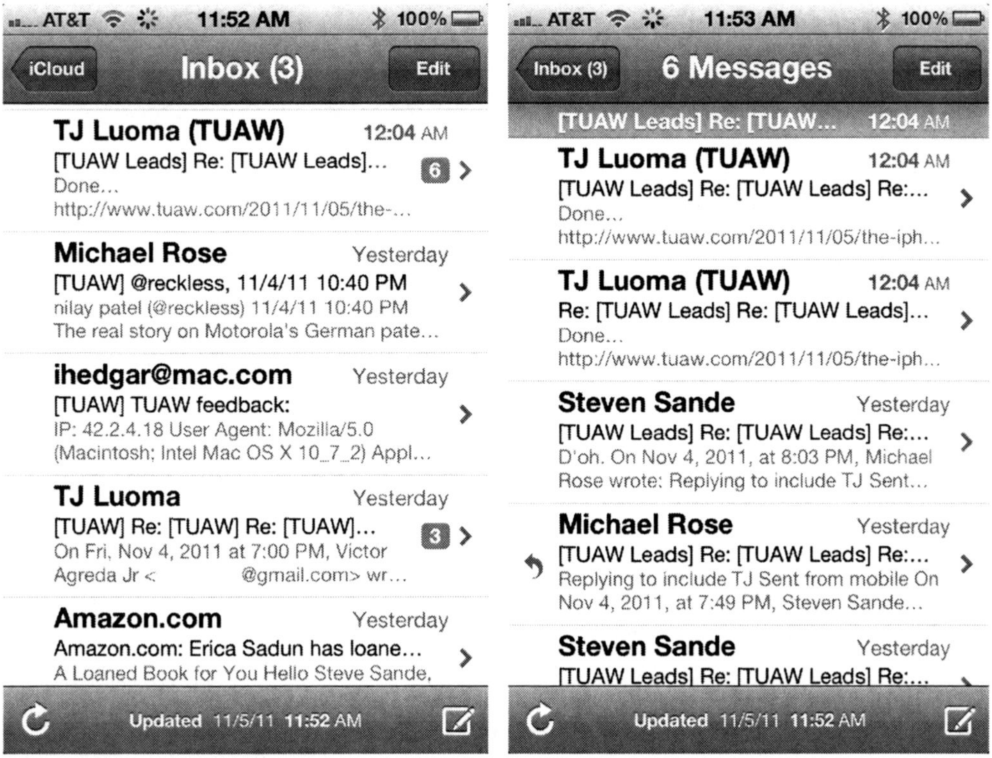

Figure 7–6. *Organize by Thread makes it easy to follow e-mail conversations by aggregating all similar e-mails into one easy-to-read thread.*

Always Bcc Myself: Some mail services put a copy of sent e-mails into a Sent Mail folder. Others do not. Enable this option to send a blind carbon copy to yourself when writing letters. The "blind" part of carbon copy means that you won't be visibly added to the recipient list. When correspondents "reply to all," you won't (necessarily) receive multiple copies of those e-mails.

Increase Quote Level: When you forward or reply to a message, Increase Quote Level adds a level of indentation to text that was already in the message so that it is differentiated from any text that you've added. This setting can be enabled or disabled.

Signature: By default, iPhones add the words *Sent from my iPhone* to all outgoing messages. To remove this tag, erase the text in the signature. You can also customize this message or replace it entirely. Perhaps you might add contact information or a favorite quote. To do this, tap the current signature. A keyboard appears and allows you to edit the text. After making your edits, tap Mail to return to the **Settings ➤ Mail, Contacts, Calendars** screen.

Default Account: Choose the default account you want to use for sending mail. This applies only to non-Mail iPhone applications such as Safari or Photos. When you pass along a bookmark or a picture you've snapped, this option sets the account used to send that message.

Audible Mail Alerts

This final pair of settings appear in **Settings ➤ Sounds**, not **Settings ➤ Mail, Contacts, Calendars**.

New Mail: Choose whether you want to hear an audible alert (Yes) or not (No) when your iPhone receives new mail. If you've enabled **Settings ➤ Sounds ➤ Silent ➤ Vibrate**, your iPhone vibrates when it plays the new mail sound.

Sent Mail: When enabled, this option plays a whoosh sound that indicates your e-mail has been successfully sent on its way to the server. It's a good idea to leave this option enabled. Sometimes, it takes time for mail to get going. You won't be able to send a new message until the first one has fully gone. By listening for the whoosh, you know when you're ready to send the next message.

Getting Started with iPhone Mail

The iPhone Mail application is initially located on the Home screen on the bottom line (see Figure 7–7). The icon is blue with clouds and a white envelope. Tap this icon to open the Mail application. As with the Phone and Messages applications, a red bubble appears to indicate the number of unread messages in all of your e-mail accounts.

Figure 7–7. *A red bubble superimposed on the Mail icon indicates the count of unread messages across all your e-mail accounts.*

When you enter Mail for the first time (and after restarting your iPhone), you're greeted by the Mailboxes screen. This screen lists every inbox on your iPhone, as well as every account you've added to your iPhone. Each inbox and account displays the number of unread messages. Tap an inbox name to open any of the individual inboxes, or tap the account names to view individual folders within an account. Return by tapping the Accounts back button at the top-left corner of that screen.

Inboxes

Each e-mail account has a number of mailboxes; Inbox, Outbox, Drafts, Sent Mail, Trash, and Junk are some of the common mailboxes you'll find. Apple separates the Mailboxes screen into an Inboxes list and an Accounts list. Most of the time, you're going to be working in the inboxes, reading and responding to mail, so they're listed on the Mailboxes screen first (Figure 7–8).

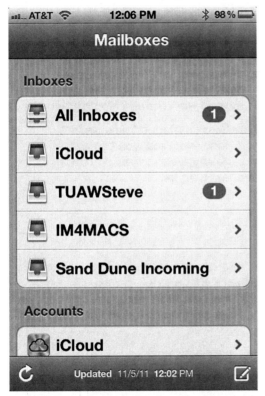

Figure 7–8. *The Mailboxes screen displays all e-mail inboxes first, followed by the accounts. All Inboxes is a global inbox that accumulates all incoming e-mail for all accounts. Numbers indicate how many unread messages are in each inbox. The Accounts section lists all the other mailboxes (including Drafts, Trash, and Sent Mail, among others), for each account.*

If you're looking for one place to read all your new e-mail, All Inboxes is that place. It is a global inbox for all of your accounts, containing all recent read and unread e-mail in a chronological order. To see only the e-mail that has come into a particular inbox, tap the inbox with the name of that account. The numbers that are listed on the right side of the inboxes indicate how many unread messages are contained in each inbox.

Accounts

Below the Inboxes list is a list of accounts. Each account may include some or many of the following standard mailboxes:

> *Inbox*: All new messages load into your inbox. You have an inbox for each account.
>
> *Drafts*: Messages that are written but not yet sent get saved to Drafts.
>
> *Sent*: If your mail account saves copies of outgoing mail, they're placed in a Sent folder.
>
> *Trash*: The iPhone stores deleted mail in Trash folders. Use **Settings ➤ Mail, Contacts, Calendars ➤ Account Name ➤ Advanced ➤ Deleted Messages** to decide if and when to remove deleted messages from Trash mailboxes. Your choices are to never remove the deleted messages from the mailbox or to remove them after one day, one week, or one month.
>
> *Other folders*: Additional folders such as Gmail's Starred folder are a feature of the mail provider and not of iPhone. Note that you can add a new mailbox in which to organize messages by tapping the Edit button while looking at your mailboxes and then tapping the New Mailbox button.

Using Mailboxes

When viewing an account's mailboxes, you can open a mailbox and view the messages stored inside by tapping the mailbox name. This links you to a new screen (see Figure 7–9) that displays the list of messages stored in that mailbox. From here, you can choose messages to display and manage your mailbox. Here are the actions you can take from this screen:

> *View a Message*: Tap an e-mail to open it for viewing.
>
> *Refresh Mail*: Tap the icon at the bottom left of the screen. It looks like a semicircular arrow. When tapped, your iPhone contacts your mail provider and requests new mail.
>
> *Compose new messages*: Tap the icon on the bottom right (a square with a pencil through it) to start writing a new message.
>
> *Edit messages*: Tap Edit to enter Edit mode. In Edit mode, you can tap the circle next to any message to delete, mark, or move it. To delete a message, select one or more messages, and then tap the red Delete button. To move a message from one existing mailbox to another, select it by tapping the circle, and then tap Move. A list of the mailboxes

appears on the screen; tap any one of them to designate the location you're moving the message to. Finally, marking a message lets you either flag a message for future reference or mark a message as unread.

> **TIP:** You don't need edit mode to delete mail. Just swipe your finger through any message to instantly bring up the Delete button, or when displaying a message, tap the garbage pail at the bottom of the screen. Some people have trouble mastering the swipe at first—they open their messages instead of deleting them. Keep trying and persist. The swipe becomes second nature after a while.

Return to the mailbox list: Tap the Back button at the top left of the screen to return from this mailbox to your account screen. The button name varies, but it's always shaped like a pentagon on its side, with the pointy bit facing left.

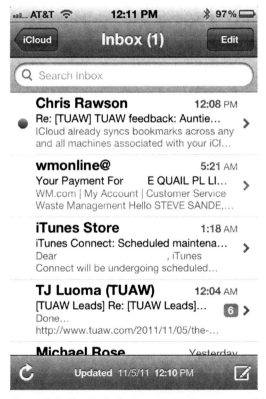

Figure 7–9. *The dot indicates an unread message on this inbox listing screen. Each message shows the recipient, the subject, and the date or time the message was sent. You control how many lines of text are shown for each message in* Settings ➤ Mail, Contacts, Calendars ➤ Mail ➤ Preview.

Reading and Navigating Through Mail

If you're used to reading e-mail on older portable devices, the iPhone's mail-viewing capabilities comes as a welcome relief. Instead of arbitrary word wrapping, missing attachments, and odd formatting, mail on the iPhone just looks...right. This being the iPhone, you can scroll up and down your e-mail—flicking if needed to move more quickly—and zoom in and out using all the standard pinching and tapping tricks described in Chapter 2.

And, as with Safari, it's not watered-down, text-only e-mail. It is fully functional e-mail that behaves the way it should. Sure, there are some missing features; you can't add attachments at will, for example, and you can't play back video files sent to you by mail without saving them to your Photo library first, but iPhone mail viewing performs to a much higher standard than most other gadgets. Unfortunately, as Figure 7–10 shows, the mail-viewing screen is littered with a proliferation of buttons and unlabeled icons. Here's a quick-and-dirty guide to your screen.

Figure 7–10. *The message display screen offers many unlabeled icons for your mail management pleasure.*

Bottom Icons

The icons at the bottom of the message display screen, from left to right, are as follows:

Refresh: The Refresh button appears at the bottom left of the screen and looks like a semicircular arrow. Tap this to request new mail from your provider.

File This Message: The folder with a small down arrow allows you to move messages from one mailbox to another. When tapped, the iPhone prompts you to "Move this message to a new mailbox." Select the mailbox you want to transfer to, and the iPhone rewards you with one of its most adorable animations. The message flies from one mailbox to the other. If you'd rather not transfer the message, tap Cancel instead.

Trash Can: Tap the small trash can in the bottom center to delete the currently displayed message. The trash lid flips up; your animated message moves down into the can. It's visually delightful. Your message moves from the Inbox mailbox (or whatever mailbox you're displaying) to the Trash mailbox.

> **TIP:** To undelete, navigate to Trash (Back, Back, Trash), select the deleted message, and file it back to the original mailbox.

Reply/Forward: The Reply/Forward icon appears just to the right of the trash can icon. It looks like a backward-pointing arrow. Tap this, and a menu appears. Tap Reply to reply to the currently displayed message, tap Reply All to respond to the sender and all of the original recipients of the message, or tap Forward to pass it along to a new recipient. There's also a Print button for printing an e-mail to any AirPrint-enabled printer.

Compose: This rightmost icon looks like a square with a pencil on it. Tap this to compose a new message.

Top Icons

The icons at the top of the message display screen, from left to right, are as follows:

Back button: Tap the Back button in the top-left corner to return from the message display to the Mailboxes screen. The button looks a signpost pointing left. The text inside the button varies according to the name of the mailbox.

Message number display: This isn't, strictly speaking, an icon. The iPhone displays the number of the current message at the top of the screen (for example, 10 of 50). Tapping an e-mail conversation (a thread of e-mails to and from you that all refer to the same topic) displays the individual messages and a header that displays the number of messages in the conversation.

Next Message/Previous Message: These two buttons appear at the top right of the screen. Tap the up triangle to move to the previous message in the current mailbox, and tap the down triangle to move to the next.

Details/Hide: This button appears just below the Next Message arrow. Tap Display to reveal your message's To and Cc lines. Tap Hide to hide them again. Details also reveals a Mark as Unread button, which does exactly what the name implies. It restores the blue dot to the message and updates the unread message count.

Embedded Links

iPhone Mail supports embedded links that you can tap from within a message. These allow you to automatically open web links in Safari or do a number of other tasks using information from message text:

Embedded Web Address: When someone sends you an embedded web address (also known as an URL), you can tap it to open it in Safari. Better yet, tap and hold that address for a second or two. A dialog box appears allowing you to either open the web page in Safari or copy the address for pasting elsewhere.

Phone Numbers: Mail is smart enough to recognize when someone has included phone numbers in a message. It underlines the number and displays it in blue—just like a normal web address link. To place a call, just tap the number. Tap and hold the phone number, and up to four buttons appear (Figure 7–11).

Figure 7–11. *Tap and hold a phone number in an e-mail message, and you can call that number, send a text message to it, add it to your contacts (if a name is included), or copy it.*

Addresses: If someone sends you a street address in an e-mail message, Mail can do a number of useful things. Tapping the address opens the Maps app to a map of the address, while a tap and hold displays the four buttons shown in Figure 7–12.

Figure 7–12. *Tap and hold an address in an e-mail, and you can open the address in the Maps app, add it to your contacts, or copy the address for pasting elsewhere.*

Events: One of the coolest things you can do with embedded links in e-mails is to automatically create events for your iPhone Calendar. The iPhone recognizes terms like "next Thursday at 7:30 PM" and displays them as links. Tapping that link displays a Create Event button to add the event to your calendar. It even gets the date and time from the e-mail and prefills that information in the Calendar app (Figure 7–13). To view the event, tap the Show in Calendar button. There's also a Copy button for grabbing the event information for pasting into another app.

Tracking Info: When you receive an e-mail with a USPS, UPS, or FedEx tracking number, tapping the tracking number launches Safari and opens a package tracking information page. This is very useful if you're away from your home temporarily and see a notice that a package is "out for delivery."

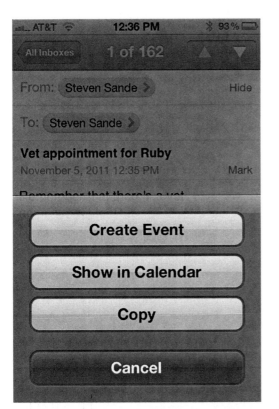

Figure 7–13. *Mail on the iPhone makes it a snap to add appointments to your calendar with a few taps.*

TRIVIA: The iPhone's ability to understand and act upon words like "next Thursday" is nothing new for Apple. The Apple Newton MessagePad (1993–1998) also understood similar phrases and would create calendar events from them. This feature is also available in Mac OS X, and Siri on the iPhone 4S knows exactly what you're saying when you tell it about time-related events.

Viewing Attachments

iPhones support many e-mail attachment file formats including Word files (`.doc`, `.docx`), Excel spreadsheets (`.xls`, `.xlsx`), PowerPoint presentations, (`.ppt`, `.pptx`), Pages documents (`.pages`), Keynote presentations (`.key`), Numbers spreadsheets (`.numbers`), many image file formats (`.jpg`, `.png`, `.gif`), some video formats (`.mov`), and PDF documents. When a message arrives with a large attachment, the iPhone shows you that the attachment is available (see Figure 7–14) and lets you choose whether to download it. If you choose to do so, tap the attachment, and wait for it to load in a new screen. After, tap Message to return to the message from the attachment viewer.

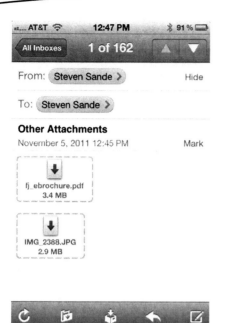

Figure 7–14. *Documents over about 1MB in size are not immediately downloaded to your iPhone. Instead, a download button appears. Tapping the button downloads the file and makes it available for viewing on your iPhone.*

Smaller documents are downloaded to Mail immediately, and they appear with buttons to tap for viewing (Figure 7–15).

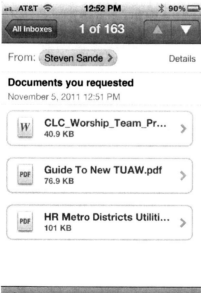

Figure 7–15. *Smaller documents attached to e-mails appear as buttons. Tap the buttons to view the documents.*

Attachments can be viewed in Mail, but if you want to edit the documents that have been sent to you, a compatible app must be installed on your iPhone. Fortunately, these apps register themselves to your iPhone, and if a compatible app is available for a certain document type, an Open In... button appears when you tap and hold the attachment button. Tapping the Open In... button displays buttons for any apps that can edit the document, and tapping one of those buttons launches a compatible app and opens the document for editing (Figure 7–16).

Figure 7–16. *Tapping the Open In... button displays a list of any applications that can open the document for viewing or editing. In this example, a .doc (Microsoft Word) document is readable in Pages but can also be opened in the Quickoffice, LogMeIn, or Dropbox apps.*

Sending Mail

The iPhone offers many ways to send mail. Unfortunately, consistency is not a strong point here. You'd imagine Apple would have designed a single universally recognized compose e-mail button and placed it more or less in the same place for each application. You'd be wrong. Here's a quick rundown of the most popular ways to ask your iPhone to create a new message across several programs:

Compose button: The Compose button, which looks like a square with a pencil through it, appears at the bottom right of many Mail screens (see Figure 7–10) and in the Messages application at the top right of the screen. In the Mail application, it creates a new letter. In Messages, it creates a new iMessage, SMS text, or MMS multimedia message.

Reply/Forward button: The Reply/Forward button appears just to the left of the Compose icon in open e-mail messages. Tap this to reply to a message or forward it on to another party.

Share icon: The Share icon appears at the bottom left of the screen in Photos and many other apps. It looks like a rectangle with an arrow jumping out of it—the arrow is basically a mirror of the Reply/Forward button. To send a picture, tap this, and then select Email Photo from the pop-up menu. As mentioned earlier, there isn't a consistent look for the icon, so in some apps, it may appear as an envelope.

Each of these (various, assorted, and inconsistent) methods requests Mail to open a new message, ready to be addressed, personalized, and sent.

Addressing E-mail

When you reach the New Message screen shown in Figure 7–17, you're ready to address your message. Start by tapping either the To or Cc/Bcc line on the New Message screen. The iPhone opens a keyboard so you can enter text. As you type, the iPhone searches its contacts list to match what you're typing to the contacts in its list. Tap in a few letters until you see the name of the contact you want to use. Tap that contact, and the iPhone automatically adds it to the field (To, Cc, Bcc) you selected.

You do not have to use an address from your contacts list. You can type in the full e-mail address (the iPhone helpfully provides you with the @ sign on the main keyboard for e-mail) and address your e-mail by hand. Also, it remembers the e-mail addresses you use. So, the second time you type *alex@nowhere.nomail.org*, the proper address pops up by the time you type *a* and *l*. As with normal contacts names, just tap an e-mail address to add it to your recipient list.

To remove a recipient from the message, select one of the blue recipient bubbles—they're labeled with a name or e-mail address—and tap Backspace.

Figure 7–17. *The New Message screen allows you to address and personalize your e-mail.*

Entering a Subject

Tap the Subject line to move the cursor to that field. Use the keyboard to enter a meaningful subject for your message.

Editing the Message

Tap in the message area to begin editing your message. A blinking cursor indicates this is where the keyboard will enter text. Use the typing skills covered in Chapter 2 to type your message. Remember to use the magnifying glass trick to move the cursor if you need to back up and make corrections.

> **TIP:** To remove an attached photo or other file from e-mail, position the cursor right after the picture, and tap Backspace.

Saving a Draft

At any time, you can take a break from editing a message and return to it later. To do this, tap Cancel. It's at the top left of the message-entry screen. A pop-up menu appears. Tap Save Draft to save the message for later, Delete Draft to abandon the message, or Cancel to return to the editing screen. When you choose Save Draft, the iPhone creates a copy of your message in the Drafts (or sometimes Sent) mailbox for your default account. Return to that mailbox when it's convenient to continue editing the message and/or to send it.

Sending E-mail

When you are done addressing and composing your letter, you can send it on its way by tapping Send. If you haven't disabled the feature, the iPhone alerts you with a whoosh sound to indicate that the message has been sent successfully to the outgoing mail server. You don't need to remain in the Mail app, because your message delivery takes place whether your phone is asleep or you are in another app. As soon as you've finished tapping Send, you can move on to another task.

Writing and Sending Mail with Siri

Siri provides new way of sending and reading e-mail messages that have been sent to you. If you have an iPhone 4S, no longer do you need to hunt and peck on the iPhone keyboard to assemble an e-mail.

Creating Mail

To create a blank mail message that is addressed to someone in your contacts, invoke Siri and say "E-mail name or nickname about subject." Telling Siri to "E-mail Erica about the book" produces the following conversation (Figure 7–18).

Figure 7–18. *A quick conversation with Siri creates a Mail message that's ready to send at your command.*

Next, Siri asks what you want in the body of the e-mail. This enables dictation, and Siri listens as you speak your message. Complete your conversation, and Siri asks if you want to send the message, at which time saying "Yes" or "Send" sends the e-mail on its way.

For people without a nickname in your Contacts, use their first and last names (e.g., Erica Sadun) to get their e-mail address. If there is more than a single e-mail address for a person, Siri prompts you to select one.

To shortcut the conversation required to create a message, tell Siri to "Mail contact about subject and say message." As an example, I could say, "Mail Barb about exercising and say you are doing well period keep up the good work exclamation point." That long statement creates a message that looks like the one shown in Figure 7–19.

Figure 7–19. *It's possible to address an e-mail, enter the subject, dictate the text, and send it, all without touching the iPhone's virtual keyboard.*

Checking Mail

Siri can also check for incoming mail and display it on your iPhone screen, although it cannot read it to you aloud. Here are some sample phrases you can try with Siri:

- Check e-mail.
- Any new e-mail from Barb today?
- Show new e-mail about the wedding.
- Show the e-mail from Michael yesterday.

At this point in time, Siri responds to requests to delete mail with a terse "I'm not allowed to delete e-mails for you" message.

Responding to Mail

When reading a Mail message, you can use Siri to respond to it several different ways. To send a reply via Mail, say something like "Reply Dear Mom thanks for sending the flowers to the hospital." If you want to call the person who sent you the message, say,

"Call [him/her/name] at [work/home/iPhone]." Siri dials the phone number of the person, and within seconds you're talking to them.

Summary

iPhone's Mail program removes many burdens associated with checking and responding to e-mail on a portable device. It provides a fully capable e-mail client that displays messages the way your senders intended you to view them. With its powerful attachment handling, the iPhone brings you one step closer to the ideal of bringing along your work or home computer in your pocket. Here are a few key points from this chapter that you might want to think about:

- Make sure to use your full iPhone interaction vocabulary of touches, pinches, and so forth, to get the most out of viewing attachments.

- It's really easy to add preexisting mail accounts using iTunes and add new ones using iPhone the Mail, Contacts, Calendars settings.

- Many corporations use Microsoft Exchange Server for mail and other groupware tasks. Be sure to ask your IT department for access to your work e-mail system if you so desire.

- If you see an underlined blue link in an e-mail, be sure to take advantage of Mail's abilities to understand the information contained in the link. This makes it easy to add new contacts or update existing contact information with a tap.

- Remember that there are many different icons and buttons used to denote how to send messages. Become familiar with these buttons in your favorite apps, because it makes it much easier to share information with the world.

- Siri is useful for creating and sending short mail messages without touching the virtual keyboard on your iPhone.

Part **IV**

Media and Shopping

Chapter 8

Touching Your Music

Your iPhone can do a thousand different things, given the right apps. One of the roles that it performs very well is that of media player, and given the family lineage of the iPhone, that's not surprising. The iPhone does this through its Music and Videos apps, which provide you with the ability to play music, show videos, function as an audiobook and podcast player, and even act as a portal to iTunes University. This chapter introduces you to the iPhone-as-iPod music player and shows you how to get the most use out of it.

The Music Application

Your iPhone's Music app brings all the functionality and ease of use you expect from a music player, but it delivers that functionality in a distinctive touch-based package. Figure 8–1 shows the Music application icon. It's easy to spot, since it is bright orange and marked with a music note. Tapping this icon launches the music player and allows you to access and play the songs you've synchronized to your device.

> **NOTE:** Do not confuse the Music and iTunes applications on your iPhone. Music is used to play your music tracks. iTunes connects you to the mobile iTunes Wi-Fi Music Store where you can shop for and purchase music and video tracks and is not a general music player.

Figure 8–1. *Launch the Music application by tapping its icon.*

If you've used pre-iOS iPods like the shuffle, nano, or classic, expect to be pleasantly surprised by the Music app. If you're new to the world of iOS, expect to be blown away. The Music app interface simplifies browsing, locating, and playing music and videos. Here are just a few ways iOS gives you your best music experience yet:

> *Touchscreen*: With the iPhone's touchscreen, there's no need for scroll wheels. Flick through your lists, and tap the items you want to play.

> *Cover Flow*: If you like Cover Flow in iTunes, you'll love it on the iPhone.

> *Alphabet index tool*: The Music application a simple alphabet index that makes searching through long, alphabetized lists a breeze.

> *Customizable button bar*: Do you prefer to search by genre or album, rather than artist or song? Just drag the items you use the most onto the configurable button bar.

And that's just a taste of the ways the Music app changes the way you use your iPhone. Read on for more details on how this program works.

Browsing Media

Tapping the orange Music icon on your Home screen takes you to the music player application. This program gives you access to all the audio media files you have synchronized to your iPhone, including songs, podcasts, and audiobooks. At the bottom of the screen you'll see blue-and-black buttons labeled Playlist, Artists, Songs, Albums, and More (see Figure 8–2). Tapping any of these buttons allows you to sort through your music. Tapping the Store button in the top-left corner of the screen takes you to the iTunes Store app (discussed in the next chapter) where you can buy music and videos.

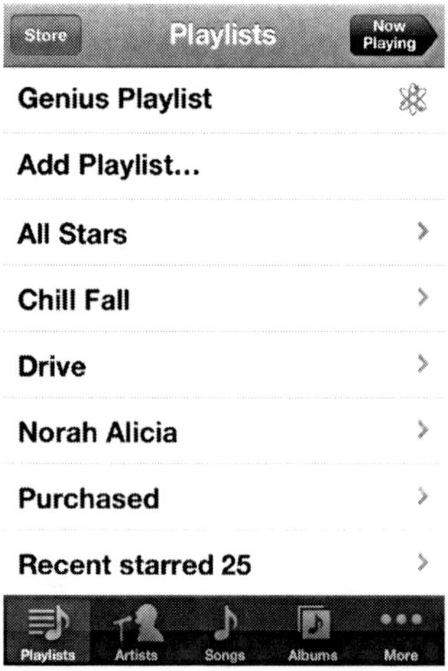

Figure 8–2. *The music player screen*

The More screen offers the best place to start exploring your media collection. Locate the More button at the bottom right of the screen, and tap it to load the screen full of categories shown in Figure 8–3.

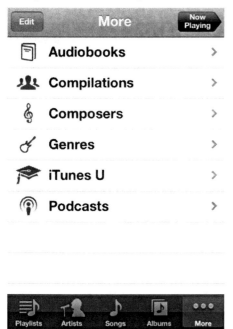

Figure 8–3. *The More screen provides an excellent jumping-off point for exploring your media. The Now Playing button appears on all category screens, including this one, and instantly takes you to the track currently playing.*

From the More screen, you can see every kind of category used to sort your songs: Playlists, Artists, Songs, Albums, Audiobooks, Compilations, Composers, Genres, iTunes U, and Podcasts. Some of these appear in the black bar at the bottom of the screen, while others appear in the list in the center of the screen. Tap any item to open that collection. For example, tap Artists to see a list of your media sorted by artists, or tap Audiobooks to view the audiobooks loaded on your system.

The black bar is your shortcuts bar or, more officially, your browse buttons bar (a name I find especially awkward, so please bear with me when I refer to it as simply the shortcuts bar). The difference between the items in the shortcuts bar and the items in the previous list is that these shortcuts appear universally in every category view. Your Music app lets you select which items you want to keep handy in that bar, as described next.

Editing Your Browse Buttons

From the More screen, tap the Edit button to open the Configure screen, as shown in Figure 8–4. This screen allows you to customize your shortcuts bar.

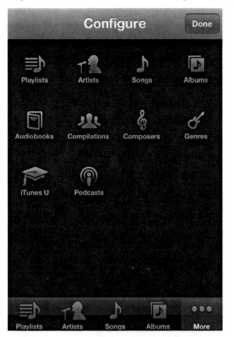

Figure 8–4. *Use the Configure screen to choose which items appear in your shortcuts bar at the bottom of the screen.*

To replace any item on the shortcuts bar, drag an icon from the center of the screen onto the item you want to replace in the bar at the bottom. Say you listen to podcasts and audiobooks more than you listen to music. Drag those two icons onto your bar to replace, for example, Artists and Albums. You'll see your shortcuts bar in every category view. Add whichever icons you use the most. You can also rearrange the icons in the bar by dragging them left or right within the bar.

The bar must always contain four—and only four—icons. You cannot drag icons off the bar, and you cannot set the bar to contain fewer than those four icons. You cannot add more than four shortcuts, and you cannot replace the More button with another item.

Here are the items you can choose from:

> *Albums*: Every album on your device, ordered by album name.
>
> *Podcasts*: A list of audio podcasts that you have chosen to sync to your device.
>
> *Audiobooks*: Every audiobook on your device.

Genres: A list of every genre—such as Classical, Rock, Pop, Country, and so on—that appears on your device. Each item leads to a list of media that belongs to that genre.

Composers: A list of media sorted by their composers. My iPhone contains listings for Bob Dylan, Wolfgang Amadeus Mozart, and more.

Compilations: A list of all media belonging to compilations—that is, albums that have been contributed to by various artists.

Playlists: A list of all the playlists you've chosen to sync to your device.

Artists: A list of your media sorted by the artist who recorded them.

Songs: Every song on your device, arranged alphabetically by song name.

iTunes U: A list of all your iTunes U lessons and lectures.

When you are finished making changes, tap Done to return to the More screen.

Navigating the Category Screens

All the category screens work in much the same way. The screen displays its members—whether podcasts, artists, or songs—as an alphabetically sorted scrolling list. If the list is long, you'll see an alphabet control on the right side of the screen, as shown in Figure 8–5. Tap a letter or scroll your finger down the alphabet to move to the section you want to view.

> **TIP:** Many category screens offer a Shuffle option as their first item. Tap it to start playing that category in random order.

When the items listed are individual songs or videos, tap any name to play your selection. When the items listed are collections, such as genres or albums, tap to open a screen that displays each item of that collection. For example, you can tap an album to list its tracks and then tap a track name to play it.

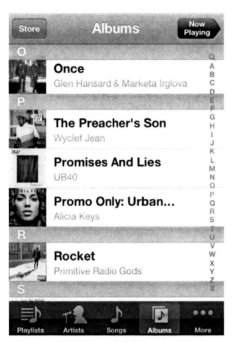

Figure 8–5. *The Albums screen lists albums in alphabetical order. When you've downloaded album art, it appears in the squares marked by the music notes.*

Playing Audio

Figure 8–6 shows the Music app's Now Playing screen. You arrive at this screen whenever you start playing a song. You can also jump to this screen from any category by tapping the Now Playing button at the top-right corner (see Figure 8–5).

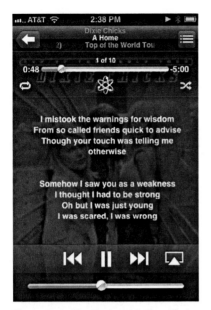

Figure 8–6. *The Music app's Now Playing screen provides an interactive screen that controls playback for the currently playing item. From this screen, you can adjust the volume, pause and resume playback, and loop the current track.*

Here are the items you'll find on the Now Playing screen and what they do:

> *Play indicator*: The right-pointing play indicator at the top right of the screen (just left of the battery status) appears universally when you're playing music. This tells you at a glance that music is playing. You'll find this especially helpful when you've removed your earbuds and placed the iPhone on a table.

> *Back button*: Tap the Back button at the top-left corner (the arrow pointing left) to return to the most recent album or playlist screen. Tapping Back does not stop playback. Your song continues to play as you browse through your categories or tap Home to do other things on your device.

> *Artist, song, and album*: These items appear at the top middle of the screen and are for information only. Tapping them does nothing.

> *Optional lyrics*: If you have saved lyrics with your album, they'll appear displayed superimposed over the album art.

> *Album View button*: This button looks like a three-item bulleted list and appears at the top right of the screen, just below the battery indicator. Tap this to switch between your Now Playing screen and its Album view (discussed in the next section).

Scrubber bar: The scrubber bar appears below the artist, song, and album name. Tap the album cover to make this control appear; tap again to hide it.

■ The number at the left of the bar shows the elapsed playback time. The number at the right shows the remaining playback time.

■ Drag the playhead to set the point at which your song plays back. You can do so while the song is playing so you can hear which point you've reached.

■ Look just below the scrubber bar to see which album or playlist track is playing. In Figure 8–6, this is track 5 of 11.

Loop control: This control, which looks like a pair of arrows pointing to each other in a circle, appears when you tap album art.

■ Tap once to loop the currently playing album or playlist. After the last song plays, the first song starts again.

■ Tap a second time to loop just the current song. The number 1 appears on the loop, telling you that the loop applies to just this song.

■ Tap once more to disable looping.

■ A blue loop (both the regular loop and the loop with the number 1) indicates that looping is enabled. A white loop means looping is switched off.

Genius button: This button looks like an atom with electrons swirling around it and lies in the center of the bottom bar. Tapping this creates a Genius playlist based on the song that is currently playing. When you navigate back to the music library, you'll see a playlist labeled "Genius" along with several other options. We'll discuss those options in just a bit.

Shuffle: The shuffle control looks like two arrows making a wavy *X*. It appears to the right of the scrubber bar and, like the loop and scrubber controls, appears only after you tap the album cover.

■ When the shuffle control is off (white), album and playlist songs play back in order.

When the shuffle control is selected (blue), the Music app randomly orders songs for shuffled playback.

Album art: When you've downloaded album art, the cover image appears just below the top bar and occupies most of your screen.

■ Tap the art area to open the gray playback controls that appear just below the artist, song, and album name.

- Tap again to hide the controls.

- Double-tapping the album art sends you to the Album view.

- Swipe to the right to return to the most recent category screen.

Rewind: The Rewind button looks like a vertical line followed by two left-pointing triangles.

- Tap to move back to the beginning of the currently playing song.

- Double-tap to move to the previous song in the album or playlist. If you are already at the start of the song, a single tap moves you back; if you're already at the first song, this works as if you had pressed the Back button—you return to the most recent album or playlist screen.

- Touch and hold to rewind through the current song. You'll hear very short snippets as you move backward through the song. This feature proves especially handy while listening to audiobooks.

Play/Pause: Play looks like a right-pointing triangle. Pause looks like a pair of upright lines. Tap this button to toggle between playback and pause modes.

Forward: The Forward button looks like the Rewind button in a mirror. The line is to the right, and both triangles point right instead of left.

- Tap once to move to the next song in the album or playlist. If you're at the last song, tapping Forward moves you back to the album or playlist.

- Touch and hold to fast-forward through your song.

AirPlay: The AirPlay button looks like a triangle pointing up inside a rectangle. It appears only when an AirPlay source is available to use such as an Apple TV. Tap the button, and select a source for your music to play through to. Choose iPhone to redirect your music back to the unit's built-in speakers.

Volume: Drag along the slider at the bottom of the screen to adjust playback volume. If you've attached an external speaker or remote control, you can use its controls to control the playback volume as well.

Album View

Tapping the Album View button at the top-right corner of the Now Playing screen switches you to an overview of the current album or playlist, as shown in Figure 8–7. This screen shows a track list with item names and durations.

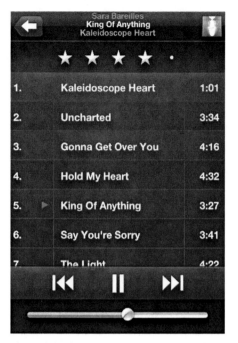

Figure 8–7. *The Album view shows a list of tracks and durations for the current album or playlist.*

Several items on this screen overlap with the Now Playing view and work in the same way. Here's a quick screen rundown:

> *Return to Now Playing*: The icon at the top right (it looks either like a music note or, if you have album art, like a wee version of the album cover) switches you back to the Now Playing screen.

> *Rate your songs with the rating stars*: Use the stars control to rate the current song, from zero to five stars. Drag your finger along the dots to form stars to set your rating. These ratings sync back to your computer, and you can use them when making Smart Playlists. For example, you might choose only your most favorably rated tracks to play. Set up this kind of playlist on your computer using iTunes. When you rate a song, it's personal and does not get sent back to the iTunes Store to be shared with the world.

> *View the entire track list*: Scroll up and down the track list to see all the items on the current playlist or album. Tap any item to start playback.

TIP: When there's empty space on the track list—for example, when you have only one or two tracks—double-tap the empty areas to return to the Now Playing screen. Alternatively, double-tap either side of the rating stars display.

Cover Flow

Tilt your device onto its side when browsing or listening to music, and you instantly enter Cover Flow mode. Cover Flow is the Music feature that allows you to view your media collection as a series of interactive album covers, as shown in Figure 8–8.

Figure 8–8. *Cover Flow presents your media library as a series of album covers.*

To use Cover Flow, simply flick your way through your collection to the left or right. The Music app provides animated, interactive feedback.

Here's what you can do in Cover Flow mode:

> *Album selection*: Tap any album to bring it to the front. Tap again to enter Album view.

> *Play/Pause*: Tap the small Play/Pause button at the bottom left of the Cover Flow screen to pause or resume the currently playing track.

> *Album view*: To enter the Cover Flow version of Album view, tap the small *i* (Info) button or the album cover. The cover flips and displays a list of tracks.

> ▓ Tap a track name to start playback.

> ▓ Tap Play/Pause to pause or resume playback.

> ▓ Tap anywhere on the screen (other than the Play/Pause button or a track name) to leave Album view.

Turn your device back to portrait orientation (with the Home button pointing down) to exit Cover Flow mode. Unless the Home button is down, you'll remain in Cover Flow mode.

Creating Playlists

The Music app on the iPhone allows you to create two kinds of playlists, Regular and Genius, right on the device itself—no iTunes required. Playlists allow you to build a selection of related songs that you can listen to without interruption, providing you with your own soundtrack throughout the day. You might want an exercise routine playlist or a "I feel depressed and want to hate the world" playlist, depending on your mood, of course. Playlists can be used for feelings, for tasks, for parties, and so on. Think of a playlist as burning your own CD of your favorite songs for a given event.

Creating a Regular Playlist

A regular playlist is simply a collection of songs of your choosing played one after the other. To create a regular playlist on your device, tap the Playlist button in the shortcuts bar at the bottom of the screen. Next, tap the Add Playlist... menu item (see Figure 8–9). A New Playlist pop-up appears asking you to name your playlist. Name the playlist whatever you like, and tap Save.

Figure 8–9. *Creating a playlist with the Add Playlist... selection.*

The song list appears next, as shown in Figure 8–10. Navigate through your entire collection, and pick which songs you want to add by tapping the plus sign (+) to the right of each track name. After making your selections, tap Done.

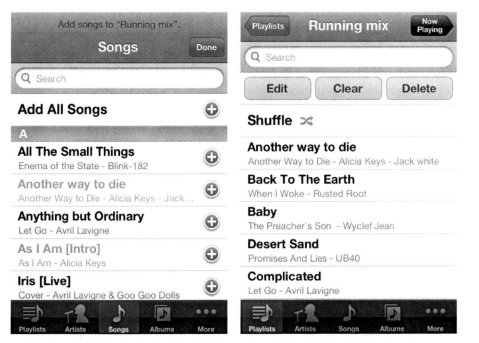

Figure 8–10. *Add songs to your playlist with this Songs selection screen (left). Tap the blue button with the + to the right of each name to add a song. Tap Done to be taken to your new playlist (right).*

Tapping Done sends you to the playlist. From here, you can tap Shuffle to begin a random playback of your playlist songs or tap Playlists to go back to the previous screen. You also have a search field to search by playlist songs if it's a long list. Finally, you can edit the playlist, clear it, or delete it by tapping the buttons above the Shuffle command. Tapping Clear removes all the songs from the playlist but leaves the name and empty playlist intact. Tapping Delete deletes the playlist. Your songs still remain on your device. You are asked to confirm your Clear and Delete selections before the commands are carried out.

To edit the playlist, tap Edit to add or remove items from your playlist. The playlist Edit mode, shown in Figure 8–11, provides all the tools you need to manage your new playlist:

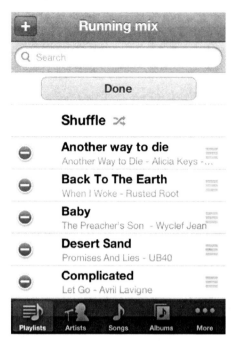

Figure 8–11. *In Playlist Edit mode, tap – to delete a song or + to add a song. Use the grab bars to the right of each song to change its order in the playlist.*

- Tap the plus sign (+) at the top left to add songs to your playlist.

- Tap Clear Playlist to remove all songs from the playlist. A confirmation dialog box appears. Confirm by tapping the red Clear Playlist option, or tap Cancel to leave your songs unchanged.

- Tap the minus sign (–) in the red circle to the left of any name to begin deletion. Tap Delete to confirm, or tap anywhere else to cancel.

- Drag the move bars (the three parallel gray lines to the right of each track name) to reorder items within your playlist. Grab a move bar, drag it to a new position, and then release.

- Tap Done to leave Edit mode and return to your playlist.

Any playlists created on the device will sync back to your iTunes library and appear in the iTunes playlist collection.

Creating a Genius Playlist

Genius is a feature in iTunes that finds songs in your music library that go together. It does this by matching rhythm, beat, artists, genres, and Internet data. A Genius playlist is a list of songs that result when you choose to run the Genius feature on a song you are playing.

Genius playlists can be created in iTunes on your computer or on the device. However, to enable the Genius feature, you need to enable it through iTunes on your computer first. To do this, launch iTunes on your computer, go to the Store menu, and select Turn on Genius. You'll need to log in with an iTunes Store account or create an iTunes account to access the Genius features. Enter your user name and password, agree to the terms and conditions, and sit back as Apple analyzes your music library.

You can create a Genius playlist by tapping the Genius icon in the center of the bar (see Figure 8–6). The icon looks like an atom surrounded by electrons. The Music app scans all your songs and compiles a new Genius playlist that collects other songs on your device that go great with your chosen song.

A new playlist named "Genius" appears on the screen (see Figure 8–12). In its list of songs, you can scroll through to see what Genius has picked out. You then have three options via three buttons at the top of the song list:

New: Tap New if you don't like the Genius playlist compilation. You'll then be presented with a list of your songs to choose a new song from.

Refresh: Tap Refresh if you want to keep the Genius playlist based on the original song you chose but want to get other songs that go well with the original one. This is good when you have listened to a playlist already (for example, Motown) and want to refresh the music that fills it without changing the theme (songs like the Jackson 5's "ABC").

Save: Tap Save once you are satisfied with the Genius playlist. After tapping Save, the Genius playlist labeled "Genius" disappears, and it is replaced by a Genius playlist that is named after the title of the song you chose to create the playlist. This playlist lives on your device and even syncs back to iTunes on your computer.

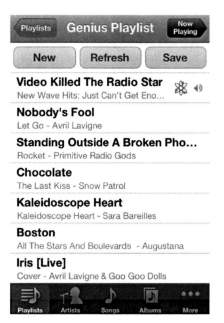

Figure 8–12. *The Genius playlist creation screen. The song with the atom icon is that which the playlist was created from.*

Editing a Genius Playlist

You have three options when editing a Genius playlist. The options appear as buttons above the song list when the Genius playlist is selected (see Figure 8–13).

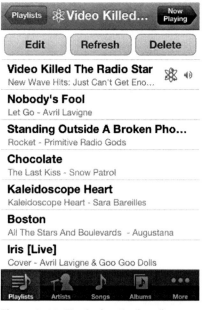

Figure 8–13. *The Genius playlist edit screen*

Edit: Tapping Edit lets you arrange your genius playlist songs in the order you want. You can also remove individual songs from the genius playlist.

Refresh: Tapping Refresh populates the Genius playlist with new songs that go well with the original one. The songs that were previously on the playlist are removed from it (but they'll still remain in the main music library).

Delete: Tapping Delete immediately deletes the saved Genius playlist. Its songs remain on your device.

> **NOTE:** Once a Genius playlist is synced back to iTunes on your computer, you will not be able to delete it on your device. Your only option will be Refresh. If you want to delete the Genius playlist, you must do so through iTunes on your computer.

Searching

The Music app has a simple yet powerful search feature that enables you to find a song quickly. To begin searching for a song, just scroll all the way up to the top of any category view (playlists, songs, artists, and so on). You'll find a search field at the very top (see Figure 8–14).

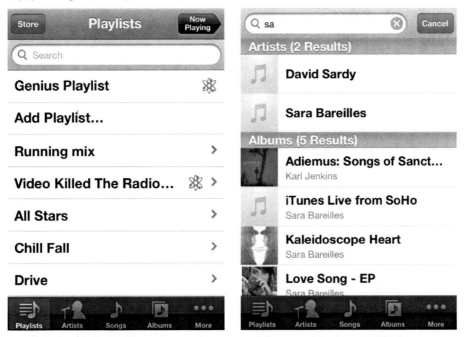

Figure 8–14. *The Music app's search function lies at the top of any category view (left). Results are displayed according to category (right).*

You can scroll through the search results as they are divided into categories by Songs, Artists, Albums, Composers, Podcasts, or Audiobooks. To play a song, simply tap it.

> **TIP:** You can also search for songs without opening the Music app. Use the iPad's Spotlight feature to the left of the Home screen to search for a song, and then tap it to begin playing.

Going Beyond the Music App

As you've seen, the Music app lets you browse through your media and play audio. But you can also work with playback in a couple ways that go beyond the Music application.

Saving Energy

You can put your device to sleep during music playback to save energy. Press the Sleep/Wake button once. This locks your device and turns off the screen but allows your music to keep playing.

To peek at the current album cover during playback, tap Sleep/Wake. When you've loaded album art for the track, the cover appears on your lock screen instead of your normal wallpaper. If your track has no art, you still see the current time and track name. Double-tap the Home button to view your playback controls, as shown in Figure 8–15.

Figure 8–15. *During audio playback, your device lock screen displays the currently playing song and, if album art is available, its album cover. The small playing icon just to the left of the battery indicates that audio is playing back. When an AirPlay destination such as Apple TV is available, the AirPlay button (white triangle inside the rectangle) appears to the right of the playback controls.*

Display Music Playback Controls When in Another App

We've already mentioned how your music, podcasts, and audiobooks keep playing even when you leave the Music app. The good news is that you don't need to go back into the Music app to change tracks. Simply press the physical Home button twice in quick succession to bring up the unit's multitasking bar (discussed in detail in Chapter 3). Swipe your finger from left to right until you see the Music controls slide onto the screen (see Figure 8–16). You can access these controls from any app or Home screen; they allow you to quickly play/pause a song, rewind or fast-forward, and skip to the next or previous song. To be taken immediately to the Music app, click the Music app icon.

Figure 8–16. *You can access the Music playback controls from any screen on the device by pressing the Home button twice. Pull the recent items to the right to reveal the controls, which lie to the left of your recent apps list.*

Adding a Sleep Timer

Unlike the Sleep/Wake button, which switches off your device screen without interrupting music playback, the Clock application allows you to "sleep" your device and tell it to end playback after a set interval. This is handy for those who like to listen to music while falling to sleep.

To set the sleep timer, on the Home screen tap Clock. Then tap the Timer icon at the bottom right of the Timer screen. Scroll the hours and minutes wheels to select a period of time after which you want the device to sleep. Tap When Timer Ends, and choose Sleep from the options list, as shown in Figure 8–17. Tap Set to set your sleep timer, and then tap the big green Start button.

Figure 8–17. *The Sleep function automatically ends music playback and locks your device.*

The device begins a timer countdown. When it reaches zero, it automatically stops music playback and locks your device.

Adjusting Music Settings

Surprisingly, for a feature-rich application like Music, iOS provides just a few settings (see Figure 8–18). You'll find these in **Settings ➤ Music**, and they work as follows:

> *Shake to Shuffle:* When this is set to On, you can physically shake your device to shuffle the current list of playing songs. You should make sure this is switched to Off if you are going to be moving while listening to music. Our technical editor had his iPhone in his pocket while walking around one day, and he couldn't figure out why his songs kept changing!

> *Sound Check*: Say you're listening to a song that was recorded way too low so you crank up the volume during playback. Then when the next song starts playing back, boom!—there go your eardrums. Sound Check prevents this problem. When you enable Sound Check, all your songs play at approximately the same sound level.

> **TIP:** You can also use Sound Check in iTunes. Choose **Edit** ➤ **Preferences** ➤ **Playback** ➤ **Sound Check** (Windows) or **iTunes** ➤ **Preferences** ➤ **Playback Sound Check** (Mac).

EQ: The iPhone offers a number of equalizer settings that help emphasize the way different kinds of music play. Select **Settings** ➤ **Music** ➤ **EQ**, and choose from Acoustic, Dance, Spoken Word, and many other presets. To disable the equalizer, choose Off.

Volume Limit: Face it—personal music players bring your audio up close and very personal. It's so up close, in fact, that your hearing may be in peril. We strongly recommend you take advantage of the iPhone's built-in volume limit to protect your ears. Navigate to **Settings** ➤ **Music** ➤ **Volume Limit**, and adjust the maximum volume using the slider, as shown in Figure 8–18. All the way to the left is mute—sure, you'll protect your ears, but you won't be able to hear anything. All the way to the right is the normal, unlimited maximum volume. If you're super paranoid or, more usually, if children have access to your device, tap Lock Volume Limit to open a screen that allows you to set a volume limit passcode. No one may override your volume settings without the correct passcode.

Lyrics & Podcast Info: Some songs and podcasts have embedded lyrics and text. When this is set to On, you'll see that embedded text over the cover art in Album view. To disable the text, set this setting to Off.

Group By Album Artist: With this option set, if a song has multiple artists, the same song appears under both artists when you are navigating your music by Artist in the music app.

Home Sharing: Enter your Apple ID and password here to activate Home Sharing on your device. Home Sharing allows you to stream music from iTunes on your computer and listen them on your iPhone. Your device and your computer must be connected to the same wireless network and iTunes must be open on your computer for your device to see its music.

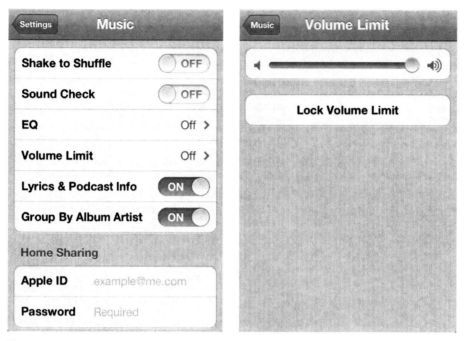

Figure 8–18. *The Music app's settings (left). Set the maximum volume for your device (right) by dragging the slider on the Volume Limit settings screen.*

Choosing Headphones

You can use virtually any headphones with your iPhone, but reviewing every headphone here would fill more pages than *War and Peace*. Just know that you don't need to use the earbuds that came with the iPhone. You could use any third-party headphone, from the cheap $2 kind you find at Walgreens to the $1,500 Shure noise-canceling earbuds.

You can also use wireless Bluetooth headphones that support A2DP (two-channel stereo audio streaming). Bluetooth headphones are great because you don't have a cord hanging over your body. On the other hand, the great thing about corded headphones is that they don't require power to work. Note that if you do use Bluetooth headphones and are going on a long jog or trip, make sure you have extra batteries or that the headphones are at least fully charged, or you could find yourself cut off from your music mid-song.

Summary

This chapter introduced all the ways you can browse and play media using the Music application. As you've seen, the new music player software is a lot more flexible and intuitive than the old click-wheel approach. With the iPhone, you can flick through your entire collection and tap your way to the media you want to use. Here are a few points to think about before you move on to the next chapter:

- Cover Flow makes browsing through your media a simple visual pleasure. Tip your device on its side to enter Cover Flow mode.

- Don't be afraid to fill your shortcut bar with the items you use the most. It's easy to customize. It's also easy to put it back the way it started.

- Save your ears. Adjust your playback volume using the built-in volume controls and limiters.

- Don't forget about double-tapping the Home button to pull up music controls, regardless of your current application.

Chapter 9

Shopping at the iTunes Store

The iTunes Store realizes the promise of mobile commerce on handheld devices. The program is beautiful to look at and easy to use. It integrates itself seamlessly into your normal iTunes experience. That being said, it is admittedly a contrivance to sell you things. But these are things that you presumably want and can use while on the road. Stuck at an airport or a coffee shop? Download some new music to enjoy, catch up on last week's episode or your favorite TV show, or watch that Hollywood blockbuster you never saw in theaters. Yes, the iTunes Store is a point of sale, but it's also a fascinating place to spend some time and an interesting application for your iPhone.

Connecting to the iTunes Store

The iTunes icon on the button bar at the bottom of your iPhone's home screen launches the iTunes Store application. It is colored purple and shows a white music note with a circle around it (see Figure 9–1).

Figure 9–1. *The iTunes application icon*

When you tap the iTunes icon, the application attempts to connect to Apple's storefront web server. Because of this, you must be located near a Wi-Fi hotspot and be connected to the Internet to use this application.

When your connection is not active or not strong enough to carry a signal, the iTunes Store application displays an error message saying your iPhone can't connect to the store. To resolve this problem, return to your home screen, and tap Settings > Wi-Fi. Make sure your iPhone is connected to a 3G or wireless network and that the signal registers at the top left of your screen with at least one arc or bar (and preferably three arcs or five bars).

Unfortunately, sometimes and iTunes Store connection issue is an Apple problem. Sometimes Apple's servers go down for a minute or two. When this happens, your only option is to check back frequently to see whether you can connect.

Signing in to Your iTunes Account

Before you can purchase anything from the iTunes Store, you need to sign in to it. To sign in, scroll to the bottom of any iTunes Store page in the app until you see the Sign In button. Tap it, and you'll be presented with two options, as shown in Figure 9–2: Use Existing Apple ID or Create New Apple ID.

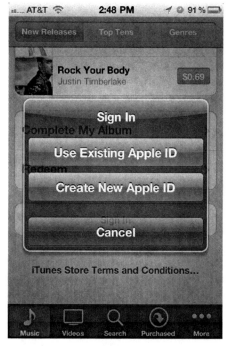

Figure 9–2. *The iTunes Store sign-in screen*

If you are signing in using an existing account, all you have to do is enter your account name (usually your e-mail address) and password. You'll then be logged in and able to purchase songs and videos. If you are creating a new account, the process is quick and easy. Choose what country you are in, agree to the license agreement, and create your user name and password.

NOTE: You may want to think about logging out of the iTunes Store if you have children who might use your iPhone and, knowingly or unknowingly, download music or video that costs you money. To log out, scroll to the bottom of a page until you see your account name. Tap it, and then tap Sign Out.

Browsing Through the iTunes Store

Figure 9–3 shows the iTunes Store application screen. At the bottom of the screen you'll see shortcut buttons to different sections of the store. By default you'll see the Music, Videos, Search, Purchased and More buttons.

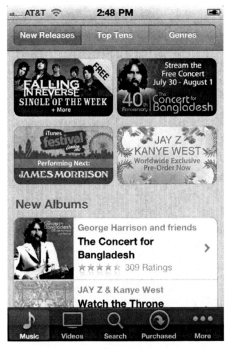

Figure 9–3. *The iTunes Store offers many ways to browse, find, and purchase music.*

If you tap More, you'll be taken to a screen that also links to the Genius, Ping, Ringtones, Podcasts, Audiobooks, and iTunes U sections of the store, as well as your current downloads. We'll talk about all those sections of the store later in this chapter. On the More screen, tap the Edit button to rearrange icons on the shortcuts bar at the bottom of the screen (Figure 9–4). You can, for example, replace the Videos shortcut button with the Audiobooks shortcut button.

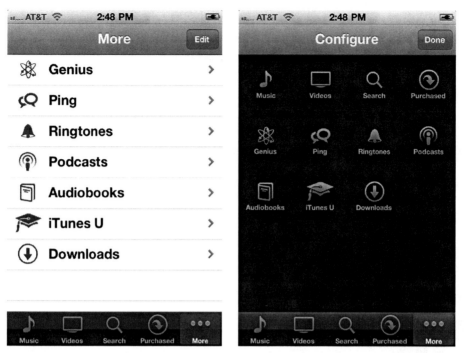

Figure 9–4. *The More screen (left) lets you access other areas of the iTunes Store. You can also rearrange shortcut buttons by pressing the Edit button (right).*

Additionally, when you're in a Starbucks coffee shop, you may see a special option. Tap the Starbucks icon in the button bar to discover which song is currently playing in your location. You can also browse the special Starbucks catalog. These Starbucks features are only available to U.S. iTunes account holders in U.S. Starbucks locations. Now, let's explore the different sections of the iTunes Store.

The Music Store

The Music section of the iTunes Store is the first one you'll see (see Figure 9–3). This section is broken down into three categories: New Releases, Top Tens, and Genres. You'll also see banner ads and album promotions.

Tap any of the buttons at the top of your screen to access the following sections:

> *New Releases*: The New Releases section includes a list of albums with recent release dates. Tap any item to open the album page and find track-by-track listings.

> *Top Tens*: The most popular-selling albums and tracks in more than 20 categories ranging from Alternative to World appear in the Top Tens section. Tap any item to move to its feature page. As you can see in Figure 9–5, Top Tens breaks down the categories into Top Songs or Top Albums.

Genres: Use the Genres list to limit your featured selections to a particular genre, such as Hip-Hop/Rap, Country, or Pop. Choosing a genre opens a screen dedicated to the biggest current hits for that kind of music (see Figure 9–5). Think of the genre sections as mini-stores for your current mood.

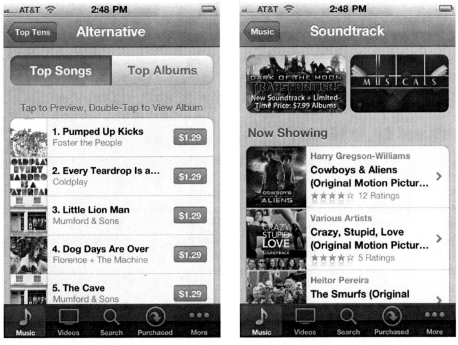

Figure 9–5. *The Top Tens section (left) allows you to view the most popular items by album or songs. This is the top-ten listing for the Alternative genre. The Genres section (right) allows you to view songs and albums in mini-stores according to genre. This is the mini-store for the Soundtrack genre.*

Exploring the Top Tens

The Top Tens section lists the best-selling albums and songs by genre, such as Alternative or Rock. It's also our favorite section and behaves like the rest of the sections in the iTunes Store, so it's a perfect place to get acquainted with. Tap any genre name to open a top-ten listing (see Figure 9–5), and then tap either Top Songs or Top Albums.

Here are a few tips for making the most of the Top Tens section:

- When viewing songs, tap any song to preview it, or double-tap to open its album.

- When viewing albums, tap the album name to open a track list, and then tap a song to preview. Previews play back for up to 30 seconds.

- View the most popular songs storewide by tapping iTunes instead of a genre. (Figure 9–5 shows the list for the Alternative genre.) It's listed as the first item in the Top Tens section before the actual genres.

- If you do not find your favorite genre on the main Top Tens screen (only Pop, Alternative, Hip-Hop/Rap, Rock, and Country are listed for the U.S. store), scroll down and tap More Top Tens for the complete list. You'll discover Reggae, R&B/Soul, and more.

- What is popular and "top" changes over time. As you navigate through these lists, you may actually see new items as the store downloads updated lists from the iTunes server.

Previewing and Buying Music

Figure 9–6 shows the layout when browsing a typical album. You're shown the cover art, the name of the artist and album, and the option to buy the entire album (in this case, for $9.99). Below the option to buy the entire album, you'll see a Like and Post button. Tapping either one of these allows you to "like" or post a link to the album on your Ping wall (we discuss Ping later in this chapter). Below the Like and Post buttons are the average user ratings and reviews. Tap the stars to read through individual reviews. You can also create your own review. Reviews are tied to your iTunes account, so you have to authenticate to leave a review. Apple does this so a single person can't leave multiple negative (or positive) reviews.

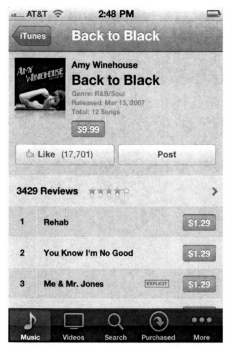

Figure 9–6. *Previewing and buying music is fun and easy.*

Tap the name of any song to listen to a preview. You'll see the track number or album image next to the name flip around to show the playback control, as shown in Figure 9–7.

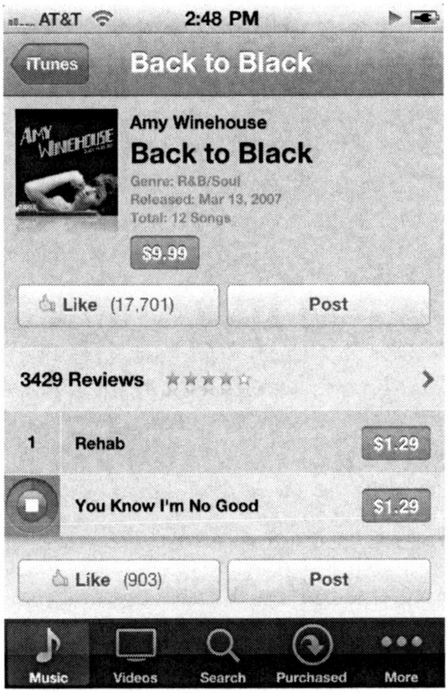

Figure 9–7. *Each song listing allows you to play a 30 to 90-second preview and lists the purchase price for the track.*

Here are a few pointers about previewing music:

- Previews are 30 to 90 seconds long seconds long, depending on the song, and generally start playback 30 seconds into the song. If a song is shorter than 30 seconds, it plays back for as long as it can. For example, search for Monty Python's "Spam" song. Select it, and its "preview" plays back the entire track.

- The dark pie wedge shows how much of the preview has played. The wedge grows over time until the preview has finished, and the wedge is a complete dark circle.

- The Stop button in the center of the control allows you to stop playback.

- You cannot pause and resume playback. Playback always starts at the same point.

- When you are previewing a song you'll have the option to "like" or post a link to that single song on your Ping wall.

To purchase music, tap the price to the right of the track name. The button expands, turns green, and changes from the price to BUY SONG. If you are purchasing an entire album, the price button examnds to say BUY ALBUM. Tap a second time to confirm that you really do want to buy the selection. In a delightful animation, your new song jumps directly into the Downloads icon at the bottom of the screen (or the More button if you don't have the Downloads shortcut showing at the bottom of the screen), and a red badge with the number of currently downloading items will appear.

If you haven't recently entered your password, the iTunes Store app prompts you to do so by opening a little dialog box alert. Type in your password, and tap OK. Pay special care while typing, because you will not be able to see the text. It appears as a series of dots instead to protect your security. Once you've entered the proper password and tapped OK, your download begins.

The Video Store

The great thing about the iTunes Store application is that all sections look and behave in the same manner. As you can see in Figure 9–8, the Video store has the same layout as the music store. The difference between the Music and Video stores are that in addition to purchasing content, in the Video store you can also rent movies and TV shows.

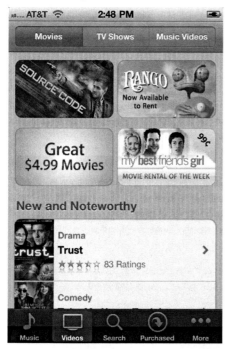

Figure 9–8. *The Video store has a similar look and feel as the other iTunes Stores.*

The video store is divided into three categories along the top: Movies, TV Shows, and Music Videos. All three categories allow you to preview and purchase videos in much the same way. Let's look at your typical movie information page.

In Figure 9–9 we've selected the excellent documentary *The Corporation*. From the *The Corporation* page, you can choose to buy or rent the movie by clicking the respective buttons. Some movies you can only buy, not rent. If you do rent a movie, you have 30 days to begin watching it, but once you begin watching it, you must complete it within 24 hours. After the 30-day and 24-hour time limits are reached, the movie is automatically deleted.

Figure 9–9. *The movie information page*

NOTE: Your iPhone is nice enough to remind you about the rental state. You'll be notified when the period is about to expire and when the periods have expired. Let's see Blockbuster do that!

You can view the movie's theatrical trailer by tapping the preview button. The movie preview will play full-screen and will automatically return you to the movie's information page when it is done playing. On the information page you can read user reviews or Rotten Tomatoes critic reviews. Finally, the summery of the movie and a list of major cast and crew are presented.

While the previews for movies are usually the full theatrical trailer, previews for television episodes and music videos run 30 seconds only.

Once you have found a video you want to purchase, simply tap the Buy button. The button expands, turns green, and changes from the price to BUY MOVIE. Tap a second time to confirm that you really do want to buy the selection. Your new video jumps directly into the Downloads icon at the bottom of the screen (or the More button if you don't have the Downloads shortcut showing at the bottom of the screen), and a red badge with the number of currently downloading items will appear.

TIP: Download times can be enormous, especially when you're on the road. Factor slow hotel Wi-Fi into your rental and purchase choices. Want to catch a nice movie on Saturday night? Your download might not finish until Sunday afternoon.

The Podcasts, Audiobooks, and iTunes U Stores

If you understand how to navigate the music and video stores, the remaining Ringtones, Podcasts, Audiobooks, and iTunes U stores will be a breeze. They are virtually arranged in the same way. One cool difference, however, is that when you preview a podcast or iTunes U lesson, you can actually watch or listen to the entire episode just by streaming it. So, if you are low on available space on your iPhone, you don't actually need to download the episode to view it. Also note that you use the iTunes Store app to buy audiobooks only, not regular books. To purchase regular books, you use the iBooks app discussed in Chapter 11.

Searching the iTunes Store

The Search screen, shown in Figure 9–10, allows you to perform a live search with instant feedback. Start typing, and the iTunes Store application shows all the matches to your search string, updating whenever you type a new character.

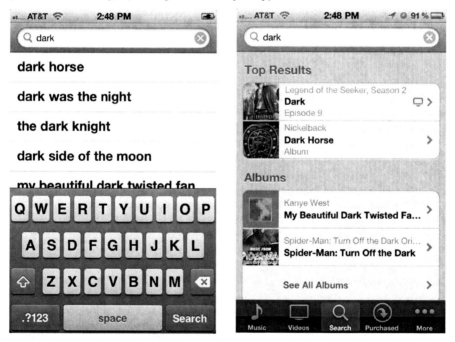

Figure 9–10. *The iTunes Store application matches your search string to available tracks as you type (left) and presents your results to you by category (right).*

When you locate an item you were searching for, simply tap its search suggestion. The store moves you to the search results page that lists all the results by categories. Tap the item you are looking for to go to its information page.

Purchased

The Purchased screen allows you to see all the songs, videos, and audiobooks you've ever bought from the iTunes Store. It doesn't matter if you bought them through iTunes on your computer, through the iTunes Store on your iPhone, or through the iTunes Store on another iOS device. If you bought any items with the Apple ID you are using on the iTunes Store on your iPhone, your entire purchase history will show up when you tap on the Purchased button (Figure 9–11).

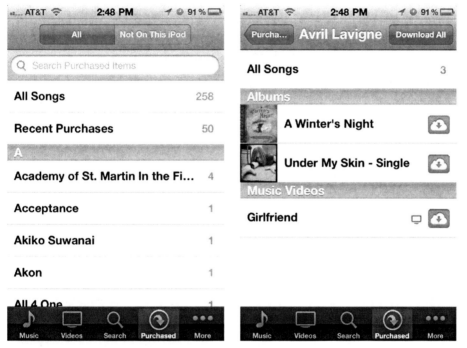

Figure 9–11. *Viewing your purchase history*

You can sort through all your purchase history, or just your purchase history for items not currently on your iPhone by tapping the "All" or "Not on this iPhone" tabs at the top of the Purchased screen (Figure 9–11 left). If you scroll through your Purchased list, you can select any item, an artist, for example, and see all the songs you've bought by that artist (Figure 9–11, right).

To redownload those songs (or videos) for free, simply tap on the button with the downward arrow in a cloud button, or to download all the items by that artist, select the "Download All" button at the top of the screen. You will not be charged again for downloading the items you already bought. This is a great feature if you're away from your computer and find you really want to listen to a song you've purchased but you forgot to sync it to your iPhone.

Downloads

The Downloads screen (see Figure 9–12) tracks the download progress for your recent purchases. Once you've completely downloaded a track, it disappears from this screen and adds itself to your iPhone's library.

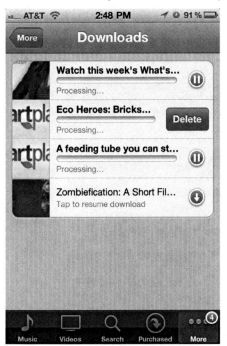

Figure 9–12. *The Downloads screen allows you to track progress as newly purchased tracks arrive on your iPhone. The red bubble on the More or Downloads button indicates the number of tracks left to download.*

You can interact with currently downloading items in three ways:

- *Pause a download:* Press the blue-and-white pause buttons (the two vertical lines) while a download is in progress. This pauses the download while the next item to be download automatically begins downloading.

- *Resume a download:* Press the blue-and-white arrow button to resume a paused download.

- *Delete a download:* Swipe your finger left to right over the download item, and a Delete button will appear. Tap the button to remove the downloading item.

At times, you may be unable to connect properly from your iPhone to the iTunes Store to complete a purchase. Then your downloads start to back up a bit. This has happened to us on numerous times. The tracks simply collect in the Downloads screen until you get a better connection or until the store resumes regular download service.

> **NOTE:** The iPhone has a 20 MB download limit over a 3G connection. If a file is larger than that, you'll have to download it over a Wi-Fi connection. This limitation is in place for a few reasons, specifically, to help you avoid data-overages charges and to help the wireless providers keep their networks from crashing.

Redeeming Codes

You can redeem gift certificates and codes on your iPhone. On the Music screen, scroll all the way to the bottom of the page until you see a blue Redeem button. Tap the Redeem button; enter your iTunes gift card, gift certificate, or other iTunes code into the text box; and tap Redeem. Your iTunes account will update, and you will be able to spend those funds directly in the iPhone iTunes Store.

Transferring Purchased Items to Your Computer

Transfering something you've purchased on your iPhone back to your computer is as simple as connecting your iPhone via the USB cable to your computer. All music, videos, and podcasts bought on your iPhone transfer back to your computer when you next sync. The tracks appear in a special playlist, which appears in the Store section of your iTunes source list. The playlist is called "Purchased on *your iPhone name*"—in my case, "Purchased on Michael's iPhone" (the name of the iPhone used), as shown in Figure 9–13.

Figure 9–13. *All iPhone purchases transfer to your computer on your next sync. You'll find all your new songs in the "Purchased on" playlist, which is automatically created during synchronization.*

> **NOTE:** The iTunes Store application is smart enough to know about the Complete My Album feature. If you've already purchased tracks on a given album, you'll be given the option to purchase individual tracks. Bonus content, such as liner notes, will be available to you when you return to your home computer, but they will not download to your iPhone.

Getting Free Music and Videos

The official iTunes Store for many countries (including the United States, Australia, New Zealand, Canada, France, Japan, the Netherlands, and the United Kingdom) offers a free single of the week each Tuesday. You can download these tracks onto your iPhone using the iTunes Store application, but you cannot find them easily. They aren't listed separately, and the application does not offer a freebies search.

Likewise with videos, there are many free video clips available on the iTunes Store; it's just rather hard finding them on your iPhone sometimes. Free videos usually are no longer than a few minutes and are really just commercials for an upcoming TV series or movie. Have a look around, but don't expect to find any truly free full-length movies or TV shows. A caveat to this are free Podcast or iTunes U videos.

Getting Social with Ping

You've probably noticed the chat bubble icon labeled *Ping* in some of the images in this chapter (see Figure 9–4). We've saved Ping to talk about until now because, frankly, it's not that cool. Ping is Apple's attempt at social media. Think of it as Facebook for iTunes account holders, except you can't share videos or photos or do most of the other things you can with Facebook.

What Ping allows you to do is follow your favorite artists to see what they're up to: concerts, new albums, and so on. You can also follow your friends to see what kind of music they are liking at the moment. To use Ping, you first have to sign into it using iTunes on your computer. To do this, open up iTunes 10.0 or newer on your computer, and select Ping from the source bar under the Store heading.

You'll be asked to turn Ping on (see Figure 9–14) and then be asked for your iTunes password. You'll then be taken to your Ping profile home page (Figure 9–15) where you can upload a profile picture, search for friends on Ping, and follow artists.

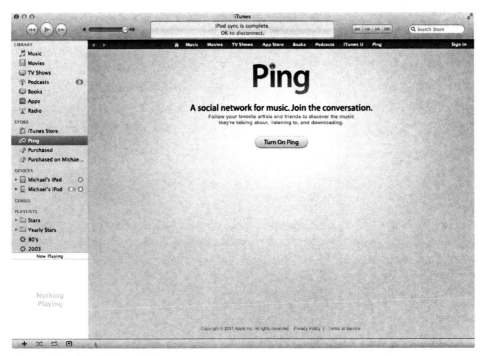

Figure 9–14. *Ping in iTunes 10*

Figure 9–15. *Ping. Meh.*

Once you've set up Ping on iTunes on your computer, you can then go back to the iTunes Store app on your iPhone (Figure 9–16) and access Ping by tapping the Ping button in the bottom toolbar. From there you can browse through Ping using the three tabs at the top:

> *Activity*: Shows you the latest status updates of the artists you are following.

> *People*: Shows you a list of everyone you follow or who follows you. It also notifies you of any "follow" requests—in other words, people who have friended you.

> *My Profile*: Shows you your Ping profile. It's kinda lame that you can't edit your profile from the app, but again, Ping is kinda lame.

Chances are, unless you are a huge music fan, Ping will not appeal to you. It's a social network for music fans; the rest of us can stick with Facebook.

Figure 9–16. *Ping in the iTunes Store app. Still meh, unless it's important to you to know a Disney star had a Holiday in Harry Potter Land.*

Summary

Not only does the iPhone's iTunes Store application allow you to buy music, videos, podcasts, and audiobooks from iTunes right now, it also shows a great deal of promise as the forerunner of a generation of future mobile points of sale. This chapter has shown you how to use this application to search, select, preview, and purchase music. Here are a few points to take away from this chapter:

- Don't confuse the iTunes Store application with the Music application. The iTunes Store app is for downloading music and videos, and the Music app is for playing your music.

- If you know how to browse through one section of the iTunes Store, you know how to browse through all the sections. Apple has done a good job at making the iTunes Store app easy to navigate.

- Any item purchased on the iTunes Store app will automatically sync back to your iTunes library on your computer. This includes movie rentals! If you started watching a rented movie on your iPhone and want to finish it on your laptop, simply sync the iPhone to your computer. You can then finish watching the rental on your computer. Just be sure to finish the movie in the 24-hour time window! After that, it is automatically deleted from all your devices.

- Make sure to transfer purchases back to your computer. If you don't and you try to redownload the song or video from the iTunes store on your computer, you will be charged again!

- Play around with Ping, but don't expect to be blown away unless you are a music freak.

Chapter 10

Shopping at the App Store

Perhaps the coolest thing about the iPhone is the multitude of apps available for it. As of this writing, more than 450,000 apps are available for the iPhone. These apps range from games to medical programs to reference utilities and more. If there's something you're interested in, there's most likely an app for it. The best news of all is that many apps are totally free, while most others are priced between 99 cents to $2 (though there are some apps that do cost hundreds of dollars). Even long after you've bought it, apps keep your iPhone fresh and new, and with the App Store on your iPhone, you can shop for apps wherever you have a Wi-Fi connection.

Connecting to the App Store

The App Store icon on the button bar at the bottom of your iPhone's home screen launches the App Store application. It is colored blue and shows a white *A* made up of a ruler, a pencil, and a brush with a circle around it (see Figure 10–1).

Figure 10–1. *The App Store icon*

When you tap the App Store icon, the application attempts to connect to Apple's storefront web server. Because of this, you must be located near a Wi-Fi hotspot and be connected to the Internet to use this application.

When your connection is not active or not strong enough to carry a signal, the iTunes Store application displays an error message saying your iPhone can't connect to the store. To resolve this problem, return to your home screen, and tap Settings > Wi-Fi. Make sure your iPhone is connected to a 3G or wireless network and that the signal registers at the top left of your screen with at least one arc or bar (and preferably three arcs or five bars).

Signing in to Your App Store Account

Before you can purchase anything from the App Store, you need to sign in to it. To sign in, scroll to the bottom of any App Store page in the app until you see the Sign In button. Tap it, and you'll be presented with three options, as shown in Figure 10–2: Use Existing Apple ID, Create Apple ID, or iForgot.

If you are signing in using an existing account, all you have to do is enter your Apple ID (usually your e-mail address) and password. You'll then be logged in and able to purchase apps. If you are creating a new Apple ID, the process is quick and easy. Choose what country you are in, agree to the license agreement, and create your user name and password. If you've forgotten your Apple ID, tap iForgot and you'll be taken through a short process to retrieve your exisiting Apple ID.

Figure 10–2. *The App Store sign-in screen*

Browsing Through the App Store

Figure 10–3 shows the App Store. Because it is dealing only with one thing—apps—and not a multitude of music, videos, podcasts, and audiobooks, and so on, the App Store has a simpler layout than the iTunes Store. At the bottom of the screen, you'll see shortcut buttons to different sections of the store. These buttons are Featured, Categories, Top 25, Search, and Updates. Let's explore the different sections of the App Store and how to navigate them.

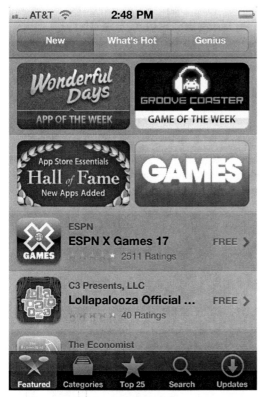

Figure 10–3. *The App Store storefront*

Featured

The Featured section of the App Store is the first one you'll see (see Figure 10–3). This section is broken down into three categories: New, What's Hot, and Genius. You'll also see banner ads for specific apps and collections of apps. For individual apps, tap any listing, and you'll be taken to its information page (discussed later) where you can read more about the app and download it.

Tap any of the tabs at the top of your screen to access the following sections:

New: The New section includes a list of the most recent apps that are available on the App Store.

What's Hot: This section features the most popular free and paid-for apps.

Genius: Genius is a feature Apple originally introduced in iTunes to recommend music you may like based on the music in your existing iTunes library. Apple has extended this Genius capability to its App Store. Tap the Genius tab, and you'll be presented with a list of free and paid apps that Apple thinks you'll like based on your previous app downloads.

In our experience, the Genius recommendations are spotty at best, but give it a try for yourself and see whether the feature works for you. You'll first need to turn on the Genius recommendations feature and agree to send information about the apps you've downloaded to Apple. This is kind of redundant since Apple already knows all the apps you've downloaded. Once you click Turn On Genius (Figure 10–4), you'll see a list of recommendations. You'll see the name of an app you've downloaded above the name of the recommended apps in which the Genius recommendation was based on. If you found an app you are interested in, tap its listing to go to its Info page.

Figure 10–4. *Turning on the Genius feature and the subsequent Genius list of apps*

Not interested in one of the recommendations and never will be? Swipe the app from left to right to reveal a red Remove button. Tap the button to remove the app from the Genius list.

Categories

The second button on the shortcuts bar at the bottom of the screen is the Categories button. This divides the Apps Store into 20 categories (see Figure 10–5). Categories is a great feature when you know you want a certain type of app but are not sure exactly what app that is. Tap any category to be taken to that category screen. On the individual category screens, you'll see three tabs labeled Top Paid, Top Free, and Release Date. The tabs are just different ways of sorting the apps in the category, with the goal of making apps easier for you to find.

> *Top Paid:* Lists the top paid apps people have purchased in that category

> *Top Free:* Lists the top free apps people have downloaded in that category

> *Release Date:* Lists the most recently released apps in that category

Figure 10–5. *The categories screen (left) and a subsequent category view showing lists of Top Paid, Top Free apps, and apps by Release Date*

As you might imagine, the Top Paid, Top Free, and Release Date lists change quite frequently. By default, 25 apps are shown on each tab. At the bottom of the 25th app, you can tap Twenty Five More to add another 25 apps to the list.

> **NOTE:** The Games category has its own category sublist ranging from Action and Arcade games to Trivia and Word games.

Top 25

The third button at the bottom of the App Store is the Top 25 button. Tap this to be taken to a list of the top 25 downloaded apps in the App Store (see Figure 10–6). The Top 25 list takes into account apps from all categories and, as you can image, will change frequently. The Top 25 categories are important because they are probably the single best way to figure out what's worth buying. It's the wisdom of the masses. If an app isn't really good, it probably won't show up in the Top 25 lists.

Figure 10–6. *The Top 25 screen in the App Store*

At the top of the Top 25 screen, you'll see three tabs labeled Top Paid, Top Free, and Top Grossing.

> *Top Paid:* Lists the top paid apps people have purchased in the App Store.
>
> *Top Free:* Lists the top free apps people have downloaded in the App Store.
>
> *Top Grossing:* Lists the biggest moneymakers in the App Store. This is a category Apple added in order to help big app developers, such as major game developers, who wanted to port their popular games to the iPhone and iPhone touch. Porting major titles to the iPhone costs a lot of money, so the developers have to charge more for the games. Top Grossing ensures that costlier apps get eye time with customers and aren't pushed out of the way by all the 99-cent games.

At the bottom of the Top 25 screens, you can tap Show Top 50 to add the next 25 apps to the list.

Exploring an App's Information Page

After browsing the App Store, you're sure to come across an app you're interested in. Simply tap the app's listing on any App Store screen to be taken to its information page (see Figure 10–7). You'll only see parts of the Info page at a time since you have to scroll through it, but in the figure, we show you what the entire Info page for an app looks like for clarity's sake.

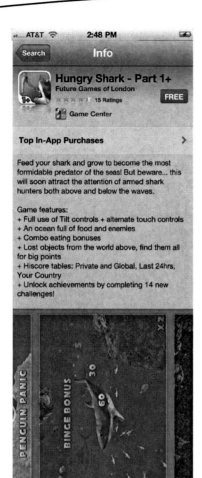

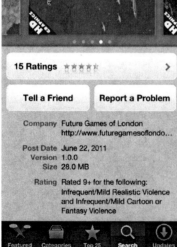

Figure 10–7. *The Info page*

The page is basically divided into three parts: the top, the preview images, and the bottom. At the top of the page you'll find the app icon and name, as well as its user ratings. You'll find a blue button either with FREE or with the price of the app in it. Tap the blue button to download the app (we'll talk more about that in a moment). The remainder of the top of the screen is dedicated to a short text description of what the app does. Beneath the price button you'll see the Game Center icon if the app or game offers Game Center support (discussed later in this chapter). Finally, you'll see a section for Top In-App Purchases if the app offers additional add-ons you can buy from within the game.

In the center of the Info screen you'll see a series of pictures. These pictures are screenshots of the app; they show you what the app looks like. Below the screenshots you'll see a series of white dots. Each dot represents a picture. Swipe to the left or right to move through the pictures.

The bottom of the screen is where you'll find a link to user reviews of the app, a Tell a Friend button that allows you to send an e-mail with a link to the app in it, and a Report a Problem button that allows you to send a note to Apple if you find a problem with the app. The remainder of the screen shows general information about the app: who made it, its size, its age rating, its posting date, and its version number.

Keep in mind ratings aren't always reliable. A developer can easily have a bunch of his friends rate his app five stars. It doesn't happen all the time, but it does happen. As we mentioned earlier, the best way to tell whether an app is really good is if it appears in a Top 25 category.

Buying and Downloading Apps

There are two kinds of apps in the App Store: paid and free. Depending on which the app is, you'll either see a either a blue FREE button or see a blue button with a price in it at the top of an app's Info page. To download the app, tap the blue button. It will turn into a green INSTALL button for free apps or a BUY NOW button for paid apps.

Tap the green button, and a confirmation window will pop up asking you to enter your iTunes account password. Enter it, and tap OK; you will then be taken to your iPhone's home screen. On that screen you will see a dimmed icon of the app you just purchased with a blue progress bar signifying the download (see Figure 10–8). Once the bar fills, your app download is complete! Tap the app's icon, and enjoy!

NOTE: If you've already bought an app, you'll only see a blue INSTALL button next to it and tapping it will immediately begin downloading the app on your device. You will not be charged again for redownloading an app you've already bought.

Figure 10–8. *After you buy an app, you are returned to your home screen where the app proceeds to download. The download is signified by the blue progress bar.*

Searching the App Store

Sometimes you may not want to browse the App Store. You may be on a mission to find a specific app or apps related to specific things. That's where the search feature comes in. The Search screen, shown in Figure 10–9, allows you to perform a live search with instant feedback. Start typing, and the App Store shows all the matches to your search string, updating whenever you type a new character.

Figure 10–9. *The App Store search feature matches your search string to available tracks as you type (left) and presents your results to you in a list (right).*

Tap the search button on the keyboard to search for your term, or tap any of the search suggestions that appear above the keyboard. You'll be taken to the search results page that lists all the results that match your query. Tap the item you are looking for to go to its information page.

Downloading Updates and Previously Purchased Apps

Developers are always updating their apps. Updates can include major new features or just subtle performance tweaks. How do you know when there's an update to one of the apps you've downloaded? A red badge with a number will appear in the corner of the App Store icon on the iPhone home screen (Figure 10–10). The number in the red button tells you how many of your apps have available updates.

Figure 10–10. *The red dot tells you how many apps have an update available. In this case, two apps have an update available.*

To download the updated apps, tap the App Store icon, and then tap the Updates button at the bottom of the App Store (see Figure 10–11). You'll be presented with a list of all the apps on your iPhone touch that need updating. Tap Update All to automatically download all the app updates. To download just one of many app updates, select the app from the Update list, and tap the blue UPDATE button that appears on the app's Info page.

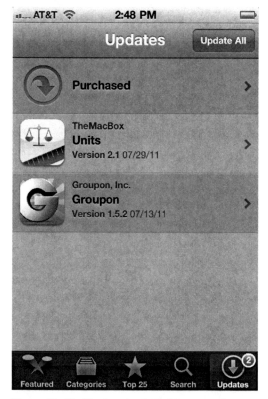

Figure 10–11. *The App store's Updates page shows you available updates for apps on your iPhone touch.*

> **NOTE:** At this time, if an app shows up in the Updates page, the update will be free. You will never be charged again for any apps that appear on the Updates page. This of course can change in the future.

From the Updates section of the App Store you can also redownload any other apps you have previously download. It doesn't matter if they were free apps or paid apps. From the Updates screen, tap the "Purchased" button (Figure 10–11).

The Purchased screen (Figure 10–12) allows you to see all the apps you've ever bought from the iTunes Store. It doesn't matter if you bought them through iTunes on your computer, through the iTunes Store on your iPhone, or through the iTunes Store on another iOS device. If you bought any items with the Apple ID you are using on the iTunes Store on your iPhone, your entire purchase history will show up when you tap on the Purchased button.

Figure 10–12. *Viewing your purchase history.*

You can sort through all your purchase history, or just your purchase history for items not currently on your iPhone by tapping the "All" or "Not on this iPhone" tabs at the top of the Purchased screen (Figure 10–12).

To redownload any of your previously purchased apps for free, simply tap on the button with the downward arrow in a cloud icon. You will not be charged again for downloading the items you already bought. This is a great feature if you're away from your computer and find you really want an app that you had download but you forgot to sync it to your iPhone. It's also a great way to check through all your apps and locate one you may have forgotten about, like a really good game.

Redeeming Gift Certificates and Codes

You can redeem gift certificates and codes on your iPhone. On the Featured screen, scroll all the way to the bottom of the page until you see a blue Redeem button. Tap the Redeem button; enter your App Store gift card, gift certificate, or other App Store code into the text box; and tap Redeem. Your App Store account will update, and you will be able to spend those funds directly in the App Store. Remember to type carefully, or else you might get a "code not valid" error. If you see an error, go back and carefully type in the code again.

Transferring Purchased Items to Your Computer

All apps bought on your iPhone transfers back to your computer when you sync the next time. Just plug in your iPhone and wait for the sync to complete. Any newly downloaded or update apps will be automatically transferred to iTunes.

Buying Apps Through iTunes on Your PC

It's important not to forget that you aren't limited to buying apps for your iPhone on your iPhone. You can also use the iTunes Store on your computer to browse for and purchase apps. We tend to browse for apps through iTunes more than the App Store app on our iPhone because our large computer screens. As you can see in Figure 10–13, the iTunes Store has a nice wide-screen layout that lets you easily navigate through all the app offerings.

Figure 10–13. *The desktop version of the App Store in iTunes*

Any apps bought in the App Store in iTunes will automatically transfer to your iPhone on the next sync. See Chapter 2 for more details.

Getting Your Game on in Game Center

Not content at stopping with Ping (see the previous chapter), with iOS 4.1 Apple introduced Game Center, which is a gaming social media application (Figure 10–14). With Game Center, you can play certain games you've downloaded from the App Store against your friends or even complete strangers from around the world. If you are a big iPhone gamer, then Game Center will appeal to you.

Figure 10–14. *The Game Center icon*

To use Game Center, you'll first need to log in (Figure 10–15). You can do so using your existing Apple ID, or you can create a new ID right inside Game Center. Once logged in, you'll be able to set your online status, see which of your friends are online or invite new friends, view all the Game Center–compatible games you have on your iPhone, view the leaderboards for those games, and view any pending friend requests.

Figure 10–15. *Log into Game Center (left) to be presented with your personal gaming stats.*

Since it's introduction in iOS 4.1, Game Center has become a big hit. Improvents to Game Center in iOS 5 include the ability to add your own profile picture, get game reccomendations from within the app, and view overall achievement scores. Needless to say, Game Center caught on as a social media platform where Ping did not.

Summary

The App Store is one of the coolest things about the iPhone. It's your gateway to hundreds or thousands of apps that constantly turn your device into an amazing new machine. Here are some tips to take away with you:

- You can download apps through the App Store on the iPhone as well as through the iTunes Store on your desktop or laptop.

- Most apps on the App Store are free or very cheap.

- Use the App Store to check for updates to your apps. All updates will always be free.

- Any item purchased on the App Store app will automatically sync back to your iTunes app library on your computer.

- App Store categories like Top 25 frequently change. Check back often for new apps!

- Use the Genius feature to find new apps you might like based on your current app downloads.

- Game Center brings social media to gaming. If you're a big gamer, it's worth a try. If you're the kind of person who just likes to play Tetris while waiting for the train to work, Game Center is a pass.

Chapter 11

Reading Books and Newspapers with iBooks and Newsstand

Not only is your iPhone a wonderful device for playing games, surfing the Web, and listening to music, but with iBooks, it's also a powerful e-book reader with a library of more than 30,000 free books at your fingertips as well as thousands more paid books, including many *New York Times* best sellers. But iBooks doesn't stop there! You can add your PDFs to iBooks so you can carry them with you on the iPhone. This allows you to access all your PDFs from the same library as your books—a great feature for those of you who regularly work with or receive PDF files. In addition to iBooks, Apple has introduced Newsstand in iOS 5. Newstand lets you view and buy all your magazine and newspaper subscriptions in one easy to access location.

In this chapter, you'll discover how to navigate your iBooks bookshelf and the books themselves. You'll also learn about bookmarking favorite passages from books, creating notes, and even having a book read to you. We'll take you through all the PDF features of iBooks. Finally, we'll explore Newstand and show you how to shop for and organize all your subscriptions. Let's get started.

iBooks App

The iBooks application does not ship on the iPhone. To use it, you must download it first for free from the iTunes Store. Alternately, the first time you launch the App Store on your iPhone, it will ask you if you want to download iBooks as well. Once you have done this, the iBooks icon will appear on your iPhone's home screen (see Figure 11–1).

Figure 11–1. *iBooks icon*

Tap the icon to launch the iBooks app. When you do, you'll be presented with your iBooks bookshelf (see Figure 11–2). The bookshelf will be populated with any e-books you have added to your books library in iTunes (more on that in a moment).

View a Book's Info Page

Figure 11–2. *The iBooks bookshelf*

Syncing Books

Before you can sync books, you need to first get some to sync. We talked about syncing books to your iTunes library in Chapter 2, but we'll touch on it again here. There are a few ways for you to obtain books to sync to your iPhone.

iBookstore

In the previous chapters, you learned how to buy music, videos, and apps using the separate applications to buy them (such as iTunes for music and movies and the App Store for apps). With iBooks, Apple has combined both the store and the reader into one app. In the upper-right corner of your bookshelf, you'll see a Store button (see Figure 11–2). Tap this button, and your bookshelf will flip around like it's a secret passageway. On the backside of the bookshelf, you'll be presented with the iBookstore. Here you can buy books, download samples, and navigate best-seller lists. Let's look at the iBookstore more closely now. As you can see in Figure 11–3, the iBookstore is laid out similarly to the iTunes and App stores.

Figure 11–3. *The iBooks bookshelf. The Featured page is the first page you'll see.*

At the top of the store you'll see a Categories button that allows you to select specific sections of the iBookstore like Mystery or Non-Fiction. The Library button on the right will flip the store around and bring you back to your iBooks bookshelf. The bottom of the screen is populated with five shortcut buttons that allow you to browse the bookstore in different ways.

> *Featured*: This is the home page of the iBookstore. On it you'll see banner ads for specific books or collections of books. Below the banner

ads you'll see individual listing of select books. Tap any listing to be taken to the book's information page. We'll talk more about a book's individual information page a little later.

Charts: This button displays two tabs at the top of the screen: Top Charts and New York Times (Figure 11–4).

Top Charts shows you the top downloaded paid and free books on the iBookstore in groups of ten. You can tap Ten More Books at the bottom of the listings to show an additional ten books.

The *New York Times* gives you a listing of its fiction and nonfiction best sellers that are available on the iBookstore. Note that only *New York Times* books that are available on the iBookstore will show in the charts. If the iBookstore doesn't sell a particular book that is on the *New York Times* list, it will not show on the screen.

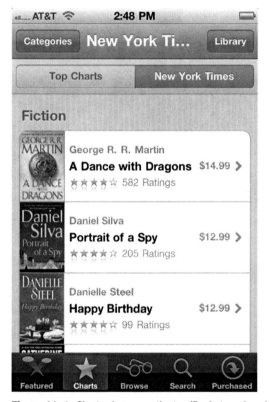

Figure 11–4. *Charts shows you the top iBookstore downloads as well as the New York Times best sellers.*

Browse: This allows you to search through the iBookstore by author (Figure 11–5). Scroll through the list with your finger, or drag your finger along the alphabet on the side to jump to a specific letter. Authors are in alphabetical order by their last names. You can choose to browse by authors of paid or free books by selecting the Top Paid or Top Free tab at the top of the screen. You can further whittle down your authors list by choosing a specific category from the categories button. For example, selecting Romance will show only romance authors.

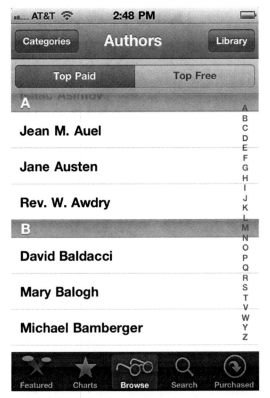

Figure 11–5. *The Browse function lets you search through the iBookstore by author.*

Search: The search function allows you to search for a book by typing in the name of the author or title (Figure 11–6).

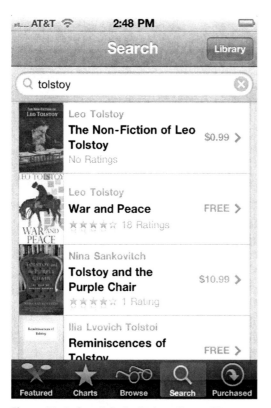

Figure 11–6. *Search for books by author or title.*

After you've entered your query, tap the search button in the keyboard, and you'll be presented with a list of results. Tap any item in the list to be taken to the book's information page.

Purchased: This page allows you to see all the purchases you have made in the iBookstore (Figure 11–7). Not only can you see all your purchases, but you can redownload them if you've deleted them from your device. Simply tap on the button with the downward arrow in a cloud icon. You will not be charged again for downloading book you already bought. Don't worry—you won't be charged again for it!

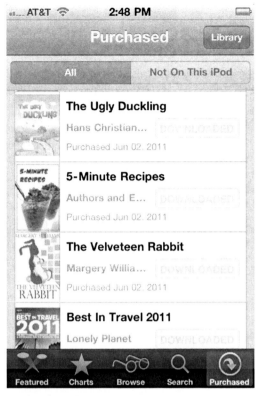

Figure 11–7. *The Purchases screen lets you view and re-download all your iBooks.*

NOTE: You don't need to spend money to enjoy reading books on your iPhone. The iBookstore offers more than 30,000 free books from the Project Gutenberg book library. Project Guttenberg is a digital collection of books that are in the public domain. The only lame thing about Project Guttenberg titles is that they're given the plain-looking brown covers you see in some of the figures. Though Guttenberg does redeem itself by making plenty of ePub books available with illustrations, there's no need to rely solely on PDFs if you want illustrations in your book.

View a Book's Info Page

Once you have found a book you're interested in, tap it to be taken to its information page. As you can see in Figure 11–8, a book's information page allows you to read a summary of the book (this is equivalent to reading what's on the book of the book in a real bookstore). It also has a link to the author's page where you can read more about the author and their other works. You can also view user ratings for the book.

Figure 11–8. An individual book's information page

As you can tell, the information page has a ton of information about the book, but the main features are the two buttons at the top. The first button in Figure 11–8 reads $11.99. This is the price button. If you want to buy the book, tap the price, and it turns into a green Buy Book button. Tap it again to purchase and download the book. You may be asked to enter your iTunes password if you haven't entered it in a while, and then the iBookstore will flip around, and the book will appear on your bookshelf with a blue progress bar (see Figure 11–9). Once the progress bar is complete, it will disappear, and you can begin reading your new book! Note that with free books, the price button will read Free. When you tap it, the button changes to Get Book. Tap it again to download the free book.

The Get Sample button shows on every book listing. It allows you to download a sample of any book on the iBookstore. Simply tap the Get Sample button; the iBookstore will flip around, and the book will appear on your bookshelf with a blue progress bar. Once the progress bar is complete, it will disappear, and you can begin reading the sample of the book. Samples always start on the first page and usually include the first chapter (or first several chapters if the book has smaller chapters).

Figure 11–9. *Downloading an iBook. Note the blue progress bar on the upper-left book. This means you are downloading the book.*

NOTE: As with the iTunes Store and the App Store, you need to sign into your iTunes account before you can buy or download any book. To sign in, simply scroll to the bottom of the iBookstore home page, and tap the Sign In button. Enter your iTunes user name and password, and you're good to go!

ePub Books

Besides using the iBookstore to read books in the iBooks app, there is a second way to get books on your bookshelf. You can download ePub-formatted books from other web sites and then drag them into your book library in your iTunes source list on your computer. Any ePub books you've added to your iTunes library will be automatically synced the next time you connect your iPhone to your computer.

What Is ePub?

ePub is a universal e-book file format. Any device capable of opening and displaying ePub files can display the book no matter where you bought the e-book. In other words, you don't need to buy your books from the iBookstore only. Several sites sell e-books in the ePub format that are compatible with the iPhone. ePubbooks (www.epubbooks.com/buy-epub-books) has an excellent list of sites that offer ePub books for sale and for free download. Once you've downloaded an ePub book, simply drag it to your iTunes library, and the book will sync to your iPhone on the next connection.

> **NOTE:** Amazon's Kindle bookstore is another popular place to buy e-books. However, Kindle books don't use the ePub format. If you buy an e-book from the Kindle store, you'll need to download Amazon's free Kindle book reader app for the iPhone to read those books. You will not be able to read a Kindle book in the iBooks app. Barnes & Noble's BN eReader for iPhone is another way to buy e-books on the iPhone, but the BN eReader app supports the standard ePub format so you can move books back and forth between various ePub readers.

ePub vs. PDF

As you'll see later in this chapter, iBooks can read both ePub books and PDFs. So, if you have a choice between buying a book in ePub format or PDF, which do you choose? Let's look at the pros and cons of each:

ePub pros:

- Selectable and searchable text in iBooks
- Smaller file sizes

ePub cons:

- Requires a dedicated ePub reader if you want to read the book on your Mac or PC. Currently there is no desktop version of iBooks available.

PDF pros:

- Can be read in iBooks or on almost any computer in the world. PDF is one of the most universal document formats.

PDF cons:

- Files sizes can be large. A 300-page book can be more than 100 MB in size, taking up valuable room on your iPhone.

- iBooks doesn't offer font adjustment, searchable text, or notes for PDFs.

After look ing at the pros and cons, I would say that if you have an option of buying a book in ePub or PDF format, choose ePub, especially if you'll be viewing the book primarily in iBooks. The ePub format offers many more feature-rich options than PDF does.

Navigating Your Bookshelf

OK, you have a bunch of books downloaded and synced. Before you start reading them, let's get a little better acquainted with navigating all your books on your bookshelf. By default, your iBooks bookshelf will look like it does in Figure 11–2. If you swipe you finger down, you'll be presented with a few more options, as shown in Figure 11–10.

Figure 11–10. *From the title bar of the iBooks bookshelf, you can access the iBookstore, navigate between your collections, and access view and edit modes.*

The title bar in the iBooks bookshelf features three buttons with an additional search field and view buttons below it:

- *Edit*: Allows you to rearrange or delete books on your bookshelf as well as sort your books into collections.

> **NOTE:** Deleting a book from the iPhone will not delete it from your iTunes library on your computer. You will be able to resync the book any time you want. You can also immediately redownload the book under the Purchased shortcut button in the iBookstore.

- *Collections*: In Figure 11–10 the collections button is labeled "Books" but the label on the button will change to whatever the name of the collection you are viewing is. The collections button displays a list of all your book collections in iBooks. By default you'll see two collections:

    - *Books*: When you tap *Books*, you'll be present with your bookshelf. This contains all the ebooks you have in the iBooks app.

    - *PDFs*: Tapping *PDFs* will take you to your PDF bookshelf. We'll talk more about the PDF features of iBooks in the second half of this chapter.

    We'll talk about collections in detail later on in this chapter.

- *Store*: As mentioned, tapping this will take you to the iBookstore where you can go shopping to expand your library.

- *Search*: If you have a large collection of books, you can use this search feature to quickly find the book you are looking for. The search feature searches all the titles on your shelf by name or author.

- *Icon View*: This is the default view of your bookshelf. The button with four white squares shows you all your books' covers in large, easy-to-see thumbnails.

- *List View*: This is the button next to the Icon View button. It has three white lines in it. Tap it to display a list view of your iBooks bookshelf (see Figure 11–11).

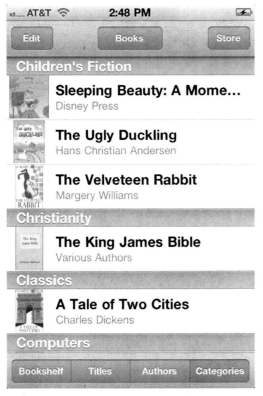

Figure 11–11. *List view with sorting options by bookshelf, title, author, and category*

When you tap the List View button, you'll notice that at the bottom of the screen you have four ways to sort your lists:

- *Bookshelf*: Displays your books in the order that they appear in icon view.

- *Titles*: Displays your books in alphabetical order by title.

- *Authors*: Displays your books in alphabetical order by name of author.

- *Categories*: Displays your books in genre groups. Books are arranged alphabetically in each grouping.

You may notice that some of your books have a blue or red ribbon in their cover's right corner. The red ribbons say Sample, and they signify the book on your bookshelf is a sample you've downloaded from the iBookstore. Samples will stay on your iPhone until you delete them or buy the full book, but they will not sync back to your iTunes book library.

Blue ribbons say New, and they signify that you have not begun reading the book yet. The New ribbon will appear until you've turned at least one page inside the book (Figure 11–12).

Figure 11–12. *Books with the New and Sample ribbons next to a previously read book*

Rearranging the Order of Your Books

iBooks allows you to rearrange the order of the books in your library. In icon view tap the Edit button, then simply tap and hold a book's cover, and drag it to a new position on your bookshelf. This is no different from the way you arrange apps on your iPhone's home screen. In list view in edit mode, you can only rearrange books in the *Bookshelf* sorting category. Tap and hold the grip bars on the right of the book's genre, and drag to your preferred position.

Deleting Your Books

Deleting books is also easy in iBooks. In icon view tap the Edit button, you'll notice a red Delete button appears in the upper-right corner of the screen. Tap the book or books you want to delete so a blue checkmark appears over them (Figure 11–13). Next, tap Delete. A confirmation dialog will appear asking if you're sure you want to delete the book. Tap Delete again to confirm.

In list view in Edit mode, you can delete books from any of the four sort views. Simply tap the the book or books you want to delete so a blue checkmark appears next to them (Figure 11–13). Next, tap Delete. A confirmation dialog will appear asking if you're sure you want to delete the book. Tap Delete again to confirm.

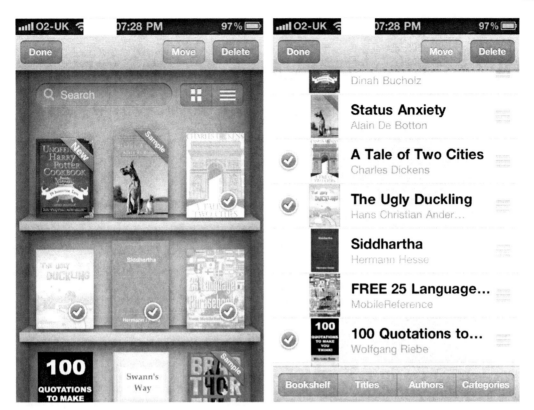

Figure 11-13. *Deleting books in icon and list views*

Sorting Your Books into Collections

iBooks does a wonderful job of displaying your books and PDFs on a digital bookshelf, however there may come a time when your book collection grows so large, seeing them all displayed on a single iBooks bookshelf might not make for the easiest browsing experience.

Luckily, Apple has a built-in feature called "Collections" that allows you to sort your books onto different bookshelves for easier orginaization. In the center the iBooks screen you'll see the Collections button. It will be labeled according to the name of the selected collection. In Figure 11-10 the collections button is labeled "Books" because that is the currently selected collection. Tap the collections button to reveal a list of book collections in iBooks (Figure 11-14).

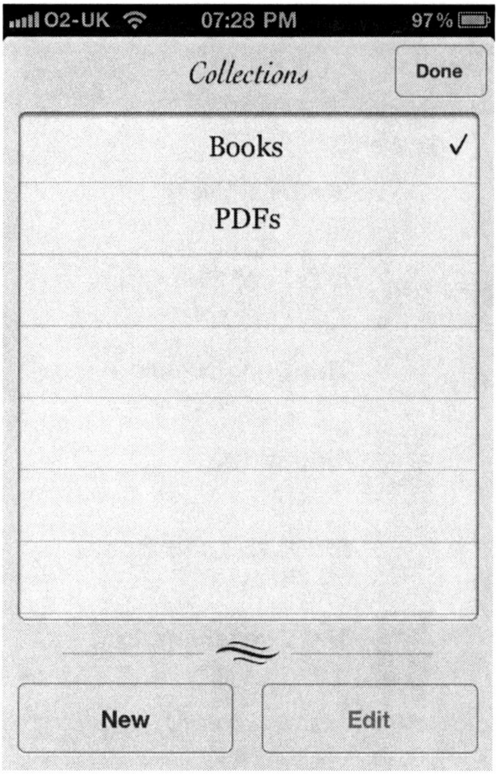

Figure 11–14. *The Collections menu.*

Be default you'll see two collections: Books and PDFs. Any ebooks you have will appear on their own bookshelf under the Books collection, and any PDFs you have will appear on their own bookshelf under the PDFs collection.

Creating New Collections

If you'd like to create new collections to better manage your library, you can do so easily:

1. Tap the Collection button so the collections menu appears.

2. Tap the "New" button.

3. A new Collections field will appear (Figure 11–15) and enter the name of your new Collection.

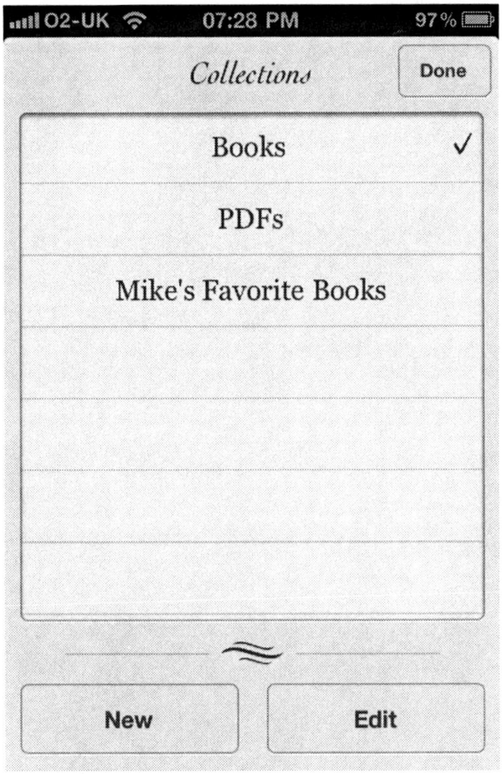

Figure 11–15. *Creating a new Collection.*

4. When you have entered your Collection's name, tap **Done** and your new Collection will be created.

Adding Books and PDFs to Your Collections

Once you've created a new collection, you need to add some books or PDFs to it. To add books or PDFs to a collection:

5. Tap the Edit button in the upper-right corner of an iBooks bookshelf.

6. Tap the book(s) or PDF(s) you want to add to a collection. The selected book or PDF's cover will fade and a blue checkmark will appear in its lower-right corner (Figure 11–16).

Figure 11–16. *Selecting books to move to a collection.*

7. Tap the Move button at the top of the iBooks bookshelf. The collections list will be displayed (Figure 11–17, left).

8. Choose the collection you want to add the selected books or PDFs to by tapping its name. An animation will show the selected collection sliding onscreen and you'll be taken to that collections bookshelf where you'll now find your selected books or PDFs (Figure 11–17, right).

Figure 11–17. *Moving books to your new collection, left, and your new collection, right.*

NOTE: You can only place the same book or PDF in one collection at a time. When you add a PDF or book to a collection, it is removed from its previous collection.

Navigating Between Your Collections

iBooks makes it easy to navigate between your collections. Matter of fact, it gives you two ways to do this:

- Tap the Collections menu and then tap on the Collection you want to view, OR

- From any Collections bookshelf, drag your finger left or right to swipe to the previous or next collection.

Editing Collections

iBooks lets you edit the names of existing Collections, arrange the collections in a specific order, and delete collections.

To edit the name of a collection:

1. Tap the Collection button so the collections menu appears (Figure 11–15).

2. Tap the Edit button.

3. Tap the collection whose name you want to edit.

4. Enter the new name of you're the Collection.

5. Tap the Done button when finished.

To arrange the order of a collection:

1. Tap the Collection button so the collections menu appears.

2. Tap the Edit button.

3. Use the grip bars to drag your collections up or down in the Collections list (Figure 11–18). You can't move the Books or PDFs collections.

4. Tap the Done button when finished.

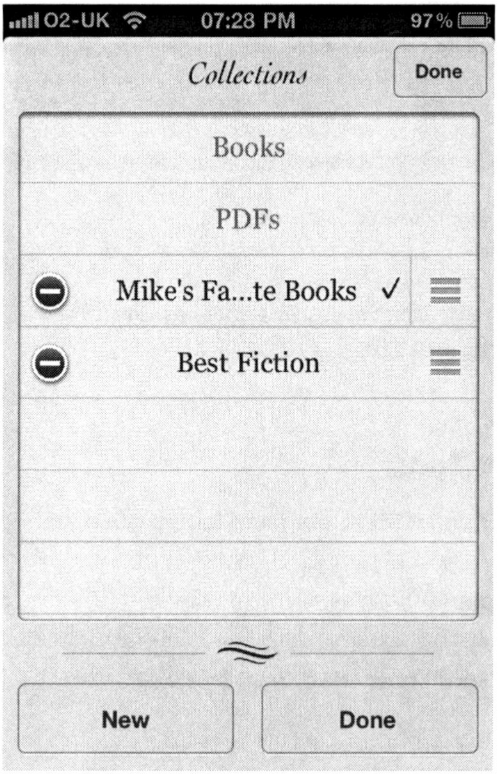

Figure 11–18. *Editing collections.*

To delete a collection:

1. Tap the Collection button so the collections menu appears.

2. Tap the Edit button.

3. Tap the red minus sign button (Figure 11–10).

4. A red delete button will appear. Tap it to delete the collection. A warning dialog will appear asking you if you want to remove the collection's items from the device or move the back to their original collections. Tap "Remove" to remove the items from your iPad or tap "Don't Remove" to keep them on the iPad and move them back to their default (Books or PDFs) collection.

Reading Books

The bookshelf displays your books in a gorgeous and easy-to-find layout, but books are meant to be read, not just ogled at on a shelf. Let's get started!

To read a book, simply tap its cover. The book will fly forward and open. If it's the first time you've opened the book, you'll be on the first page. If you have opened the book before, it will open on the page you left off on.

While reading a book, you can choose between landscape or portrait orientation. As you can see in Figure 11–19, landscape mode shows you about a paragraph of text on average, while portrait mode shows you slightly more text. You can navigate between the two modes by simply rotating your iPhone.

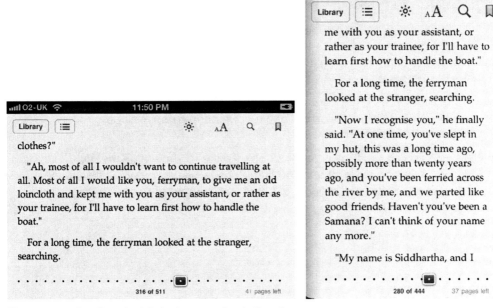

Figure 11–19. *Reading a book in landscape and portrait modes*

At the top of any book's page, no matter what orientation you are in, you'll notice a menu that contains a series of buttons (see Figure 11–20). We will get to using all these features momentarily, but we'll familiarize you with the menu first.

Figure 11–20. *A book's menu buttons*

- *Library*: Tapping this effectively closes the book and takes you back to your bookshelf. The next time you open this book, you'll be taken to the page you were on when you left it.

- *Table of Contents/Bookmarks*: This button is signified by three dots, each with a line after them. Tap this button to be taken to the book's Table of Contents/Bookmarks page.

- *Brightness*: This is the button that looks like the sun and changes the screen brightness while inside the iBooks app only.

- *Font*: This button, symbolized by a small and big *A*, allows you to change the font of the book's text as well as the font size. This is helpful for those people who need larger text while reading, such as older people or anyone with sight difficulties. You can also change the background of the book's page to a sepia tone.

- *Search*: The magnifying glass button allows you to search through a book's text.

- *Bookmark*: Tap the bookmark ribbon to lay down a red bookmark in the upper-right corner.

- *Page scrubber*: This is the series of dots that run along the bottom of a book's page (see Figure 11–22). Tap and hold the square button that sits on the dots; then drag it left or right to quickly navigate through the book's pages.

- *BUY*: A Buy button appears when you are reading a sample book. Tap the Buy button to purchase the book. Your sample copy will be replaced with the full copy.

While reading, you can tap the center of a book's page to show/hide the menu bar and page scrubber. You'll be left with only the title of the book and name of the author (in landscape view) at the top of the page and the page number at the bottom.

Turning Pages

You have three ways to move through a book's pages:

- Tap and hold the side of a page; then drag your finger across, and the page will curl on the screen (see Figure 11–21). When you lift your finger, the page turn will be complete.

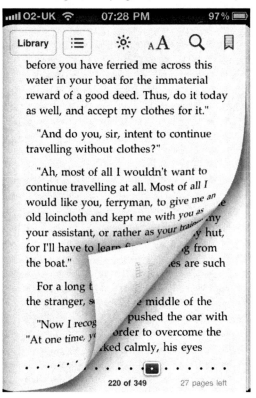

Figure 11–21. *You get cool eye candy when turning a page.*

- Tap the right or left side of the screen to move forward or backward. This accomplishes the same function as the previous one, but with less interactive eye candy.

- Tap and hold the scrubber bar at the bottom of a page (see Figure 11–22); then slide your finger in either direction. The name of the chapter and the page number will appear above the scrubber as you slide. When you've found the right page, remove your finger from the scrubber, and the page will flip, taking you to the page you've selected. The scrubber lets you go to a specific page number quickly without having to flip through all the pages of the book.

Figure 11–22. *The page scrubber shows the page number and chapter title.*

Adjusting Brightness

Depending on your eyes, you may find it easier to read text with a brighter or darker screen. To adjust the iPhone's screen brightness while reading a book, tap the Brightness button (the one that looks like a sun) in the menu bar. A drop-down menu will appear with a slider in it (see Figure 11–23).

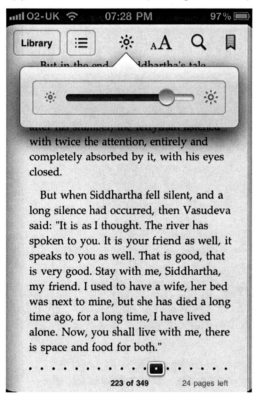

Figure 11–23. *The brightness slider*

Slide to the left to reduce brightness and to the right to increase it. When adjusting the brightness in the iBooks app, the entire screen will brighten or dim according to your slider settings, but once you leave the iBooks app, the screen brightness will return to the settings you have specified in the iPhone's Settings application. This is a great feature because you can instantly switch between brightness levels when you enter or exit the iBooks app without having to reconfigure them each time.

To change your iPhone's overall brightness levels, go into Settings on the iPhone's home screen, and choose Brightness. Adjust the slider there to set your preferred brightness.

Adjusting Font, Font Size, and Page Color

Depending on your eyesight, you may want to adjust the font size of the text. Tap the double-*A* font button to be presented with the font menu (see Figure 11–24). Tap the small *A* to decrease the font size and the large *A* to increase it. Increasing or decreasing the font size will result with fewer or more words on a page, respectively.

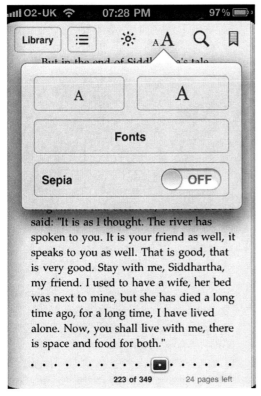

Figure 11–24. *The font panel*

Below the font size controls, you'll see a Fonts button. Tap this to select from six font types (see Figure 11–25). Different font types can affect the number of words you see on the screen slightly. Why change the font? Some people have an easier time reading different fonts, especially serif or sans serif fonts. A sans-serif font is like the font of the text of this book; there are no little lines hanging off the letters. A serif font is one like Times New Roman.

Below Fonts, you'll see the Sepia button. Tap to toggle on or off. When set to ON, the entire book will take on a yellow-brown tone, similar to how pages in an old paper book start to turn color after a while. Some people find reading from a sepia screen easier on the eyes since you aren't staring at a bright white background.

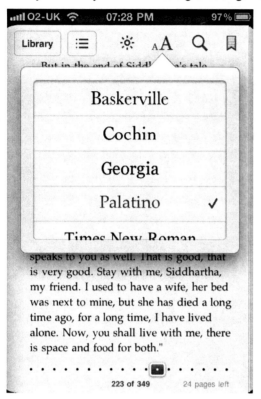

Figure 11–25. *The fonts you can choose from*

Searching Text

You can search for any word or text in the book you are reading by simply tapping the magnifying glass icon. A search field will pop up along with the keyboard. Type any search term you want, and you'll be presented with a list of results, displayed by order of page number (see Figure 11–26). Tap any result to be taken instantly to that page. On the page, your search term will have a brownish yellow bubble over it.

You can also perform a Google or Wikipedia search for your word or phrase. Below the search results, you'll see a Search Google button and a Search Wikipedia button. Tap either to leave the iBooks app. You'll be taken to Safari where the Google search results or Wikipedia entry page will be presented.

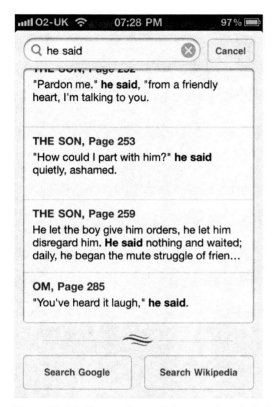

Figure 11–26. *The search panel lets you perform in-text searches as well as quickly link to Google and Wikipedia searches on the Web.*

Bookmarking a Page

Tapping the bookmark icon will cause a red bookmark to be laid down at the top of the page (see Figure 11–27). Laying down a bookmark adds a shortcut of the page to the Table of Contents/Bookmarks page so you can quickly access the bookmarked page later. Bookmarking in iBooks isn't really like using a bookmark in a physical book. In the iBooks app, the bookmarking feature is more akin to dog-earing a page on a real book, since you aren't limited to one bookmark. You can bookmark as many pages as you want. To unbookmark a page, tap the red bookmark ribbon.

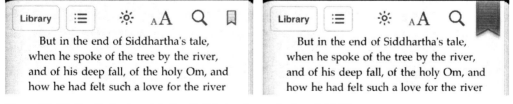

Figure 11–27. *Tap the bookmark button (left) to lay down a bookmark (right).*

Interacting with Text

Your interaction with the book's text isn't limited to search. What we'll show you next is one of the reasons why e-books are superior to traditional paper books. However, paper books still have a leg up on e-books in many ways. See the article about the two formats here: www.tuaw.com/2010/05/08/a-tale-of-two-mediums-despite-the-iPhone-traditional-books-aren/. Paper books have the advantage over e-books that they are relatively cheap (especially if you buy them used), and you don't need to be afraid to take them to a park or a beach. Sand or dirt isn't going to affect the usability of a paperback like it will an electronic device like the iPhone. Also, while reading in public, paper books are a much lower theft target than Apple's latest gadget wonder.

While on any page, press and hold your finger to the screen, and a spyglass will pop up on the page. To move it around, simply drag your finger. Below the spyglass, a single word will be highlighted in blue. When you've found the word you want, remove your finger from the screen. The spyglass will disappear, and the word will be highlighted with grab bars on either side. Drag the grab bars to select more than one word, such as a sentence or entire paragraph.

With your selection confirmed, you'll be presented with five text-selection tools from the black pop-up menu that appears (see Figure 11–28). Alternately, you can double-tap a word to bring up the contextual menu.

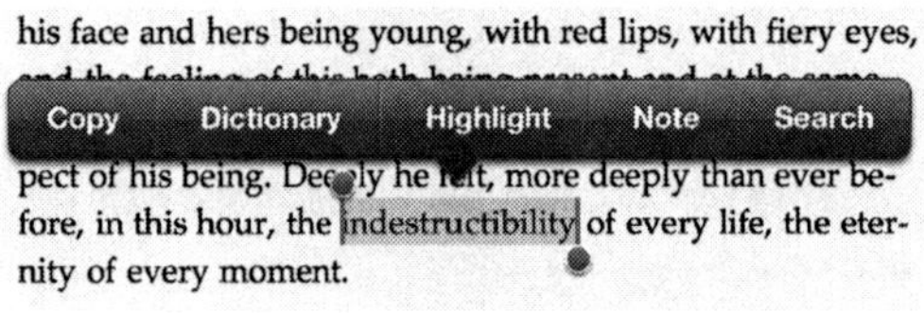

his face and hers being young, with red lips, with fiery eyes,

| Copy | Dictionary | Highlight | Note | Search |

pect of his being. Deeply he felt, more deeply than ever be-fore, in this hour, the indestructibility of every life, the eter-nity of every moment.

Figure 11–28. *The text selection tools*

- *Copy*: Select to copy the text so you can paste it into another application or the search field.

- *Dictionary*: This is our favorite feature of the iBooks app because it shows you one of the primary advantages—and ease-of-use features—that e-books have over traditional paper books. When reading a paperback book, if you don't know a word, you need to put the book down and grab a dictionary. On the iPhone, if you don't know a word in a book, you can simply select it and tap the Dictionary button. The first time you tap the dictionary command you'll get a notice that iBooks need to download a dictionary. Tap the download button to download the dictionary. This needs to be done only once. After that, a page will appear with the definition of the word (see Figure 11–29). You can then tap Done on the page to close the dictionary window and get back to reading the book. Simple.

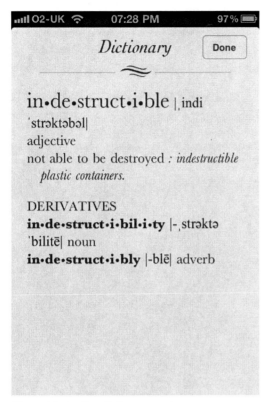

Figure 11–29. *The dictionary panel*

- *Highlight*: Tapping highlight will mark the text as if it's been highlighted by a highlighter (see Figure 11–30). Apple has outdone itself here, because the highlighting actually looks the same as it does on physical paper.

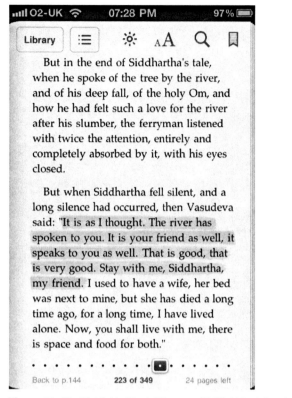

Figure 11–30. *Highlighted text. When you highlight text, it automatically gets added to the bookmarks page.*

If you tap the colored highlight, another pop-up menu appears that allows you to change the color of the highlight, create a note to go along with the highlighted text, or remove the highlight (see Figure 11–31). Color selections are yellow, green, blue, pink, and purple. Any newly selected text you choose to highlight will be highlighted the color of your last choosing. Any text you highlight will show up in a list on the bookmarks page (which we'll get to in a moment).

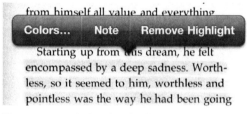

Figure 11–31. *Options for highlighted text*

■ Note: Tapping Note will automatically highlight the selected text and then cause a Post-it note to fly forward on the screen and the on-screen keyboard to appear (see Figure 11–32). You can type as much as you want in the note and scroll up and down using your finger. The color of the note will be based on the color you chose for your highlight. Tap the note's Done button to close the note. You'll see a small note icon appear on the side of the page (see Figure 11–32). Tap the note's icon to edit the note. Tap the text's highlight, and select Remove Note to delete the note.

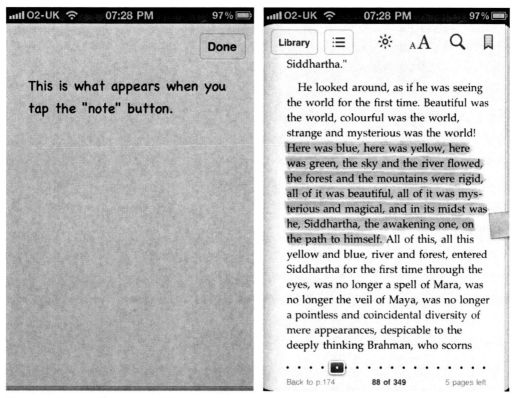

Figure 11–32. *Creating a note and the note icon in the margin of the page after creation. The note is tied to the highlighted text.*

■ *Search*: Tapping Search will open the magnifying glass search window in the upper-right corner of the page. The text you selected will be automatically filled in as the search query.

Accessing the Table of Contents, Bookmarks, and Notes

Tap the Table of Contents/Bookmarks button (the button that has three dots followed by three lines; see Figure 11–19) at the top of your page to be instantly taken to the Table of Contents/Bookmarks page (see Figure 11–33).

The Table of Contents/Bookmarks page is, unsurprisingly, divided into Table of Contents and Bookmarks sections; each has their own tab.

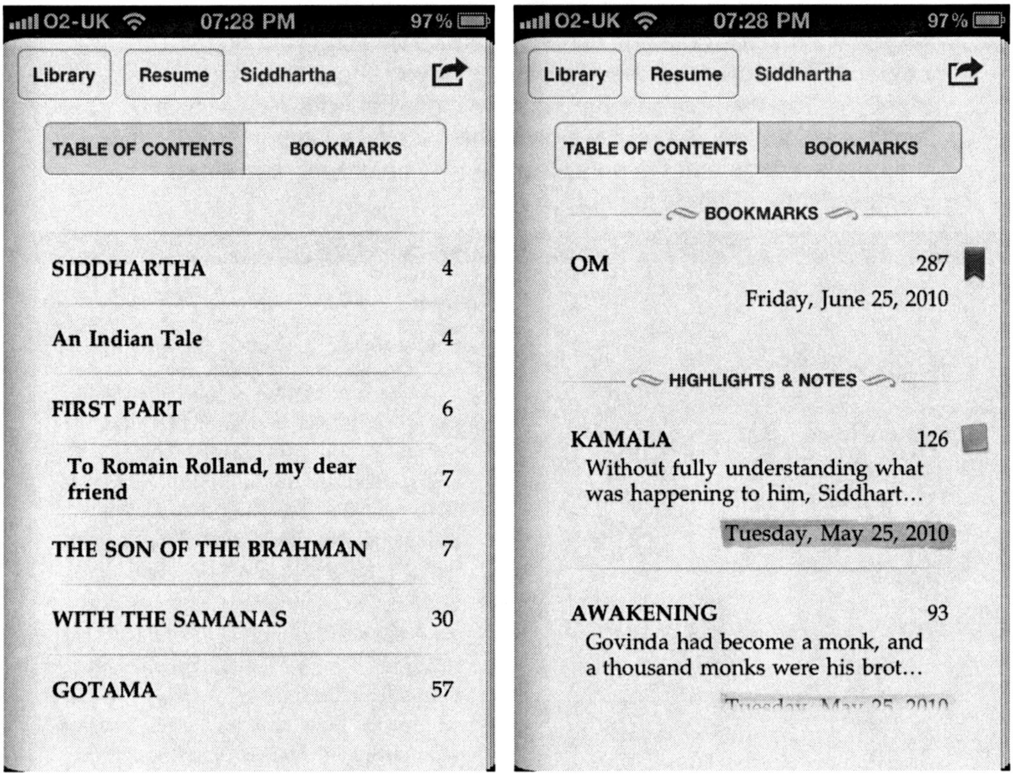

Figure 11–33. *The Table of Contents/Bookmarks page. Switch between the two by tapping the appropriate tab. Return to your last position in the book by tapping the Resume button.*

The Table of Contents tab displays the book's table of contents as a scrollable list. Tap any item in the table of contents to be instantly taken to it.

The Bookmarks tab displays all your bookmarks, highlights, and notes. They are divided into two sections: Bookmarks and Highlights & Notes. Under the Bookmarks heading, you'll see a list of chapter names or numbers that hold the bookmark, as well as the page number of the bookmark and the date you bookmarked the page. A red ribbon representing the bookmark lies next to the bookmark's page number. Tap any bookmark to jump to the bookmarked page.

Under the Highlights & Notes heading, you'll see a list of all the highlights and notes you've created. For each highlight and note, you'll see the beginning of the first sentence that the highlight or note appears in, as well as the chapter name or number and also the page number and the date you marked the page. The date is highlighted in the color that you choose to highlight the text in. This is a nice feature if you use different colors for different bookmark classifications, such as quotes from the antagonist in blue and from the protagonist in pink.

Remember than whenever you create a note, a highlight is automatically created. You can distinguish between a highlight and a note easily. Any note has a tiny sticky note icon in the right margin. To be instantly taken to any highlight or note, tap it in the list. To read a note you created without leaving the Table of Contents page, tap the note icon in the margin. The note will spring forward on the screen. You can then tap the note to bring up the on-screen keyboard to edit it. Tap the Done button on the note to close the note.

At the top of the Table of Contents and Bookmarks page you will notice a Share button in the top-right corner. Tap it to insert the TOC and your notes into an email message or print the TOC and your notes to a wireless AirPrint printer.

To exit the Table of Contents/Bookmarks page, tap the Library button to return to your bookshelf, or tap the Resume button to return to your last position in the book.

Having a Book Read to You

Not only can you read books on the iPhone, but also you can have the iPhone read books to you. Using iPhone's VoiceOver screen reader technology, you can make the iPhone read any text to you, including the text of an entire novel. We'll talked about VoiceOver in detail in the final chapter of this book, but for now we'll touch on how to activate it for iBook reading.

1. Turn VoiceOver on. Go your iPhone's home screen, and tap Settings; then choose General Accessibility VoiceOver. Tap the ON button.

2. Return to your book in iBooks. To have everything on the page read to you, use two fingers held together and flick up. Everything from the top of the screen down will be read. When VoiceOver reaches the bottom of the page, it will automatically turn it for you and continue reading.

3. To stop VoiceOver reading, tap anywhere on the screen with one finger. It would also be a good idea to return to Settings and turn VoiceOver off, unless you want to continue using VoiceOver gestures.

Now, you might be wondering why you would have VoiceOver's mechanical voice read you a book when you can just buy an audiobook and sync it to the iPhone. The simple answer is because not all books are in audiobook format. It should also be noted that the iBooks VoiceOver ability isn't a feature intended to appeal to a large number of readers but an accessibility option to help those who are hard of sight read their favorite books.

Syncing PDFs

You have two ways of syncing PDFs to iBooks on your iPhone: using iTunes or using the iPhone's Mail app. To sync PDFs via iTunes, simply drag any PDFs you want to sync into your iTunes library. They will automatically be added to the Books section of your iTunes library. The next time you sync your iPhone to iTunes, your PDFs will sync as well.

You can also add PDFs to iBooks through the iPhone's Mail app. To do this, open Mail, and select an e-mail that has a PDF attachment. Tap the attachment in the body of the e-mail to see it previewed full-screen. While previewing it full-screen, you'll see a *Share* button in the upper-right corner. Tap this button, and select *Open in "iBooks"* from the pop-up list (see Figure 11–34). Mail will close, and the PDF will automatically open in iBooks and be added to your PDF bookshelf. When you sync your iPhone with iTunes, any PDFs you have added to iBooks in this manner will be added to your iTunes books library.

Figure 11–34. *Opening a PDF in iBooks using Mail*

Navigating the PDF Bookshelf

To see all your PDFs that iBooks contains, open iBooks, and tap the Collections button in the iBooks menu bar (see Figure 11–10). From the collections menu (Figure 11–14) tap the PDFs collection. Doing so will take you to your PDF bookshelf. As you can see from Figure 11–35, the PDF bookshelf is similar to the regular bookshelf. The PDF bookshelf will be populated with any PDFs you have added to iBooks.

Figure 11–35. *The PDF bookshelf is identical to the regular bookshelf. If you know how to navigate one, you know how to navigate the other.*

Just like with the regular bookshelf, you can choose to view your PDFs as icons or in a list. In list view you will find you can sort your PDFs by titles, authors, categories, or bookshelf (the way they are arranged in icon view). List view also presents you with a search field so you can search your PDFs by name or author. The PDF bookshelf works just like the regular bookshelf in editing and deleting items as well. Simply tap the Edit button to rearrange or delete PDFs.

Navigating and Reading PDFs

To read a PDF, simply tap its cover. The PDF will fly forward and open. If it's the first time you've opened the PDF, you'll be on the first page. If you have opened the PDF before, it will open on the page you left off on.

You can view PDFs in portrait or landscape mode (see Figure 11–36).

Figure 11–36. *Viewing PDFs in iBooks*

At the top of any PDFs page, no matter what orientation you are in, you'll notice a menu that contains a series of buttons with the name of the PDF document in the center. These buttons will already be familiar to you because they are similar to the ones you see while reading an e-book.

- *Library*: Tapping this closes the PDF and takes you back to your PDF bookshelf. The next time you open the PDF, you'll be taken to the page you were on when you left it.

- *Contact Sheet*: This button is signified by three dots, each with a line after them. Tap this button to be presented with a contact sheet—a series of thumbnails of all the pages in a PDF.

- *Share*: Tap this button to email or print the PDF.

- *Brightness*: This is the button that looks like the sun and changes the screen brightness while inside the iBooks app only.

- *Search*: The magnifying glass button allows you to search through a PDF's text. It also has quick links to search Google and Wikipedia for your selected search term.

- *Bookmark*: Tap the bookmark ribbon to bookmark the current page you are on. Remember that iBooks uses bookmarks differently than traditional bookmarks are used in a paper book. Bookmarking a page in iBooks means you have effectively "dog-eared" the page. You can have multiple bookmarks in the same document. To remove a bookmark, tap the bookmark icon again.

- *Page scrubber*: This is the series of page icons that run along the bottom of a PDF's page. Drag your finger across the thumbnails to quickly navigate through the PDF's pages. You'll see the page number of the page currently selected float overhead. You can also just tap any thumbnail to jump right to that page.

While reading, you can tap the center of a book's page to show/hide the menu bar and page scrubber. While on a page, you can double-tap it to zoom in or, for more control, you can use a pinch gesture to zoom in or out. To navigate the pages of a PDF, simply swipe your finger to the left or right to move forward or backward one page. You can also tap the margins of a page to move forward or backward, or you can use the page scrubber at the bottom of the page. Alternately, you can scroll through large thumbnails representing all the pages in the PDF document by using the contact sheet.

Using the Contact Sheet

As you can now see, you already know how to use the PDF menu bar because it is so similar to an e-book's menu bar. The only feature that is slightly different is the Table of Contents button, which has been replaced with a contact sheet button (though both icons are identical—three dots, each followed by a line).

Tap the contact sheet button, and you'll see all the pages in the PDF document presented to you in large thumbnails that you can then scroll through with the swipe of your finger (Figure 11–37). This is useful when you are dealing with a very large document with lots of diagrams or images. It allows you to quickly search the PDF by eye. When you find the desired page, tap it, and you'll be instantly taken to that page in the document.

You'll also notice that some contact sheets might have a little red bookmark in their upper-right corner. This means you've bookmarked that page by tapping the bookmark button in the PDF menu bar (see Figure 11–36). To see only your bookmarked pages, tap the bookmark button in the upper-right corner of the contact sheet menu (see Figure 11–38). Any page without a bookmark will be hidden from view.

Figure 11–37. *The contact sheet lets you see all the PDF's pages as large thumbnails.*

Figure 11–38. *The contact sheet bookmarked pages view*

To leave the contact sheet, you can tap the Library button to return to your PDF bookshelf, you can tap the Resume button to return to the page you were on when you navigated to the contact sheet, or you can tap any page to be taken to that page.

TIP: Want to create a PDF on your computer? On a Mac, if you can print it, you can PDF it. Simply choose what you want to turn into a PDF, and then from the File menu of the application you are in (Word or Firefox, and so on) choose Print. You'll see a PDF button in the lower-left corner of the Print dialog box. Click it, and select Save as PDF from the drop-down menu. Name the PDF, click Save, and then drag it to your iTunes library. On your next sync, your new PDF will appear in iBooks. If you own a Windows computer, there are several options to turning documents into PDFs. You can find one such solution at `www.primopdf.com`. Google "print to PDF" to find the right solution for you.

Settings

There are a few external settings for the iBooks app. Navigate to Settings from the iPhone's home screen, and select iBooks from the Apps header on the left side. You'll see three settings (see Figure 11–39):

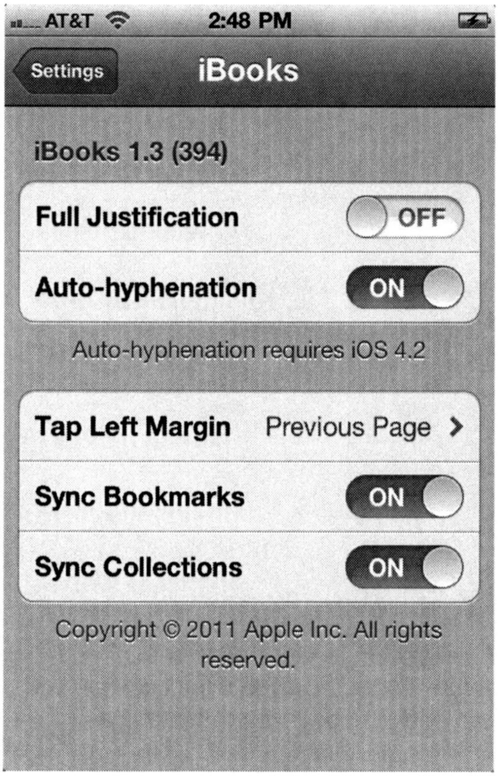

Figure 11–39. *The iBooks app settings*

Full Justification: When this set to ON, the text on a book's page will fill the width of the page evenly. When full justification is set to OFF, the text on the right side of the page will be ragged (see Figure 11–40).

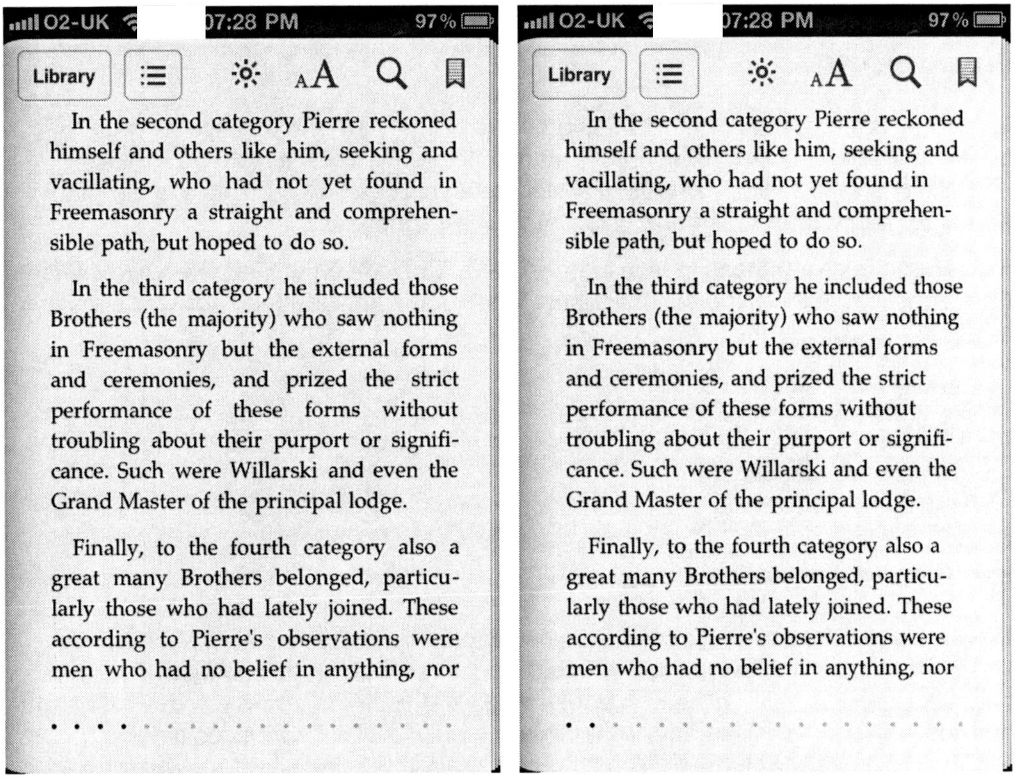
02-UK
07:28 PM
97%
Library
AA
In the second category Pierre reckoned himself and others like him, seeking and vacillating, who had not yet found in Freemasonry a straight and comprehen-sible path, but hoped to do so.
In the third category he included those Brothers (the majority) who saw nothing in Freemasonry but the external forms and ceremonies, and prized the strict performance of these forms without troubling about their purport or signifi-cance. Such were Willarski and even the Grand Master of the principal lodge.
Finally, to the fourth category also a great many Brothers belonged, particu-larly those who had lately joined. These according to Pierre's observations were men who had no belief in anything, nor
02-UK
07:28 PM
97%
Library
AA
In the second category Pierre reckoned himself and others like him, seeking and vacillating, who had not yet found in Freemasonry a straight and comprehen-sible path, but hoped to do so.
In the third category he included those Brothers (the majority) who saw nothing in Freemasonry but the external forms and ceremonies, and prized the strict performance of these forms without troubling about their purport or signifi-cance. Such were Willarski and even the Grand Master of the principal lodge.
Finally, to the fourth category also a great many Brothers belonged, particu-larly those who had lately joined. These according to Pierre's observations were men who had no belief in anything, nor

Figure 11–40. *The same page with full justification on (left) and full justification off (right)*

Auto-hypenation: When this is set to ON, iBooks will automatically hyphenate words, allowing more words to be displayed on a single page.

Tap Left Margin: You can set this to Previous Page or Next Page. If you set it to Next Page, tapping the left margin of a book will advance you to the next page in a book instead of taking you back one page. This setting might be nice while reading a book on the iPhone at odd angles, like in bed. With Next Page selected, the only way to go back one page in your book is by using the page scrubber bar at the bottom of the page.

Sync Bookmarks: When set to *ON*, this will sync a book's bookmarks, highlights, and notes between devices. This is nice if you are using iBooks on an iPad and iPhone. When you create a note or bookmark in the book on one device, it will appear on the other.

Sync Collections: When set to *ON*, this will sync your iBooks collections. This is nice if you are using iBooks on an iPad and iPhone. When you create or modify a collection on one device, it will appear the exact same on the other.

Newsstand

Newsstand is a new feature of iOS 5 that allows you to view and manage all your magazine and newspaper subscriptions in one place. We call it a *feature* because Newsstand isn't technically an app. It looks like an app, but it's actually a folder that resides on your home screen and holds all your subscriptions.

You can see the Newsstand icon in Figure 11–41. The icon on the left shows you what Newstand looks like with no subscriptions. When you start download subscriptions they appear in the icon (right).

Figure 11–41. *The Newsstand icon.*

Unlike books in iBooks, magazines and newspapers in Newsstand aren't actually text-based ePub files. Each magazine or newspaper subscription is its own individual app. What this means is that, unlike with books in iBooks, each magazine you download and view can look and act differently. Again, this is because all subscriptions are just individual apps, they all happen to just be contained in the dedicated Newsstand folder.

To open Newsstand, simply tap it, and your home screen splits to display the Newsstand shelf filled with all of your subscriptions (Figure 11–42).

Figure 11–42. *The Newsstand shelf*

The Newsstand store is part of the App Store, and it's where you'll find all of the magazine and newspaper subscriptions you can buy. To quickly get to the Newsstand section of the App Store from your Newsstand shelf, tap the Store button, and you'll be instantly taken there.

Once you have subscribed to the magazines or newspapers of your choice, the newest issues are automatically downloaded as they become available and are placed in your Newsstand. The cover of the most recent issue or the front page of the most recent newspaper is displayed at the top of that periodicals subscription stack on your Newsstand shelf.

To read an issue, tap it, and that periodical's app will open as a normal app would.

Summary

In addition to doing so many other things, the iPhone is also a breakthrough e-book and PDF reader. iBooks, the all-in-one application that lets you buy books and read, search, and mark them up, is an elegant yet powerful tool for discovering new titles and taking your entire book library with you and Newsstand allows you to subscribe to and automatically download the latest issues of your favorite magazines and newspapers. Here are a few key tips for you to carry away with you:

- You aren't limited to buying books from the iBookstore. Many web sites sell books in the ePub format that you can download and sync to the iPhone. A great place to start is `www.gutenberg.org`. Also, Googling *free e-books* will return a host of results of sites that let you download e-books for free.

- iBooks has a powerful dictionary-lookup feature that gives you the definition of a word right on the screen.

- iBooks bookshelf has many views and a search function to help you navigate your books library.

- No audiobook? No problem. You can use the iPhone's built-in VoiceOver technology to read any book out loud to you.

- Choose different colors for your notes and highlighting. Maybe use blue for passages you like and green for something you want to reference later. See all your bookmarks, notes, and highlights in one easy place (the Bookmarks page, of course!), and tap any one to instantly jump to it in the book.

- iBooks isn't limited to reading e-books. It's also a PDF reader. Now you can organize, view, and easily navigate all your PDFs—even while on the go!

- Newsstand automatically downloads your latest subscriptions in the background, so when you wake up in the morning the day's paper will be there waiting for you.

Photos, Video and the Camera

Chapter 12

Touching Your Photos and Videos

Free your photos from your home computer! Why huddle around a computer screen, when you can pass your photos from hand to hand? You can touch, explore, and interact with your captured images in a completely new way and share that experience with others. This chapter introduces you to iPhone photo and video navigation and helps you discover how to make the most of these incredibly sophisticated presentation features both for personal enjoyment and for sharing.

The iPhone's Retina display offers beautiful, clear images at higher resolutions than ever before. Its touchscreen provides intuitive interaction controls. Its wireless Internet capabilities allow you to access a huge range of still and moving content—from YouTube to the Internet archive to your own personal computer. With your iPhone, video has entered the Internet age. This chapter introduces you to both the expected and unexpected ways you can use images and video on your iPhone.

Working with Photos

Sure, you can snap lots and lots of pictures using the onboard cameras, but you may also want to transfer images shot elsewhere to the device. There are many ways you can do this: syncing photos from your computer, saving photos from e-mailed messages, saving images found on web pages, and capturing screenshots. This chapter focuses (if you pardon the pun) on the image experience instead of using the camera. The iPhone's camera features are introduced in Chapter 13.

Syncing Photos from Your Computer

iTunes synchronizes your iPhone with pictures stored on your computer. This allows you to bring your photo collection with you and share it using the iPhone's unique touch-based interface. Who needs to carry around thick and heavy physical photo albums when you have an iPhone with its thin body and vibrant display?

To get started, connect your iPhone to your computer, and launch iTunes. Select your iPhone from the source list (the blue column at the left side of the iTunes window), and open the Photos tab. Check the box labeled "Sync photos," and then choose the location of the photos you want to sync (see Figure 12–1). Your choices depend on your operating system.

On a Windows computer, your options are Adobe Photoshop Elements (3.0 or newer) or any folder on your computer, such as My Pictures. On the Mac, your options are iPhoto (4.0.3 or newer), Aperture (3.0.2 or newer), or any folder on your computer. On a Mac you'll also need iPhoto (5.0 or newer), if you want to sync videos you've taken with your digital still camera.

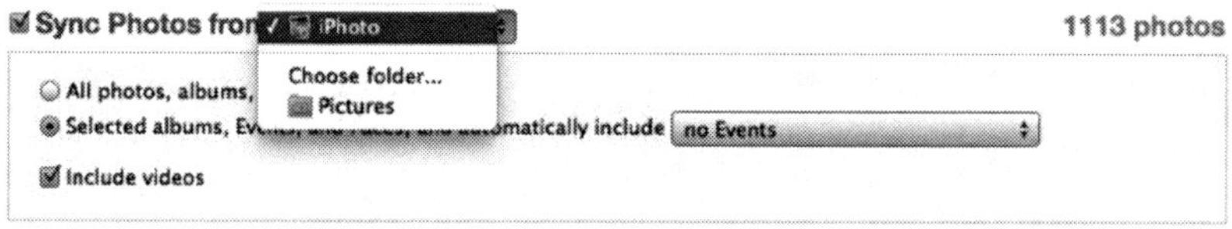

Figure 12–1. *Syncing your photos through iTunes*

After choosing where to sync your photos from, select whether to sync your entire photo collection (a good choice for relatively small libraries) or individual albums (better for large libraries that might not fit on the iPhone's limited storage space). In the latter case, pick only those albums you want to copy to your iPhone.

If you are using a Mac and iPhoto or Aperture, you'll also have the option to sync Faces (iPhoto '09 or newer) and Events (iPhoto '08 or newer) albums. Faces are smart photo albums that contain all the photos that have a selected individual's face in them. iPhoto uses built-in facial recognition software. The software "learns" as you tell it that it has or hasn't matched the right image to the person. Faces in iPhoto doesn't get the right match all of the time, but its accuracy isn't too bad given that it's an automated process. Events are another type of smart album that groups photos together that were taken on the same day. This helps eliminate clutter and keeps your photo library organized.

To finish, click Apply to save your changes and then sync.

Saving Photos from Mail and Safari

You can save photos and web page images on your iPhone without importing them from your computer or taking them with the iPhone's camera. Here's how you do this for each situation, using a tap-and-hold gesture to reveal a save menu.

When someone e-mails you a photo, the photos appear in the body of the message in the iPhone's Mail app. Tap and hold your finger on any photo. A pop-up appears allowing you to save that one photo or all the photos contained in the e-mail (see Figure 12–2). The photo or photos you've selected to save appear in the Camera Roll in the iPhone's Photos app.

In the iPhone's Safari web browser, you can tap and hold your finger on any photo in a web page and select the Save Image pop-up that appears (see Figure 12–2). That photo is saved to the Camera Roll in the iPhone's Photos app.

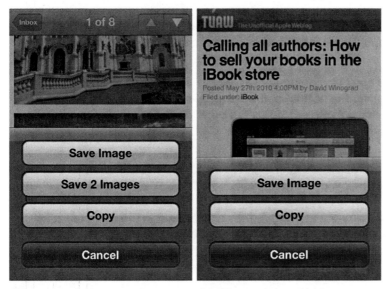

Figure 12–2. *Saving photos from an e-mail (left) or a web page (right)*

> **NOTE:** Some third-party apps including web browsers and magazines also allow you to save images to your iPhone. Some apps may introduce their own, unique way of saving images, but many follow the example set in Mail and Safari.

Navigating Your Photos in the Photos App

Once your iPhone's photo albums are populated with images, it's time to exploring the Photos app. To launch the app, tap the Photos icon on the Home screen. It's the one with a bright yellow sunflower on it, as shown in Figure 12–3. This is where the fun begins.

Figure 12–3. *The Photos app icon has a yellow dandelion on it.*

When you touch your digital photos for the first time, you feel like you've finally stepped properly into the 21st century—that promised utopian future where technology merges with your fondest memories, where you can go back and relive and explore them like never before. When you start pinching, dragging, and expanding your photos and albums, you'll feel like a child again who's just been given his first bag of marbles, spread them on the ground, and is staring wide-eyed at the colors and shapes that he can control before him.

Figure 12–4 presents the main Photo app screen, which is displayed when the app is first launched. Running along the bottom of the app is a toolbar that allows you to switch between the different ways your photos are organized. To select a view, tap its button in the toolbar.

> *Albums*: This view displays your photos in their albums as you've arranged them on your computer (see Figure 12–4). You will also see a Camera Roll album if you've saved images from the Web or if you've received them in e-mail on your iPhone. If your iPhone has a camera and you've taken any photos with it, they also appear in the Camera Roll along with any screen captures you may have taken.

Albums	Edit
Camera Roll (5)	>
Photo Library (447)	>
Favorites (9)	>
Cool pics (9)	>
2010 (17)	>

Figure 12–4. *The Photos app in album view*

> **NOTE:** Did you know you can take screenshots of your iPhone? A screenshot, or a screen capture, is an image iPhone's screen contents at the moment you snap it. To capture a screenshot, press and hold the power button on the iPhone. While holding the power button, press and release the home button. The iPhone's screen flashes white, and you'll hear a shutter click sound effect. Once you hear that sound, you can let go of all the buttons. The newly captured screenshot appears in your Camera Roll album. Use screenshots to save images of web pages (great for remembering movie show times) or show off that high score in a video game. Most of the images in this book were taken using the iPhone's screen capture function.

Events: This view organizes your photos as a series of events (see Figure 12–5). Events, which are used in Aperture 2 and iPhoto '08 and newer, are a way to automatically arrange your photos by the date they were taken. Events helps you keep large photo libraries in easy-to-navigate shape. Events is a Mac-only feature. You will not see this tab if you are syncing your iPhone with a Windows computer.

Figure 12–5. *Events view*

Faces: This view displays your photos grouped into an individual's "face" album (see Figure 12–6). If you are using iPhoto '09 or Aperture 3 on a Mac, the programs use built-in facial recognition software to establish albums of individuals and groups. It's an amazing and fun way to see all the photos of a certain friend or family member. Faces also works to some extent on cats and dogs. You will not see this tab if you have not tagged any faces or if you are syncing your iPhone with a Windows. Like Events, Faces is a Mac-only feature.

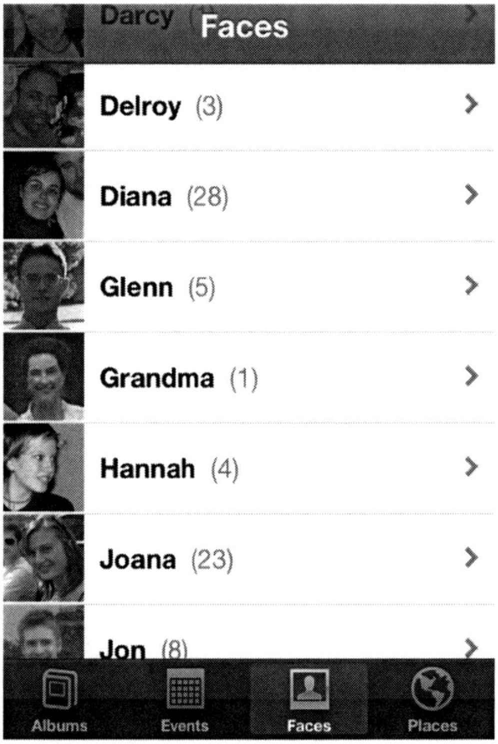

Figure 12–6. *Faces view*

Places: The iPhone's camera offers geotagging, a popular feature these days. When authorized to do so by the user, geotagging encodes the photo with the location coordinates where it was taken. The Places tab uses photo coordinates to display them on a Google map (see Figure 12–7). This is arguably the snazziest feature of Photos on iPhone because it lets you navigate your photos on a map that you can view from a global level to a street level. It's an especially cool feature for travelers: you can see at a glance where you have been and just how much of the world is left to explore.

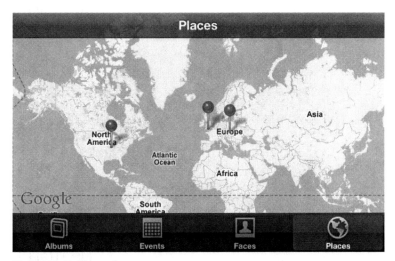

Figure 12–7. *Places view*

Red pins appear on the map signifying the geographic location of your photos. You can pinch and zoom on the map to get closer. As you do, you may see more pins appear on the map, signifying greater accuracy of the photo's coordinates (see Figure 12–8).

Figure 12–8. *More pins may appear as you zoom into an area of the map, signifying greater accuracy of the photo's coordinates.*

Tapping a pin allows an album pop-up to appear (see Figure 12–9). Tap the blue-and-white chevron button to view the Places album associated with the geographical location in question. You can then explore all the photos that were taken in that location. Places requires an Internet connection to display the Google map.

Figure 12–9. *Tap a pin to see an album and thumbnail of photos that were taken at that location.*

As you can now see, the iPhone's Photos app uses its tabs to organize your photos for easy navigation. You may not see all the views on your iPhone. Categories depend on whether you are using a Mac or a Windows computer, whether you have chosen to sync albums from each category view, and whether your photos are tagged with geocoordinates.

As long as you have one photo on your iPhone, you'll always have access to the Albums tab. For Events and Faces, you'll need to sync the data that powers them from your computer using the software that creates those special albums. You don't need to do anything to sync Places; its tab will appear automatically whenever your album any photos tagged with geocoordinates.

Touching and Viewing Your Albums and Photos

Navigating your photo collections is just the start of enjoying your photos. Get ready now to touch and view them. Remember all the gestures covered in Chapter 3? When viewing a collection of albums or a single image full-screen, the iPhone allows you to interact with that album or photo using a number of these gestures.

Touching and Viewing Albums

For this section, an *album* refers to any kind of album in Photos. The interactions with a regular album, an Events album, or a Faces album are all the same. As you can see in Figure 12–4, your iPhone might play host to many albums of many kinds. To open any album, tap it, and you'll be taken to the album page (Figure 12–10). This page contains thumbnails of all the images inside that album.

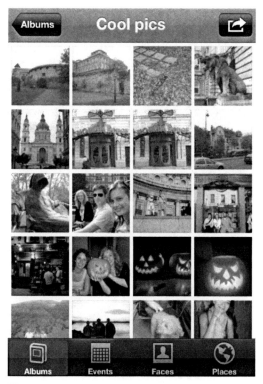

Figure 12–10. *Photos inside an album*

The menu bar at the top of the screen displays the name of the album, with a back button that takes you to the category view you were previously in. It also presents a Share button (the arrow in the box in the top-right corner), which allows you to present your photos and share them with others.

To exit the album, tap the back button. The back button uses the album's category name. In Figure 12–10, the "Favorite photos" album is part of the Albums category. The back button is always on the top left and is shaped as a five-sided pentagon, pointing left. Tap it to go back one step.

On the Places tab, the red pins on the map act as albums. This is a slightly different way of presenting albums to you. Each pin contains all the photos taken there. Tap the pin to be presented with an album thumbnail (see Figure 12–9), and then tap the thumbnail to view the album of that location.

Touching and Viewing Photos

Each album displays thumbnails of the photos it contains (see Figure 12–10). To view a photo full-screen, tap the photo once. As you can see from Figure 12–11, you can view the photo in portrait or landscape mode. Simply tilt the iPhone from horizontal to vertical or vertical to horizontal. The iPhone automatically updates the presentation to match the device orientation. If the photo was shot using landscape orientation, it fits itself to the wider view.

Figure 12–11. *Viewing a photo in landscape and portrait modes*

Interacting with Photos

Once you select and display a photo, you have several ways to interact with it. Use standard iPhone gestures to do the following:

- Pinch to zoom into and out of the photo. Pinches change the scale interactively, so you can fine-tune exactly how much to zoom.

- Double-tap to zoom into the photo using a preset zoom factor. Double-tap again to zoom out to the normal full presentation.

- Drag with your finger to re-center a zoomed-in image. After zooming into a specific face, you can move that face to the center of the screen, for example.

- When your image is displayed at the normal full-screen (zoomed-out) size, drag to the left or right to move to the previous or next image in the album. (When zoomed into an image, dragging the photo pans across it instead of moving to the next image.)

Tap any image once to invoke the image overlay shown in Figure 12–11. This overlay features a menu bar at the top and bottom of the screen, allowing you to access Photos features specific to the image being displayed. The overlay menu bar at the top of the screen indicates the number of the selected image out of the total number of images in the album and the back button to return to the album. At the bottom of the screen is the Share button and also back, play, and forward buttons. The back and forward buttons move the photos in your album back or forth one at a time. The play button allows you to start a slideshow.

You may also see an AirPlay icon (Figure 12–12, top). Looking like an upward-pointing triangle in a white rectangle, the AirPlay feature allows you to send a single photo or a slideshow to an AirPlay-enabled device, such as Apple TV (Figure 12–12, bottom). The AirPlay icon appears when you're on the same network as an AirPlay device.

Figure 12–12. *The AirPlay icon allows you to share photos and slideshows with AirPlay enabled players such as Apple TV. Tap the icon to select a destination for your photo to display on.*

Viewing Your Photos as a Slideshow

When viewing the contents of any album or a single image in any album, the Share and Slideshow buttons appear at the bottom of the screen. As the name suggests, the Slideshow buttons display the contents of a photo album, one image after another as a presentation. You can play these images back locally to the iPhone screen, over a cable to an external connected TV or monitor, or wirelessly using AirPlay.

Playing slideshows on your iPhone is as easy as tapping a single button, namely, the play button that resides at the bottom center of the screen. When you tap it, your slideshow begins displaying one photo in the selected album after the next. To stop a slideshow, tap the screen.

Upon tapping the play button, the Photos application presents you with the Slideshow Options screen (Figure 12–13). Here, you can pick the presentation style and whether to play music during the slideshow.

The Transitions options vary, depending on whether you're playing video back locally or via AirPlay to Apple TV. Apple TV offers a much wider range of slideshows (including Origami, Photo Mobile, and Ken Burns) than the relatively limited set of onboard styles (Dissolve, Ripple, and Wipes).

When you choose to play music, a new option appears on the screen called (quite obviously) Music. Tap this to open a iPod-style browser, where you can select from Playlists, Artists, Songs, and all the other built-in iPod music-selection features.

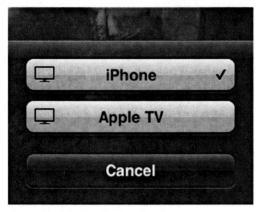

Figure 12–13. *The slideshow's options*

Other Slideshow Settings

In addition to the options you see at the commencement of your slideshow, you'll find several others in the Settings app in the Photos pane. Here, you can choose the default length of time to play each slide for (2, 3, 5, 10, and 20 seconds), whether to repeat the slideshow indefinitely, looping it at the end back to the beginning, and shuffle, which mixes up the slide playback for you.

> Apple's new Photo Stream automatically uploads all new photos to iCloud, downloading them to each of your iCloud-enabled devices. You can enable this feature in **Settings ➤ Photos**.

Slideshow Tips

Slideshows offer a terrific way to share your photos with your friends and family. Remember, however, that our images are associated with our personal memories, so they are always going to be more pleasant for us to watch than for others. All you have to do is remember a time you were stuck looking at someone else's photos, when the seconds ticked by as if they were hours. To keep your slideshows exciting for your viewers, keep a few things in mind:

Shorter is better: The average shot (a clip of video displayed between cutting away to another shot) in a movie or TV show is less than two seconds nowadays. Back in the 1950s, the average shot was 30 seconds long. Watch an episode of *Friends* and then an episode of *I Love Lucy*, and you'll see exactly what we mean. *Lucy* seems to trudge along so slowly by today's standards. As the world—and media—got faster, our attention spans shrunk. This applies to viewing still images too. People can take in a lot from an image in just two or three seconds. If they are forced to look at an image any longer, they start to get bored. Keep the time a single image is displayed short. Also, keep the entire length of the slideshow short. When you watch a movie trailer in the cinema, its time is exactly two minutes and twenty seconds—a perfect amount to whet the appetite, show people the best shots, and leave them feeling fulfilled but not exhausted.

Transitions help too: A transition is the effect that occurs when moving from one image to the next. It adds some visual flare to the change of images. Photo's slideshows allow you to choose between a number of transitions. Use them as eye candy to keep your audience entertained, but don't use any of the flashier ones if your slideshow is really long and people are forced to sit down and watch it directly. Stick to something simple (like dissolve); others will get tiring. If you plan to play slideshows in the background on a passive TV at a party, then Apple TV's Ken Burns effect offers a simple presentation that offers delicious wall candy without being too distracting.

Play it in the background: If you are having a party, a great way to show off your photos without wrangling up all your guests and forcing them to sit and watch is to project your slideshow on a TV and set it to repeat. That way, your slideshow is constantly playing in the background, and your guests can continue to catch glimpses of it as they mingle. Images on slideshows playing in the background are great conversation starters and allow you to play much longer slideshows and display individual images for longer, since you don't have to worry about a captive audience. If you are going to play your slideshows in the background, you can choose to show several thousand images for as long as five or ten seconds each; the entire show could run for hours, and it won't get boring or tedious.

Sharing Your Photos

You have a number of ways to share photos you have on your iPhone. To access all the ways you can share your photos, bring up a photo full-screen, and tap the Share button, which looks like a curved arrow breaking free from a small box (see Figure 12–11). You'll be presented with a pop-up menu of sharing options (see Figure 12–14).

Figure 12–14. *The sharing photos menu pretty much takes up the entire screen.*

E-mail Photo: Tap this to open a new e-mail composition screen. The photo is automatically copied into the body of the e-mail. Enter the recipient's e-mail, a subject, and somebody text, and then tap Send; your photo is on its way!

Alternatively, you can e-mail up to five photos at a time from within the Photos app. While in an album, tap the Share button, and you'll see the album menu renamed to Select Photos. Tap up to five photos that you want to send, and then tap the Share button at the bottom of the screen (see Figure 12–15). A pop-up menu appears with a button that says Email. Tap this button, and an e-mail compose window appears on the screen with the photos in the body of the message.

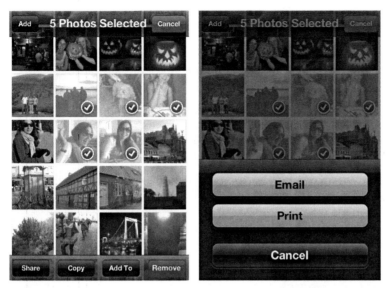

Figure 12–15. *You can e-mail up to five photos at a time from within the Photos app.*

Tweet: Tapping Tweet opens a Twitter upload screen. This allows you to tweet your picture directly to your Twitter account, which you have set in **Settings ➤ Twitter**. Add a short message to the photo and (optionally) your current location (see Figure 12–16), and you're ready to share your picture with the world.

Figure 12–16. *Tweeting a photo*

Assign to Contact: This option allows you to assign a photo to an address book contact. Tap Assign to Contact, and then select the contact's address book entry from the pop-up menu. Move and scale the thumbnail of the photo that appears, and then tap the Set Photo button.

The next time you view the contact in the iPhone's Contacts app, the image you selected for them appears next to their name. This image syncs with their contact info in Address Book, Entourage, and Outlook on a Mac, and Outlook on a Windows computer.

Use as Wallpaper: Tap this button to use the selected image as wallpaper on your iPhone. Move and scale the image, and then tap Set. From the pop-up menu (see Figure 12–17), you can select whether you want to use the image for the iPhone's lock screen, the Home screen, or both.

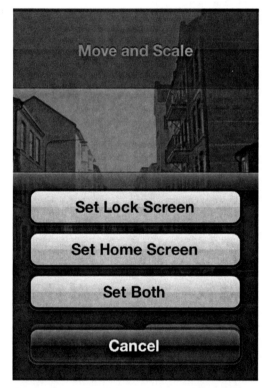

Figure 12–17. *The wallpaper menu bar options let you select which screen you want to use the photo as wallpaper for.*

Print: Tapping this prints your selected photo to an AirPrint wireless printer. Alternatively, you can print multiple photos from within the Photos app. While in an album, tap the Share button, and you'll see the album menu renamed to Select Photos. Tap up to five photos that you want to send, and then tap the Share button at the bottom of the screen (see Figure 12–14). A pop-up menu appears with a button that says Print. The photos are sent to your wireless AirPrint printer. We use Ecamm's $20 Printopia product (`www.ecamm.com/mac/printopia`) to enable AirPrinting to a Brother printer. It acts as an AirPrint server and then redirects any print requests to the normally non-AirPrint-enabled hardware. Printopia also allows us to "print" my photos to Dropbox, which is also quite handy, especially for saving paper.

Managing Photos

Each album offers a photo management screen, which is shown in Figure 12–18. You enter this mode by tapping the Share button at the top-right corner of the screen. The button looks like a curved arrow escaping from a rectangle. From here, you can copy items, move them to new albums, delete them, or share them with others.

In this screen, tapping a photo selects it. A red-circled check mark appears over the image thumbnail. Tapping a second time deselects the photo. The check mark disappears.

Your management options appear in a bar at the bottom of the screen. From here, you can tap Share, Copy, Add To, or Delete/Remove.

Share allows you to share you photos with others. Tap it to choose from sharing options including Email, Message, Print, and Tweet. The last of these, the Tweet option, does not appear when you have selected multiple images because you are allowed to send only a single image at a time to the Twitter social networking service.

The Copy option allows you to copy up to five photos at a time from your photo albums. This saves the images to your clipboard for use in pasting into other applications. You can paste photos into e-mails and Pages documents, for example. If you have selected more than five photos, the Copy option grays out.

The Add To button lets you copy the selected photos to new or existing albums. When tapped, a menu appears letting you choose how to do this. Select whether your destination is a new album (you will be prompted to enter a new name) or an existing one (you will have to select the album from a pop-up). This action does not affect the original album. The new copy is added without removing the original.

Choose Delete when you want to remove the selected items from the Camera Roll. When viewing an album other than the Camera Roll, this button is replaced by Remove. Photos prompts you to confirm that deletion (by tapping Delete Photo or Remove From Album), and you can cancel out at any time before confirming. Once deleted, you cannot undo that action.

Figure 12–18. *This photo management screen appears when you tap the Share button. Delete is replaced with Remove in individual albums.*

Deleting Photos

Apple made it so you can only fully delete photos that are part of the Camera Roll album. Otherwise, you "remove" them from the current album. The Camera Roll album contains any photos you have saved from the Web or an e-mail or that you took with your iPhone's camera. Apple disabled photo deletion from your other albums synced to your iPhone because it didn't want users accidentally deleting photos they had stored on their computer; so, you can remove those items but not delete them.

In addition to using the photo management screen discussed earlier in this section, you can also delete photos using the individual display screen shown in Figure 12–19. A garbage pail appears at the bottom right of the display. As with the management screen, the role of this button depends on the current album. Tap the garbage pail when in the Camera Roll, and you're prompted to delete everywhere. From another album, the prompt is Remove from Album.

Figure 12–19. *The trash can icon in the lower-right corner of a photo allows you to delete it or remove it from an album.*

To delete other photos on your iPhone, you must delete them on your computer first and then resync the iPhone.

Editing Your Photos

With iOS 5, Apple has introduced photo editing to the Photos app. The photo-editing features aren't especially advanced, but they do allow you to make some nice adjustments to your photos. Apple included four editing tools: rotate, enhance, redeye reduction, and cropping. To edit a photo, select a photo from your albums, and then click the Edit button in the top-right corner to enter Edit mode.

Figure 12–20. *Editing a photo. The tools, from left to right: rotate, enhance, redeye reduction, and crop.*

Figure 12–20 shows what edit mode looks like in the Photos app. The four editing tools are displayed along the bottom of the screen. Each of them offers a way to tweak your photo.

> *Rotate*: Rotating a photo is something almost everyone has done or needs to do. Usually when a photo needs to be rotated, it's because you took it in portrait, or vertical, orientation with your camera, but it was imported in the standard landscape, or horizontal, orientation. Tap this button (it looks like a curved arrow) to rotate the photo in 90-degree increments. Click the yellow Save button when you've finished rotating your photo.

> *Auto-Enhance*: Sometimes you might take a beautifully composed photo, but the color or exposure may be off. When this happens, there's no need to panic! The Photos app offers a one-click fix for most photos with ailments such as poor saturation or contrast; it's called the Enhance button, and it works almost like magic. Tap the enhance button (it looks like a magic wand) to auto-enhance your photo. Enhancing a photo can really bring out details that would normally have remained hidden without doing advanced manual adjustment techniques on it in a

dedicated photo editing app. Click the yellow Save button when finished enhancing your photo.

Red-eye reduction: Ah, red-eye—the scourge of photographers everywhere. We're all familiar with red-eye. It's the thing that makes us look like demons in photographs—the red halo that appears in people's eyes that is caused by the way the human eye reflects the camera's flash. Luckily, most of the cameras on the market today offer built-in red-eye reduction, but the iPhone does not. It won't reduce red-eye while you're taking the picture, but if your iPhone takes photos in which your friends look like they're about to unleash some heat vision, the Photos app's red-eye reduction tool makes it easy to eliminate the red tint.

To eradicate red-eye in your photos, tap the red-eye tool (it looks like a red dot with a line through it). Next, tap each eye of the person (Figure 12–21). Like magic, their red eyes gain a more natural color. Click the yellow Apply button when finished.

Figure 12–21. *Reducing red-eye in your photos. In this photo, the right eye has had red-eye reduction applied, while the left eye has not.*

Crop: Crop your photos to remove unwanted portions of them. To do this, tap the crop button (it looks like a square). Crop gridlines appear, helpfully laid out using rule-of-thirds proportions (Figure 12–22).

One of the rules for good composition is truly "classic." The ancient Greek and Egyptian philosophers discovered an important feature about beauty. Much of what we find attractive and beautiful incorporates a specific ratio, which is approximately 3:2. They called this ratio Phi (rhymes with "tie"), the "golden ratio," or even the "divine ratio." You can find this mathematical relationship abundantly in nature, such as in the way a tree grows, flowers bloom, or our body parts (fingers, hands, arms, and so on) are laid out.

The ancients incorporated this idea into their art and architecture. It was this transference from nature into art that came to be known as the rule of thirds. Basically, the rule is that things that are split into thirds, with features placed at the one-third mark and/or two-thirds mark, look better than things with more arbitrary placements. It's as simple as that.

When you place features along the rule-of-thirds lines, especially at the four intersections, you'll end up with better-composed scenes. Drag the gridlines around until you've selected the portion of the photo you want to crop. Click the yellow Crop button to apply the crop.

Figure 12–22. *Cropping a photo. Notice how the major features have been adjusted to fit the rule-of-thirds grid lines.*

You can also constrain the aspect ratio of the crop so you'll know the exact ratio between the height and width of the photo once you are done cropping it. To constrain a photo's aspect ratio, click the Constrain button at the bottom of the crop screen (Figure 12–22). The constraints screen appears (Figure 12–23).

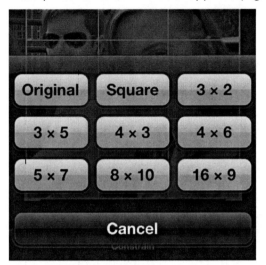

Figure 12–23. *Constraining a crop's aspect ratio*

Tap the desired aspect ratio. This matches the crop box to the specific ratio you selected. The rule-of-thirds grid updates to the new aspect. You can then drag the constrained crop box around knowing that no matter where you crop, the photo will match the selected ratio. Beware: If you drag the handles at the edges of the constrained box, you will lose that aspect ratio. To get it back, tap Constrain one more time, and again select the desired aspect.

Tap the yellow Crop button when ready to crop your photo, and then tap the yellow Save button to save your cropped photo.

> **NOTE:** You can straighten a photo while in crop mode. With the crop grid in place, use two fingers to "twist" the image left or right. As you do, additional grid lines appear to help you align your photo.

iPhone Video Applications

Video forms such a basic component of your iPhone that you shouldn't think about it as just a single application. Apple provides the base technology used by several different programs. You'll find several applications that support video playback on your iPhone (see Figure 12–24).

Figure 12–24. *Your iPhone provides not one but three primary applications that support video playback: Safari, YouTube, and Videos. What's more, there are any number of third-party apps that play videos as well.*

Videos: The Videos application appears on the Home screen of your iPhone. The icon looks like a traditional clapperboard, with a black-and-white striped top over a blue base. This application plays back TV shows, movies, podcasts, iTunes U lessons, and music videos you've synchronized from your home iTunes library.

YouTube: You'll find the YouTube application icon next to the Videos app in Figure 7-1. The icon looks like an old-fashioned TV, complete with a greenish screen and brown dials. YouTube connects to the Internet and allows you to view videos from YouTube.com. You can navigate to http://youtube.com in Safari on the iPhone and browse and watch YouTube videos that way, but the iPhone's YouTube app wraps http://youtube.com in such a nice and easy-to-navigate package, you'll find it is leaps and bounds better than using YouTube in a web browser.

Safari: Safari, which you read about in depth in Chapter 4, offers a third way to view videos. Like its computer-based equivalents, the Safari app allows you to watch embedded movie files. Safari's icon looks like a light blue compass with a needle pointing to the northeast.

In addition to the three apps that play video that come with the iPhone, there are thousands of other apps that play video. You can discover all these apps in the iTunes Store. Some of our personal favorites are YXPlayer, which allows you to view videos from a personal camcorder (it records in AVI format), the BBC News app to view news footage, and the Weather Channel app to watch weather-related news stories and Doppler video.

NOTE: Apple's latest iPhone officially supports the following video formats: H.264 video up to 1080p, 30 frames per second using High Profile level 4.1 AAC-LC audio. This includes up to 160 Kbps, 48kHz, stereo audio in .m4v, .mp4, and .mov file formats; MPEG-4 video up to 2.5 Mbps, 640 by 480 pixels, 30 frames per second; Simple Profile with AAC-LC audio up to 160 Kbps per channel, 48kHz, stereo audio in .m4v, .mp4, and .mov file formats; Motion JPEG (M-JPEG) up to 35 Mbps, 1280 by 720 pixels, 30 frames per second, audio in ulaw, PCM stereo audio in .avi file format.

You can use AirPlay Mirroring up to 720p, 30 frames per second, normal video mirroring and video out up to 1080p using the Apple Digital AV Adapter and Apple VGA adapter, up to 576p and 480p with the AV Component cable, and 576i and 480i with the AV Composite cable.

For all that the iPhone brings to video, it has limits. Your iPhone plays files using H.264 MPEG-4 video and its immediate family, and that's pretty much it. You cannot use your iPhone to natively view Flash/Shockwave videos or animation; to play AVI videos or DivX, Xvid, Matroska video; or to play any of the other dozens of popular formats. If your video isn't in MPEG-4 H.264 format, by default, your iPhone won't understand it.

That doesn't mean you cannot purchase a third-party product to handle some of these playback duties, but there's usually compromises involved especially for flash media playback.

We am very fond of the VLC/FFMPEG families of video players based on GNU-licensed open source media players. Unfortunately, because of licensing issues, the best of these clients—the official (and free) Video Lan Client app—was pulled from the App Store. We have had good success using YXPlayer, and there are any number of other smart media players as well. Check the reviews carefully when making your purchases.

For the most part, it's very easy to play AVI and MKV video on the iPhone using one of these third-party players. Pretty much universally, they permit you to add files in iTunes—whether they are from your personal video recorder or from a Windows-based capture card—and play them back on your iPhone on the road. You can then delete them from within the application as you're on the go, to free up space as needed.

Another solution is provided by transcoding servers like AirVideo and StreamToMe. For a few dollars, they provide an iPhone-based client that you purchase and a free server component that you install on your home computer, be it a Mac or Windows system. (There are even a few Linux-based solutions out there.) The server uses transcoding— converting the data in real time from its native format like AVI to an iPhone-friendly MPEG-4 version, which you can watch as it streams over a Wi-Fi connection.

Both of these approaches, a native multiformat player and the streaming transcoder, are traveler friendly, whether you're commuting on the train or bus or on a business trip.

Video Playback

iPhone video is primarily a wide-screen feature, unlike audio, which plays back in both portrait and landscape orientations. You must usually flip your iPhone on its side to view TV shows, video podcasts, movies, and music videos. Select any video—from Safari, YouTube, or Videos—to begin playback, and then flip your iPhone on its side to watch. The Home button goes to your right. Safari and YouTube provide exceptions to the landscape-only rule; in those applications, you can also watch videos in portrait orientation.

Depending on the app you are watching it in, you may see more options for the video being played or for the app itself. However, most apps display the same elements in the video interface, meaning once you know how to control video playback in one app, you know how to do it in the rest of them. Here is a quick overview of those controls, which are shown in Figure 12–25.

Figure 12–25. *The iPhone's video playback controls allow you to control playback as you watch.*

Play/Pause: Play/Pause appears as either a right-pointing triangle (Play) or a pair of vertical lines (Pause). Tap this button to pause or resume video playback.

Rewind: The Rewind button appears as two triangles pointing left to a line. Tap it to return to the start of the video, or press and hold the button to scan backward.

Fast-Forward: The reverse of Rewind, the Fast-Forward button's triangles point to the right instead of the left. Press and hold this button to scan forward. Tap it to skip to the next video track.

AirPlay: A rectangle outline with a solid triangle at its base, this option allows you to select an AirPlay destination for your video, typically an Apple TV. Choose iPhone from this menu to revert video display back to the device screen. You'll find the AirPlay button at the right side, just above the volume control. You will not see this option when you do not have a secondary AirPlay destination connected on your current network.

Scrubber bar: The scrubber bar appears at the top of your screen. It is a long line with a small knob that you can drag. (The volume control is the thicker bar at the bottom.) Drag the playhead along the scrubber bar to set the current playback time.

Zoom: The Zoom button looks like two arrows pointing away from each other, at the top-right of your screen. Either double-tap the screen or tap the Zoom button to switch between full-screen mode and original aspect ratio. To get back into the original aspect ratio's view, double-tap the screen again, or tap the zoom button again. You'll note that the zoom button changes slightly when viewing a video full-screen: the arrows have turned into a letterbox icon. When viewing in full-screen mode, you use the entire iPhone screen, but some video may be clipped from the top or sides of the video. In original aspect ratio, you may see either letterboxing (black bars above and below) or pillarboxing (black bars to either side), which results from preserving the video's original aspect ratio.

Volume: The volume control is the large line below the play/pause buttons. Drag the volume control knob to adjust playback volume. Of course, you can always use the dedicated physical volume button on the side of the iPhone as well.

Audio tracks and Subtitles: If alternate audio tracks or subtitles are available in the video you are watching, you'll see an icon that looks like a speech bubble appear in the play/pause bar. Tap this icon to select from a pop-up list of audio tracks and subtitles.

Done: The Done button appears on all video application screens. Tap Done to exit video playback. Press the physical Home button on the iPhone's bezel to quit the app and return to your Home screen.

While you're playing a video, the iPhone automatically hides your video controls after a second or two. This allows you to watch your video without the distraction of on-screen buttons. Tap the screen to bring back the controls. Tap the screen again to hide them, or leave them untouched for a few seconds, and they once again fade away.

YouTube

The YouTube app requires an Internet connection, so as long as you have a Wi-Fi connection, you're all set. But to take full advantage of the YouTube app, you'll want to have a YouTube account. You don't *need* a YouTube account to use the app, but having one makes the app that much more powerful. With a YouTube account, you can view and bookmark your favorite videos; subscribe to YouTube users videos; see all the videos you've uploaded to YouTube with the tap of a button; and share, rate, and flag videos—all from within the YouTube app. Creating a YouTube account takes only a few minutes and can be done at www.youtube.com/create_account.

To launch the application, tap the YouTube icon, which looks like a retro-styled TV set (see Figure 12–26). When launched for the first time, the application displays the Featured screen, as shown in Figure 12–27. This screen showcases YouTube's notable videos.

Figure 12–26. *The YouTube app*

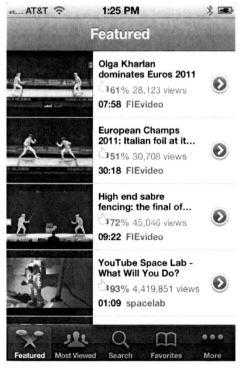

Figure 12–27. *YouTube's Featured screen provides a video showcase.*

Here are a few interaction elements you'll find on most YouTube video-listing screens:

> *Play a video*: Tap the image or name of a video to begin playback. Your iPhone connects to YouTube, downloads the video, and plays it for you.

> *View a video's info screen*: Tap the More Info button (the blue circle with the right-pointing white chevron) to learn more about the video. Read more about the info screen later in this chapter, in the "Viewing Video Info Screens" section.

> *Select another listing screen*: Choose any button along the bar at the bottom of your screen. You'll jump to the associated built-in YouTube screens: Most Viewed, Search, Favorites, and so on. Each of these screens helps you find and view YouTube videos. You can customize this buttons bar to change the buttons it contains.

Playing YouTube Videos

To play a video, tap the name or image of the video. The video appears in full-screen, as shown in Figure 12–28.

Figure 12–28. *Playing a YouTube video*

From this screen you can interact with the video in the following ways:

> *Scrubber*: At the top of the screen you'll see the scrubber bar. This allows you to *scrub*, or advance or go back, through a video. The silver dot symbolizes where you are in the video, and the white part of the scrubber bar symbolizes how much of the video has downloaded. You can skip ahead to undownloaded portions of the video, and the YouTube app starts downloading the video from that point on.

Bookmark: The bookmark button looks like a book and allows you to save a video to your favorites for easy, quick access. It is found above and to the far left of the volume bar.

Rewind, play/pause, and fast-forward: These standard buttons allow you to rewind, play or pause, and fast-forward through a video.

AirPlay: Use the AirPlay button (rectangle with up-pointing triangle) to redirect your video to an external AirPlay-enabled destination, typically Apple TV. You will not see this option if an AirPlay destination is not available on your network.

Share: This Share button allows you to send an e-mail with a link to the YouTube video in the body of the message. You can also add the video to your Favorites or tweet a link to the video. This allows you to share your favorites immediately after you watch them.

Volume slider: Located at the bottom of the screen, this allows you to adjust the volume of the video to the most comfortable audio levels.

Done: Tap this button in the upper-left corner to exit the video and return to its Info page.

Finding YouTube Videos

Each button on the buttons bar offers a different way to list YouTube videos. To find videos, tap any of these buttons:

Featured: This screen lists videos reviewed and recommended by YouTube staff. These are usually pretty high quality and worth checking out.

Most Viewed: This screen lists the most popular videos of the day, week, or all time. The All Time screen is great, because it's interesting to see a list of the planet's most-viewed videos.

Search: On this screen, enter a keyword or two, and then tap Search to look through YouTube's entire collection.

Favorites: This screen is for a collection of videos you've selected and bookmarked. Easy access to your favorite videos is always a plus because it saves you time from searching for them again.

More: Choose from six more viewing choices or customize the display:

- *Most Recent*: Showcases YouTube's newest items. Some might be good; others not.

- *Top Rated*: Lists YouTube's collection of videos that have garnered the most viewer support. This is the wisdom of the masses, so starred videos might not equal quality in every case.

- *History*: Displays recently viewed items. This is handy if you remember you watched a hilarious video but can't remember the exact name of it.

- *My Videos*: Displays all the videos you've uploaded to YouTube. This feature requires you to be logged in to your YouTube account.

- *Subscriptions*: Allows you to subscribe to another YouTube user's videos so you can keep up-to-date with the latest videos they've posted. Any subscriptions you have show up on this screen. Tap the name of the user to see all their videos displayed to the left of the list. This feature requires you to be logged in to your YouTube account.

- *Playlists*: Creates playlists of videos. When signed in, you can see any playlists you've created on YouTube.com. Playlists are handy because it lets you group related videos together (for example, exercise videos).

- *Edit* lets you choose which items appear on your shortcuts bar and which appear on the More screen.

On each of these screens, you can scroll up and down the listings and play back any video by tapping its name or icon.

Customizing the YouTube Buttons Bar

The buttons bar at the bottom of your screen is fully customizable, so it can provide quick access to the categories you view the most. Tap More ➤ Edit to make changes. Available categories appear in the screen above the bar, as shown in Figure 12–29. Select the ones you want to use, drag them down to the buttons bar, and then tap Done.

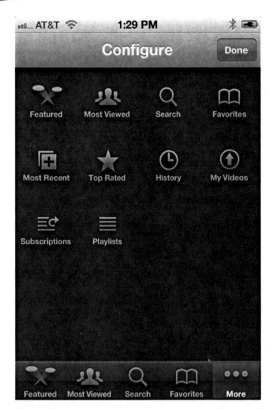

Figure 12–29. *Use this Configure screen to choose which buttons appear in the bar at the bottom of the YouTube application.*

Here are a few pointers about how this customization works:

- The buttons bar always contains four category buttons plus the More button. You cannot add more buttons or remove buttons to display fewer options.

- You cannot replace More with another button.

- If you replace a button with an item already in the buttons bar, the two items switch positions.

- There is no "revert to defaults" option. The original order is Featured, Most Viewed, Search, and Favorites.

- The items you do not include in the buttons bar appear as a list when you tap More. You can select them from that list. It's an extra step, but all the options are still available.

Viewing Video Info Screens

Video information screens provide a detail view for each video. Figure 12–30 shows a typical info screen. Here, you'll find the name of the video, its rating (in stars, from zero to five), the number of times the video has been viewed, its run time, and more. Scroll down the screen to find YouTube's suggestions for related videos.

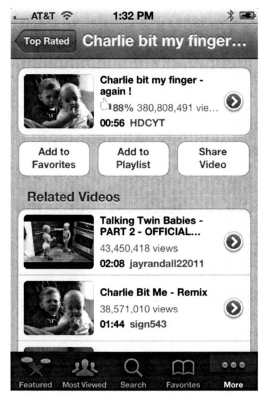

Figure 12–30. *A video info screen offers information about the video and the option to bookmark the video.*

Here is also where you'll find the Add to Playlist and Share buttons.

> *Add to Favorites*: Marks the video as one of your favorites and adds it to your Favorites bookmark list.
>
> *Add to Playlist*: Adds the video to one of your YouTube playlists
>
> *Share Video*: Creates an e-mail with a link to the YouTube video in the body of the e-mail. You can also tweet a link to the video.

To get more information about the video, tap the blue-and-white chevron button. This takes you to the More Info screen (Figure 12–31). From this screen you can read more about the video; read comments; and rate, comment, or flag the video. Tap the More Videos tab to see move videos from the user.

Figure 12–31. *A video's More Info screen gives you information about the video, links to more videos by the same uploader, and (if you scroll down) user comments.*

The Videos App

Long gone are the days when keeping entertained on long car trips required a portable DVD player and a case of discs. The iPhone's Video app lets you carry around your favorite movies, TV shows, and podcasts in your pocket and switch between them with a tap of your finger.

The Videos application icon (Figure 12–32) is colored blue and has a traditional, striped clapperboard top. Tap it to launch the program. This opens the screen shown in Figure 12–33.

Figure 12–32. *The Videos app*

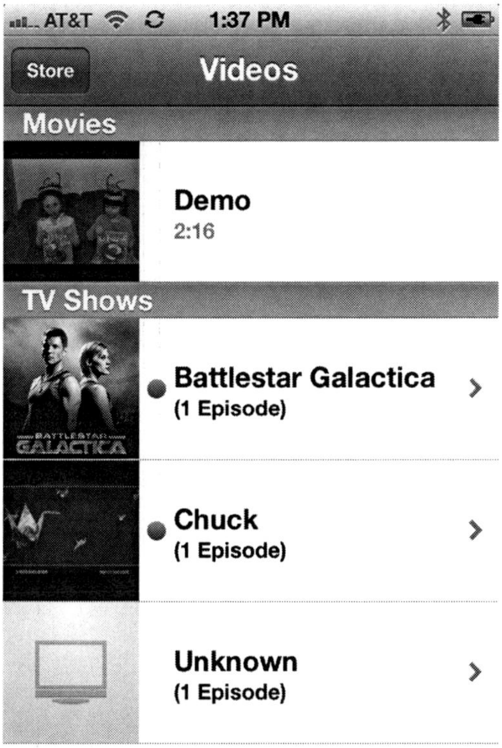

Figure 12–33. *The Videos app offers a list of music videos, TV shows, movies, and video podcasts you've synchronized to your iPhone. Episodes that are currently syncing (see the sync icon in the status bar) appear as "Unknown" until the data is finished downloading.*

As you can see, the Videos interface couldn't be simpler. It displays a series of thumbnail images representing the music videos, TV shows, podcasts, and movies you've synchronized to your iPhone (Chapter 2 introduces the art of synchronizing these items). Tap any item to begin playback. Your screen clears, and the video loads and automatically begins playing. Tap Done to return to the list screen, or press Home to quit and go to your Home screen.

Tapping the Store button in the top-left corner of the screen takes you to the iTunes Store app (discussed in Chapter 7) where you can buy music and videos.

If you tap a TV show or podcast, you'll be taken to an additional page (Figure 12–34) that lists all the episodes for the TV show or podcast that you have on your iPhone before the video begins playing. From this screen, tap the episode you want to play or tap the Get More Episodes... button to be taken to the show's iTunes Store page where you can download additional episodes.

Figure 12–34. *A TV show's page in the Videos app*

Deleting Videos on the Go

The iPhone allows you to recover space on the go by deleting videos after you've watched them. To take advantage of this feature, go to the Videos screen and swipe through the name of any video. A red Delete button appears to the right of the video name. Tap Delete to remove the video, or tap anywhere else on the screen to cancel and keep the video.

Choose your videos wisely. Even with newer iPhones with expanded memory, videos can quickly eat up your free space. And don't be shy about deleting your videos on the go. You can always sync them back on your home computer.

Getting Videos

The easiest way to get compatible official videos on your iPhone is to buy or rent them from the iTunes Store. Check out Chapter 7 for more details on buying and renting movies. You can also rip DVDs you own using desktop applications like Handbrake (http://handbrake.fr). Keep in mind local laws may prevent you from ripping DVDs, even if you own them.

If you take home movies using small portable "flip"-style video recorders, your video may not be compatible with Apple's Videos software. In this case, you can use Handbrake-style tools to convert them to H.264 compatible movies, or you can purchase third-party applications that handle their format natively. Typically they record using AVI. Bringing home movies along to share on trips can be a great way to share your life with others, but plan in advance so your video formats don't trip you up during playback. Another great way, of course, to virtually "share" your kids, your spouse, and your friends is to use FaceTime for live video conferencing between iPhones.

Video Settings

Several settings affect your video playback. These settings are accessed through the iPhone's Settings application (see Figure 12–35) and control how your video is played on your iPhone and when your iPhone is connected to your TV. Choose **Settings ➤ Video** to view them.

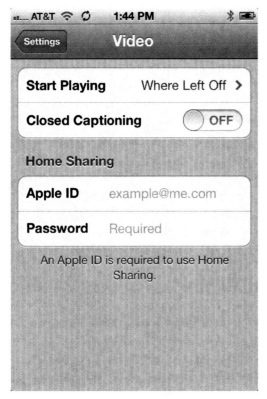

Figure 12–35. *The Video app's settings*

For your iPhone video settings:

> *Start Playing*: Choose whether to start playing videos from the beginning or where you left off. If you do a lot of product demos, set this option as "from the beginning." That way, each time, you're ready to demonstrate using freshly queued up videos. If you're a commuter who catches just a bit of your favorite show at a time, leave it set as "Where left off." This allows you to keep watching sequentially, picking up each time from your previous stopping point.

> *Closed Captioning*: If your video contains embedded closed captions, you can view them by switching on the Closed Captioning option. Switch the option from Off to On. Closed Captions aren't just for the hard of hearing. They can help out when you're viewing videos in noisy conditions such as on public transportation or when your training seminar accidentally got scheduled next to a construction zone.

Home Sharing allows you to share media assets over a local network without having to sync those items over to your iPhone. It provides a live feed of data from any home computer registered to your Apple ID. For your Home Sharing settings to work, your iPhone and computer must be connected to the same wireless network, and iTunes must be open on your computer for your iPhone to see its videos.

> **NOTE:** Unfortunately, the iPhone does not allow you to turn off your screen and continue listening to the audio track from your video. Tap the Sleep/Wake button, and your video playback ends. You can, however, diminish the screen brightness levels in **Settings ➤ Brightness**. This is not much of a win. Your iPhone continues using (energy-consuming) video decoding to play back video as well as audio.

Watching Videos on the Web with Safari

Video on the iPhone isn't limited to special-purpose applications. You can also watch MPEG-4 movie files with the iPhone's Safari application. Chapter 4 introduced Safari. Here you'll see how you can connect to video on the World Wide Web and watch it in your Safari browser.

Many web sites besides YouTube feature embedded video. For example, go to virtually any news site, and you're sure to find embedded video. The iPhone, and thus Safari, does not support Flash playback natively, which limits the iPhone's ability to display every single video on the Web. However, many web sites now serve HTML5 and MPEG-4 videos, and these are fully iPhone-compliant. HTML5 is particularly exciting because it's an open web standard that allows developers to create fully interactive content that is optimized and compatible to today's (and tomorrow's) touchscreen devices. HTML5, unlike Flash, does not require that the user download and install a special plug-in to view video content.

For example, the web site TED (www.ted.com) where you can watch videos of some of today's greatest minds talk about science, education, technology, and art is fully iPhone-compatible, and it achieves this by being written in and having the videos encoded in HTML5. Figure 12–36 shows this site's video of author Elizabeth Gilbert talking about creativity playing back in the iPhone's Safari web browser.

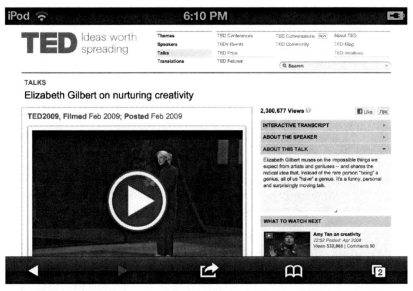

Figure 12–36. *Many videos on the Web can be played natively in the Safari web browser.*

Tap an embedded video to begin playing it. The video opens in the usual video playback window, and you'll have the option of using AirPlay to redirect the video to an AirPlay-compatible destination if one is available on your local network. Depending on the speed of your Internet connection, it may take a few seconds before the video begins playing. Watch the video, and when you're done, tap the Done button in the video playback screen to return to the Safari web page.

Streaming Video to Your Apple TV with AirPlay

Just as Home Sharing allows you to stream video from your iTunes library on your computer to your iPhone, another technology called AirPlay lets you stream video from your iPhone to your AppleTV.

An Apple TV is an inexpensive (US$99) set-top box that you plug into your HDTV. With this box, you can rent movies and TV shows from the iTunes Store directly on your TV. The Apple TV connects to the Internet wirelessly and also communicates with your computer, iPhone, iPhone, or iPad wirelessly. Once you have your Apple TV set up, start watching a video on your iPhone, and then tap the AirPlay icon (Figure 12–37) that appears in a video's control bar to instantly stream that video to your TV.

Figure 12–37. *The AirPlay icon appears in a video's control bar when your iPhone detects nearby AppleTVs or potentially other AirPlay receivers when third-party units become available.*

AirPlay is, essentially, the opposite of Home Sharing. Instead of sending data from a nearby computer to your iPhone, AirPlay allows you to redirect video or audio to an external player. It's a particularly handy feature because you can start watching a video on your iPhone on your commute home from work, and when you get home, you can finish watching the video on your TV with the tap of a button.

AirPlay also allows you to mirror your iPhone 4S screen to the big-screen TV for live gaming and product demos. This option is not available on earlier iPhone units. To access this option, you'll need to follow these steps. First, double-click the Home button to reveal the recent applications tray. Swipe your finger from left to right twice. The first swipe brings you to playback controls. The second to volume and AirPlay (see Figure 12–38).

Here, you'll find yet another AirPlay control. Tap it to select your AirPlay destination. Instead of rerouting video, however, it will mirror your entire screen.

Some applications are smart enough to use this feature in another way. Instead of standard mirroring, they treat that external AirPlay destination as a second—very large—output screen, allowing you to use your iPhone for game controls and your home HDTV for game play.

This feature is just coming online as this book was being written, so we do not as-yet have specific games to recommend, but keep your eye out for this option. It's going to be one of the most compelling reasons to purchase the iPhone 4S model because nothing beats gaming on a very, very, very big screen.

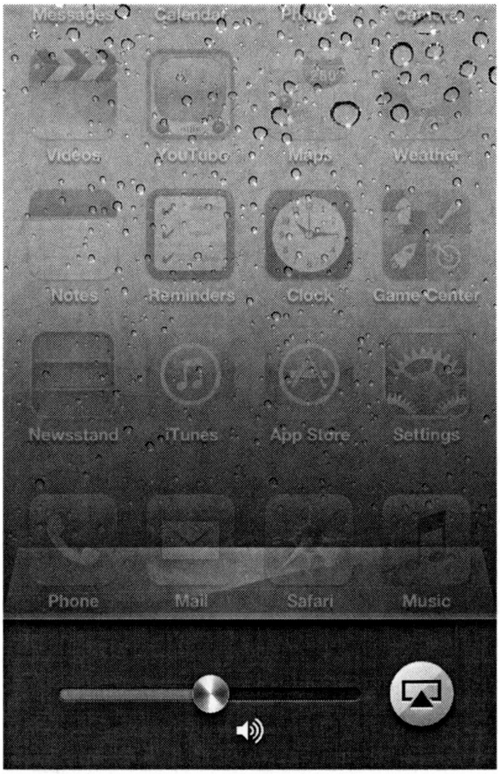

Figure 12–38. *AirPlay mirroring is available exclusively on the iPhone 4S and newer and the iPad 2 and newer.*

Video Accessories

As far as video goes, there are several iPhone accessories besides the AppleTV you may consider purchasing.

> *Stands*: Several companies make them, and they range in price, typically from $5 to $30. Whatever stand you choose, if you are planning to prop the iPhone up while watching video, make sure it holds the iPhone steady in landscape mode. By the way, business card holders make excellent stands for use while you're traveling on airplanes.

> *iPad Dock Connector to VGA Adapter* ($29): Yes, its name says "iPad," but it works just fine with the iPhone. The VGA end of the adapter can be connected to external monitors, some TVs, and PC projectors. You'll need this or the cables below to connect your iPhone to your home television.

> *Apple Component AV Cable* ($49) and *Composite AV Cable* ($49): These also work with the iPhone, providing two more methods of linking external monitors and projectors to the device.

Apple Digital AV Adapter ($39) This cable links your iPhone to HDMI output, so it can be used with most HDMI television sets.

Each of these cables are types of physical video connectors that link devices to TVs.

- *VGA* is a 15-pin connector that you can still find on the back of many PCs. It supports resolutions up to 2048x1536.

- *Composite* is a video connector that channels three video source signals through a single connection. It's the oldest of the three technologies but still supports a resolution of up to 720x576i.

- *Component* is a video connector that takes three video source signals and outputs them through three different connections. It's basically a Composite cable with three heads, but Component offers a much better resolution, up to 1920x1080p (otherwise known as "Full HD"). The Apple adapter can output up to 576p, even though the format is more capable than that.

- *The Apple* Digital AV Adapter provides HDMI-compatibility with up to 1080p output. It is also compatible with the fourth-generation iPod touch and all models of iPad.

Many modern TVs provide compatibility with some or all these connections. Check your TV's manual to see which yours supports.

Summary

This chapter introduced you to the iPhotos app of the iPhone and showed you how to navigate your photo collections in a variety of ways. It also demonstrated how your iPhone's wide-screen video features and interactive touchscreen are in a class of their own. They offer clear, easy-to-watch video on a (relatively) large screen. In this chapter, you've seen how to watch video from YouTube, the Videos application, and Safari. Here are a few points you should take away and consider:

- The iPhone's Photos application offers some of the most instantly appealing ways to show off the power of your iPhone. You can scroll through your albums, zoom in and out with a pinch or double-tap, and flip the unit on its side. These features all deliver the iPhone wow factor.

- You aren't limited to just viewing photos on your iPhone, you can also apply simple edits to them to make them look their best and use AirPlay to send slideshows to your Apple TV.

- You have several ways to navigate your photos: by album, by face, by event, or by place. By far the coolest way is Places, which shows you your photos on a map, based on the location where they were taken.

- Consider investing in an inexpensive business card holder as a stand for your iPhone. It makes watching slideshows on your iPhone a lot easier, especially for more than one person at a time. A video-out cable from Apple increases the fun by sending the slideshows to a TV screen.

- Apple TV may seem like a $99 boondoggle, but once you have one, you'll discover just how wonderful it is to be able to redirect your iPhone 4S's video output to the big screen. Plus, being able to present slideshows at parties is a great way to add a unique personal touch to your decorations.

- Pick the YouTube listings that you like best. The buttons bar at the bottom of the screen is fully customizable. If you prefer to view the Top Rated videos over the Most Viewed, feel free to drag that option to your bar.

- Use the red Clear button at the top-right corner of the History screen to erase your YouTube viewing history. People don't have to know you've been watching that skateboarding dog.

Chapter 13

Photographing and Recording the World Around You

Every iPhone since 3G offers two cameras—one in the front and one in the rear. These cameras represent two of the most significant features of the iPhone: the ability to take photos and record high-definition video and the ability to place FaceTime video calls. Each generation represents a major improvement in technology over the hardware that preceded it, and each camera upgrade has provided a significant advancement in technology.

With the iPhone 4S, the primary iPhone camera on the reverse of the unit has gone from excellent to amazing. With 8 megapixels and improved optics, Apple isn't far off when it states in its marketing text that this might be the best camera ever on a mobile phone.

The 8-megapixel camera provides 60 percent more pixels than the iPhone 4 ever did, and that camera was engineered with amazing light collection features. Its quick responsiveness and improved optics mean you can capture pictures better and more beautifully than ever before. You can catch images of water as it splashes and leaves as they twirl down from the trees, and you can do all this without blurring and fuzziness. With its incredible dynamic range, you can capture pictures in candlelight and full daylight.

The Camera Hardware

The iPhone features two cameras—one front and one rear. The lower-resolution front camera is meant for video conferencing and social use. The high-end rear camera helps you snap photos and record high-definition video for your personal memories.

Front Camera

The front camera is located at the top of the iPhone, directly in the center of the iPhone's upper bezel. If you shine a light directly on your iPhone, you can make out a tiny opaque dot about the size of a pencil tip. Behind this dot lies the front-facing camera.

This camera opens up the world of FaceTime video calls (see Chapter 14), although you can also take photos and record video with it. It's also a great tool for taking self-snapshots for profile pictures for social networking sites. No more shooting your picture in a bathroom mirror or turning the camera around and hoping you get yourself in the shot! With the front camera, you can see and compose the shot as you take it.

The front-facing camera isn't as powerful as the rear camera. It doesn't record high-definition (HD) video. High-definition video is defined as video that has at least 720 lines of resolution. The more lines of resolution, the sharper the picture. Although the front camera can record video, its resolution is limited to standard-definition (SD) VGA-style video at up to 30 frames per second. SD video has a resolution of 640x480.

Why didn't Apple use an HD camera in the front? Well, it would be unnecessary. The front camera was designed for video calling and playing around, not for recording video. The image quality while video calling on a small device like the iPhone is more than good enough using an SD camera.

Rear Camera

The rear camera is the primary one you will be using to take photos and record video. If you flip your iPhone over, you'll see the rear camera in the top-left corner of the device.

The iPhone 4S rear camera will record videos in 1080p HD resolution at 30 frames a second; that's HDTV-quality video. Its still-camera capabilities are far better than the front-facing camera; the rear-facing camera can take 8-megapixel photographs, a massive improvement over the previous iPhone 4 model.

This high-quality camera means that the iPhone 4S is ready to snap good-quality pictures suitable for framing. You can bring your iPhone on vacation for once-in-a-lifetime nature photography, to social events to capture moments from your wedding, or even to your baby's birth. The iPhone 4S is completely up to the task.

NOTE: What's the *p* stand for in 720p? you ask. P means progressive. When HD video is displayed on a screen, it shows either all 720 lines of resolution at a time or just half of them. If it shows only half of them, this is known as *interlace video* and is denoted with an *i*. Simply put, progressive video generally looks sharper because it shows you all the data (or lines of resolution) in a single frame at a time, and interlace shows you only half the data at a time (followed quickly by the other half). Interlace video used to be the norm when bandwidth issues were more of a factor, but as bandwidth increased, progressive video slowly took over.

Real-World Use

In real-world use, the iPhone 4S does a superior job at recording HD video and still photographs. The iPhone uses a light-sensitive sensor, which can be used in a wide range of lighting situations. This sensor allows for the best image quality the hardware can record. Because of this sensor, even in low-light conditions, the quality is still very good.

Navigating the Camera App

To launch the Camera application, tap the Camera icon. It looks like a gray button with a camera lens on it (see Figure 13–1). The camera can be used in either portrait or landscape mode. Simply rotate your iPhone to switch between the two orientations.

Figure 13–1. *The Camera app*

Figure 13–2 shows the standard layout of the Camera app. With the exception of the Switch Camera and Options buttons at the top of the screen, all the camera controls reside in the gray bar at the bottom of the screen in portrait orientation. When you rotate into landscape orientation, the Switch Camera and Options buttons remain at the top of the screen, but the camera control bar shifts to the left (or right) of the screen. The icons on the control bar simply rotate to match your iPhone's orientation.

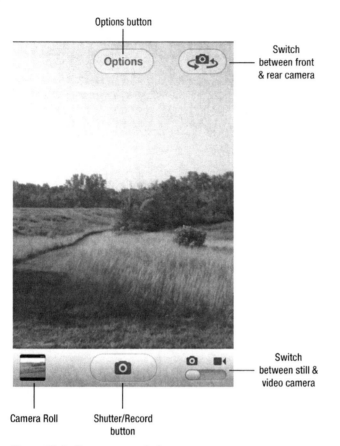

Options button

Switch between front & rear camera

Switch between still & video camera

Camera Roll

Shutter/Record button

Figure 13–2. *The camera controls*

The camera controls are as follows:

Switch between still and video camera mode: Tap the slider that lies below icons of a still and video camera in the right of the control bar. The camera icon with the slider button below it is the mode the camera is in (in Figure 13–2, the slider is below the still camera, so you know that you are in still-camera mode).

Switch between cameras: Tap the Switch Camera icon in the top right of the screen to switch between the front and rear cameras. The icon looks like a traditional still camera with swirling arrows on either side. You'll see a 2D animation of the screen flipping between cameras.

Select flash mode: Tap the flash mode toggle at the top left of the screen to choose the flash mode. Options include Auto, On, and Off. In Auto mode, the iPhone detects the light levels. In On mode, the flash is always used when snapping photographs. In Off mode, the flash is disabled.

Options: This button allows you to access the camera gridline overlay that helps you compose images using the classic rule of thirds and the HDR toggle. With High Dynamic Range (HDR), the camera captures three photographs from your one shot, each with a different exposure level. It then combines these shots to create a single photo, capturing the best quality elements from each of the component shots. The iPhone can save both the original image and the HDR-enhanced photo to your camera roll (via an option in **Settings ➤ Photos**), so you can see the difference that HDR makes.

Shutter button: Tap the oval button with the icon of a traditional still camera in the center of the control bar to take a still photograph. This button changes to an oval button with a red dot in the center when you are in video camera mode. Tap the button to record video. Tap again to stop recording. If you have your finger on the Shutter/Record button but then change your mind about photographing or recording your subject, you can slide your finger off the button and no image will be taken, nor will video begin being recorded.

Access the Camera Roll: Tap the square button on the left of the control bar. The square will be filled with an icon of the last image or video recorded. Once tapped, your Camera Roll will slide up on screen. This is a great feature for reviewing your last photo or video. It saves you a lot of time since you don't have to leave the Camera app to check out your Camera Roll in the Photos app.

Taking Still Pictures

Taking a still photograph couldn't be easier. Point your camera at what you want to take a picture of, and tap the shutter button. You can also press the topmost volume button on the side of your iPhone. While in camera mode, the topmost volume button acts as a shutter button. You'll hear a shutter click sound effect and see a brief animation of a lens's iris quickly closing and then opening. After that, the still image you just took will jump down into the Camera Roll icon.

> **NOTE:** Some people find that tapping the on-screen shutter button to take a still photo causes their composition to get messed up. A neat trick Apple included to counteract any accidental nudging when you tap the shutter button is this: tap and hold the shutter button and *then* compose your shot. When you are ready to take the photo, simply remove your finger from the shutter button, and the shot will be recorded.

Autofocus and Exposure

You can set the exposure of the camera by tapping anywhere on the screen. You'll see a white box with crosshairs quickly appear. The iPhone's camera reads the exposure setting of the part of the image inside the box and adjusts the image accordingly.

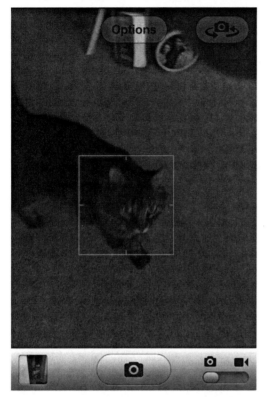

Figure 13–3. *Tap the screen to autofocus and set the exposure.*

Setting the exposure helps when you are shooting an image of a cloudy sky, for example. If you want the sky to appear other than blinding white, tap the area of the image on your iPhone's screen, and the exposure will adjust accordingly. When you tap any portion of the image, the camera will also autofocus on the part of the image.

Composing Shots with Gridlines

There's a tenet in photography called the "rule of thirds," which was first introduced in Chapter 12. It states that pictures that are split into thirds, with features placed at the one-third mark and/or two-thirds mark, provide better composition than images with more arbitrary placements.

When you place features along the rule-of-thirds lines, especially at the four intersections, you'll end up with better-composed scenes. You can also use the rule of thirds to sequester items; that is, you can limit the subject of your shot to one-third of the screen—preferably the outer edges—to make for a much more interesting shot. Both sequestering and composition can be helped when you can see a grid on your screen.

With this in mind, Apple built gridlines into the Camera app. To turn on Gridlines, tap the Options button (Figure 13–2) and set Grid to On (Figure 13–4). Gridline will appear on your screen dividing it into nine squares. Tap Done to exit the options menu. To turn off Gridline, go back into options and set Grid to Off. While gridlines appear on your iPhone screen, they will not appear in your photographs. They are provided for composition only.

Figure 13–4. *Turning on gridlines helps you compose your shots using the rule of thirds.*

Pinch to Zoom In and Out

To zoom in or out, simply pinch the screen with two fingers. The zoom slider appears (Figure 13–5). This zoom bar allows you to adjust the digital zoom settings of the photograph; it lets you zoom in and out on your subject. Slide your finger along the bar to zoom in or out. You can also tap the + or – button to zoom in or out in increments or simply continue pinching in or out

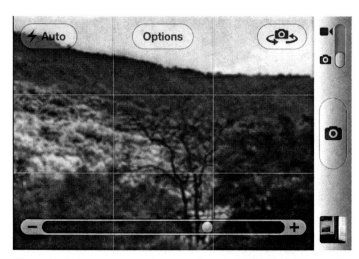

Figure 13–5. *The zoom controls appear above the control bar while tapping the screen in still-camera mode.*

> **NOTE:** You can zoom in only while in still-camera mode using the rear camera. You cannot zoom using the front-facing camera. There is also no zoom while in video camera mode.

Recording Video

To record video, set the slider in the control bar to video camera mode. The camera's shutter button will be replaced with a recording button (see Figure 13–6). Tap the record button to begin recording your video. The red dot on the record button will begin to glow, and a time code stamp will appear in the upper right of the screen showing the hours, minutes, and seconds that have elapsed since recording began. To stop recording, tap the record button again. While recording, double-tap the screen to enter the 16:9 aspect ratio.

Just how much video can you record on your iPhone? That depends on the size of your iPhone and how much space you have available. If you have a 32GB iPhone but have only 10GB of free space on it, you'll be able to record only 10GB of video. The rear camera with its 1080p video recording can eat up your available storage very quickly. The front camera will be far more forgiving.

Figure 13–6. *The video-recording screen shows the time elapsed while recording. Double-tap the screen to enter 16:9 aspect ratio.*

> **TIP:** If you are going to be using the recorded video in a movie or be viewing it on your TV, you might want to make sure you are recording in landscape mode. You can record in portrait mode, but portrait mode is a weird aspect ratio to view videos in.

Changing the Autofocus and Exposure

As with still images, you can set the autofocus and exposure of recorded video. You'll see a white box with crosshairs quickly appear. The iPhone's camera reads the exposure setting of the part of the image inside the box and adjusts the video's exposure settings accordingly. When you tap any portion of the image, the camera will also autofocus on the part of the image.

Accessing Your Camera from the Lock Screen

An amazing new feature of iOS 5 is the ability to quickly access your camera from your iPhone's lock screen. This feature eliminates precious time wasted from having to unlock your iPhone, then swipe to the Camera app, and the tap its icon to open it. Now you can simply access the camera from the lock screen and get that spontaneous shot.

To access your camera from the lock screen, simply double-press the physical home button on your iPhone. Doing so brings up audio playback controls on the lock screen and a shortened slider bar. As you can see in Figure 13–7 there's also a camera icon next to the slider bar. Tap it to be immediately taken to your camera.

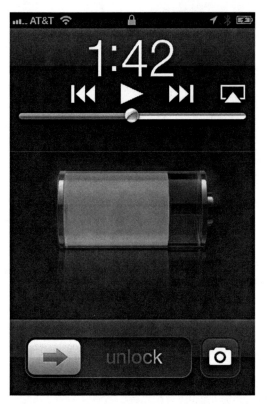

Figure 13–7. *Accessing the camera from your iPhone's lock screen*

Viewing Your Camera Roll

To view all the photos you have taken and the videos you have recorded, tap the Camera Roll icon in the left of the control bar. The last image or video you recorded will appear on the screen. Tap the Camera Roll arrow to be taken to the Camera Roll (Figure 13–8).

Figure 13–8. *The Camera Roll contains all the photos and videos you have taken with the iPhone's camera.*

To view any individual photo or video, simply tap its thumbnail. Photo thumbnails appear as a picture square, while video thumbnails appear as squares with a single frame of the recording representing the video. A small camera icon with the length of the video in minutes and seconds overlays a video thumbnail's image.

> **NOTE:** When accessing the Camera from the lock screen, you'll only be able to view Camera Roll items that you take from the lock screen. Other items in your Camera Roll remain hidden for privacy purposes.

Viewing Individual Photos

When in your Camera Roll, you will see thumbnails of the photos it contains (see Figure 13–8). To view a photo full-screen, tap the photo once. As you can see from Figure 13–9, you can view the photo in portrait or landscape mode.

Figure 13–9. *Viewing a photo in landscape and portrait modes*

Once you display a photo full-screen, you have several ways to interact with it:

- Pinch to zoom into and out of the photo.

- Double-tap to zoom into the photo. Double-tap again to zoom out.

- When your image is displayed at the normal zoomed-out size, drag to the left or right to move to the previous or next image in the album. When zoomed into an image, dragging the photo pans across it.

While viewing individual photos, flip your iPhone onto its side to have your photo reorient itself. If the photo was shot using landscape orientation, it fits itself to the wider view. Tap any image once to bring up the image overlay, as shown in Figure 13–9. The image overlay features a menu bar at the top and bottom of the screen.

The image overlay menu bar at the top of the screen shows you the number of the selected image out of the total number of items in the Camera Roll and shows you the back button, labeled Camera Roll, to return to the album. You can tap the Done button to exit the Camera Roll and return to the Camera app.

At the bottom of the screen you'll see the Share button (it looks like an arrow breaking free from a small box) and also a play button. The play button allows you to start a slideshow. Tapping the trash can icon will bring up a deletion confirmation menu. Tap the red Delete Photo button to delete the selected photo.

Viewing Videos

To view any video you have recorded, simply tap its thumbnail in the Camera Roll. The video will appear with a big play button in the center. Tap any area of the screen once to bring up the on-screen video controls (Figure 13–10).

Figure 13–10. *Displaying video from the Camera Roll. Tap once to bring up the on-screen menus.*

Once you display a video full-screen, you have several ways to interact with it:

- Tap the video once to play it. Tap again to pause it.

- Scrub through the video by tapping and holding the silver drag bar in the scrubber bar. The scrub bar shows you segments of the video represented by thumbnails for those segments.

- Hold your finger on the scrub bar for a few seconds, and you'll see the scrub bar stretch out. This gives you finer control over finding a specific spot in the video.

The video overlay menu bar at the top of the screen shows you the number of the selected video out of the total number of items in the Camera Roll and shows you the back button, labeled Camera Roll, to return to the main Camera Roll. You can tap the Done button to exit the Camera Roll and return to the Camera app.

At the bottom of the screen you'll see the Share button and also a play button. The play button allows you to start playing the video. Tapping the trash can icon will bring up a deletion confirmation menu. Tap the red Delete Video button to delete the selected video.

The AirPlay button (the rectangle with the embedded triangle) appears only when there's a valid AirPlay destination (typically an AppleTV) on your local network. To play the video out to AirPlay, tap the button and select the destination from the pop-up menu. Choose iPhone to restore the video to the built-in device screen.

Editing Your Video

Apple has included limited video-editing functionality in the Camera app. Video editing isn't exactly the right word, though. *Trimming* is more accurate because you can shorten, or *trim*, the video at the front and end of the clip.

To trim a video, bring up the video menu overlays (see Figure 13–11). Next, grab the beginning of the scrub bar, and pull it to the right. This activates trim mode (Figure 13–14).

Figure 13–11. *Video trim mode*

In trim mode, you can drag the ends of the scrub bar, now outlined in yellow, toward the center. Dragging the ends shortens the clip at the beginning and the end.

Trimming is a great feature that allows you to highlight just the really good portions of your video clips. When you've adjusted your trim commands, tap the yellow Trim button to bring up a Trim pop-up menu (Figure 13–12).

Figure 13–12. *The Trim pop-up menu lets you trim the original or save the trim as a new clip.*

The Trim command presents you with three options:

> *Trim Original*: This replaces the original video recording. It will permanently delete the sections of video you have trimmed out.

> *Save as New Clip*: This leaves your original video intact and creates a completely new video file of just the trim you specified.

> *Cancel*: This closes the menu and returns to the clip with your trim points still set.

Remember that if you choose to keep the original clip, storage space on your iPhone can quickly fill up. A one-minute clip took up a whopping 120MB of space on our iPhone.

Sharing Your Video

While viewing any single video clip, you have several sharing options. To bring up the sharing menu, tap the Share button, which looks like an arrow breaking free from a small box (see Figure 13–10). You'll be presented with a pop-up menu of sharing options (see Figure 13–13).

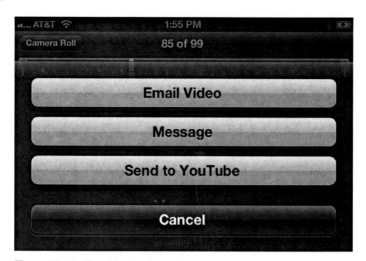

Figure 13–13. *The video sharing options*

Email Video: Selecting this command compresses the video clip as a QuickTime movie file. A new message window will appear with the movie clip attached to the body of the message.

Depending on the length of your video clip, you may get an error message that says "Video is Too Long." If you see this, your iPhone will ask you whether you want to select a smaller clip from the video to e-mail. Tap OK, and you'll enter trim mode, which will allow you to cut down the length of the clip.

Once you have trimmed your video, tap the yellow Email button above the scrub bar. A blank e-mail with the video in the body of the message should appear.

Message: Choose this option to send your video as an attachment for a message. Messages may be sent directly to other iMessage users using Apple's internal infrastructure or sent to phone numbers using multimedia MMS text messaging. Charges may apply to both your and the recipients' phone accounts.

Send to YouTube: Selecting this option will allow you to upload your video to YouTube right from your iPhone. On the screen that appears (Figure 13–14), enter a name and description for your video, select to upload it in standard- or high-definition, add tags, and finally select a YouTube category and then tap Publish. You must have a YouTube account to upload videos to YouTube.

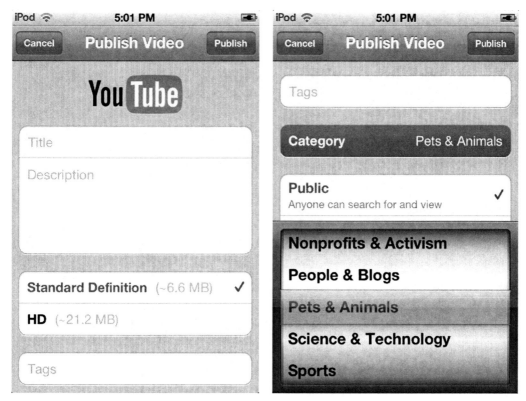

Figure 13–14. *Publishing a video to YouTube*

Uploading Images to Your Computer

Although it's nice to e-mail and Tweet photos and upload videos to YouTube, most people primarily viewing their images on their computers. To get your pictures and videos off your iPhone and onto your computer, simply plug your iPhone into your computer via the USB-to-dock cable.

On a Windows computer, your photo software such as Picasa or Adobe Photoshop Albums should recognize the iPhone as just another camera and import the photos and videos as the application normally would. On a Mac, iPhoto will detect that your iPhone is connected and ask whether you want to import the videos and photos from the iPhone's Camera Roll. You can also import media using OS X's Image Capture utility. This utility (found in the Applications folder on your Mac) allows you to choose the default import application (see Figure 13–15).

Figure 13–15. *Choose your default iPhone import application in OS X's Image Capture utility.*

> **NOTE:** iCloud's new PhotoStream simplifies sharing your photos with all your devices. Snap them using your iPhone's fantastic camera and view them on your iPad, your Mac, or your Windows PC.

Summary

The front and rear cameras add many nice features to your iPhone. The HD video-recording capabilities are amazing, and the still photography is breathtaking. Here are a few key tips for you to carry away with you:

- If you're going on vacation, leave your bulky HD video camera at home. Your iPhone 4S lets you record great-quality video at 1080p. Just be sure to bring a laptop so you can dump your video off on its hard drive and make way for more video on your iPhone.

- The iPhone 4S's updated video camera makes it the perfect companion for any aspiring photographer. You can catch that beautiful sunset over the ocean without having to lug along a point-and-shoot camera.

- Need a new profile picture for Facebook? The front camera on the iPhone makes it easy to take self-shots.

- You can zoom in while in still camera mode, but there is no zoom option while recording video.

- Each minute of 1080p video takes up a *lot* of space on your iPhone. Keep this in mind if you are going to be recording a lot of video because you'll need a lot of free space on your iPhone. Consider using the other camera for casual video use.

- Apple has imposed a seemingly arbitrary limit on e-mailing videos. A video clip must be 54 seconds long or shorter in order for you to e-mail it. If it's 55 seconds or longer, you'll be asked to trim the clip before you e-mail it.

- If you are taking pictures or recording video within range of a Wi-Fi network, the iPhone's Camera app will tag your photos and videos with geodata. Applications such as Apple's iPhoto can then display your photos on a map.

Part VI

Accessories

Chapter 14

Staying on Time and Getting There with Clock, Calendar, and Maps

We admit it—the iPhone has become a major player in the organizer/PDA world. It plays music and video. It lets you send and receive e-mails, read books, takes photos, and play games. Given all that, it should be no surprise that the iPhone offers several very nice utilities that allow you to manage your time, keep track of your appointments, and set alarms. This chapter introduces you to the Clock, Calendar, and Maps applications and shows you how to get the most from them.

Using the Clock Tools

Your iPhone comes with a Clock application. This application is far more flexible and useful than you might first imagine. Although you may think that it would show only a clock face and maybe set a timer, it actually provides *four* separate and useful time tools.

To launch the application, tap the white clock face icon on the black background, as shown in Figure 14–1.

Figure 14–1. *The Clock icon*

Along the button bar at the bottom of the Clock application screen, you'll find icons for each of the four utilities (see Figure 14–2).

Figure 14–2. *The four Clock utilities appear in a button bar at the bottom of the application screen.*

> *World Clock*: Use this application to monitor the time for multiple clocks around the world.
>
> *Alarm*: Set your alarms, both one-time and repeating, with this utility.
>
> *Stopwatch*: Time events with the iPhone's built-in stopwatch.
>
> *Timer*: Set a timer to go off after a specific interval with this utility.

NOTE: All clock utilities continue in the background, even if you're not in the Clock application itself. You can start an alarm, a timer, or the stopwatch and go off to other iPhone applications. The utility will keep ticking away as you work on other things.

World Clock

The iPhone World Clock utility keeps track of time zones around the world. It's really handy if, for example, you regularly travel or make phone calls across time zones. The iPhone's World Clock can instantly tell you the time in another city. Load it with your favorite cities, and you have an at-a-glance reference that keeps track of the times and time zones for you.

This utility is smart enough to take into account daylight saving time and other quirks, such as New Delhi being 30 minutes off standard. As Figure 14–3 shows, white clock faces indicate daytime, and black clock faces indicate night.

Figure 14–3. *The iPhone World Clock utility monitors time around the world.*

Adding Cities

Tap the + at the top right of the screen to add new cities to the World Clock. A search field pops up, prompting you to search for a city. Tap a few letters of the city name. As you type, a list of matching cities appears below the search field. When you find the city you want to add, tap it. Your new clock appears at the bottom of the World Clock screen.

> **NOTE:** World Clock uses a limited database of cities. You may not find a specific city, town, or village. Instead, look for the nearest large city in the same time zone. For example, if you are interested in the time in Massapequa, Long Island, you'll need to use New York City instead.

Reordering Cities

If the cities do not appear in the order you prefer, tap the Edit button at the top left of the World Clock screen. Grab handles (three parallel gray bars) appear to the right of each clock. Drag these handles to reorder your clocks into any position you like. Tap Done when finished. The World Clock screen updates to reflect your new ordering.

Removing Cities

You can easily remove any or all city clocks from your World Clock screen. Tap Edit (again, at the top left of the screen) to reveal the red remove controls to the left of each city name. Tap any red circle. A Delete button appears to the right of the selected clock. Tap Delete to confirm removal, or tap anywhere else on the screen to cancel the action. Tap Done to leave edit mode and return to the normal World Clock screen.

Alarm

The Alarm utility allows your iPhone to alert you at a specified time. Use alarms to wake up in the morning or remember business meetings. Unfortunately, the external speaker for the iPhone is extremely limited. It's tinny and not very loud, and the set of alarms is minimal. Keep in mind that the alarm works better in quiet locations than in loud ones, and avoid using it for mission-critical events.

Creating Alarms

Create alarms by tapping the + on the Alarm screen. This opens the Add Alarm screen shown in Figure 14–4. From this screen, you can set your alarms as follows.

Figure 14–4. *Create custom alarms that play sounds at a given time.*

Set a time: Spin the wheels to specify the time for the alarm to sound. Drag your finger up and down, and the wheel spins with you. Flick your finger, and the wheel continues spinning, even after your finger leaves the screen. If you like, you can also tap a number rather than spin to it.

Make an alarm repeat: Alarms are day-specific. You must choose days of the week for repeating events. For a daily alarm, select every day from Monday through Sunday. For a weekday alarm, use Monday through Friday instead. I use a weekday-only alarm to remind me ten minutes before I need to pick up my kids at the bus stop.

Select a sound: Choose any of the built-in sounds. They are all quiet. They are all tinny. You'll hear them better if your iPhone is plugged into an external speaker system.

Allow snooze: The Snooze button, as you might expect, allows you to delay an alarm and repeat it ten minutes later. To enable this, set the Snooze option to ON. To disable snoozing, set it to OFF.

Label an alarm: Give your alarm a custom label by tapping its name and entering text with the keyboard. This helps you differentiate your alarms at a glance. So, you know which one is "Pick Up Kids at Bus Stop" and which one is "Leave for Dental Appointment."

Save an alarm: Tap Save to store your new alarm, or tap Cancel to exit the Add Alarm screen without saving the alarm.

Managing Alarms

The main Alarm screen lists all the alarms you've added to your iPhone. To manage your alarms, you can do the following:

Activate alarms: Use the ON/OFF toggles to activate or deactivate each alarm.

Remove alarms: To remove an alarm, tap Edit, tap the red button to the left of the alarm name, and then tap Delete. This permanently removes the alarm from your iPhone. Tap Done to return to the main alarm screen.

Edit alarms: To edit an alarm, tap Edit, and then tap the gray reveal button (>) to the right of each name. The Edit Alarm screen opens. It looks similar to the Add Alarm screen (Figure 14–4). Make your edits, and tap Save.

Stopwatch

The iPhone Stopwatch utility (see Figure 14–5) allows you to time events. On the Stopwatch screen, tap Start to begin the timer, and tap Lap to mark the latest lap time. The laps appear as a scrolling list at the bottom of the screen. Tap Stop to pause. Tapping Reset returns the timer to 00:00.0.

Figure 14–5. *The Stopwatch application allows you to keep track of lap times in a scrolling list at the bottom of the screen. Tap Start to start, Stop to stop, Lap to end a lap, and Reset to return the time to zero and erase the lap times.*

Timer

The iPhone Timer utility (Figure 14–6) plays a sound after a set period of time. Unlike alarms, timers are not tied to a particular time of day. Use alarms for appointments; use timers for cooking eggs. On the Timer screen, set the amount of time you want to pass (three minutes, ten minutes, one hour, and so on), and then tap Start. After the timer counts down, it plays one of the standard alert tones you've selected and shows a pop-up message noting that timing has concluded if the Clock app is in the background.

> **TIP:** During the timer countdown, you can select a different alarm tone or cancel the timer before it finishes.

Figure 14–6. *Use the Timer application to play an alarm after a set period.*

Working with the Calendar

The iPhone Calendar application allows you to keep track of your appointments while on the go. With it, you can view your existing events and add new ones.

Launch Calendar by tapping the white-and-red icon that looks like a page from an old-fashioned, tear-off calendar (see Figure 14–7). The day and date are current and update every day.

Figure 14–7. *The Calendar icon appears on the top row of your iPhone home screen and shows the current date.*

Switching Calendar Views

The Calendar application offers four views: List, Day, Week, and Month. Each of these helps you locate and review your appointments.

List View

The List view does exactly what the name suggests. It displays your calendar events as a scrolling list. The list is ordered by day and time, as shown in Figure 14–8. The easy-to-follow formatting groups all events on a single day together. All events are listed, providing a powerful overview of all upcoming happenings.

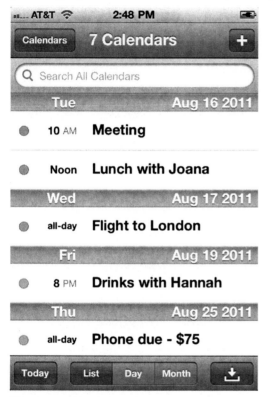

Figure 14–8. *Use the List view to see your appointments as a scrolling list.*

Here are a couple of points about the List view:

- Tap any event to view it in more detail.

- As you scroll, the currently displayed date "sticks" at the top of the screen, even as you scroll through it. It's a very cool but subtle effect.

Day View

Calendar's Day view shows your day's events in day-planner style (see Figure 14–9). Each event occupies a certain amount of space on the layout and is marked with the event and location.

Figure 14–9. *View a day at a time with the Day display.*

Here are some things you need to know about Day view:

■ Tap the previous and next arrows to scroll through your calendar a day at a time.

■ The day starts and ends at 12 a.m. So if you schedule your New Year's Eve party from 11 p.m. on December 31 until 2 a.m. on January 1, the Calendar application will split it into two Day views, even though it's a single event.

■ Tap an event to open its detail view.

Week View

When you rotate your iPhone to a landscape position Calendar's Week view appears (see Figure 14–10). You must rotate your iPhone to see the week view. There is no button in the Calendar app that activates it.

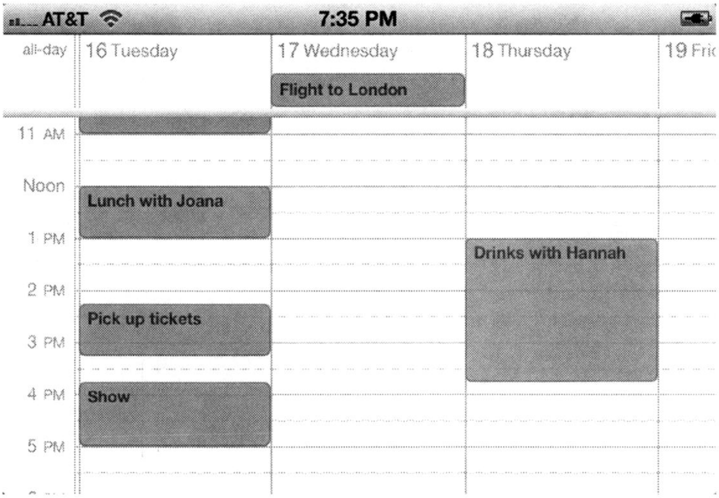

Figure 14–10. *View a week at a time with the Week display.*

Here are some things you need to know about Day view:

- Swipe left or right to move through the week.

- Swipe up and down to movie through the hours of the day.

- Tap an event to open its detail view.

Month View

The month-at-a-time view highlights all days with appointments (see Figure 14–11). A small dot appears below all days containing appointments. Tap any marked day to view a scrolling list of events at the bottom of the screen. As with the other views, tap those events to view their details.

Figure 14–11. *The Month view marks a dot under all dates that contain events.*

Here are some things you need to know about Day view:

- The darkened, recessed square represents the current date.

- A blue square represents the date you have selected.

- Tap an event to open its detail view.

The Today Button

Clicking the Today button in any view automatically jumps you back to the display for the current day but preserves whichever view you are using. So, you'll see the current month for Month view or recenter the list in List view.

The Calendars Button

The Calendars button at the top left of the screen allows you to choose which calendars you want to show (see Figure 14–12). A calendar with a check mark will show events in any of the calendar views. To hide a certain calendar, tap it to uncheck it.

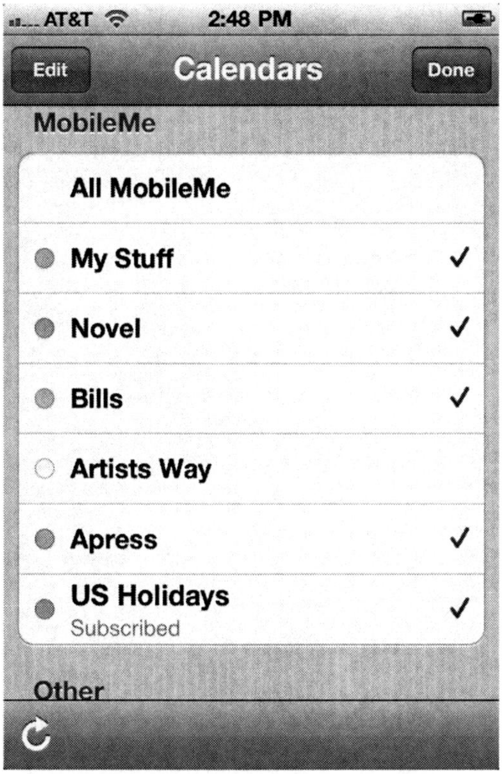

Figure 14–12. *The Calendars button screen allows you to choose which calendars you want to show.*

You can create new calendars right on your iPhone. To do so tap the *Edit* button in the Calendars window (Figure 14–12). Next, tap *Add Calendar* and then enter the name of the new calendar and the color you want to use for it. You can also delete and rename any calendar from the same calendar edit screen. Tap *Done* when finished.

Adding Events

Your iPhone allows you to add calendar events on the go. This lets you adjust and update your schedule when you are away from your computer. You have two ways to add events. In Day or Week view you can simply tap and hold on the screen and a new event bubble will appear (Figure 14–13). Drag the grab circles to adjust the times that the event covers. In week view you can also drag an even from one day to another.

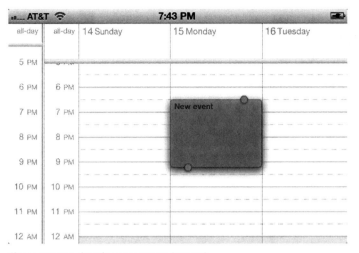

Figure 14–13. *Creating new events by touch*

If you are in the List, Day, or Month view you can also add a new event by tapping the + button at the top right of the screen. The Add Event screen opens, as shown in Figure 14–14.

Start by entering a title and location for the event. Tap in either field, and use the keyboard to enter a name and place. To finish naming your event, tap Done, or tap Cancel to leave the screen without adding a new event.

Once you have named your event and tapped Done, you are returned to the Add Event screen. Here, you can update the event name and/or location and specify when the event starts and ends, specify its time zone, specify whether it repeats,, when to play an alert to notify you about the event, and specify what calendar the event should appear on (Work, Bills, and so on). You can also add a URL and note to the event. Customize any or all of these options, as described in the following sections, and then tap Done to finish adding the event. Tap Cancel if you want to return to the List, Day, Week, or Month view without adding that event.

Figure 14–14. *Add new events directly on your iPhone.*

Updating an Event Name or Location

Tap the name and location line (just below the Add Event title) to open an editor that allows you to update the event's name and location text. After making your changes, tap Done to save your changes, or tap Cancel to return to the Add Event screen without applying those changes.

Setting the Event Start and End Times

Tap the Starts/Ends field to open the screen that allows you to set these times. You enter the time by way of a scroll control. This control contains date, hour, minute, and a.m./p.m. wheels. You set the start and end time by scrolling your way to the proper combination.

Tap either Starts or Ends to switch between the two times (when the event begins and when it ends) and make your adjustments as needed.

The basic scroller is great for relatively near-term appointments. It is not so great when you're scrolling six months into the future for your next tooth cleaning or your child's commencement schedule. It can take an awful lot of scrolling to get to the date you want. For quicker access to future dates or for all-day events (such as when you go on vacation or will be out of town on a business trip), set the All-day indicator from OFF to ON. The scroll wheel updates, replacing the date/hour/minute wheels with month/day/year wheels. You can schedule appointments this way, all the way up to December 31, 2067. (Don't count on me to be there. I have a tooth-cleaning appointment that afternoon.) You can also set the time zone for the event on this screen.

Tap Done to confirm your settings, or tap Cancel to return to the Add Event screen without changing the start and end times.

Setting a Repeating Event

When your event repeats, you can select from a standard list that defines how often: Every Day, Every Week, Every Two Weeks, Every Month, or Every Year. To make this happen, tap the Repeat field on the Add Event screen, select a repetition interval, and tap Done. To return to the Add Event screen without adding a repeated event, tap Cancel. To disable repeats, tap None, and then tap Done.

Adding Alerts

Add event alerts to notify you when an event is coming due. For example, you may want a one-hour notice for those dental appointments and a two-day notice for your anniversary. The iPhone provides a nice selection of options. These include five, fifteen, and thirty minutes before the event; one or two hours before the event; one or two days before the event; and on the date of the event itself.

Tap the Alert field to set an event alert. After selecting an event alert time, tap Done. To cancel without setting the alert time, tap Cancel. To remove event alerts, tap None and then Done.

Once you've saved your first alert, the iPhone offers you the option to add a second one. This allows you to remind yourself both a day before an event and a few minutes before you need to leave. This is a particularly useful feature for people who need extra reminders.

> **NOTE:** Unfortunately, there are no "snooze" options for calendar events.

Assigning Event to a Specific Calendar

You can select which calendar the event is assigned to by tapping Calendar and then selecting which calendar the event belongs on from the checklist.

Adding URLs

If there is a website associated with the event, you can type in its web address URL in the URL field.

Adding Notes

You can also add a free-form note to your event. Tap the Notes field at the bottom of Add Event screen, and use the Notes screen with its built-in keyboard to set the details for your event, such as phone numbers or names. As with all the other customization options, tap Done to save the note, or tap Cancel to return to the Add Event screen without saving it.

Editing and Removing Events

Tap any event in any view (List, Day, Week, or Month) to edit it. This opens an event detail view. On this screen, you'll see an Edit button at the top-right corner. Tap it to open the Edit screen. This screen is a near twin to the Add Event screen (Figure 14–14) and offers all the same customization options found there.

To remove any event, select it, go to its detail view, and tap Edit. The Edit screen opens. Scroll to the very bottom of the screen, and locate the red Delete Event bar. Tap it. The iPhone prompts you to confirm. Tap the red Delete Event bar a second time to remove the event, or tap Cancel to cancel deleting the event.

Synchronizing Calendars with Your Computer

Once you set up iTunes, you can synchronize your iPhone to your Microsoft Outlook calendars (Windows) or iCal and Microsoft Entourage calendars (Macintosh). We've told you how to do this in Chapter 2 already, but here's a quick overview.

In iTunes, choose your iPhone in the source list, and click the Info tab. Scroll down to find the Calendars section (see Figure 14–15), and use the settings there to specify how your touch synchronizes with your computer-based calendars.

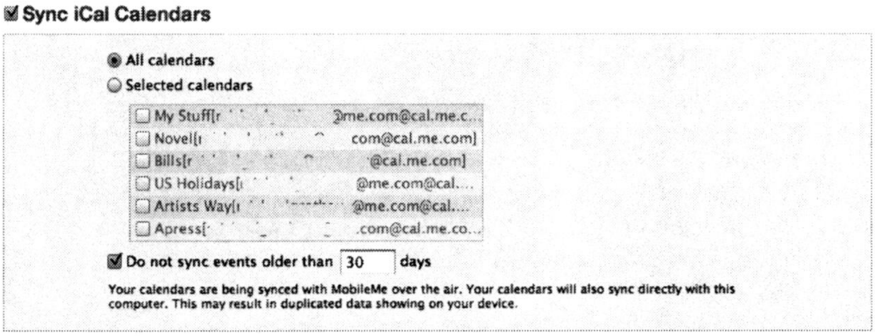

☑ **Sync iCal Calendars**

- ◉ All calendars
- ○ Selected calendars

  | ☐ My Stuff[r · ' · · · · ˀ · · · · 𝟑me.com@cal.me.c... |
  | ☐ Novel[r · · · · · · · ˄ · com@cal.me.com] |
  | ☐ Bills[r · · ' · · · · · ˄ · · · @cal.me.com] |
  | ☐ US Holidays[ı · · ˀ · · @me.com@cal.... |
  | ☐ Artists Way[ı · · ' · · · ˈˢᵗ· · @me.com@cal... |
  | ☐ Apress[· · · · · · · · · .com@cal.me.co... |

☑ Do not sync events older than ⎡ 30 ⎤ days

Your calendars are being synced with MobileMe over the air. Your calendars will also sync directly with this computer. This may result in duplicated data showing on your device.

Figure 14–15. *Choose how to synchronize your iPhone calendars to your computer by using the Info tab in iTunes.*

Select the top check box to enable calendar synchronization. Then choose whether to synchronize all calendars or just those calendars you specify. You can also set a statute of limitations on how far back you want to synchronize events. The default settings do not sync events older than a month.

These settings also let you specify the calendar to which you want to add new events from your iPhone. You don't have multiple calendars on the touch, but you can control the way the touch interacts with multiple calendars on your computer. Simply select the calendar using the pop-up list.

If, at any time, you want to completely update the calendars on your iPhone, scroll down to the bottom of the Info screen and locate the Advanced options. Check the box that indicates you want to replace information on this iPhone for calendars. After setting this option, the next time you sync (and only during that next sync), iTunes completely replaces the calendar on your iPhone with the information from your computer. Use this option when you set up your iPhone with a new home computer after it was previously synchronized to another host.

Exploring with Maps

Maps uses Google Maps interactively to find and display locations using map and satellite imagery. With Maps (Figure 14–16), you can get directions, view traffic, and more. Launch the app by tapping the Maps icon. It looks like a small map and actually shows the location of Apple on 1 Infinite Drive in Cupertino, California. This takes you into the Maps application, where you can view and explore geography from around the world.

Figure 14–16. *The Maps icon*

Getting Around the Maps Screen

Figure 14–17 shows the basic Maps interface. It consists of the following:

■   *Search field*: Marked with a spyglass, the search field allows you to enter addresses and other queries. You can type an entire address ("1600 Pennsylvania Avenue, Washington, DC") or search for contacts ("Bill Smith"), landmarks ("Golden Gate Bridge"), or even pizza places in your local zip code ("Pizza 11746").

■ *Bookmarks button*: This blue book-looking button lies within the search field. Tap it to select addresses from your bookmarked locations, your recent locations, or your contact list.

■ *Map*: The map itself appears in the center of your screen. It's fully interactive. You can scroll by dragging your finger along the map, or zoom in and out using pinches and double-taps. (Use a single-fingered double-tap to zoom in and a double-fingered tap to zoom out.)

■ *Red pushpins*: The red pushpins indicate locations found by the application after a search. For example, Figure 14–17 shows a café called Curved Angel Café. Tap a pushpin to view a location summary, and then tap the blue > icon for more details and options. These options include directions to and from that location, bookmarking the location, and assigning the location to contacts. Tap the orange-and-white icon with a man in it to enter Street View.

■ *Purple pushpins*: The purple pushpins show where you've dropped pins onto the map to add your own user-defined locations.

■ *Locate Me button*: Tap the arrowhead button at the lower-left side of the screen to contact Google and search for your location. Google uses a kind of pseudo-GPS position based on your Wi-Fi signal. Some local Wi-Fi networks can return approximate locations within about a half-mile and help you determine your location. Other times, Maps thinks you're in Cleveland when you're actually in Arizona. So, don't count on this service; your results will vary.

■ *Search/Directions buttons*: The two buttons at the bottom of the screen switch between normal mode and directions mode. Tap Directions to enter start and end locations for your trip or scroll through the stages of your current trip. The directions appear at the top of the screen, along with Previous and Next buttons. When viewing directions, tap the curvy arrow to switch your start and end points and get reverse directions.

■ *Options button*: Marked with a page curl icon, this button reveals options hiding below your map. (The map actually bends back to reveal the options.) The list includes the following options:

   ■ Switch between the standard map, satellite, and hybrid imagery or show your directions as a text list, such as "Go west for 5.4 miles."

   ■ The drop pin feature lets you include additional feature points without needing to enter an address. This is perfect for when you need to remember where you parked the car or saw a cool product in a shop window while walking.

- Choose Show Traffic to request traffic conditions along your route. This feature is limited to certain regions, mostly major metropolitan areas.

- Tap the Print button to print your map and directions to an AirPrint printer.

Figure 14–17. *The Maps application (left) allows you to interactively view and search standard and satellite maps. The red pushpins show the locations found by your search. Tap the page curl icon in the lower-right corner to be presented with your Maps options (right).*

Navigating Maps

The Maps app makes it so you can explore the world from the comfort of your palm. Like any other app, you navigate the map using gestures. You can also view the map in different modes.

Gestures

On maps you use gestures to zoom in, zoom out, pan, and scroll.

Zoom in: You have two ways of zooming in. Either pinch the map with two fingers, or use one finger and double-tap the location on the map that you want to zoom in on. Double-tap again to zoom in even closer.

Zoom out: You can zoom out in two ways. Either reverse-pinch the map with two fingers, or use two fingers double-tap the map. Double-tap with two fingers again to zoom even farther out.

Panning and scrolling: Touch and drag the map up, down, left, or right to move the map around and view another location.

Changing Map Views

The default map view is Google's classic road map with orange, yellow, and white streets. But the Maps application also allows you to view the map in four additional views as well as with traffic overlay.

To access these features, tap or tap and drag the page curl at the bottom of the maps screen. The map will curl up, and you'll be presented with the Map settings page (see Figure 14–17). Your settings include map views, overlays, and a special feature called "Drop Pin," which places, or "drops," a pin anywhere on the map. These dropped pins let you easily mark a business, street corner, beach, or any other kind of location on a map.

> *Standard*: This is the classic default map view. It uses Google's standard road map.

> *Satellite*: This view shows you the world using satellite imagery. It's perhaps the coolest maps view because you can zoom in on streets and see little blips of people walking the day the satellite imagery was taken. No labels appear in satellite view.

> *Hybrid*: This view combines Classic and Satellite. You see the map in satellite imagery, but it has labels, roads, and borders overlaid on it.

> *List*: This view shows you your location or direction using a list.

> **TIP:** The standard map view uses orange, yellow, and white to color streets. Orange indicates interstate highways. Yellow indicates state highways and county parkways. White indicates local and private streets.

> *Show Traffic*: Tap to turn Traffic ON. While on, the current traffic conditions will be overlaid on the map. To see current traffic conditions, you will need to be connected to a Wi-Fi network. We'll talk more about traffic later in this chapter.

Drop Pin: Tapping this button causes the page to uncurl and drops a location pin in the center of the map. Use a dropped pin to easily mark a business, street corner, beach, or any other kind of location on a map. You can also drop a pin by touching and holding anywhere on the map. We'll talk more about dropping pins later in this chapter.

You'll notice we said that the Maps app allows you to view the map in standard map view as well as four additional views, so there are five views total. The fifth view is called Street View, and you access it from a search results or dropped pin. We'll talk more about Street View later in this chapter.

Finding Locations

The Maps app gives you multiple ways to find locations. You can search for locations using the search field, automatically find your current location using the iPhone's Skyhook location services, or even just zoom in and browse the map like a bird flying overhead.

Depending what you are looking for, some types of search are better than others. For example, if you are looking for your favorite spot on a beach, chances are it doesn't have an address or name, so your best bet is to navigate to the beach and then zoom in and scroll around in satellite view until you find that favorite spot.

Search

You'll find most of your locations through the search field at the top of your screen (see Figure 14–17). Tap the search field, and a keyboard appears. There are many ways to search for a location. You can type an entire address (1600 Pennsylvania Avenue, Washington, DC) or search for contacts on your iPhone by typing in their name (Bill Smith), landmarks (Eiffel Tower), or even pizza places in your local zip code (Pizza 60605).

Enter your search query and one or more red pin will fall onto the map. Imagine you're taking a trip next week to Chicago. As you'll see in Figure 14–18, we searched for "Pizza Chicago." Several red pins populate the map, all representing pizza places.

Figure 14–18. *Search result pins on the map*

When you touch one of the red pins, you get the pin's information bar (see Figure 14–19). The information bar tells you the name of the establishment (a pizzeria, in this case) and displays an icon on either side. Those icons represent the Information window and Street View.

Figure 14–19. *A search result pin's information bar shows the name of the establishment with a Street View icon on the left and an Information icon on the right.*

Information Window

Tap the white-and-blue > on the pin's information bar to make the Info window slide open. The Info window (see Figure 14–20) displays information for the establishment, such as its phone number, web page, and physical address and gives you several options on how you can use this location further on your iPhone.

Figure 14–20. *The Info window*

Phone: The establishment's phone number. Touch and hold to copy the number to the clipboard.

Home page: The establishment's web address. Tap it to close Maps and be taken to the web address in Safari.

Address: The establishment's address. Touch and hold to copy the address to the clipboard.

Directions To Here: Tap here to be taken to the directions toolbar. The address of the establishment will be populated in the second (end destination) directions field. We'll talk more about directions later in this chapter.

Directions From Here: Tap here to be taken to the directions toolbar. The address of the establishment will be populated in the first (origin destination) directions field.

Add to Contacts: Tapping this button will add the name of the establishment, the phone number, the web address, and the physical address to a contact. You have the options Create New Contact or Add to Existing Contact.

If you choose Create New Contact, a new contact window will slide up (see Figure 12-12) in the Info window populating contact fields with information and also allowing you to add more information to the contact. Tap Done to save the new contact.

If you choose Add to Existing Contact, a list of all your contacts from your address book will slide up in the Info window. Tap the contact you want to add the information to. The information will be added, and the contacts list will slide away.

Share Location: Tapping this button will allow you to e-mail a link of the establishment's name, Google Maps link, and attach a vcard (a virtual business card the receiver can choose to add to his address book).

Add to Bookmarks: Tapping this button will allow you to save the location to your Maps bookmarks. You'll be able to name the bookmark, so you can change "Pizano's Pizza & Pasta" to "My favorite pizza joint." We'll talk more about bookmarks in a moment.

Tap Map to close the information window and return to the map.

Street View

Street View uses Google technology to display 360° panoramic views of the location you are at. To enter Street View, tap the white-and-orange Street View icon in the pin's information bar (see Figure 14–19). Your map will begin to zoom in on the pin and then tilt up and present you with a street-level panoramic view (see Figure 14–21).

Figure 14–21. *Street View fills the entire screen. Tap the white arrow on the road to move forward down the street. Tap the map navigation icon to return to map view.*

Google has had Street View available on the Web for some time, but using it on the iPhone brings it to a whole different level. The fact that you can touch and drag and pinch and zoom around the street gives Street View an immediacy it's never had.

While in Street View, drag your finger around to experience the 360° panoramic views. Pinch or double-tap the screen to zoom in. Reverse-pinch to zoom back out. To "walk" down the street, find the big white arrows at the end of a street label and tap them. You'll then move that direction.

The small circular navigation icon sites at the bottom right of a Street View map. It shows you the direction you are looking in. Tap the icon to return to your last map view location.

Street View isn't available in all cities yet, but it is in most major North American and European ones. Street View is a wonderful tool because it lets you check out what a place or area looks like in advance. Thinking of moving to a new area of town? You can virtually scroll down the street in Street View to see whether you like the looks of it before you take the time and trouble to start searching for houses in the neighborhood.

Current Location

Curious about where you are in the world? The Maps app allows you to find your current location with a tap of a button. The current location button is located in the bottom left of the screen (see Figure 14–22). It looks like an arrowhead. Tap it to jump to your current location on the map.

Your current location, as determined by the onboard GPS receiver, is indicated by a blue dot. This dot appears to be pulsing when the iPhone's location services are fixing your position. The blue circle surrounding the pin is indicative of the error in the GPS system; you are most likely somewhere in the area defined by the circle.

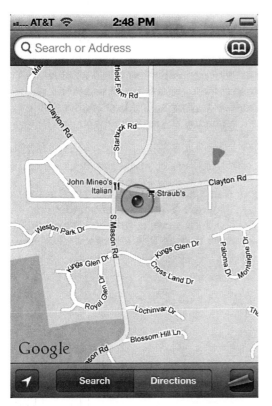

Figure 14–22. *The blue dot surrounded by the circle represents your approximate location.*

Your current location is signified by a blue dot, as in Figure 14–22. If the Maps app can't determine your exact location, a blue circle appears around the dot. The circle can range in size depending on how precisely your location can be determined. What the circle means is you are somewhere in that location. The smaller the circle, the more precise the current location marker.

NOTE: Location Services must be turned on for your iPhone to find your current location. To turn on Location Services, go to **Settings ➤ Location Services ➤ ON**.

When you are in Current Location mode, the current location icon in the toolbar turns blue. After you've found your current location, if you drag the map around, you can simply tap the current location button again to have the map center back on it.

You can tap the blue current location dot on the map to bring up Current Location information bar. The address of the current location will be displayed. Tap the > button to get the information window for the location, including the ability to get directions to/from the location, bookmark it, add it to contacts, or e-mail the location; or tap the Street View button to enter Street View (if available in the area).

Bookmarking and Viewing Saved Locations

There are two ways you can bookmark locations you've navigated to in Maps: dropping a pin or tapping the Add to Bookmarks button in the location's information window. Dropping a pin allows you to mark any location on a map, regardless of whether it has a physical address; you can then add the pin's location to your saved bookmarks. Once you've saved locations, you can view them all in the handy Bookmarks menu.

Dropping a Pin

Navigate to a point of interest on the map without doing a search for something. In the example in Figure 14–23, we found a location by Chicago's Shedd Aquarium that has beautiful views of the sunrise over Lake Michigan. To drop a pin, all you have to do is press and hold your finger on the map where you want to drop it. After a second or two, a purple pin will fall and stick in the map.

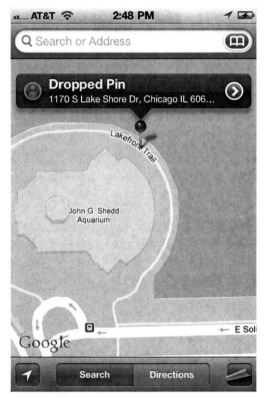

Figure 14–23. *A dropped pin and its information bar with the approximate address*

The pin's information bar will appear with the approximate address of the pin as well as the usual icons for Street View and the information window. If the pin's location isn't exactly where you want it, you can tap and hold the purple pin's head and drag it to the location you want. Remove your finger to sink the pin into the map.

Tap the > button to get the information window for the pin's location, including the ability to get directions to/from the location, bookmark it, add it to contacts, or e-mail the location; or tap the Street View button to enter Street View (if available in the area).

You can also drop a pin in the center of the map by accessing the Maps settings page behind the page curl in the lower-right corner. Tap the page curl at the bottom of the maps screen and tap the Drop Pin button. The settings page will uncurl, and a pin will drop in the center of the map. You can then tap and drag the pin to move it to anywhere you want on the map.

Dropping pins might seem like a nice but unnecessary feature at first. Why, if you can search maps with the apps powerful search features, would you manually add locations? Again, dropped pins are great because it allows you to mark locations that do not have a fixed address, such as a good trail in the mountains, the sight of your first kiss (for the romantic among you), or even the location of your favorite bench in Central Park.

Bookmarking

So far in this chapter we've shown you several ways to bookmark locations, whether it be by a dropped pin or the information windows of a business, friend, or address you looked up. But where are all those bookmarks you've saved? In the bookmarks window, of course!

Tap the bookmarks icon that's located in the search field (see Figure 14–17). It looks like a book folded open. The bookmarks window will appear. The bookmarks window presents three views: Bookmarks, Recents, and Contacts (see Figure 14–24).

Bookmarks: This lists all the bookmarks you've saved in the Maps app. Tap any bookmark to jump to it on the map. Tap the Edit button to delete a bookmark, move it up or down the bookmarks list, or change the name of the bookmark.

Recents: This lists all the resent search queries, driving directions, and dropped pins you've made. Tap any item on the list to jump to it on the map. Press the Clear button to remove all items from the list. Remember, clearing your Recents list will ensure that people who use your iPhone can't spy on locations you've searched for. Be aware, however, it will also clear your direction routes. Routes can't be bookmarked, so the only way to quickly access them is through the Recents window. If you clear the window, you'll need to perform your route searches from scratch.

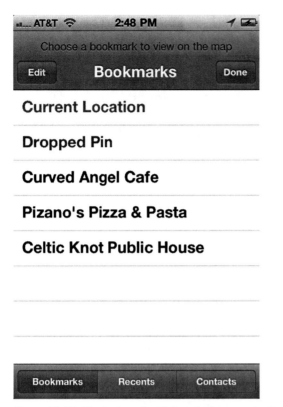

Figure 14–24. *The bookmarks window displays your bookmarked locations, recent locations, and contact's locations.*

Contacts: This list shows you all the contacts who you have addresses for. Tap any contact on the list to jump to their address on the map. If a contact has more than one address, you'll be asked to choose which address to navigate to. Tap the Groups button to navigate through your contact groups.

Directions and Traffic

The iPhone Maps app lets you search for directions and view current traffic conditions. Like the Maps app itself, directions and traffic require an Internet connection. Since the iPhone only has a Wi-Fi connection, you'll need to look up the directions before you leave home.

Directions

To get directions, tap the Directions tab in the Maps bottom toolbar (see Figure 14–17). You'll notice that the search field becomes a double field to enter your start and end locations (see Figure 14–25). The Maps app will put your current location, if available, as the starting location. If you don't want to use your current location as the starting address, tap it in the first search field, and press the *X* to remove it and type in whatever address you want.

Figure 14–25. *The Maps search field changed to directions input when you tap the directions button.*

NOTE: You can also begin a directions search from any pin's information window.

To enter an address from one of your contacts, tap the bookmarks icon, and then choose a contact. You'll be asked to choose whether you want Directions to Here or Directions From Here. Choose, and the contact's address will be populated in the appropriate directions field. To reverse the start end points, tap the curvy, sideways S-arrow to switch the points (and get reverse directions). The reverse directions feature is nice because sometimes the route you came isn't the quickest route back. Reverse directions will show you whether another route home is quicker.

When you have selected both a start point and an end point, one or more blue lines will appear on the map showing you suggested routes you can take (see Figure 14–26). Tap on the route label ("Route 1," "Route 2," etc) to select a route. A green pin represents your starting location on the map, and a red pin indicates your end location. You'll also notice a blue directions bar has appeared at the top of the screen. The directions bar lets you choose between driving (car icon), public transit (bus icon), or walking (person icon) directions. These different modes of transportation may give you different direction routes on the map between the exact same two locations. This is because people aren't allowed to walk on highways and cars aren't allowed to drive on pedestrian streets and on certain bus routes, depending on the city you live in.

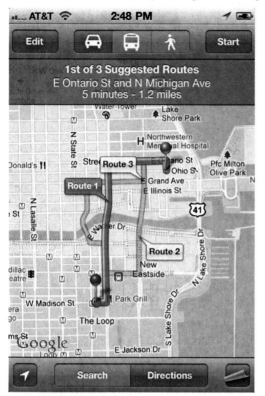

Figure 14–26. *The map with the car route showing three possible routes*

Driving or Walking Directions

Tap either the driving or walking icon. You'll see the length of the route and the estimated time it will take to get there. If traffic data is available, the estimated journey time will adjust accordingly.

To navigate through the directions step-by-step, tap the blue Start button in the upper-right corner. The directions bar will change to the one in Figure 14–27.

If you'd like to navigate through the directions step-by-step in the map, tap the right-pointing arrow on the bar. Each subsequent tap will bring you forward one step in the route. To move back a step, tap the left arrow.

Figure 14–27. *Tap the left or right arrow to move through the directions step-by-step.*

Public Transit Directions

Tap the public transit button. In the blue directions bar you'll see the estimated time it will take to get there. If traffic data is available, the estimated journey time will adjust accordingly.

Tap the clock icon to display a list of departure times and schedules (see Figure 14–28). Tap Depart to choose a date and time. The Depart field defaults to the current date and time unless you change it. Below the depart time you'll see a list of alternate schedules. Select one, and then tap the Done button.

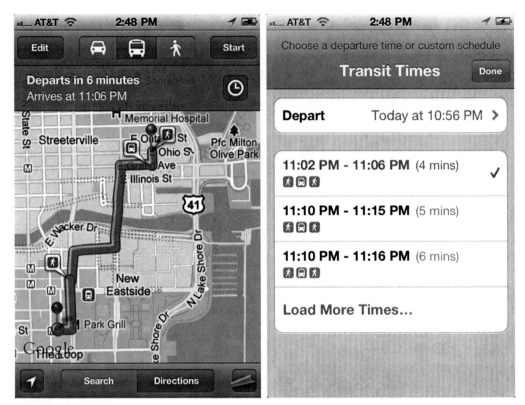

Figure 14–28. *The directions bar shows public transit routes (left). The clock icon allows you to select between different transit schedules (right).*

To navigate through the directions step-by-step, tap the blue Start button. If you'd like to navigate through the directions step-by-step in the map, tap the right-pointing arrow on the bar. Each subsequent tap will bring you forward one step in the route. To move back a step, tap the left arrow.

> **NOTE:** We've mentioned it before, but unfortunately, you can't bookmark routes. That's a pity because it would be nice to be able to quickly pull up traffic conditions on your favorite routes. Ideally Apple will add this feature in the future.

Traffic

The Maps app can display traffic conditions that help you when planning an immediate journey. To turn on traffic conditions, tap the page curl at the bottom of the maps screen, and then tap Show Traffic to ON (see Figure 14–17). Back on the map you'll notice that green, yellow, and red lines have appeared over some of the roads (see Figure 14–29).

Just how on Earth does the Maps app know what the current traffic conditions are? Most major U.S. cities have sensors embedded in the highways and major roads. These sensors feed data back, in real time, to the Department of Transportation (DOT). The DOT uses this information to update digital traffic signs that report local traffic conditions (like those bright Broadway-like signs that hang from overpasses on major metro highways that tell you how long it will take to get to a certain exit). The DOT also shares this data, which Google collects and uses to display near real-time traffic maps.

Figure 14–29. *Traffic overlays on the map*

Green lines indicate traffic is flowing at least 50 mph. Yellow ones mean that traffic is flowing between 25 and 50 mph. Red highways mean that traffic is moving slower than 25 mph. A gray route indicates that traffic data is not available for that street or highway.

The traffic feature is limited to certain regions, mostly major metropolitan areas in the United States, France, Britain, Australia, and Canada, but new cities and new countries are frequently added. If you don't see traffic conditions, try zooming out on the map. If you still don't see any, they aren't available in your area yet.

Maps Tips

Here are some tips for using Google Maps on your iPhone:

- When a person or business is in your contacts list, save yourself some time. Don't type in the entire address. Just enter a few letters of the name, and select the contact.

- URLs that link to Google Maps automatically open in the Maps application, whether they are tapped in Safari or Mail.

- Tap individual items on the directions list to jump to that part of your route.

- The Recents screen (in Bookmarks) shows both recent locations *and* recent directions.

Find a Lost iPhone

Have you lever lost your iPhone? Horrible, right? Don't worry! Now Apple has created a free app called Find My iPhone (Figure 14–30) and you can use it should you ever lose your iPhone again. Yes, it says "iPhone" but it works for iPads, iPod touches, and Macs as well. Using this app, you can locate all your iDevices from any iPhone, iPad, or iPod touch, or by logging into your iCloud account at www.icloud.com.

Figure 14–30. *The Find My iPhone icon.*

Before you can find a lost iPhone, you need to make sure you've installed and set up the Find My iPhone app on the device. Therefore, it's best to do that as soon as you get your iPhone. Once you've set up Find My iPhone to work with your iPhone and other iOS devices, launch the app and sign in. You'll then be presented with the screen shown in Figure 14–31.

Figure 14–31. *The Find My iPhone app lists all your devices. Select one to see its location on a map.*

You can choose what Mac or iOS device you want to see the location of. Select a device and it will be located on a map. An iPhone will be represented by a tiny iPhone icon. Tap the icon to see the name of the device, then tap the blue Info button to display a window that shows you the various actions you can perform with the device:

- *Play Sound or Send Message*: This lets you display a text message on your iPhone or play a sound at full volume for two minutes (even if the iPhone is muted). The sound feature is great if you don't know where in the house you have left your iPad or iPhone.

- *Remote Lock*: Use this to set up a remote passcode lock on your device or initiate your current passcode lock. This will keep anyone out of the device who doesn't know the passcode.

- *Remote Wipe*: This is a worst-case scenario feature. If your iPhone has been stolen and you don't want to play detective and track it to the perpetrator's house, you can remote wipe your iPhone. Remote wiping your iPhone will permanently erase all your personal data on it, ensuring that whoever has or finds your iPhone can't commit identity theft against you.

Find a Friend

Your iPhone is so amaing that not only can it help you find other iOS devices and Macs you own, it can help you find friends as well! Well, not "find friends" as in make new ones, but it can help you find the frineds you already know. It does this through an app (and iCloud service) called Find My Friends (Figure 14–32).

Figure 14–32. *The Find My Friends icon.*

Using Find My Friends, you can instantly see the location of any of your friends who have iPhones, iPod touches, or iPads. That is, you can see where they are as long as they've given you presmission. The Find My Friends app allows you to also share your location. It's a great way to see where you are in location to your friends. Perhaps you're out shopping and you're thinking of grabbing a coffee. Just open Find My Friends and looks for any buddiess that are near you to meet up for a quick drink.

As you can see in Figure 14–33, all your friends who have allowed you to know their location show up in a list. Tap the friend's name to get the address of where they are and also view their location on a map.

And for those of you concerned about privacy know that Apple has built in a great many of privacy options into the app. For instance, you can choose to only share your location for a certain period of time, like three hours; or a certain time of day, like from noon to five pm. You can also revoke all location invitations at any time, which will disable any of your friends from following you.

The Find My Friends app is a great new social netowrking app that's a free download in the App Store. The only requirement is that you have a free iCloud account. Get one at www.icloud.com.

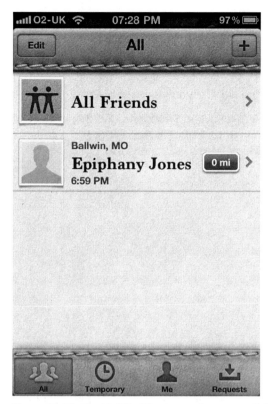

Figure 14–33. *The Find My Friends app shows you a list of the locations of all your friends.*

Summary

As you can now see, the iPhone offers you tools to stay on time and get to places you need to be! Its Clock and Calendar applications certainly complement the other onboard applications and expand usability in a vague time-management way. Maps is the world in your pocket. With it, you can now find directions to your favorite pizza joint, get an instant fix on your current location, or check out what the tops of the Pyramids of Giza look like without leaving your living room. You've learned how to use maps to find public transport times and routes, current traffic conditions, or just virtually stroll down the street of a neighborhood you are thinking of moving to.

Before we move on to the next chapter, here are a few key points to keep in mind:

- The sound levels for the iPhone's built-in speaker are pretty good. Still, if you are going to rely on your iPhone as your only alarm, you may want to buy an iPhone speaker system with built-in dock. You'll get much louder sounds, and your iPhone will charge while plugged in!

- Calendar has four views: List, Day, Week, and Month. Get used to them all because they all provide unique ways of planning and viewing your events.

- You don't have to pop over to Google every time you want to check what time it is in London. Set up the World Clock utility and have that information just a couple of touches away.

- Street View is not only fun; it's useful if you want to explore an area of your city—or almost any major city in the world—you've never been to.

- Using your iPhone's built-in GPS features, an iCloud account, and the free Find My iPhone and Find My Friends apps from the App Store, you can now find your missing iOS devices, Macs, and friends all right from your phone.

Using Your Desk Set: Contacts, Calculator, Notes, Weather, Stocks, Voice Memos, and Reminders

The iPhone is your digital gateway to more tools and apps than you could ever imagine. Chapter 10 taught you how to navigate and download apps from the App Store; this chapter shows you how to use many of the productivity apps that come preinstalled on the iPhone, namely, Contacts, Calculator, Notes, Weather, Stocks, Voice Memos, and Reminders.

Synchronizing Your Address Book with Your Computer

Before you even get to the iPhone, start thinking about your contacts while you're at your computer. In iTunes, the Info tab controls how and when your iPhone syncs its contacts with those stored on your computer. You can sync your iPhone with contact information from Windows Address Book or Microsoft Outlook (Windows) or Address Book or Microsoft Entourage (Mac).

Choosing Sync Options

In Chapter 2, we already told you how to sync your contacts from your computer with your iPhone, but let's quickly look at it again. In iTunes, click the Info tab, and locate the Contacts section—it's near the top of the screen, as shown in Figure 15–1. To synchronize your address book, you must select the "Sync contacts" check box. Then all the grayed-out options turn dark black, and you can select your settings.

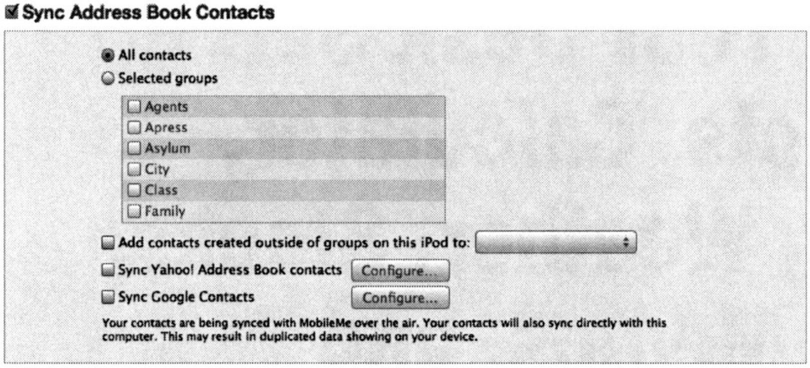

Figure 15–1. *Unless you check the "Sync contacts" check box, your contacts will not copy over to your iPhone.*

Choose where to sync your contacts from (and, for that matter, to). iTunes looks for address books on your system and lists those available in a drop-down list. The list varies by system and by your installed software.

Then choose whether to use all contacts or select a group like Home or Work to sync. If you do not divide your contacts into groups, just leave the default option, "All contacts." You can also sync contacts from your online Yahoo! or Google contacts. Select either box, and then enter your Yahoo! or Google ID and password.

After making your choices, tap Apply to save your changes. The button is located at the bottom right of the iTunes screen.

> **NOTE:** If you are syncing your contacts through iCloud (see Chapter 2), you don't need to worry about any of these steps.

Replacing Contacts

At times, you may want to replace the information on your iPhone entirely with the contact information from a computer. For example, you may be reparenting your iPhone after upgrading your system to a new machine, or you might be reassigning the iPhone from one employee to another.

Start by locating the Advanced Info options for your iPhone, at the very bottom of the Info tab. Scroll all the way down using the scroller at the right side of the iTunes window. In that section, select the Contacts box under "Replace information on this iPhone," and then click Apply.

During the next sync—and the next sync only—iTunes will completely wipe the contact information off your iPhone and replace it with the information found on the computer.

Working with the Contacts Application

The Contacts application appears on the top row of your iPhone home screen. It looks like a brown, spiral-bound address book with tabs (see Figure 15–2). Tap this icon to open the Contacts application.

Figure 15–2. *Use the Contacts application as a palm-top address book. You can search for existing contact information and add new contacts directly from your iPhone.*

Finding Contacts

When you launch the Contacts app the first time, you'll be presented either with the Groups screen, which lists all your contacts by groups, or with the All Contacts screen, which lists all your contacts alphabetically. The screen you see will depend on whether you have contact groups set up. If you do not, then you will be presented with the All Contacts screen. As Figure 15–3 shows, both the Groups and All Contacts screens are quite basic. The Groups screen consists of an alphabetical listing on all your groups, while the All Contacts screen consists of a scrolling list of names, an alphabetic index, and an Add button. You can scroll, drag, or flick up and down the screen to move through your entire groups or contacts collections. On the contacts screen you can also tap a letter to move instantly to that part of the address book or drag your finger up and down the alphabet to jump through the names. Tap the refresh button in the upper-left corner to make sure you've synced the latest contacts.

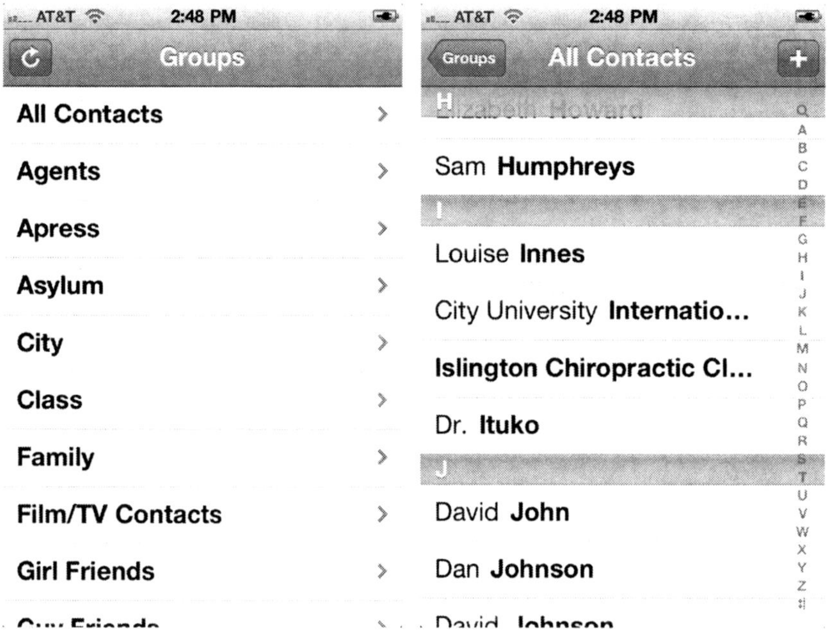

Figure 15–3. *The Groups (left) and Contacts (right) application screens*

Ordering Your List

You can choose how Contacts orders your contacts list: by first name and then last, or by last name and then first. How you set this up depends on whether you want to search for your friends and business acquaintances informally or formally or whether your country uses a non-English ordering method, as in Japan or China.

To change your settings, navigate to Settings ➤ Mail, Contacts, Calendars, and choose an ordering method for sorting and for displaying.

Viewing Contact Details

Tap any contact name to view its information screen. Figure 15–4 shows a contact information screen for Apple's mythical John Appleseed. The level of detail and the amount of information shown depends on how much information you've entered into the address book. A contact may include a physical address, a web site URL, e-mail address, phone numbers, and more.

Figure 15–4. *The Info screens contains as much or as little contact information as you have set.*

A contact's info screen isn't just to be looked at; it's interactive. Tap and hold a phone number to copy it to the clipboard. Tap and e-mail address to be taken to a new compose mail message screen with the e-mail address filled in the To field. Tap a web link to open the Safari browser to that web address. Tap a physical address to open the address in the Maps app. Tap and hold other information on the page to copy its text to the clipboard. Finally, tap Share Contact to compose an e-mail with the contact's information attached as a VCF (virtual business card file) to the body of the e-mail. The recipient of the e-mail can then add the card to their address book.

Adding Contacts

One of my favorite iPhone features is its ability to add contacts on the go. When I'm talking with another parent and trying to set up a play date or when I'm in a business meeting, I can pull out my iPhone and enter contact information right where I am. When I return to my computer or sync to iCloud, I sync that information into my main computer-based address book.

Contacts you create or edit on your iPhone will sync back to your computer and update the information there. If you've set the Sync contacts option in iTunes, all changes made on your touch will synchronize to your computer and reflect your updates.

Tap the (+) button at the top right of the screen to create a new contact. A detail screen opens, as shown in Figure 15–5. Here, you can enter all the information for your new contact. Fill in the fields, as described in the following sections, and then tap Done to add your new contact to the list.

> **TIP:** Once you've added a field to your contact, the green + next to each defined field turns into a red −. Erase any field by tapping the red button and then tapping Delete.

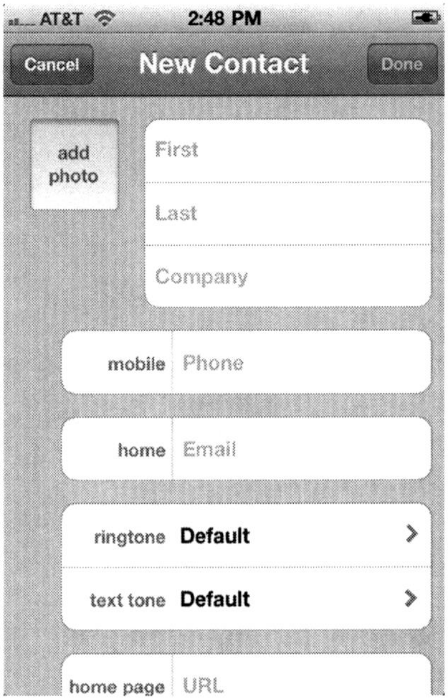

Figure 15–5. *Use the New Contact screen to add information about your new contact.*

Adding a Contact Name

As you can see, adding a contact name is straightforward. Type in their first name, and then touch the last name field to enter their last name. One caveat is when you are entering a business name. Here you have a choice. You can enter a name and a company ID, just one, or just the other. For example, you might add a contact for your favorite pizza parlor using just its company name, without adding a contact name for that establishment.

After entering the new information, tap Done. This returns you to the New Contact screen.

> **NOTE:** The iPhone expects you to separate a contact's first and last names into separate fields so that it can properly alphabetize the results.

Adding a Contact Photo

The Contacts application can take advantage of any photos you have synchronized to your iPhone. Tap the Add Photo box at the top left of the New Contact screen, and then tap Choose Photo from the pop-up menu that appears to assign a photo to your new contact. The Photo Albums screen opens. From there, navigate to a photo thumbnail, and tap it to display it. Move and scale that photo as desired, and then tap Set Photo. The iPhone saves the picture and adds it to your contact.

You can also take a photo on the contact if you happen to be with them. Tap the Add Photo box at the top left of the New Contact screen, and then tap Take Photo from the pop-up menu that appears. Snap your pic, move and scale it, and then tap Use Photo to assign the photo to your new contact.

Adding Phone Numbers

The Contacts application supports not one or two but *eight* different kinds of phone numbers. And on top of that, it also offers a free-form phone number label. You can enter almost unlimited quantities of phone numbers and assign them to standard types, including mobile, home, work, pager, and more.

Tap the Phone field, and the iPhone opens an Edit Phone screen. Enter a phone number. You can then tap the current label of that phone number (such as "mobile" or "iPhone") to get a pop-up list of labels you can choose from. The label defines the kind of number you're using, such as "work" for work numbers and "home" for home numbers. In addition to the standard labels (mobile, home, work, main, home fax, work fax, and page), you can also add custom labels to your heart's content. See the upcoming section on managing custom labels to learn more about adding and editing labels.

Tap Done to save your new phone number for the contact, or tap Cancel to go back to the New Contact screen without adding that number.

Adding E-mail Addresses and URLs

The E-mail and URL fields allow you to add Internet addresses for your contacts. Tap either option, enter the e-mail or web address desired, and tap Done. As with phone numbers, you can set standard labels for these items or enter custom ones as needed.

Adding Addresses

The address fields refer to a contact's physical location, including street address and city. As with all the other contact information, you can add more than one address to a contact and label these items as home or work or with a custom label.

The Contacts application is smart enough to adjust the address fields based on the country you pick. So for Australian addresses, you're prompted for suburb, state, and postal code. Japanese addresses include postal code, prefecture, and county/city.

Adding Other Fields

In addition to the standard name, phone, and address fields, you can add a number of other predefined fields to a contact's information. Tap Add Field, and choose from Prefix, Middle, Suffix, Phonetic First Name, Phonetic Last Name, Nickname, Job Title, Department, Birthday, Date, and Note. The Note field allows you to enter a free-form note and can prove very handy.

Adding Outside Data to an Existing Contact

If someone who is already in your contacts list sends you an e-mail with their address or phone number or if you find contact information on the Web for someone you already have in your address book, tap and hold that information, be it a phone number or address, and wait for the Add to Existing Contact menu pops up. Tap Add to Existing Contact, and then choose your contact from your address book. When their address card opens, the new phone number or address will populate the respective field. Add more information if you like, and then press the Done button.

Managing Custom Labels

There's a big world out there that goes beyond "home fax" and "work address." The Contacts application allows you to add custom labels to your phone numbers, e-mail addresses, URLs, and physical addresses. Manage these labels using any of the label-selection screens, each of which contains an Edit button. Tap this Edit button—it is at the top-right corner of the screen—to switch to edit mode, as shown in Figure 15–6.

In edit mode, you can perform the following actions to add and remove custom fields to and from your iPhone:

> *Add a field*: Tap the green + button at the bottom of the edit list to add a new custom field. A Custom Label screen opens. Here, you can type in the name for the new label. Tap Save to add the label.

> *Remove a field*: Tap the red button next to any custom field you want to remove. A Delete button appears at the field's right. Tap Delete to confirm deletion, or tap anywhere else on the screen to cancel. Once removed, all phone numbers, e-mail addresses, and so forth, that have been labeled with that custom item are renamed to the generic "label." You will not lose phone numbers and other data items you've entered.

To finish making your edits, tap Done.

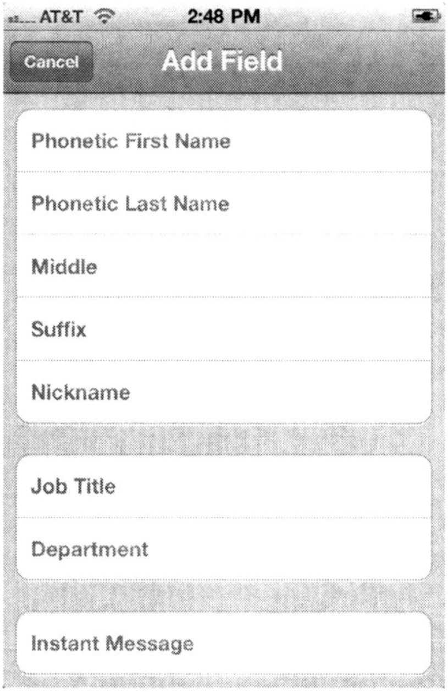

Figure 15–6. *Contacts allows you to interactively manage your custom fields.*

Editing and Removing Contacts

To edit a contact, first select it in the contacts list, and tap it to open its Info tab. There, tap the Edit button in the top-right corner. This sends you to an edit screen that is functionally nearly identical to the New Contact screen (Figure 15–5). Make your changes, and then tap Done to finish and save them.

A Delete Contact button appears at the bottom of the edit screen. To remove a contact from your address book, scroll down to the red button, and tap it. A confirmation dialog box appears. Tap Delete Contact again, and Contacts removes the item from your address book. Tap Cancel to retain the contact.

As you can see, Contacts are a big part of the iPhone experience. Not only does the app help you manage all your contacts, it's fully integrated into iOS itself. You contacts appear in other Apple and third-party iOS apps such as Maps, Messages, Calendars, Facebook, and more. Get used to adding and organizing your contacts because the payoff in user experience is huge! Now, let's move on to some other desk set apps, which will help you in your everyday tasks.

Using the Calculator

iPhone's Calculator app provides a thorough interactive calculator with a simple memory. The icon on your home screen looks like four calculator buttons. It appears on the second row of the home screen, the second icon in. You can see this icon in Figure 15–7.

Figure 15–7. *The Calculator icon*

When you launch the Calculator app, you'll see a simple calculator that allows you to add, subtract, multiply, and divide (Figure 15–8). When you tap an operation button, a white circle appears around the button to let you know which operation will be carried out. But remember, many apps have multiple views depending on which way you are holding your iPhone. Rotate the iPhone into landscape mode to reveal the built-in scientific calculator!

Figure 15–8. *The iPhone Calculator application allows you to use your iPhone as a calculator (left) when you're on the go. Rotate the iPhone vertically to reveal the scientific calculator (right).*

The Calculator application allows you to add, subtract, multiply, and divide (and much more if you're in scientific mode). When you tap an operation button, a white circle appears around the button to let you know which operation will be carried out.

Use the memory buttons to add to the stored number (m+) or subtract (m–). Once a number is stored in memory, the button highlights with a white circle. Tap mr to recall the stored number. Tap mc to clear the number from memory.

> **TIP:** If you're more interested in splitting a restaurant bill with friends than doing advanced math, you may want to use one of the many free online tip and bill-splitter calculators instead when visiting restaurants. Search the App Store for *tip calculator*.

Taking Notes

The iPhone Notes application allows you to jot down quick notes on the go. This application isn't meant to be a full-powered word processor. It just provides a simple way to create notes and bring them with you.

To launch Notes, tap the yellow notepad-styled icon on your home screen (Figure 15–9).

Figure 15–9. *The Notes icon*

Figure 15–10 shows the Notes screen. From this screen, you can add and manage notes as follows.

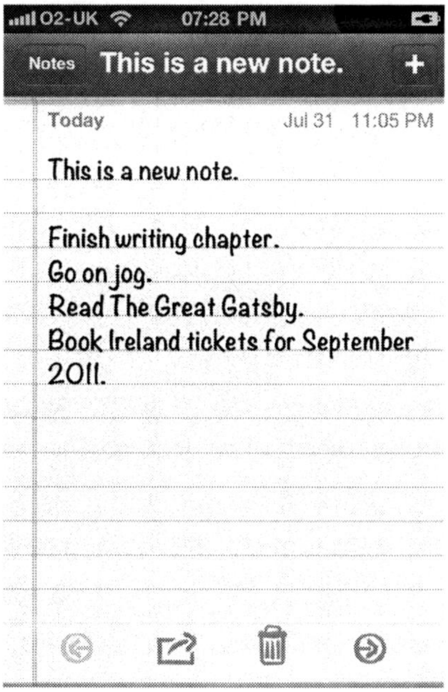

Figure 15–10. *Use the Notes screen to write quick notes. You can e-mail your notes to others.*

Create new notes: Tap the + button to add a new note.

Enter and edit text: Tapping in the text area summons the keyboard. Type your note, make any changes, and then tap Done to dismiss the keyboard.

Delete a note: Tap the garbage can icon, and then tap Delete Note.

Navigate between notes: Use the left and right arrows to move between notes, or tap Notes in the upper-left corner and select the note you want to view from the list.

E-mail notes: Tap the envelope, enter an address, and tap Send. The text from the note will be pasted into the body of the e-mail.

In Chapter 2, we talk about setting up a Bluetooth keyboard. If you are using Notes a lot, you might want to think about investing in one.

Syncing Notes

If you like, you can sync notes between your iPhone and your computer. To sync notes, you'll need to be using Mail.app, Entourage 2008, or Outlook 2011 on a Mac or Microsoft Outlook 2003 or newer on a Windows computer. Again, if you are using iCloud, your Notes will sync over the air automatically. You can also sync notes with various e-mail providers such as Gmail, Yahoo!, and AOL. To sync notes with those e-mail accounts, navigate to **Settings ➤ Mail, Contacts, Calendars**, and choose your e-mail account. Where you see the Notes icon, tap the switch to ON. Syncing notes allows your notes to be viewed and edited in Mac OS X's Mail app or Windows Outlook.

If you are using multiple note accounts, you'll see the option of viewing all notes together or just notes from a certain account on the Accounts screen (Figure 15–11).

Here are some tips on using the Notes application:

- Although your Notes files are backed up, you cannot sync your notes to text files on your personal computer. Use e-mail to send yourself your notes if you want to sync them to your computer.

- To search through your notes, navigate to a notes list screen (the second image in Figure 15–11), and swipe down to reveal the search field at the top. The results screen will populate with any notes that match your search criteria.

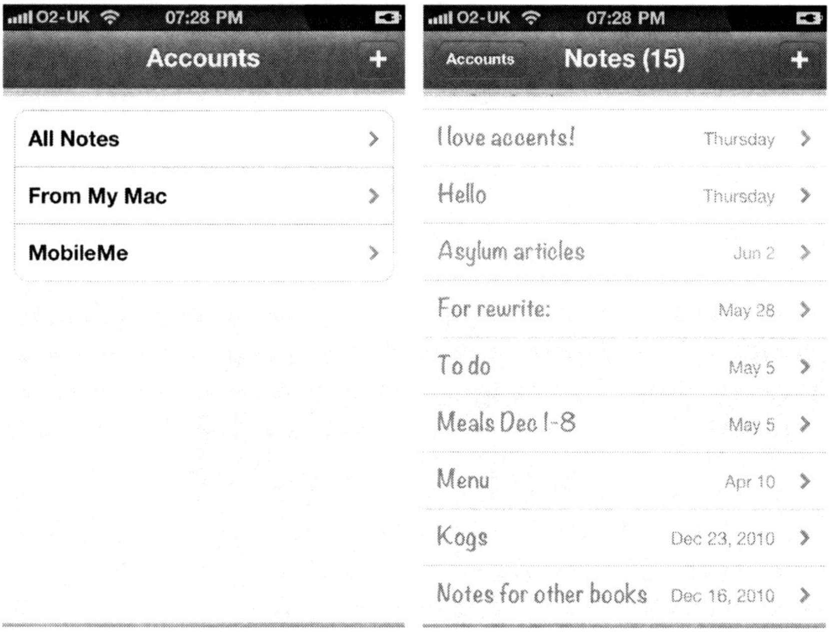

.ıll O2-UK 🛜 07:28 PM 🔋	.ıll O2-UK 🛜 07:28 PM 🔋
Accounts **+**	**Accounts** **Notes (15)** **+**
All Notes >	I love accents! Thursday >
From My Mac >	Hello Thursday >
MobileMe >	Asylum articles Jun 2 >
	For rewrite: May 28 >
	To do May 5 >
	Meals Dec 1-8 May 5 >
	Menu Apr 10 >
	Kogs Dec 23, 2010 >
	Notes for other books Dec 16, 2010 >

Figure 15–11. *Use the Accounts screen (left) to view all your notes together (right) or on a per-account basis.*

> **NOTE:** Unfortunately, there's no easy way to change the dreadful default font for Notes. Also, currently, you cannot print your notes directly from the iPhone to a printer.

Checking the Weather

The iPhone Weather application allows you to view the current temperature and six-day forecast for each of your favorite cities. Weather uses forecast data from Yahoo! and the Weather Channel to provide up-to-the-minute data on your iPhone. To launch Weather, tap the blue icon with the sun on your home screen (Figure 15–12).

Figure 15–12. *The Weather icon*

Viewing Weather Info

Figure 15–13 shows a typical Weather screen. From here, you can flick left and right to scroll between your cities. The bright dot at the bottom of the screen shows which item you're viewing. The dim dots show the other cities you've added to the Weather app. The arrowhead in front of the line of dots is the current location weather. This weather screen shows you the wether for whatever location you are currently located in. Cities that are experiencing daylight have a blue background, and cities where it is already dark have a purple background. Tap any weather screen to see an hourly forecast for the selected city.

Figure 15–13. *The iPhone Weather application provides six-day forecasts for your favorite cities and your current location. Tap the weather screen to see an hourly forecast.*

When you're ready to specify your cities, tap the small *i* at the bottom right of any Weather screen. This flips from the forecast to the city-management screen. From this screen, you can customize your cities:

> *Local Weather: Toggle this On or Off to show the current location weather screen.*
>
> *Add a city*: Tap the + button, enter the city name, tap Search, and then tap the city you want to add. You cannot find every city. Only those supported by Yahoo! and the Weather Channel are available.
>
> *Remove a city*: Tap the red – button next to any city name, and then tap Delete.

> *Reorder cities*: Use the grab controls to the right of each name to drag your cities into a new order.
>
> *Switch between Fahrenheit and Celsius*: Tap °F or °C.

Tap Done to return to the forecast screen.

Weather Tips

Here are some tips for using the Weather application:

- As Figure 15–13 shows, based on the dots at the bottom represent how many cities you've added. The first "dot" will be an arrowhead, which is the weather for your current location..

- Tap the Y! icon to visit Yahoo Weather in Safari.

- You don't need to keep the Cupertino forecast. Although the iPhone offers Cupertino as its default forecast, feel free to add your own city and remove Cupertino from the list. Apple will never know.

Monitoring Stocks

You can use your iPhone to keep track of the stock market so you could see how much you've made (or lost!) that day. The Stocks icon looks like a blue-and-gray stock ticker (Figure 15–14). Tap it to go to the application that monitors your favorite stocks using 20-minute delayed data from Yahoo!

Figure 15–14. *The Stocks icon*

The Stocks screen, shown in Figure 15–15, consists of a list of stocks above a historic graph. Current prices appear to the right of each name, with the changes listed in green (positive) or red (negative). From this screen, you can view and customize stock information as follows.

Figure 15–15. *Yahoo! Finance powers the iPhone Stocks application using 20-minute-delayed data.*

View a stock: Tap any stock to load its associated graph.

Choose the history length: Choose the length of time over which you want to view a stock's history. Pick from one day (1d), one week (1w), one month (1m), three months (3m), six months (6m), one year (1y), and two years (2y).

Customize: You can add or remove stocks from your list by tapping the *i* icon at the bottom right of your screen. This opens the customization screen (Figure 15–16).

Figure 15–16. *Customizing the stocks app*

- To add a stock, tap the + button and either search for a company name or enter the stock symbol directly.

- To remove a stock, tap the red – button, and then tap Delete.

- Reorder stocks by using the drag controls to the right of each stock name.

- The %, Price, and Mkt Cap buttons switch between the percentage gained or lost, the current price, and the market cap of the stocks.

- Tap Done to return to the main Stocks screen.

Notice the three dots below the chart in the stocks app (see Figure 15–15)? If you swipe left or right, you can also view the summary and news headlines for a specific stock (Figure 15–17). When viewing the news headlines, scroll up or down to see more. Tapping a headline will open up the news article in the Safari browser.

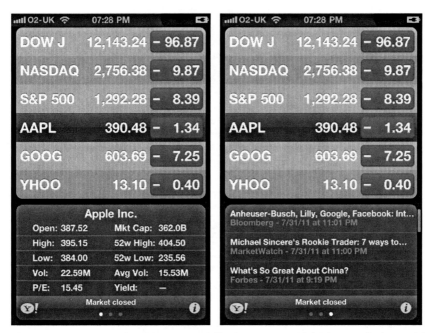

Figure 15–17. *You can view the summary (left), chart, or news (right) for a particular stock by swiping left or right.*

The Stocks app also support landscape mode. Turn your iPhone on its side to be presented with an interactive chart of a particular stock (Figure 15–18).

Figure 15–18. *Rotate the iPhone to landscape mode to see the interactive chart.*

Use the time buttons (1 day, 3 months, and so on) to show a specific time frame. Drag your finger across the chart to see the precise stock price for any given time. Drag two fingers along the chart (Figure 15–19) to show the price difference between any two different points in time. Finally, swipe left or right to switch to another stock's chart.

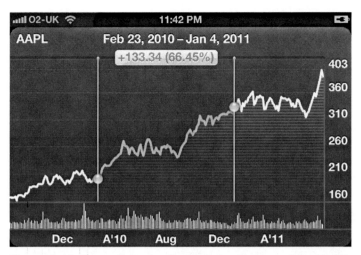

Figure 15–19. *Place and drag two fingers on the chart to see the price difference between any two points.*

Here are some tips for using the Stocks application:

- Tap Yahoo! Finance at the bottom of the customization screen to jump directly to the Yahoo! Finance web site. You can also tap Y! at the bottom left of the main Stocks screen to get to this web site.

- Stock quotes are delayed according to the rules of the stock exchange. This provides an advantage to on-floor traders and allows vendors to charge for premium real-time quotes.

- You don't need to press the customization button to switch between percentage, price, and market cap views; you can just tap the value column (red and green squares) to switch between views.

We are sure there's a limit to how many stocks you can add to your list, but we have yet to personally encounter that limit.

Dictating Voice Memos

When Apple decided to include the Voice Memos app (Figure 15–20) on the iPhone, we thought we would never use it. Now, however, it's one of the apps we turn to most. With voice memos, you can quickly record ideas or entire classes or meetings with the tap of a button.

To use the Voice Memo app, your iPhone will need a microphone. Obviously, all iPhones have a built-in microphone that enables you to talk, but the earbuds that came with the iPhones also have built-in mics for hands-free talking. Other hands-free iPhone-compatible mics can be purchased at http://store.apple.com.

Figure 15–20. *The Voice Memos icon*

Tap the Voice Memos icon to launch that app. You'll be presented with a screen that shows a large, old-fashioned radio mic from the 1930s. The radio mic is just for show. You interact with the Voice Memos app using the two buttons, situated on either side of the audio level meter (Figure 15–21).

Figure 15–21. *The Voice Memos app*

To record a memo, tap the red-and-silver record button on the left of the screen. A red bar will appear at the top of the screen with the word *Recording* in it followed by the recording time that has elapsed (Figure 15–22). You'll also notice that the record button has changed to a pause button. Tap it to pause the current recording. Tap it again to resume recording. To stop a recording, tap the silver-and-black stop button on the right side of the screen.

Figure 15–22. *Recording a memo*

To view and listen to all your recordings, tap the Memos button. The Memos button has three horizontal lines and rests in the lower-right corner in Figure 15–21. The Voice Memos screen will appear (Figure 15–23).

From the Voice Memos screen, you can play back any memo you've recorded.

> *Play a Memo*: Tap the memo you want to play so it is highlighted in blue. Then tap the memo again to play it.

> *Scrub through a memo*: Use the slider at the bottom of the screen to scrub through your memos. This is particularly helpful for long recordings.

> *Share a memo*: Select a memo, and then tap the Share button. A pop-up menu will appear asking you whether you want to share your memo using e-mail or in a message. Tap E-mail, and a new email compose screen will appear with the recording attached to the body of the e-mail. Tap Message, and a new message compose screen will appear with the recording attached to the body of the message. We discuss the Messages app in Chapter 6.

> *Deleting a memo*: Select a memo, and then tap the Delete button. Tap the Delete Voice Memo pop-up that appears to confirm your deletion.

Figure 15–23. *The Voice Memos screen lists all your memos.*

You can also label and edit voice memos by navigating to their information screen. To do this, tap the blue-and-white > button next to a voice memo. You'll be taken to that voice memo's information page (Figure 15–24).

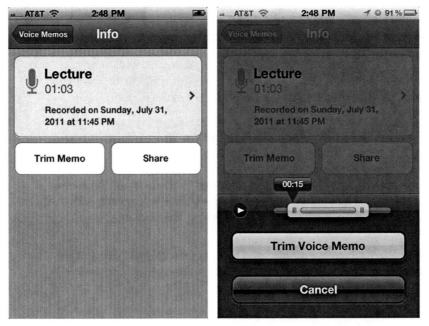

Figure 15–24. *A memo's information page (left) and trimming options (right)*

From this page you can do the following:

> *Label the voice memo*: Tap the field with the microphone icon in it (next to the time stamps) to be taken to the labels screen. From this screen you can select from the following labels: Podcast, Interview, Lecture, Idea, Meeting, or Memo. You can also name your memo anything you want by tapping the Custom button and entering a name. To keep length of time of the memo as its name, select None as the label.

> *Trim the voice memo*: You can actually edit your voice memos right on the iPhone. Tap Trim Memo, and a black-and-yellow trim menu will appear (Figure 15–25). Adjust the beginning and end times by using the yellow and blue slider, and tap Trim Voice Memo to trim the selection. The trim feature is a great way to cut out the usual dead air times at the beginning or ending of a recording. However, you cannot edit out snippets of the recording piecemeal. You can only trim its edges. Also, note that edits you make *cannot* be undone.

> *Share*: This button functions the same as the Share button on the main information page. Tap Share, and then tap E-mail, and a new message compose screen will appear with the recording attached to the body of the e-mail.

iTunes automatically syncs any voice memos you have created the next time you connect your iPhone to your computer. The memos are stored under a playlist that is created called Voice Memos (see Figure 15–25).

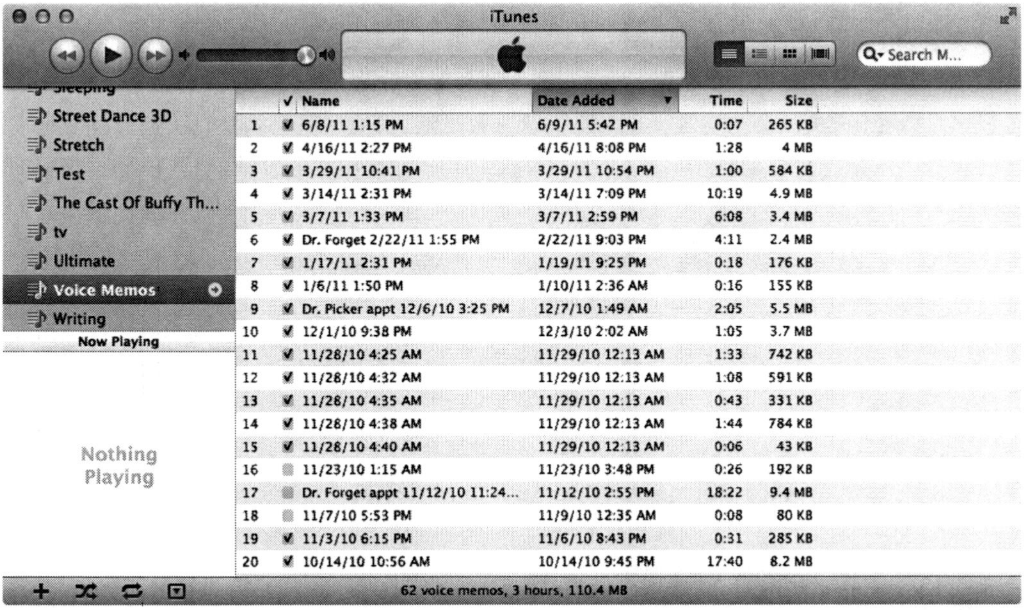

Figure 15–25. *iTunes automatically creates a playlist called Voice Memos when it detects a voice memo on your iPhone.*

When you sync voice memos to iTunes, they still remain on the iPhone until you delete them. Deleting them on the IPhone will not delete them from iTunes; however, deleting a voice memo from iTunes will also delete it from the iPhone on the next sync.

Setting Reminders

Reminders is a brand new app included on every iPhone. It's a to-do app that lets you create lists and set reminders so you never forget anything again. To launch Reminders, tap its on your home screen (Figure 15–26).

Figure 15–26. *The Reminders icon*

When you launch the app you'll first see a looseleaf piece of paper with the title "Reminders" at the top. This is your main reminders list (Figure 15–27). To create a reminder, tap the + button and enter a name or description for the reminder. Tap Done when you have finished naming the reminder. In Figure 15–27, one of our reminders is to "Buy flowers."

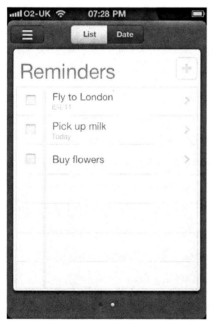

Figure 15–27. *The Reminders app*

But Reminders isn't just an app that helps you create lists. It's called "Reminders" for a reason. You can set a number of ways to be reminded to do something on your list. Reminders will remind you of your to-do list items via the notifcations center and you can set reminders to notify you based on date and time.

To set details and notifications for your reminders, tap an item from your Reminders list. On the details screen that appears (Figure 15–28) you can set the time and date you want to be reminded at, the time and date the item is due, whether the item on your list is a one-time even or a repeating event (such as weekly), when to end the repeating reminders, the priority of the to-do item (None, Low, Medium, High), and even add notes to the reminder to give it more details.

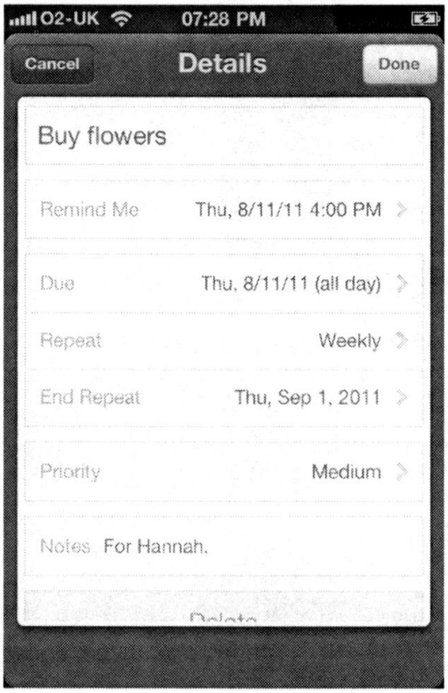

Figure 15–28. *Setting the details of a Reminders event*

When you are done entering details about a reminder event, tap the Done button. To delete a reminder, tap the red delete button that appears at the bottom of the Details screen.

Besides viewing your reminders as a list, you can also view them by date. Simply tap the Date button at the top of the screen (Figure 15–27) and you'll be taken to the date view (Figure 15–29). In date view you can swipe left and right between days, or tap the calendar button in the top-left corner to view monthly calendars. Tap any date on the calendar to be taken to its date page.

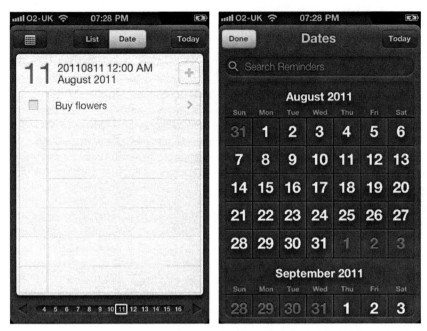

Figure 15–29. *Browsing Reminders by date. Day view, left; calendar view, right.*

When you complete an event in your reminders list, tap the checkbox to mark it off
(Figure 15–27). The event will be removed from your Reminders list and added to your
Completed list (Figure 15–30). To view your Completed list, swipe right on the
Reminders screen or tap the lists button.

Figure 15–30. *The Completed list*

The lists button appears at the top-left corner of the screen and has three lines on it. Tap it to reveal all your lists (Figure 15–31). Tap a list to jump right to that list. To create a new list, tap the edit button on the list screen and then tap "Creat New List." Multiple lists can be very handy. You can create on for work, one for groceries, one for your personal life, etc.

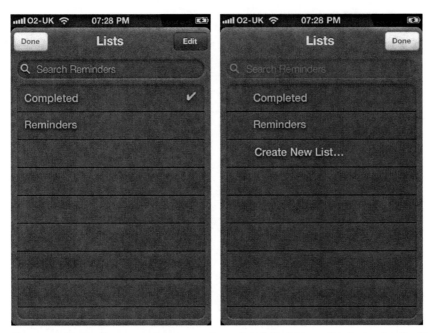

Figure 15–31. *The lists screen shows you all your lists (left). Add new lists by tapping the "Create New List" button, right.*

Summary

As you can now see, the iPhone includes several useful tools for the user, whether they are a business professional or a student. The Notes, Voice Memos, and Reminders applications provide helpful on-hand references for when you need a quick jog to your memory in written or audio form. The Contacts app also lets you expand your address book while on the go and synchronize it to your home computer. The Calculator is always there to get you out of a jam when you realize you didn't pay attention in Algebra 101 and Stocks and Weather lets you check both your current and future financial and climate forecasts.

Here are a few last thoughts:

- Although the iPhone does not have an onboard phone, it's easy enough to look up numbers on the iPhone and type them into your cell phone.

- It's *really* nice to have all your numbers and addresses in one place. Because our iPhones sync to our computers, we don't have to keep a half dozen separate address books, each on a separate device. We can rely on the iPhone's version instead.

- The iPhone's calculator is a lifesaver when you realize math isn't your strong suit.

■ The Stocks and Weather applications provide great ways to keep up with real-time information using classic Apple design.

■ Although the Notes application is limited, it offers a convenient way to jot down notes in a central and easy-to-remember location.

■ How many times have you been in a class or meeting and wish you had a voice recorder with you? With your iPhone, now you do.

■ Reminders is a wonderful app that can help those of us with poor memories when things need to get done.

Part **VII**

Preferences

Chapter 16

Customizing Your iPhone

The iPhone has many settings allowing you to customize how the device works and looks. These settings are all customizable in the Settings app on the Home screen of your iPhone. The iPhone's Settings application offers many ways to enhance your iPhone experience, in addition to those options tied to a particular application. These general settings control everything from screen brightness to sound effects to keyboard tricks. I've explored various options in the Settings app throughout this book. This chapter covers the remainder of these extra settings and discusses how you can use them in your day-to-day routine. I'll start this chapter by showing you the top five settings people use the most.

Tap the Settings app icon shown in Figure 16–1, and you'll be presented with the Settings screen, which is a list of preferences for the iPhone and other applications that are installed on it (see Figure 16–2). To select an app's settings, tap the name of the app.

Figure 16–1. *The Settings app icon*

Figure 16–2. *The Settings screen*

Not all of the settings that are controlled within the Settings app are covered in this chapter, because they vary by iPhone model and installed applications.

Six Important Settings

The Settings app lets you really customize your iPhone to its fullest. However, most people won't be messing around with all the advanced settings. Before I launch into explaining all of the general settings, let's go through the top six settings people use the most.

Airplane Mode

This one is for all your frequent fliers and business travelers. Airplane Mode puts your iPhone into a configuration that allows you to use it on a plane without the flight attendant telling you to turn your device off. To enable Airplane Mode, tap the switch to On (Figure 16–3). You'll notice that an orange airplane icon appears in the upper-left status bar where the signal strength bars and carrier abbreviation usually are.

Figure 16–3. *Airplane Mode. Note the airplane icon in the top-left menu bar.*

When Airplane Mode is on, no Bluetooth or Wi-Fi signals emanate from the iPhone. In other words, Airplane Mode disables antennas that can interfere with flight instrumentation. When Airplane Mode is enabled, you are not able to use wireless Bluetooth headsets or use in-flight Internet on your iPhone. You can reenable Wi-Fi when the plane is in flight, even while using Airplane Mode. This allows you to purchase and use in-flight Wi-Fi and even have a video chat with your friends and family back home if you own an iPhone that can run the FaceTime app.

Note that during takeoff and landing, you are instructed to turn off all portable electronics, regardless of whether they are in Airplane Mode or not. After you're back on the ground, turn Airplane Mode off by tap the switch to Off. Since all of your iPhone's wireless transmitters are turned off, turning on Airplane Mode also improves your battery life significantly.

Twitter

In case you haven't heard, Twitter is the Internet social network and micro-blogging service that allows users to instantly send messages to friends and followers in 140 characters or less. It seems like the whole world is tweeting these days, from your next-door neighbor to celebrities and politicians. As you've seen throughout this book, Twitter is highly integrated into iOS 5. You can tweet directly from Photos, Safari, YouTube, Camera, and Maps, plus many other third-party apps.

Before iOS 5, you had to log into your Twitter account in every app that supported tweeting. With iOS 5, there's just a single login location for Twitter, and that means your Twitter account ID is integrated systemwide for easy tweeting.

To set up your Twitter account, go to Twitter in the Settings app. In the Twitter settings (Figure 16–4), enter your Twitter ID and password, and then tap Sign In. If you don't have a Twitter ID, tap the Create New Account button and set up a new Twitter account right in the Settings screen.

Figure 16–4. *Settings for Twitter. In this figure, the Twitter app is installed, and two accounts have been enabled.*

Once you are signed into Twitter, you'll be able to tweet directly from iOS 5's built-in apps like Safari, Maps, YouTube, and more. Also, on the Twitter Settings screen you can tap the Install button to immediately download and install the official Twitter app, which lets you fully interact with Twitter.com and all your friends and followers.

In Twitter Settings, tap your account name for additional settings. These include the ability to let your friends find you on Twitter using your e-mail address and automatically tweeting your location when you post a tweet. Finally, you can tap Update Contacts to add Twitter usernames to the people in your Contacts lists.

Sounds

The Sounds settings enable you to select which ringer and alerts sound effects you hear while interacting with your iPhone (Figure 16–5). These settings are useful when you are using your iPhone in a public place like a library or a coffee shop or attending a meeting.

> *Vibrate*: If Vibrate is turned on, your phone will vibrate when receiving a call or other notification. If you've enabled the Mute switch on the side of the phone, the vibration is the only way you'll know that a call is coming in. If the Mute switch is off, your iPhone will both ring and "buzz."

Volume slider: This slider allows you to turn your ringer volume up or down. The ringer volume refers to the level of sound that you hear when someone calls you or initiates a FaceTime call with you.

Change with Buttons: When this is switched to On, you can use the physical volume buttons on the side of your iPhone to adjust the volume level of the ringer and alerts. When set to Off, the volume of the ringer and alerts is separate from the volume of the other sounds (like music playback) on your iPhone.

Ringtone: This allows you to choose your ringtone from one of Apple's built-in ringtones. If you've synced your own ringtones from iTunes (see Chapter 2), you can also select that ringtone here.

Alerts: By default the iPhone plays a sound effect whenever you send or receive mail, have a calendar alert, lock your iPhone (by pressing the Sleep/Wake button on the top of the iPhone), press a key on the on-screen keyboard, and more. On the Sounds settings screen, you can choose to change any of these sound effects or even disable them entirely. Tap the sound effect you want to change and then select a replacement sound effect from the list of effects or choose None.

Figure 16–5. *Use Settings ➤ Sounds to choose how your iPhone plays back system alert sounds.*

Brightness

Choose Settings ➤ Brightness (see Figure 16–6) to control your iPhone's screen brightness intensity. The slider at the top of the Settings screen lets you manually set exactly how bright your screen is, from very dim (on the left) to very bright (on the right).

A lot of people who jog or walk at night benefit from turning down the brightness on their iPhone. Why? Your eyes adjust to the darkness, and when you look at your iPhone to read a message or change songs, the screen can temporarily blind you if it's set too bright. I've had friends trip and fall while jogging at night because of the sudden blinding light from their iPhone screen.

Figure 16–6. *The Settings ➤ Brightness control allows you to set the overall screen intensity for your iPhone.*

The Auto-Brightness option, beneath the brightness slider, controls another light-level feature. It determines whether your iPhone samples the ambient light when it wakes up as you slide to unlock. When enabled, it adjusts the screen according to the light it senses in the room. If you're in a dim room, it lowers the brightness of the screen. In a brightly lit room, the brightness is enhanced for readability.

Wallpaper

Although this was covered in Chapter 3, setting your iPhone's wallpaper is an important and easy way to personalize your iPhone, so I'll cover it briefly one more time.

The **Settings ➤ Wallpaper** screen allows you to set your system wallpaper from a library of commercial-grade photos that shipped on your iPhone. You can also select wallpaper from any image, such as your personal photos, on your iPhone. Select Wallpaper to see your current lock and Home screen wallpaper settings (Figure 16–7). To change either wallpaper, tap the lock and Home screen image, and you'll be presented with a list of all the photos on your iPhone. The Wallpaper collection is full of images that came with your iPhone. Below it is a list of all of your photos, both on your iPhone's Camera Roll and in your Photo Stream.

> **NOTE:** Unlike the images in your Photos library, you cannot move and scale the iPhone's built-in library of Wallpaper pictures. They are sized at 640-by-960 pixels, perfectly matched to your screen.

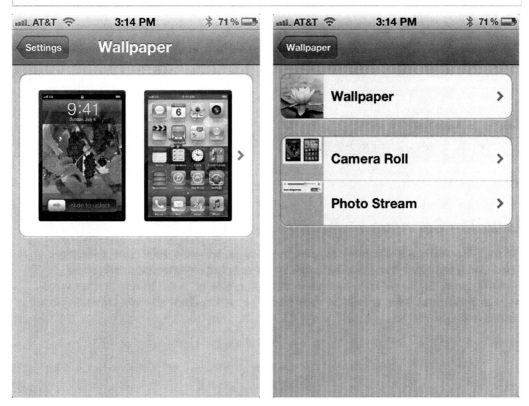

Figure 16–7. *Settings ➤ Wallpaper offers the ability to set wallpaper for the lock screen and the Home screen on your iPhone (left). Select from Apple-supplied wallpapers or use photos from your own collections (right).*

When you find the image you want to use, move and scale it with your fingers and then tap the Set button (Figure 16–8). From the pop-up menu, choose to use that image as the lock screen wallpaper, as the Home screen wallpaper, or as both wallpapers.

Figure 16–8. *Move and scale your image (left), and then choose to use it as wallpaper for the lock screen, Home screen, or both.*

Location Services

On the iPhone there are dozens of apps that rely on knowing your current location. These include Maps, time zone settings, Weather, photo geolocation, and more. However, in today's privacy-sensitive world, people want to be able to control what apps or processes have access to their current location. That's where Location Services comes in (Figure 16–9).

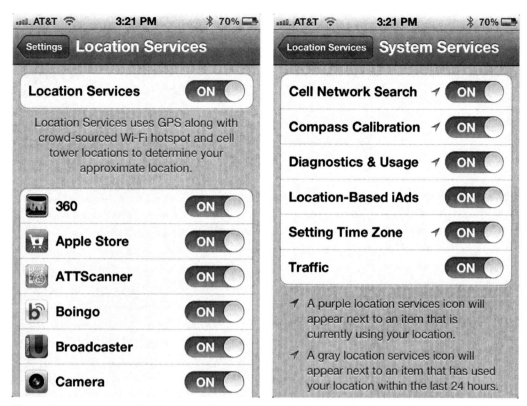

Figure 16–9. *Left, the Location Services settings can be used to disable all location services or just disable some apps from reading your current location. Right, the System Services screen gives you control over iOS 5 location services.*

To control location information on your iPhone, navigate to **Settings ➤ Location Services**. If Location Services is set to On, any apps that can automatically find your location (like the Maps app) are able to do so. Any app that has permission to read your current location shows up in the list. But before any app can access your current location, you must give it approval to do so. A pop-up notification automatically appears when an app requests your current location (see Figure 16–23).

Apps can use your location in any number of ways. The Facebook app, for example, uses your location to tell your friends where you are posting from and the Maps app uses your location in order to help identify where you are on a map.

Location services are very handy. However, today it's easy to get paranoid about people finding you based on your device's location. To turn all location services off, tap the Location Services switch to Off (Figure 16–9). Alternatively, leave location services on, but disable location services on a per-app basis.

> **NOTE:** When an app has used your current location in the past 24 hours, you'll see a tiny gray arrowhead icon next to its name in the Location Services settings. When an app is using your current location now, the tiny arrow next to it on this screen is purple. Whenever an app is currently using your location, that tiny arrowhead also appears in the menu bar.

You can also control the amount of access other iOS services have to your location. On the Location Services screen, tap the System Services button, and then toggle on or off services such as location-based iAds, traffic, and diagnostics.

Other Good-to-Know Settings

Under **Settings ➤ General**, you'll find that the General settings (Figure 16–10) are the "meat" of settings that have to do with the iPhone itself, like Siri, networking, and security.

Figure 16–10. *The General settings screen*

"About" Your iPhone

Your iPhone summarizes its capabilities and storage levels, listing the number of songs, videos, photos, and other important information on the **Settings ➤ General ➤ About** screen (see Figure 16–11). Here, you'll find basic details about the space available and remaining on your iPhone, as well as other details such as the model of your iPhone, the serial number, and more.

Figure 16–11. *The Settings ➤ General ➤ About screen lists basic information about your iPhone.*

At the top of the screen, tap Name to change your iPhone's name. If you scroll all the way down to the bottom of the About screen, you'll see a link labeled Legal. Tap this to jump to an insanely long list of Apple legal notices. It's a boring document to read, but it's an amazingly good place to get some practice flicking your screen. You almost never run out of text to scroll through.

Software Update

New to iOS 5 is the ability to update the iOS software without having to plug your iPhone into iTunes and download the software from there. These automatic updates are referred to as *over-the-air* (OTA) updates. Now any time a software update is available for iOS, a red badge appears on the corner of the Setting icon. You can also manually check for iOS software updates by navigating to **Settings** ➤ **General** ➤ **Software Update**. Any available IOS software updates are listed there.

Usage

Usage is another new Settings screen that allows you to see how much storage is being used by each app on your iPhone. View your usage at **Settings** ➤ **General** ➤ **Usage** (Figure 16–12).

Figure 16–12. *Viewing how much storage space each app is consuming*

In Figure 16–12 you can see that the Navigon app is taking up the most storage space on my iPhone. If I tap Navigon, I can see documents and data (primarily personal settings) are taking up only 172KB of storage, while most of the 1.7GB must be the app and its built-in maps. You can delete entire apps (but not the ones that shipped on your iPhone) to free all the space they take up.

Usage is handy if your iPhone is almost full but you want to download a movie at the airport to watch on the plane. You can free up some songs or other content in apps to get enough space to download that movie.

iTunes Wi-Fi Sync

As I mentioned in Chapter 2, you can now sync your iPhone wirelessly when it's in range of your computer and on the same Wi-Fi network. When you plug your iPhone into a power source, it automatically syncs over the network. You can also manually initiate syncing from your iPhone at any time by going to **Settings ➤ General ➤ iTunes Wi-Fi Sync** (Figure 16–13) and tapping the Sync Now button.

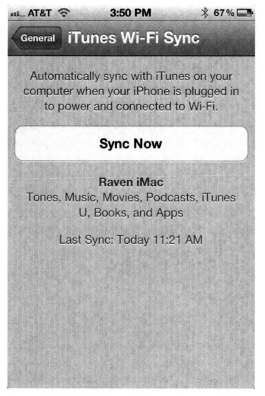

Figure 16–13. *Initiating a Wi-Fi sync from your iPhone*

Network

The settings found on the **Settings ➤ General ➤ Network** screen duplicate the Wi-Fi settings covered in Chapter 4. They also include a switch to enable, disable, and customize virtual private network (VPN) connections as well as turn your iPhone into a Personal Hotspot.

A VPN is usually used for secure communications over public Internet connections. When this option is enabled, you can configure your VPN account settings with the Network settings screen. Consult your IT department or network provider for details on how to set up your iPhone for a VPN connection.

Personal Hotspot turns your iPhone into a Wi-Fi hotspot anywhere you have a 3G data signal. This feature, which has an extra carrier cost associated with it, means that your cellular data connection can be shared with up to five other users.

Bluetooth

The Bluetooth settings allow you to turn the iPhone's Bluetooth signal on or off. This is also where you'll find a list of Bluetooth-compatible devices that your iPhone is aware of. To pair a Bluetooth device, select it in the list, and then enter the pairing code. For keyboards, a random code is usually generated. For devices such as Bluetooth headsets, look for the code on a label on the headset. Note that some newer Bluetooth devices no longer use pairing codes, show up in your pairing list automatically, and ask whether you want to give the device access. To unpair a Bluetooth device, select it from the list, and choose Forget this Device.

If you aren't using any Bluetooth devices with your iPhone, keep Bluetooth turned off to preserve battery life. Don't forget to switch it back on when you want to use Bluetooth headsets, use external keyboards, or play games between iPhone devices.

Auto-Lock

Use the Settings ➤ General ➤ Auto-Lock screen (see Figure 16–14) to determine the period of time after which your iPhone automatically locks. Autolocking is an energy-saving feature. When locked, your screen turns off—although music playback continues—and you must swipe to unlock and return to any previous activities. Choose from 1, 2, 3, 4, or 5 minutes, or choose Never to leave your screen always on. This last option wears down your battery very quickly indeed.

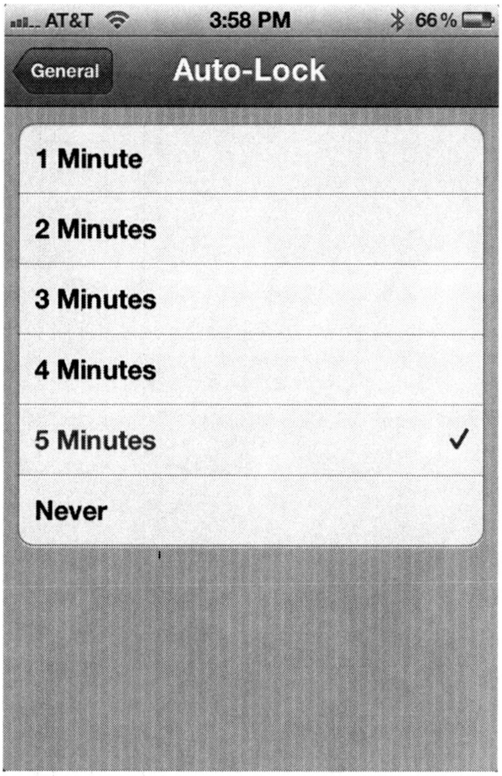

Figure 16–14. *Save your battery and save your screen by setting an autolock time in Settings ➤ General ➤ Auto-Lock.*

Restrictions

If you share your iPhone with your family or have purchased one for your children, you may want to limit what they can do on it. The Restrictions settings (Figure 16–15) lets you restrict access to Safari, YouTube, the iTunes Store app, the ability to install apps, the Camera and FaceTime apps, and the ability for apps to use location services. In addition, you can also choose what content you want allowed on the iPhone. Settings include restricting In-App purchases and limiting access to movies, music, TV shows, and apps that surpass your chosen ratings. Finally, you can also limit multiplayer gaming in Game Center.

> **TIP:** Enabling restrictions for YouTube or Facetime is a great way to "remove" factory-installed apps from your iPhone! They're still there; you just won't be able to see their icons on the Home screen!

Figure 16–15. *The Restrictions settings*

As you can see, Restrictions is all about protecting your children not only from age-inappropriate music and movies but also from potential outside threats such as strangers calling them on FaceTime or apps that post their current location online. When you enable restrictions, you'll be asked to enter a four-digit passcode. You (or your children) need this passcode to change or disable any restriction you've set up. The only way your kids can get around these restrictions is if they completely restore the iPhone to factory conditions. However, if they do this, they lose all their music and movies on the iPhone.

Date and Time

The settings found on the Settings ➤ General ➤ Date & Time screen (see Figure 16–16) allow you to specify how you want your system to handle time. Here, you can choose between a 12-hour (9:30 p.m.) and a 24-hour (21:30) clock, set your time zone, or override the system clock to set a new date and time.

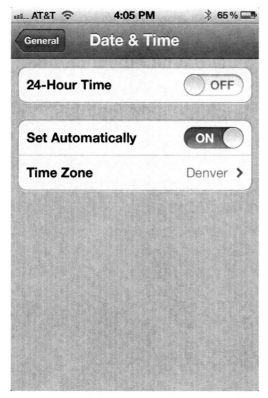

Figure 16–16. *Most of the time, you'll want to let your iPhone set the internal clock and time zone automatically.*

Keyboard

You'll find five very clever and helpful typing settings on the **Settings ➤ General ➤ Keyboard** settings screen (see Figure 16–17).

Figure 16–17. *Use Settings ➤ General ➤ Keyboard to set several handy typing shortcuts.*

Auto-Capitalization: When this feature is set to On, the iPhone is smart about guessing when you're at the start of new sentences. After detecting a period, question mark, or other sentence-ending punctuation, it automatically presses the Shift key for you.

Auto-Correction: When this feature is set to On, the iPhone suggests words to you as you type. Switch it to Off to get rid of those word pop-ups.

Check Spelling: When this is set to On, the iPhone spell-check feature underlines misspelled words in red. Tap the underlined word to see spelling suggestions.

Enable Caps Lock: When selected, Enable Caps Lock treats all taps on the Shift key as the Caps Lock function—setting it either on or off. When it's disabled, you must press the Shift key before each capitalized letter. The Shift key switches itself back off after each use.

"." Shortcut: Enabling the period shortcut feature lets you add a period and then a space to the end of sentences by double-tapping the spacebar.

Also, as discussed in Chapter 3, this is the place where you can set text shortcuts that enable you to type using acronyms that expand to full phrases (in other words, typing **ttyl** will expand to "talk to you later").

The International Keyboards option on the Keyboard settings screen allows you to set the language for your keyboard. This setting is identical to the one found on the International settings screen we'll discuss now.

International

On the **Settings ➤ General ➤ International** screen (see Figure 16–18), you'll find all the settings you need if you want your iPhone to operate in a different language.

Language: The primary system language determines how all your menus and buttons display. Whenever an iPhone application supports multiple languages, your setting here tells that application which words and phrases to use, internationalizing that application appropriately.

Voice Control: Choose the language you'll be speaking your voice commands in.

Keyboards: The keyboard language sets the default keyboard layout for when you type. If you use a lot of foreign phrases, you may want to switch to an international keyboard for certain tasks. Be aware that the keyboard automatically changes when you set a system language. The rather mysterious number shown on the settings screen (1 in Figure 16–17) indicates the chosen keyboard.

Figure 16–18. *International settings let you set your system language, regional keyboard, and date/time formats.*

NOTE: You can also choose keyboards in Settings ➤ General ➤ Keyboard ➤ International Keyboards. The two options lead to identical settings screens.

Region Format: The region format switches the standards for how dates, times, and phone numbers display. November 5, 2011, for the U.S. region would display as 5 November 2011 for the U.K. region. Use this setting to augment your language settings with a country norm.

Calendar: This setting changes the calendar format according to which calendar you follow. Select from Gregorian, Japanese, or Buddhist.

Accessibility

Apple wanted to make sure everyone could use the iPhone as easily as possible. To that end, Apple built in accessibility features to help people with disabilities use the iPhone. To see all the accessibility options, on the iPhone go to **Settings** ➤ **General** ➤ **Accessibility** (see Figure 16–19). Let's go through these settings one by one.

Figure 16–19. *The Accessibility settings*

As you can see when looking at the Accessibility settings, Apple has divided the options into three main categories: Vision, Hearing, and Physical & Motor.

VoiceOver

With VoiceOver turned on, a user simply touches the screen to hear a description of what is beneath his finger and then double-taps to select the item. With VoiceOver enabled, the iPhone speaks when the user has a new e-mail message and can even read the e-mail to the user. This is in addition to the ability for Siri to read e-mail messages, as discussed in Chapter 7.

It's important to remember that when VoiceOver is turned on, the iPhone's Multi-Touch gestures change. As a matter of fact, when VoiceOver is enabled, pretty much all of the gestures we've taught you in this book are irrelevant. The Voice Over settings are also where you can pair your iPhone with a Braille device.

VoiceOver Gestures

I list common VoiceOver gestures here, but be sure to carefully read Apple's VoiceOver article at `http://support.apple.com/kb/HT3598` for complete VoiceOver gesture controls.

> *Tap*: Speaks the selected item.
>
> *Double-tap*: Activates the selected item.
>
> *Triple-tap*: Acts as a double-tap normally would. Triple-tapping an item when VoiceOver is enabled effectively double-taps that item.
>
> *Flick right or left*: Selects the next or previous item.
>
> *Two-finger tap*: Stops speaking the current item.
>
> *Two-finger flick up*: Reads all text or items from the top of the screen.
>
> *Two-finger flick down*: Reads all text or items from the current position.
>
> *Three-finger flick up or down*: Scrolls one page at a time.
>
> *Three-finger flick right or left*: Goes to the next or previous page (such as the Home screen pages, Weather pages, or Safari web pages).

Zoom

Zoom allows those impaired vision to magnify their entire screen. This is different from the standard pinch-and-zoom features of the iPhone's regular software. Accessibility Zoom magnifies everything on the screen, allowing the user to zoom into even the smallest of buttons. When this option is selected, the user double-taps any part of the iPhone's screen with three fingers to automatically zoom in 200 percent. When zoomed in, you must drag or flick the screen with three fingers. Also, when you go to a new screen, zooming always returns you to the top middle of the screen.

Large Text

Large Text allows those with vision impairments to enlarge the text in alerts, Contacts, Mail, and Notes. They can choose from 20-, 24-, 32-, 40-, 48-, or 56-point text (12-point text is the normal text you see on a web page).

White on Black

For some people with vision difficulties, inverting the color of a computer screen so it resembles a photographic negative allows them to read text better. Turning on White on Black does just this.

Speak Selection

With this option selected, any selected text (such as the text you select when copying and pasting) is spoken aloud.

Speak Auto-text

With this option selected, any autocorrection text (such as the spell-check pop-ups that appear when you are typing) is spoken aloud.

Mono Audio

With this selected, the stereo sounds of the left and right speakers or headphones are combined into a mono (single) signal. You can then choose which speaker, the left or the right, you want to hear the mono audio come from. This option lets users who have a hearing impairment in one ear hear the entire sound signal with the other ear.

Assistive Touch

Apple recognizes that for people who have limited motor skills, using a small multitouch screen like the one found on the iPhone can be difficult. With this in mind, Apple created Assistive Touch. When Assistive Touch is enabled, a black-and-white dot is always displayed on the iPhone's screen.

Tapping the dot displays an on-screen menu overlay (Figure 16–20) that allows users to tap icons that represent gestures. Instead of tapping or swiping with two fingers, Assistive Touch allows the user to simply tap a button that performs the gesture automatically.

Figure 16–20. *The Assistive Touch on-screen menu*

Triple-Click Home

If you are sharing an iPhone with someone with disabilities, selecting this option allows users, by triple-clicking the iPhone's physical Home button, to quickly toggle VoiceOver, Zoom, White on Black, or Assistive Touch on or off. You can also set it so triple-clicking the Home button causes a pop-up to appear on-screen asking the user what accessibility feature they want to use (Figure 16–21).

Figure 16–21. *The Accessibility Options pop-up menu*

NOTE: With the exception of the triple-click home feature, all of these accessibility settings can also be configured from within the iPhone iTunes Preferences window on the Summary tab (see Chapter 2). Click Configure Universal Access to choose your settings.

Reset

At times, you may need to reset certain iPhone features via **Settings ➤ General ➤ Reset** (see Figure 16–22). Each of the following options offers a slightly different twist on restoring your iPhone to factory conditions and provides a different degree of security.

Figure 16–22. *The Settings ➤ General ➤ Reset screen allows you to return your iPhone to factory-fresh settings.*

Reset All Settings: This option returns all settings to those that are factory installed.

Erase All Content and Settings: This option deletes all content from your iPhone—music, calendar events, videos, contacts, and so forth—and resets your settings at the same time.

Reset Network Settings: This option restores your Wi-Fi network settings to the defaults. This ensures that your iPhone will not automatically connect to any "known" but dangerous network you might have once encountered.

Reset Keyboard Dictionary: This option "forgets" all words you have typed into your iPhone. The onboard keyboard dictionary is smart about learning the words and names that you type, but it also learns a lot of personal information (including passwords) at the same time. Tap this option to delete this dictionary from your system.

Reset Home Screen Layout: This resets your Home screen icon arrangement to the default one that shipped on your iPhone. Any third-party apps appear in alphabetical order starting on the second Home screen page. Any Web Clips also appear in alphabetical order mixed in with the third-party apps. Finally, any folders you created are deleted, and their apps all appear on the Home screens.

Reset Location Warnings: Any time an app (such as Facebook, Starbucks, Maps, and so on) wants to use your current location, it must first ask you for permission, as shown in Figure 16–23. Resetting the location warnings means every app on your iPhone has to ask for your permission again before it can use your current location.

Figure 16–23. *The Current Location warning pop-up*

iCloud

As previously mentioned, iCloud is Apple's cloud-based services that offers users free e-mail, calendar, and contacts on the Web. iCloud also allows you to automatically sync documents between all your devices, like your Mac or PC, your iPad, and your iPhone. iCloud works automatically and effortlessly in the background.

To enable iCloud on your iPhone, go to **Settings ➤ iCloud** and enter your Apple ID and password. That's it. Now all your documents, e-mail, contacts, and calendars are synced wirelessly across all your iCloud-capable devices.

Third-Party App Settings

The remainder of the settings in the Settings app deal with third-party application settings. Any apps that adhere to Apple's developer policies keep their settings here (see Figure 16–24). Most apps do, but some don't. A lot of users think an app's settings should be contained in the app itself, and many developers end up doing just that. With that in mind, it's a good idea to check the Settings app to see whether you favorite apps have additional settings that aren't contained in the app. Also, note that virtually all games have their settings stored within the app, rather than under the iPhone Settings app.

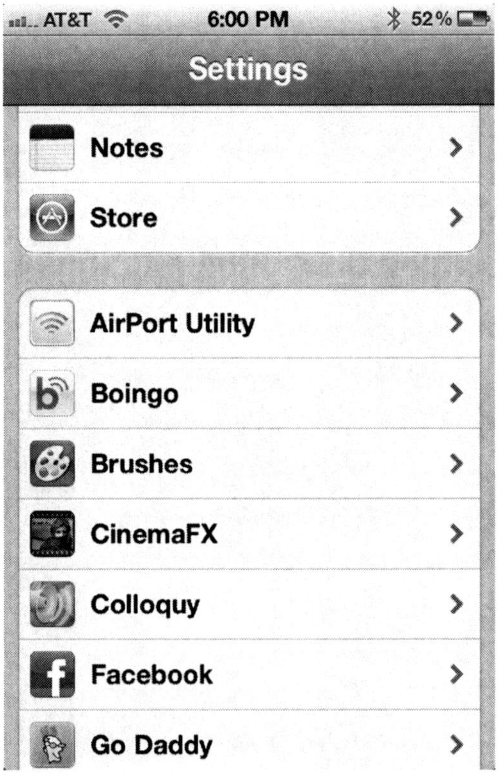

Figure 16–24. *The Settings app houses most third-party app settings as well.*

Summary

The settings screens discussed in this chapter allow you to customize your iPhone to your personal needs and conditions. Here are a few thoughts to take away with you from this overview:

■ The Settings app also contains the settings screens for many third-party apps.

- If younger children have access to the iPhone, you might want to seriously consider activating the Restrictions settings.

- Your Auto-Lock settings are a highly personal choice. Delay locking for long enough that you don't get frustrated with screen locks, but keep the autolock time short enough that you don't needlessly kill your battery.

- Don't sell or pass along your iPhone without using the Reset settings to erase your personal data. You can also do a complete system restore via iTunes.

- Use the **General ➤ About** screen to quickly access your iPhone's serial number. This is handy if you are talking to AppleCare over the phone and need the serial number to identify your device.

The iPhone has a number of accessibility options for people who are hard of sight or hearing.

Index

■Special Characters and Numerics

+ (plus) symbol, 105, 226, 228

■A

A-GPS (Assisted GPS), 73
About screen, 467
accelerometer (tilt sensor), 70
Accept Cookies setting, 153
accessibility, 476–480
    Assistive Touch option, 479
    Large Text option, 478
    Mono Audio option, 479
    Speak Auto-text option, 479
    Speak Selection option, 479
    Triple-click Home option, 480
    VoiceOver feature, 477–478
    White on Black option, 478
    Zoom option, 478
accessorizing iPhone
    Apple iPhone Dock, 23
    bumpers and cases, 21
    car chargers, 23
    Component AV Cable, 24
    Composite AV Cable, 24
    Dock Connector to USB cable, 24
    Dock Connector to VGA Adapter, 24
    docks, 23
    GelaSkins, 22
    Micro Auto Charger, 23
    PowerJolt, 23
    skins, 22
    USB Power Adapter, 23
Accounts list, 195

activating iPhone, 10, 15
Activity tab, 254
Add Bookmark button, 134
Add Bookmark menu, 147, 151
Add Bookmark option, 147–148
Add Contact button, 104
Add contacts created outside of groups
       on this iPod to check box, 56
Add to Home Screen feature, 148
Address bar, 134–135
address book, synchronizing with
       computer, 425–427
    options for, 426
    replacing contacts, 426–427
addresses, in Contacts app, 431–432
Airplane Mode, 102, 458–459
AirPlay button, 223, 232
AirPlay feature, streaming video to
       AppleTV with, 359–360
Alarm utility
    alarms, 388–390
    overview, 388–390
Album art, 222
Album view, 223–224
Album View button, 221, 223
albums, and photos, touching and
       viewing, 328–333
Albums screen, 220
alerts
    for events in Calendar app, 400
    ringtones and, 119–120
All books radio button, 51
All Inboxes, 195
All photos, albums, events, and faces
       radio button, 53
Alphabet index tool, 216

ambient light sensor, adjusting
brightness of iPhone display, 71
Answer button, 110
App Store, 257–273
Ad Hoc Helper app, 36
browsing, 259–270
apps, 263–265, 267–270
Categories button, 261–262
Featured section, 259–261
searching App Store, 266–267
Top 25 button, 262–263
buying apps through iTunes Store on
PC, 270–271
connecting to, 257–258
Game Center app, 271–272
redeeming gift certificates and
codes, 270
signing in to account, 258
transferring purchased items to
computer, 270
Apple icon, 80–81
Apple ID, 13, 160–162
Apple iPhone Dock, 23
Apple Self Solve website, 35
Apple Wireless Keyboard, 93
AppleCare, 20
Apple's Limited Warranty, 20
AppleTV, streaming video to with
AirPlay feature, 359–360
Apply button, 32
apps
App Store, 92
apps with geolocation features, 73
backgrounding, 79
buying and downloading, 265
buying through iTunes Store on PC,
270–271
Compass, 72
deleting, 67
Documents To Go, 95
downloading updates and previously
purchased, 267–270
Flick Fishing, 70
Geocaching, 73
idle apps and memory availability, 79
information page, 263–265

iPod, 79
moving app icons around, 67
organizing apps with folders, 82
processor usage and power
consumption during
multitasking, 79
running multiple apps
simultaneously, 79
third-party, customizing settings for,
484
turning off app, 79
viewing a list of active apps, 79
You Gotta See This!, 73
Apps box, 43
apps, for video, 343–345
Apps tab, 149
Apps tab, in iTunes Device window,
40–43
creating folders for, 42
file sharing for apps, 43
syncing apps, 41–42
Ask to Join Networks feature, 131
Ask to Join Networks option, 130
Assisted GPS (A-GPS), 73
Assistive Touch option, 479
AT&T
complimentary telephone support,
20
data plans, 16
insuring and repairing your iPhone,
20
messaging plans, 17
tethering, 17
voice plans, 16
attachments, in Messages app, 178
audio playback, 232
audio, playing, 220–232
Album view, 223–224
Cover Flow mode, 225
playlists, 226–231
search feature, 231–232
audiobooks, 215, 218
Audiobooks check box, 52
Audiobooks shortcut button, 241
Auto-Lock screen, 470

autobrightness feature, toggling off and
on, 71
autocapitalization, 91
AutoFill button, 139
AutoFill setting, 153
autofocus, and exposure
for recording video, 373
for still pictures, 370
autolocking, disabling, 74
Automatically fill free space with songs
check box, 46
Automatically include check box,
47–48, 50
automatically scanning, for Wi-Fi
networks, 130–131
Automatically sync new apps check
box, 41

B

Back button, 69, 146–147, 221, 223
backgrounding, 79
Backspace/Delete key, 91
Block Pop-ups setting, 154
Bluetooth headset, 77
Bluetooth keyboard, setting up, 93
Bluetooth settings, 470
bookmark creation menu, 147
bookmark ribbon, 296, 311
bookmarks
accessing when reading, 305–307
placing on pages, 301
in Safari, 143
editing, 145–147
saving, 147–149
selecting, 144
saved locations, 412–414
Bookmarks button, 134
bookmarks editor, 146
Bookmarks screen, 145
Bookmarks tab, 306
books
adding to collections, 291–292
deleting, 288
ePub vs. PDF, 284–285
having read to you, 307

reading, 295–307
accessing table of contents,
bookmarks, and notes, 305–307
adjusting brightness, 298–299
adjusting font, font size, and
page color, 299–300
bookmarking page, 301
text, 300–305
turning pages, 297
rearranging, 288
sorting into collections, 289–295
creating new, 290–292
navigating between, 293–295
syncing, 276–280
ePub books, 283–285
iBookstore app, 277–280
viewing book information page,
282–283
Books tab, in iTunes Device window, 52
bookshelves, navigating, 285–288
deleting books, 288
PDF, 309
rearranging books, 288
brightness, adjusting, when reading,
298–299
Brightness button, 298
Brightness settings, 462
bringing iPhone in for service, 20
bumpers and cases, 21
buttons bar, for YouTube app,
customizing, 351–352
Buy button, 247
BUY NOW button, 265

C

Calculator app, 433–434
Calendar app, 392–402
events, 397–401
alerts, 400
assigning to specific calendar,
400
editing and removing, 401
name and location of, 399
notes, 401
repeating, 400

start and end times of, 399–400

URLs, 401

synchronizing with computer, 401–402

views, 393–397

  Calendars button, 396–397

  Day, 394

  List, 393

  Month, 395–396

  Today button, 396

  Week, 395

Calendars button, 396–397

Call button, 103–104, 112

call, placing on hold, 112

call waiting, 113

calls, 101–123

  advanced phone preferences, 121

  basic tasks, 102–114

    answering calls, 109–110

    Favorites screen, 114

    GSM versus CDMA, 106–107

    launching Phone app, 102–103

    placing calls, 103–109

  checking cell network indicator, 101–102

  codes, 121–122

    functionality information, 122

    service shortcuts, 122

  in FaceTime, 167–171

  returning, 118

  ringtones and alerts, 119–120

    custom ringtones, 119–120

  Visual Voicemail app, 115–118

    accessing voicemail files, 118

    choosing greeting, 116

    managing voicemail messages, 116–118

    sending voicemail indirectly, 118

    setting up voicemail passcode, 115–116

Camera app, 367–373

  recording video, 372–373

  taking still pictures, 369–371

    autofocus and exposure, 370

    composing shots with Gridlines feature, 370–371

zooming, 371

Camera Roll feature, viewing photos with, 374–375

cameras, 365–382

  accessing from lock screen, 373

  hardware, 365–367

    front camera, 366

    real-world use, 367

    rear camera, 366

  navigating Camera app, 367–373

    recording video, 372–373

    taking still pictures, 369–371

  uploading images to computer, 381

  viewing photos

    with Camera Roll feature, 374–375

    individual, 375–376

  viewing videos, 377–380

    editing, 378–379

    sharing, 379–380

Cancel button, 140

Capacity bar, 28, 32

Caps Lock, toggling on and off, 91

car chargers, 23

carrier locked, 107

Categories button, 261–262

category screens, navigating, 219

CDMA (Code Division Multiple Access), GSM vs., 106–107

cell network indicator, 101–102

changing wallpapers, procedure for, 81

charging iPhone, 9

Check for Update button, 36

cities, in World Clock utility, 387–388

  removing, 388

  reordering, 387–388

Clear All option, 153

Clear Cookies button, 153

Clear History button, 153

clipboard, 88

Clock app, 385–391

  Alarm utility, 388–390

  Stopwatch utility, 390

  Timer utility, 391

  World Clock utility, 386–388

Close button, 143

Code Division Multiple Access (CDMA), GSM vs., 106–107
codes, 121–122
    redeeming, 251–252, 270
        free music and videos, 252
        transferring purchased items to computer, 251
    service shortcuts, 122
    for viewing functionality information, 122
Collection button, 290, 294–295
collections
    editing, 293–295
    sorting books into, 289–295
        creating new collections, 290–292
        navigating between collections, 293–295
Collections feature, 286, 289–291, 293–294, 309, 315
Compass app, 72
Complete My Album feature, 251
Completing Activation screen, 18
Component AV Cable, 24
Compose button, 206
Composite AV Cable, 24
computer system requirements, 5
computers
    synchronizing address book with, 425–427
        options for, 426
        replacing contacts, 426–427
    synchronizing Calendar app with, 401–402
    transferring purchased items to, 251–270
conference calling, 112
Configure screen, 218
Configure Universal Access button, 39
connecting a new iPhone to your computer, 14–15
connection status, for Wi-Fi, 128
considerations, before purchasing iPhone, 3–5
contact information, reviewing, 118
Contact Sheet button, 310–311

contact sheets, 311–313
contacts
    Contacts app, 427–433
        finding, 427–429
        new, 429–432
        ordering list of, 428
        viewing details for, 428–429
    in FaceTime, 164–167
        favorites, 164–165
        recents, 166
    in Messages app, attaching, 178
    replacing in address book, 426–427
Contacts app, contacts, 427–433
    finding, 427–429
    new, 429–432
    ordering list of, 428
    viewing details for, 428–429
Contacts icon, 102, 113
Contacts list, 108, 114
Contacts screen, 105
contractions, 89
conversations, in Messages app
    deleting, 177
    reading, 174–175
Convert higher bit rate songs to 128 kbps AAC check box, 38
Copy button, 140
Copy command, 88
Cover Flow mode, 216, 225, 237
coverage map, 101
Create Event button, 202
Create New Account button, 13
Customizable button bar, 216
customizing, 457–485
    accessibility, 476–480
        Assistive Touch option, 479
        Large Text option, 478
        Mono Audio option, 479
        Speak Auto-text option, 479
        Speak Selection option, 479
        Triple-click Home option, 480
        VoiceOver feature, 477–478
        White on Black option, 478
        Zoom option, 478
    iCloud service, 483
    Reset screen, 481–483

settings, 458–466
    About screen, 467
    Airplane Mode, 458–459
    Auto-Lock screen, 470
    Bluetooth, 470
    Brightness, 462
    Date & Time screen, 473
    International screen, 475–476
    Keyboard screen, 474–475
    Location Services, 464–466
    Network screen, 469–470
    Restrictions, 471–472
    Software Update screen, 467–468
    Sounds, 460–461
    for third-party apps, 484
    Twitter account, 459–460
    Usage screen, 468
    wallpaper, 463–464
    Wi-fi Sync screen, 469
Cut command, 88

D

dark pie wedge, 245
data detectors, 105
data plans, 16
data transfer. *See* transferring media
Databases setting, 154
Date & Time screen, 473
Day view, in Calendar app, 394
default search engine option, 137
Delete Backup button, 61
Delete button, 68, 146
Delete Draft button, 208
Deleted Messages list, 117
deleting
    downloads, 250
    in Messages app
        conversations, 177
        individual messages, 175–176
desk set apps, 425–453
    Calculator app, 433–434
    Contacts app, 427–433
        contacts, 427, 432–433
        managing custom labels, 432

Notes app, 435–436
Reminders app, 448–451
Stocks app, 439–443
synchronizing address book with computer, 425–427
    options for, 426
    replacing contacts, 426–427
Voice Memos app, 443–448
Weather app, 437–439
    tips for using, 439
    viewing weather info, 438–439
Device backups section, 59
Devices icon, 59
Devices preferences window, 59
digital compass (magnetometer)
    Compass app, 72
    recalibrating, 71
    using near a strong magnetic field, 71
directions, getting from Maps app, 414–418
    driving or walking, 416
    public transit, 417–418
DNS (Domain Name System), 129
Do not sync events older thcheck box, 57
Dock Connector to USB cable, 24
Dock Connector to VGA Adapter, 24
docks, 9, 23
Documents box, 43
Documents list, 43
Documents To Go app, 95
Domain Name System (DNS), 129
Done button, 138–139, 143, 147
double-tapping, Safari and, 66
Download All button, 249
Downloads icon, 246–247
Downloads screen, 250–251
dragging, moving quickly through index, 67
driving directions, 416

E

e-mail addresses, and URLs, 431
e-mail, and Safari browser, 322–323

earbuds, 9
Edit Bookmark screen, 146
Edit button, 145, 241–242, 288, 291,
       294–295, 309
Edit Folder screen, 146–147
Edit mode, 115, 145–146, 227–228, 288
embedded links, 200
End Call button, 113
energy, saving, 232
Entire music library radio button, 46
Entourage, 12
Episodes check box, 48, 50
ePub, 281, 316, 318
ePub books
    overview, 283–285
    vs. PDF books, 284–285
Erase Data button, 77
events, in Calendar app, 397–401
    alerts, 400
    assigning to specific calendar, 400
    editing and removing, 401
    name and location of, 399
    notes, 401
    repeating, 400
    start and end times of, 399–400
    URLs, 401
exposure
    autofocus and
       for recording video, 373
       for still pictures, 370

F

FaceTime app, 4, 157–182
    calling options, 170–171
    contacts in, 164–167
       favorites, 164–165
       recents, 166
    front camera, 157–158
    placing and receiving calls, 167–169
    rear camera, 158
    settings for, 172–173
    signing in, 158–163
       creating account, 162–163
       with existing Apple ID, 160–162
FaceTime control, 168

FaceTime video chat, 113
favorites
    adding, 114
    in FaceTime, 164–165
    removing, 114
    reordering, 114
Favorites screen, 105, 114
feature overview (iPhone 4), 9
Featured section, 259–261
file sharing, for apps, 43
firmware version, displaying, 34
Flash videos, 154–155
Flick Fishing game, 70
flicking, 68
folders
    creating, Apps tab in iTunes Device
       window, 42
    organizing apps with folders, 82
    renaming, 83
font panel, 299
fonts, adjusting when reading, 299–300
Fonts button, 299
Forward button, 223
forwarding, in Messages app, 175–176
Fraud Warning setting, 154
friends, finding with Maps app, 422
front camera, 157–158
full justification, 314–315
functionality, codes for viewing
       information about, 122

G

Game Center app, 271–272
GelaSkins, 22
Genius Bar, 112
Genius button, 222
Genius feature, 260
Genius playlists, 228–231
Genres list, 243
gestures
    controls, for VoiceOver feature, 478
    in Maps app, 404–405
    in Safari, 141–142
Get Sample button, 283
gift certificates, redeeming, 270

Global System for Mobile Communications (GSM), vs. CDMA, 106–107
Gmail, 185
Go button, 139
GPS receiver
    apps with geolocation features, 73
    Assisted GPS, 73
    Geocaching app, 73
greetings, choosing in Visual Voicemail app, 116
Gridlines feature, composing shots with, 370–371
Group By Album Artist option, 235
GSM codes, 121–122
GSM (Global System for Mobile Communications), vs. CDMA, 106–107

▉H

HandBrake tool, 31
headphones, choosing, 236
headsets, 9, 95
Hearing section, 40
Hide Keypad button, 112
highlighting text, 304
Highlights & Notes heading, 306
History button, 134
holding, moving app icons around, 67
Home button, 67
    pressing, 66
    unlocking iPhone, 74
Home screen, 66, 69, 102, 116
Home Sharing, 235
HTML5, 154–155

▉I

iBooks app, 51
iBooks App, 275–318
    books
        having read to you, 307
        reading, 295–307
        sorting into collections, 289–295
        syncing, 276–280

navigating bookshelf, 285–288
    deleting books, 288
    rearranging books, 288
PDFs
    bookshelf, 309
    navigating and reading, 310–313
    syncing, 307–308
settings, 314–315
iBookstore app, 32, 277–280
iCal app, 12
iCloud service, 483
images, uploading to computer, 381
IMAP (Internet Message Access Protocol)
    description of, 184
    downloading headers, messages, and attachments, 184
    Gmail, 185
    push e-mail, 185
    Yahoo!, 185
Inboxes list, 195
Include Audiobooks from Playlists check box, 52
Include Episodes from Playlists check box, 50
Include Movies from Playlists check box, 47
Include music videos check box, 46
Include video check box, 54
Include voice memos check box, 46
Info page, 260, 263–265, 268
Info tab, in iTunes Device window, 58
    replacing information on iPod, 58
    syncing bookmarks, 57–58
    syncing calendars, 56–57
    syncing contacts, 55–56
    syncing mail accounts, 57
    syncing notes, 58
Info window, in Maps app, 407–409
information pages
    for apps, 263–265
    for books, 282–283
INSTALL button, 265
insuring your iPhone, 20
interactive gestures

detecting electrical charge from skin contact, 65
double-tapping, 66
dragging, 67
flicking, 68
holding, 67
Home button, pressing, 66
pinching, 69
single-finger interactions and Multi-Touch technology, 65
stopping, 68
swiping, 68
tapping, 66
two-fingered tapping, 66
unpinching, 69
international calls, 105–106
International screen, 475–476
Internet browser window, 133
Internet Message Access Protocol (IMAP)
description of, 184
downloading headers, messages, and attachments, 184
Gmail, 185
push e-mail, 185
Yahoo!, 185
iOS 4
computer system requirements, 5
considerations before purchasing iPhone, 3–5
memory and storage recommendations, 3
multitasking, 79
organizing apps with folders, 82
iPhone
accessorizing
Apple iPhone Dock, 23
bumpers and cases, 21
car chargers, 23
Component AV Cable, 24
Composite AV Cable, 24
Dock Connector to USB cable, 24
Dock Connector to VGA Adapter, 24
docks, 23

GelaSkins, 22
Micro Auto Charger, 23
PowerJolt, 23
skins, 22
USB Power Adapter, 23
activating, 10, 15
ambient light sensor, adjusting brightness of display, 71
Apple iPhone Dock, 23
bringing in for service, 20
charging, 9
connecting to computer, 14–15
feature overview, 9
finding lost, 420–421
insuring, 20
iPhone 3GS, 69, 71
powering off and on, Sleep/Wake button, 80
purchasing
activating iPhone, 10, 15
Apple Online Store, 7
Apple Store, 6
AppleCare, 20
Apple's Limited Warranty, 20
bringing iPhone in for service, 20
buying in person at a store, 5
charging iPhone, 9
Completing Activation screen, 18
connecting a new iPhone to your computer, 14–15
considerations before, 3–5
data plans, 16
docks, 9
earbuds, 9
headset, 9
insuring and repairing your iPhone, 20
messaging plans, 17
microphone, 9
organizing and synchronizing your media library, 12
PayPal, 14
returns and exchange policies, 7
Sleep/Wake button, 9, 15
Subscriber Identity Module, 9

synchronizing with
computer-based calendars, 12
synchronizing with iTunes for first
time, 11–14
tethering, 17
touchscreen, 9
transferring your existing
contacts and e-mail addresses,
11
unpacking and setting up, 7
updating a Macintosh to OS X
10.5.8 or newer, 12
updating to iTunes 9.2 or newer,
12
upgrading to a newer iPhone, 11
USB cable, 8
USB Power Adapter, 9
voice plans, 16
putting to sleep, 75
rebooting, 81
restoring to factory defaults, 78
securing with passcode lock, 76
synchronizing with iTunes, 11–14
unlocking
disabling autolocking, 74
pressing Home button, 74
screen locking and power saving,
74
upgrading to newer iPhone, 11
iPhone 3GS, 69, 71
iPhone 4 (feature overview), 9
iPod app, 79
iPod box, in Summary tab, 34
IR beam, 70
iToner2, 119
iTunes
Ad Hoc Helper app, 36
adding existing mail accounts with
iTunes, 186
Apple ID, 13
Apple Self Solve website, 35
connecting iPad to a computer, 27
Create New Account button, 13
displaying your firmware version, 34
displaying your unique device
identifier, 34

iBookstore, 32
launching, 27
offloading local storage to remote
servers, 30
PayPal, 14
Project Gutenberg, 32
registering iPad for developer beta
tests, 36
renaming iPad, 34
settings pane
displaying your firmware version,
34
displaying your unique device
identifier, 34
offloading local storage to remote
servers, 30
renaming iPad, 34
Sign In button, 13
synchronizing new iPhone for first
time, 11–14
unlocking iPad, 28
updating to iTunes 9.2 or newer, 12
iTunes Device window, 28–32, 58
applying changes, 32
Apps tab in, 40–43
creating folders for, 42
file sharing for apps, 43
syncing apps, 41–42
Books tab in, 52
Info tab in, 58
replacing information on iPod, 58
syncing bookmarks, 57–58
syncing calendars, 56–57
syncing contacts, 55–56
syncing mail accounts, 57
syncing notes, 58
Movies tab in, 46–47
Music tab in, 45–46
Photos tab in, 54
Podcasts tab in, 49–50
preferences for, 58–62
Ringtones tab in, 45
sources for data, 30
Summary tab in, 33–40
iPod box in, 34
Options box in, 37–40

Version box in, 36–37
TV Shows tab in, 49
which data to sync, 30
iTunes icon, 239
iTunes Store, 239–255
    browsing through, 241–249
        Music store, 242–243
        Podcasts, Audiobooks, and
            iTunes U Stores, 248
        Search screen, 248–249
        Top Tens section, 243–246
        Video store, 246–247
    buying apps through on PC,
        270–271
    connecting to, 239–240
    Downloads screen, 250–251
    Ping social network, 252–254
    Purchased screen, 249–250
    redeeming codes, 251–252
        free music and videos, 252
        transferring purchased items to
            computer, 251
    signing in to account, 240
iTunes U Store, 246–247

J

JavaScript setting, 154

K

Keyboard screen, 474–475
keyboards
    adding international keyboards, 90
    Apple Wireless Keyboard, 93
    autocapitalization, 91
    automatic correction, 85
    Backspace/Delete key, 91
    Bluetooth keyboard, setting up, 93
    Caps Lock, toggling on and off, 91
    Copy command, 88
    Cut command, 88
    displaying and removing virtual
        keyboard, 86
    entering accented letters, 90
    entering contractions, 89

erasing multiple words at a time, 91
    features of, 85
    making keyboard entry faster and
        easier, 89
    offset correction, 85
    Paste command, 88
    positioning cursor using magnifying
        glass (loupe), 86
    predictive zones, 85
    punctuation dragging, 90
    Replace command, 88
    selecting text, 86
    turning off autocorrection, 85
    typing using onboard dictionary, 85
Keypad icon, 104, 112
Kindle app, 32

L

labels, in Contacts app, managing
    custom, 432
Large Text option, 478
Library button, 277, 307, 313
Like and Post button, 244
links, in Safari, 139–140
list of voice commands, 96
List view, in Calendar app, 393
Location Services, settings for, 464–466
locations
    bookmarking saved, 412–414
    current, 410–411
    finding, 406–410
        Info window, 407–409
        search field, 406–407
        Street View, 409–410
lock mode
    disabling autolocking, 74
    pressing Home button, 74
    screen locking and power saving, 74
lock screen, accessing cameras from,
    373
Loop control, 222
loupe (magnifying glass), 67, 86
Lyrics & Podcast Info, 235

▓M

magnetometer (digital compass)
Compass app, 72
recalibrating, 71
using near a strong magnetic field, 71
magnifying glass (loupe), 67, 86
Mail app
Accounts list, 195
adding a new account directly to your iPhone, 187
adding existing mail accounts with iTunes, 186
addressing e-mail, 206
Advanced settings, 186
All Inboxes, 195
Back button, 199
choosing messages to display and manage a mailbox, 196
compatibility with major e-mail providers, 183
Compose button, 206
Compose icon, 199
Create Event button, 202
creating and sending mail, 205
creating events automatically for your iPhone Calendar, 202
customizing your preferences for checking and displaying mail, 191–194
Delete Draft button, 208
disabling e-mail account without removing it, 191
editing a message, 207
embedded links, 200
entering a subject, 207
Inboxes list, 195
Mail Accounts settings, 186
Mailboxes screen, 194
message display screen, bottom icons, 199
message display screen, top icons, 199
Microsoft Exchange, 183
moving messages from one mailbox to another, 199

New Message screen, 206
Next Message button, 200
Open Inà button, 205
opening embedded web address in Safari, 200
opening inbox, 195
opening Mail app, 194
overview of most popular e-mail standards, 183
Previous Message button, 200
reading and navigating through your e-mails, 198
Refresh button, 199
removing a recipient from a message, 206
removing e-mail account from your iPhone, 190
Reply/Forward button, 199, 206
Save Draft button, 208
saving a message draft, 208
Send button, 208
setting audible alerts, 194
setting up account information for preferred providers, 188
Share icon, 206
standard mailboxes, list of, 196
supported file formats for e-mail attachments, 203
using trash cto delete currently displayed message, 199
viewing attachments, 203
viewing individual folders within account, 195
Mail Link to this Page button, 149
Manually manage music and videos check box, 39
map views, 405–406
Maps app
bookmarking and viewing saved locations, 412–414
finding friends, 422
finding lost iPhone, 420–421
getting directions, 414–418
driving or walking, 416
public transit, 417–418
Maps interface, 402–404

navigating, 404–411
    gestures, 404–405
    locations, 406–411
    map views, 405–406
    tips for using, 420
    traffic conditions, 418–419
Maps interface, 402–404
media, browsing, 216–219
    editing buttons for, 218–219
    navigating category screens, 219
memory and storage recommendations,
    3
Merge Calls button, 112
messages
    managing with Visual Voicemail app,
        116–118
    playing, 117
Messages app, 173–181
    attaching
        contacts, 178
        photos, 178
        videos, 178
    deleting
        conversations, 177
        individual messages, 175–176
    forwarding, individual messages,
        175–176
    reading conversations, 174–175
    sending messages, 177–178
    settings for, 180–181
    using with Siri voice assistant,
        181–182
messaging plans, 17
Micro Auto Charger, 23
microphone, 9, 111
Microsoft Exchange, 12, 183, 185
Microsoft Outlook, 11
minus sign, 228
MobileMe, 12
Mono Audio option, 479
Month view, in Calendar app, 395–396
More screen, 217–219, 241–242
Move button, 292
Movies check box, 47
Movies library, 31

Movies tab, in iTunes Device window,
    46–47
Multi-Touch technology, 65
multitasking, 79
music, 215–237
    adjusting settings, 234–235
    browsing media, 216–219
        editing buttons for, 218–219
        navigating category screens, 219
    choosing headphones, 236
    displaying playback controls from
        any app, 233
    free, 252
    Music app, 215–216
    playing audio, 220–232
        Album view, 223–224
        Cover Flow mode, 225
        playlists, 226–231
        search feature, 231–232
    previewing and buying, 244–246
    saving energy, 232
    sleep timer, 233–234
Music app, 215–216
Music store, 242–243
Music tab, in iTunes Device window,
    45–46
Mute button, 111
My Info box, 153
My Profile tab, 254

■N

navigating, 321–363
    bookshelf, 285–288
        deleting books, 288
        rearranging books, 288
    between collections, 293–295
    Maps app, 404–411
        gestures, 404–405
        locations, 406–411
        map views, 405–406
    photos, 321–323
        editing, 339–343
        in Photos app, 323–328
        saving from mail and Safari
            browser, 322–323

sharing, 333–339
syncing from computer, 321–322
touching and viewing albums
and, 328–333
video
accessories for, 361–362
apps for, 343–345
playback, 346–347
streaming to AppleTV with
AirPlay feature, 359–360
Video app, 354–358
watching on web with Safari
browser, 358–359
YouTube app, 348–353
Network screen, 469–470
networks, Wi-Fi
automatically scanning for, 130–131
connecting to, 128–129
protected networks, 129–130
New Message screen, 206
New Page button, 143
New Releases section, 242
New section, 260
Newsstand app, 275, 316–318
Next button, 138
Next Message button, 200
Noise Cancellation microphone, 74
notes, accessing when reading,
305–307
Notes app, 435–436
Now Playing button, 217, 220
Now Playing screen, 220–221, 223–224
Now Playing view, 224

O

offloading local storage to remote
servers, 30
Open button, 140
Open in New Page button, 140
Open iTunes when this iPod is
connected check box, 37
Optional lyrics, 221
Options box, in Summary tab, 37–40
orientation, for Safari, 141

P

Page scrubber, 296, 311
pages
bookmarking, 301
color of, adjusting when reading,
299–300
turning, 297
Pages button, 134, 142–143
Parts check box, 52
passcode lock
assigning, 76
Erase Data button, 77
Passcode Lock screen, 77
removing a passcode, 78
Require Passcode button, 77
restoring iPhone to factory defaults,
78
setting a new passcode, 76
simple and regular passcodes, 76
Simple Passcode switch, 76
testing a passcode, 78
Turn Passcode Off button, 78
Turn Passcode On button, 77
Voice Dial switch, 77
passcodes, for Visual Voicemail app,
115–116
Paste command, 88
pausing downloads, 250
PayPal, 14
PCs (personal computers), buying apps
through iTunes Store on,
270–271
PDFs (Portable Document Formats)
adding to collections, 291–292
books, ePub books vs., 284–285
bookshelf, navigating, 309
navigating and reading, 310–313
syncing, 307–308
People tab, 254
personal computers (PCs), buying apps
through iTunes Store on,
270–271
Phone app, launching, 102–103
phone calls. *See* calls
phone numbers, in Contacts app, 431
Photo Library, 81

photos, 321–323
    in Contacts app, 431
    editing, 339–343
    in Messages app, attaching, 178
    in Photos app, 323–328
    saving from mail and Safari browser,
        322–323
    sharing, 333–339
    still, 369–371
        autofocus and exposure, 370
        composing shots with Gridlines
            feature, 370–371
        zooming, 371
    syncing from computer, 321–322
    touching and viewing albums and,
        328–333
    uploading to computer, 381
    viewing, 377–380
        with Camera Roll feature,
            374–375
        editing, 378–379
        individual, 375–376
        sharing, 379–380
Photos app, 323–328
Photos tab, in iTunes Device window,
    54
pinching, zooming out of apps, 69
Ping profile, 252, 254
Ping social network, 252–254
pins, dropping in Maps app, 412–413
placing call on hold, 112
Play indicator, 221
playback controls, displaying from any
    app, 233
playing messages, 117
playlists, 226–231
    Genius, 228–231
    regular, 226–228
plus (+) symbol, 105, 226, 228
Podcasts check box, 50
Podcasts Store, 246–247
Podcasts tab, in iTunes Device window,
    49–50
POP (Post Office Protocol)
    advantages and disadvantages of,
        184

description of, 183
Portable Document Formats (PDFs)
    adding to collections, 291–292
    books, ePub books vs., 284–285
    bookshelf, navigating, 309
    navigating and reading, 310–313
    syncing, 307–308
Post Office Protocol (POP)
    advantages and disadvantages of,
        184
    description of, 183
powering iPhone off and on,
        Sleep/Wake button, 80
PowerJolt, 23
predictive zones, 85
preferences, for iTunes Device window,
    58–62
Preferences menu option, 58
Prevent iPods, iPhones, and iPads from
        syncing automatically check
        box, 61
Previous button, 138
Previous Message button, 200
Project Guttenberg, 32, 281
protected networks, connecting to,
        129–130
proximity sensor, 70
public transit directions, 417–418
punctuation dragging, 90
purchase history, 249
Purchased button, 269
Purchased screen, 249–250, 269
purchasing iPhone
    activating iPhone, 10, 15
    Apple Online Store, 7
    Apple Store, 6
    AppleCare, 20
    Apple's Limited Warranty, 20
    bringing iPhone in for service, 20
    buying in person at a store, 5
    charging iPhone, 9
    Completing Activation screen, 18
    connecting a new iPhone to your
        computer, 14–15
    data plans, 16
    docks, 9

earbuds, 9
headset, 9
insuring and repairing your iPhone, 20
messaging plans, 17
microphone, 9
organizing and synchronizing your media library, 12
PayPal, 14
returns and exchange policies, 7
Sleep/Wake button, 9, 15
Subscriber Identity Module (SIM), 9
synchronizing with computer-based calendars, 12
synchronizing with iTunes for first time, 11–14
tethering, 17
touchscreen, 9
transferring your existing contacts and e-mail addresses, 11
unpacking and setting up, 7
updating a Macintosh to OS X 10.5.8 or newer, 12
updating to iTunes 9.2 or newer, 12
upgrading to a newer iPhone, 11
USB cable, 8
USB Power Adapter, 9
voice plans, 16
push e-mail, 185
putting iPhone to sleep, 75

Q

quitting running apps, 79

R

reading conversations, in Messages app, 174–175
rear camera, 158
rearranging icons, 241
rebooting iPhone, 81
Recents icon, 102, 105
recents, in FaceTime, 166
Redeem button, 251
Release Date tab, 261

Reload button, 134
Reminders app, 448–451
removing voicemail, 117
renaming iPad, 34
Replace command, 88
Reply/Forward button, 199, 206
Require Passcode button, 77
Reset screen, 481–483
Restore button, 37
Restore from Backup context menu option, 61
restoring
    iPhone to factory defaults, 78
    iPod, 61
Restrictions settings, 471–472
resuming downloads, 250
Return to Now Playing icon, 224
reviews, 244, 247
Rewind button, 223
ringer, silencing, 110
ringtones, and alerts, 119–120
Ringtones box, 45
Ringtones tab, 45, 120

S

Safari, 133–142
    bookmarks in, 143
        editing, 145–147
        saving, 147–149
        selecting, 144
    double-tapping in, 66
    e-mail and, saving photos from, 322–323
    entering text in, 138–139
    entering URLs, 135–136
    and Flash videos, 154–155
    gestures in, 141–142
    links in, 139–140
    orientation for, 141
    Pages button in, 142–143
    searching in, 136–137
    settings for, 152–154
    watching video on web with, 358–359
    zooming in and out, 66

Safari Settings window, 152
Save Draft button, 208
Save Image button, 81
Save to button, 43
saving bookmarks, in Safari, 147–149
scanning, for Wi-Fi networks
        automatically, 130–131
screen orientation, for Safari, 141
scrubber bar, 222
search bar, 136
Search button, 136, 139
Search Engine setting, 153
search features, for audio, 231–232
search field, in Maps app, 406–407
Search Google button, 300
Search screen, 248–249
Search Wikipedia button, 300
searching, in Safari, 136–137
securing iPhone, with passcode lock,
        76
Seeing section, 39
Selected albums, events, and faces,
        and automatically include radio
        button, 54
Selected books radio button, 51
Selected playlists, artists, albums and
        genres radio button, 46
Send button, 208
sending
    incoming call to voicemail, 95
    in Messages app, 177–178
sensors
    ambient light sensor, 71
    digital compass (magnetometer), 71
    GPS receiver, 73
    IR beam, 70
    Noise Cancellation microphone (top
        microphone), 74
    proximity sensor, 70
    three-axis gyroscope, 73
    tilt sensor (accelerometer), 70
service shortcuts, 122
setting new passcode, 76
settings, 458–466
    About screen, 467
    Airplane Mode, 458–459

Auto-Lock screen, 470
Bluetooth, 470
Brightness, 462
Date & Time screen, 473
for FaceTime, 172–173
International screen, 475–476
Keyboard screen, 474–475
Location Services, 464–466
for Messages app, 180–181
Network screen, 469–470
Restrictions, 471–472
for Safari, 152–154
Software Update screen, 467–468
Sounds, 460–461
Twitter account, 459–460
Usage screen, 468
wallpaper, 463–464
Wi-fi Sync screen, 469
Settings app, 152
settings pane (iTunes)
    displaying your firmware version, 34
    displaying your unique device
        identifier, 34
    offloading local storage to remote
        servers, 30
    renaming iPad, 34
Shake to Shuffle, 234
Share button, 307–308
Share icon, 206
shortcuts, service, 122
Show closed captions when available
        check box, 40
Shows check box, 48
Shuffle option, 219, 222, 227
Sign In button, 13, 240
silencing ringer, 110
SIM (Subscriber Identity Module), 9
Simple Mail Transfer Protocol (SMTP),
        184
Simple Passcode switch, 76
Siri voice assistant
    placing calls with, 107–108
    using in Messages app, 181–182
sleep mode, 75, 109
sleep timers, 233–234

Sleep/Wake button, 9, 15, 75, 78, 80, 110, 232–233
SMTP (Simple Mail Transfer Protocol), 184
Software Update screen, 467–468
Sound Check, 234–235
Sounds pane, 119
Sounds settings, 460–461
source list, 28
Speak Auto-text check box, 40
Speak Auto-text option, 479
Speak Selection option, 479
Speaker icon, 112
speaker, toggling, 117
speakerphone, 112
SpringBoard, 69
Sprint, 101, 106–107, 121–122
stars control, 224
still pictures, 369–371
    autofocus and exposure, 370
    composing shots with Gridlines feature, 370–371
    zooming, 371
Stocks app, 439–443
Stop button, 134, 245
stopping, combining with scrolling, 68
Stopwatch utility, 390
Store button, 216
Street View, in Maps app, 409–410
Subscriber Identity Module (SIM), 9
Summary tab, in iTunes Device window, 33–40
    iPod box in, 34
    Options box in, 37–40
    Version box in, 36–37
swiping, functions of, 68
Sync Address Book Contacts check box, 56
Sync Audiobooks check box, 51
Sync Bookmarks check box, 58, 315
Sync Books check box, 51
Sync Collections, 315
Sync Google Contacts check box, 56
Sync iCal Calendars check box, 57
Sync Movies check box, 47
Sync Music check box, 45

Sync only selected songs and videos check box, 38
Sync Photos from check box, 53
Sync Ringtones check box, 45
Sync Yahoo! Address Book contacts check box, 56
synchronizing, 12–14
    Apps tab in iTunes Device window, apps, 41–42
    books, 276–280
        ePub books, 283–285
        iBookstore app, 277–280
        viewing book information page, 282–283
    Calendar app with computer, 401–402
    Info tab in iTunes Device window
        bookmarks, 57–58
        calendars, 56–57
        contacts, 55–56
        mail accounts, 57
        notes, 58
    new iPhone with iTunes, 11
    PDFs, 307–308
    photos, from computer, 321–322
    Wi-fi Sync screen, 469

▪T

Table of Contents/Bookmarks page, 296, 301, 305–307
Table of Contents tab, 306
tables of contents, accessing when reading, 305–307
tapping, functions of, 66
tethering, 17
text
    entering in Safari, 138–139
    interacting with, 302–305
    searching, 300
third-party apps, customizing settings for, 484
three-axis gyroscope, 73
tilt sensor (accelerometer), 70
Timer utility, 391
Today button, in Calendar app, 396

Top 25 button, 262–263
Top Free tab, 261, 279
top microphone, 74
Top Paid tab, 261, 279
Top Tens section, 242–246
touchscreens, 9
traffic conditions, 418–419
transferring media, 62
    iTunes Device window for, 28–32, 58
        applying changes, 32
        Apps tab in, 40–43
        Books tab in, 52
        Info tab in, 58
        Movies tab in, 46–47
        Music tab in, 45–46
        Photos tab in, 54
        Podcasts tab in, 49–50
        preferences for, 58–62
        Ringtones tab in, 45
        sources for data, 30
        Summary tab in, 33–40
        TV Shows tab in, 49
        which data to sync, 30
    restoring iPod, 61
Triple-click Home option, 480
Turn Passcode Off button, 78
Turn Passcode On button, 77
turning off app, 79
TV Shows tab, in iTunes Device
    window, 49
Twitter account, 459–460
two-fingered tapping, 66

U

UDID (unique device identifier),
    displaying, 34
Uniform Resource Locators (URLs)
    e-mail addresses and, in Contacts
        app, 431
    entering in Safari, 135–136
    for events in Calendar app, 401
unique device identifier (UDID),
    displaying, 34
Universal Access box, 39
unlocking iPhone, 74

unpinching, zooming in on apps, 69
UPDATE button, 268
updates, downloading, 267–270
upgrading to a newer iPhone, 11
URL-entry screen, 135
URLs (Uniform Resource Locators)
    e-mail addresses and, in Contacts
        app, 431
    entering in Safari, 135–136
    for events in Calendar app, 401
Usage screen, 468
USB cable, 8
USB Power Adapter, 9, 23
Use mono audio check box, 40
Use white-on-black display check box,
    40

V

Verizon, 101, 106–107, 112, 121–122
Version box, in Summary tab, 36–37
Video app, 354–358
    deleting videos on go, 356
    video settings, 357–358
video calls, 4
Video store, 246–247
videos
    accessories for, 361–362
    apps for, 343–345
    free, 252
    in Messages app, attaching, 178
    playback, 346–347
    recording, 372–373
    streaming to AppleTV with AirPlay
        feature, 359–360
    Video app, 354–358
        deleting videos on go, 356
        video settings, 357–358
    watching on web with Safari
        browser, 358–359
    YouTube app, 348–353
        customizing buttons bar,
          351–352
        finding videos, 350–351
        playing videos, 349–350
        video info screens, 353

Videos shortcut button, 241
viewing list, of active apps, 79
views
    in Calendar app, 393–397
        Calendars button, 396–397
        Day view, 394
        List view, 393
        Month view, 395–396
        Today button, 396
        Week view, 395
    map, 405–406
Visual Voicemail app, 115–118
    accessing voicemail files, 118
    choosing greetings in, 116
    managing messages with, 116–118
    passcodes for, 115–116
    sending voicemail indirectly, 118
Voice Control, 9
    controlling iPhone using voice
        commands, 95
    enabling when iPhone is locked, 77
    list of voice commands, 96
    placing calls with, 108–109
Voice Dial switch, 77
Voice Memos app, 443–448
Voice-over-IP (VoIP), 106
Voice Over radio button, 40
voice plans, 16
voicemail
    accessing files, 118
    removing, 117
    sending incoming call to voicemail,
        95
    sending indirectly, 118
Voicemail account, 110
VoiceOver feature, 477–478
VoIP (Voice-over-IP), 106
volume controls, 110
Volume Limit, 235–236

W, X

walking directions, 416
wallpapers
    procedure for changing, 81
    settings for, 463–464
    standard wallpaper on iPhone 4, 81
Weather app, 437–439
    tips for using, 439
    viewing weather info, 438–439
Web Clip icon, 148
Web Clips, 148–149
Week view, in Calendar app, 395
What's Hot section, 259–260
White on Black option, 478
Wi-Fi, 127–131
    automatically scanning for networks,
        130–131
    connecting to network, 128–130
    connection status, 128
Wi-Fi hotspot, 257
Wi-Fi Networks settings screen, 130
Wi-Fi settings screen, 130
Wi-fi Sync screen, 469
Wireless Keyboard, 93
World Clock utility, cities, 386–388
    removing, 388
    reordering, 387–388

Y

Yahoo! Address Book, 11
Yahoo! Mail, 12
You Gotta See This! app, 73
YouTube app, 348–353
    customizing buttons bar, 351–352
    video info screens, 353
    videos
        finding, 350–351
        playing, 349–350

Z

Zoom option, 478
Zoom radio button, 40
zooming, 371

CPSIA information can be obtained at www.ICGtesting.com
Printed in the USA
LVOW130246301211

261708LV00006B/1/P